THE

GREAT

DEPRESSION

AND

THE NEW DEAL

A seven volume series reproducing nearly one hundred and fifty of the most important articles on all aspects of the Great Depression

Edited with introductions by

Melvyn Dubofsky
State University of New York at Binghamton

Stephen Burwood
Alfred University

A GARLAND SERIES

THE

GREAT DEPRESSION

AND THE

NEW DEAL

6

WOMEN

AND

MINORITIES

DURING

THE

GREAT DEPRESSION

Edited with an introduction by

Melvyn Dubofsky
and
Stephen Burwood

GARLAND PUBLISHING, INC.
NEW YORK & LONDON
1990

49508

Library of Congress Cataloging-in-Publication Data

Women and minorities during the Great Depression : selected articles on gender,
race, and ethnicity / edited, with an introduction, by Melvyn Dubofsky and Stephen
Burwood.
p. cm. — (The Great Depression and the New Deal ; 6)
Includes bibliographical references.
ISBN 0-8240-0898-7 (alk. paper)
1. United States—Social conditions—1933–1945. 2. Women—United States—Social
conditions. 3. Minorities—United States—History—20th century. 4. Afro-Americans—History—20th century. 5. Depressions—1929—United States. 6. New Deal,
1933–1939. I. Dubofsky, Melvyn. II. Burwood, Stephen. III. Series.
HN57.W66 1990
305.42'0973'09043—dc20   89-71395

Printed on acid-free, 250-year-life paper
Manufactured in the United States of America

CONTENTS

Introduction

INTRODUCTION

Much controversy surrounds the question of the impact of the Great Depression on women and minorities, especially African-Americans. In politics, the New Deal certainly had an enormous impact on the voting behavior of minorities and it offered a larger role to women in the making of policy than any previous national administration. Between 1932 and 1936, for example, African-Americans en masse transferred their political loyalty from the party of Lincoln, the Republicans, to the party of Roosevelt, the Democrats. Women, who had been at the heart of the struggle for social reform and an American version of the Welfare State since the turn of the twentieth century, found a warm welcome in the New Deal as symbolized by the appointment of one of them, Frances Perkins, as secretary of labor, the first female cabinet member in United States history. And the nation's new first lady, Eleanor Roosevelt, exemplified the concern the new administration felt for its heretofore neglected, exploited, or oppressed citizens.

Undoubtedly, Roosevelt's New Deal practiced the symbolism of minority politics better than any previous administration in American history; female reformers and nonwhite voters became a vital constituent element in the Democratic electoral coalition. To what extent the New Deal's policies and practices actually changed the situation, material standards, and life chances of women and minorities, however, remains a hotly disputed subject.

The articles and essays collected in this volume represent an effort to grapple with the real impact of the depression and the New Deal on the lives of women and minorities. As might be expected, a number of scholars explore the situation of African-Americans during the 1930s. Some see the New Deal experience as a positive blessing for black people while others perceive it as a continuation of more traditional racist practices in a modern guise. William Muraskin, Darlene Clark Hine, and Joel Schwartz discuss how the Great Depression and the New Deal stimulated militancy and direct action among African-Americans. By contrast, August Meier and Eliott Rudwick examine the tortured relations between a radical trade union, its white leaders, and the black community.

Not only did the New Deal, in the words of the historian Harvard Sitkoff, promote a "new deal for blacks," it also became associated with a "new deal" for Native Americans. The articles by Graham D. Taylor and Charles J. Weeks scrutinize the impact of the New Deal upon Native Americans, Taylor by portraying the influence of social scientists on general policy and Weeks by examining a group of Native Americans in North Carolina.

Women, to be sure, cannot be considered a minority in the same sense as nonwhites. Historically, however, women in comparison to men had suffered a form of second-class citizenship at home, at work, and in the public arena. Women of color, moreover, experienced the handicap of race as well as gender. While Susan Ware probes the broad contours of the role women played in the New Deal, Lois Rita Hembold compares and contrasts the situation of black and white working-class women; Beverly W. Jones suggests how race and gender intersected in the lives of black tobacco workers; Sharon Hartman Strom describes the relationship among women, feminism, political radicalism, and the new industrial unionism; and Evelyn Nakano Glenn offers glimpses into the lives of Japanese-American domestic workers. Through these articles we learn whether or not the New Deal moved women toward first-class citizenship and also discover the differential impact of reform on women of different classes and colors.

THE HARLEM BOYCOTT OF 1934: BLACK NATIONALISM AND THE RISE OF LABOR-UNION CONSCIOUSNESS

By WILLIAM MURASKIN

This article is concerned with the Harlem Jobs-For-Negroes Boycott of 1934 and its aftermath. The targets of the boycott movement were the white merchants who occupied and monopolized Harlem's commercial hub. Representing the first "united front" campaign of New York Negroes, the boycott effectively employed such aggressive tactics as mass picketing to break the job ceiling which barred Negroes from white-collar positions. But two separate ruptures within the movement, at the very moment of victory, split the "united front," producing two new organizations: one was led by the radical agitator Sufi Abdul Hamid, the so-called "Black Hitler" of Harlem, and the other by Ira Kemp and Arthur Reed. It is with the activities of the latter group that we are particularly concerned. Both revolts represented bids for power by the most militant wing of the original movement, which hoped to divert the boycott into more aggressively "nationalistic" channels.

In order to capture the boycott movement, Sufi, Reed, and Kemp employed propaganda techniques which had special attraction for Harlem's masses: for Sufi the device was anti-Semitism; for Reed and Kemp it was the issue of intra-Negro color discrimination. Their rhetoric had little relevance to the ultimate goals of their organizations, and these goals were not clearcut. But the demands of power forced both groups to create a more realistic ideology, one which put labor union organization at the heart of their plans.

The labor situation in Harlem before 1934 was intolerable. New York's color bar was so rigid that it excluded blacks from white-collar

WILLIAM MURASKIN *is Assistant Professor of Urban Studies, Queens College, The City University of New York.*

1

positions in the heart of their own Ghetto, along 125th Street. Employment as a lowly grocery clerk became a desirable position, and even newsworthy. The New York *Age* of May 26, 1934, featured the news that there was "another Negro Clerk in 125th Street," a Negro woman who had obtained employment as a salesgirl in a music store. On June 23 it carried a similar item in which the fortunate girl — the daughter of a bandleader, no less — was congratulated for her good fortune. Such were the aspirations of the Negro social elite: the lower-class never dreamed so ambitiously.

There were those who tried to raise Harlem's low level of aspiration. They sought to create a greater self-awareness among New York's Negroes so that they might produce a boycott movement similar to the successful one in Chicago in 1929. One such agitator was Arthur Reed, a fiery step-ladder orator who pleaded for the creation of Negro business.[1] Like Marcus Garvey in the 1920s, Reed felt that the only hope for the black man was a self-sustained Negro economy. He was joined by another street-corner speaker, Ira Kemp, and together they formed the African Patriotic League. An offshoot of the Garvey movement, it emphasized economic activity in America rather than the politico-economic doctrine of Back-To-Africa.[2]

Agitation by Kemp and Reed, and also by Sufi Abdul Hamid, created an atmosphere conducive to change. Indeed, Sufi, who in 1933 started aggressive picketing of stores above 125th Street, may have been the major catalyst of the mass boycott movement. But the immediate impetus for the 1934 movement was supplied by Reverend John H. Johnson of Saint Martin's Protestant Episcopal Church. His church, with its conservative and established parishioners, many of them being professionals, was one of Harlem's leading religious institutions.[3] According to Reverend Johnson himself, he initiated the actions which ultimately led to the boycott after receiving a series of complaints from his congregation protesting the lack of Negro salesgirls on 125th Street. His first attempt to correct this situation involved no coercion. He asked the parishioners to collect sales slips over a short period of time, after which he went to

---

[1] Writer's Program. New York [City]. [Negroes of New York]. *Negroes of New York (an informal history)*, edited by Roi Ottley, (1942?), memorandum entitled "Activities of Ira Kemp and Trade Unionism," by Ellis Williams. The collected studies will henceforth be referred to as "Writer's program" [n.d.].

[2] Interview with James Blades, Business Manager of the Harlem Labor Union, in March 1966.

[3] Writer's Progrm, "The Church in New York," research memorandum on St. Martin's Protestant Episcopal Church, by Ted Yates [n.d.].

Blumstein's Department Store (the largest in Harlem, and a perfect test case) and presented its management with proof that blacks accounted for most of its income.[4]

Initiating his mission of peace with naive expectations of success, Reverend Johnson was soon disillusioned. The store's proprietors, William Blumstein and his sister-in-law Mrs. L. M. Blumstein, saw no reason for complaint against their hiring practices. They employed Negroes as janitors, floor-sweepers, and other menials — in fact one Negro college graduate worked the elevator[5] — and refused to meet Reverend Johnson's unreasonable request for more jobs for blacks. As a result, Reverend Johnson despaired of achieving concrete results by himself and sent out notices to many of Harlem's civic leaders, proposing the formation of a "united front" against the merchants of 125th Street.

This "united front" which came out of Reverend Johnson's appeal took the name "The Citizen's League for Fair Play." While it attempted to represent a cross-section of the community, and included such non-elite members as Arthur Reed and Ira Kemp, its membership was predominately upper-class and control remained in conservative hands. Sixty-two Harlem social, religious, and business groups, according to Claude McKay, responded to the call.[6]

After fruitless negotiations between the League and Blumstein's, the black leaders decided that a boycott was their only recourse. It began in June 1934, and lasted for six weeks.

The major voice of the movement was the New York *Age,* one of two leading Negro weeklies published in Harlem. Fred R. Moore, its editor, occupied a pivotal position in the League. His newspaper carried front-page exhortations encouraging its readers to support the boycott of Blumstein's, and its editorial and feature columns, especially those of Vere Johns, gave added support. The other major weekly, the New York *Amsterdam News,* was hostile to the movement. Its columnists, who included such men as George Schyler, noted for his caustic wit, mercilessly attacked the boycott leaders. They charged that its supporters were leading Harlem to disaster, since the white merchants were sure to institute a counter-boycott against Negroes who worked downtown.[7] That it

---

[4] Interview with Reverend John H. Johnson, April 1966.
[5] New York *Age,* May 26, 1934. Henceforce called *"Age."*
[6] Claude McKay, *Harlem: Negro Metropolis* (New York, 1940), 193. McKay was a noted black poet during this period. *Age,* June 23, 1934, stated that 300 organizations joined the League.
[7] For example, see Theophilus Lewis' column in the *Amsterdam News,* July 21, 1934.

3

printed the bulk of Blumstein's advertising before, during, and after the boycott, as well as the majority of all 125th Street advertising, provided one compelling reason for the *News*'s unique position as the major black voice opposing the Jobs-For-Negroes campaign.

The Citizen's League, while generally peaceful and orderly, as Reverend Johnson had hoped, did not refrain from using less "Christian" methods than picketing. Vere Johns recently recalled one technique which the boycotters employed in order to stop Negro women from crossing the picket line: "Half a dozen of us would watch for coloured shoppers coming out of Blumstein's, trail them to the corner, destroying their purchases, and slap them around a little to teach them national pride. I suppose it was a bit of gangsterism, but we lived in a gangster age. . . ."[8] The League also used moral as well as physical intimidation. One device was to take a picture of a shopper coming out of Blumstein's and publish it on the front page of the New York *Age*.[9] According to Ludlow Werner, grandson of Fred Moore, such shoppers were afraid to show their faces outdoors for fear of bodily assault.[10]

Owing to community support, and to such tactics as mass picketing, Blumstein's capitulated. The agreement, which was reached on July 26, 1934 (though not made public for over a week) read as follows:

> L. M. Blumstein [the full name of the store] has always employed colored help and has never practiced any racial or other form of discrimination.
> In recognition of the principles asserted by Rev. Dr. J. H. Johnson . . .
> L. M. Blumstein has decided to increase the personnel of its working staff by employing colored clerical and sales help and will take on fifteen (15) between now and August 15th and twenty (20) more in the month of September, and thereafter such number as in the judgment of the management business conditions will warrant . . . .[11]

Leaguers were exuberant: it would be easy, now that the giant had been conquered, to repeat the process.[12]

---

[8] This quote is from an article written by Vere Johns for the *Star* (December 1965), a newspaper printed in Kingston, Jamaica. The article was shown to the present author by Reverend Johnson. It has no date or page number.

[9] *Age*, July 14, 1934.

[10] Interview with Ludlow Werner, April 1966. Mr. Werner was later Editor of the New York *Age*.

[11] *Age*, August 4, 1934. The representatives of the Citizen's League who met with William Blumstein on July 26 were not satisfied with only thirty-five positions, but since the accord promised to increase the number as conditions warranted, they accepted it.

[12] *Age*, August 11, 1934. The Blumstein boycott had a direct effect on a number of other stores which, during and immediately after the boycott, decided to hire colored help: Mayfair Cleaners (*Age*, June 30), Bush Credit Jewelers (*Age*, August 4), and Lerner Shops (*Age*, September 1). The last-named store consented to take four girls whom the League would recommend.

4

But further victories were not forthcoming. Rather success brought disunity, and the League ceased to exist as an effective fighting force. Its breakup resulted from two separate ruptures: Sufi Hamid, who was never actually within the League, attacked it from outside, while at the same time a power play was staged from within by Ira Kemp and Arthur Reed, considered its sincerest supporters.[13] No single leader, however, could on his own attract a large grass-roots following. The conservative and highly respectable Citizen's League had done what the agitation of this trio of critics could never do. They had been forced into uneasy harmony with Harlem's upper-class throughout the boycott, but victory created an opportunity for each to strike out on his own.

The crisis developed when the first fifteen girls to be employed in Blumstein's were chosen. The New York *Age* published a photograph of the new employees and, to the dismay of many, the group appeared Caucasian.[14] In mid-September 1934 Ira Kemp, head of the League's picketing committee, accused Fred Moore of being responsible for the gross discrimination against dark-skinned Negro girls in the Blumstein accord. Not only were light girls chosen over dark ones, but the former had not even participated in the picketing, since "high-yellow" Negroes felt such activities were beneath them.[15] The picketing committee, with its entire corps of loyal workers, detached itself from the parent body — though still retaining its name, since the League was not incorporated — and proceeded to function as an autonomous body. Within a short time, Arthur Reed became associated with the "Rebel Picketing Committee," and shortly thereafter became one of its leaders, thus associating his African Patriotic League with this new group.[16] The Committee then proceeded to picket many of the small stores along 125th Street. A major result of this new boycott, according to the New York *Age,* was the firing of one salesgirl because she was light complexioned,[17] and it dubbed the group the "Renegade 'Boycott' Committee,"[18] and later the "Racket Committee . . . on Foul Play."[19] Both Fred Moore and Vere

[13] Interview with Reverend Johnson, March 1966.
[14] Age, September 15, 1934. There is a disagreement concerning the actual color of the girls. Adam Clayton Powell, Jr., in his book *Marching Blacks* (New York, 1945), claims that the picture was a misprint which distorted the true complexion of the girls (p. 81). However, Reverend Johnson admitted that the girls "could not be distinguished as Negro"; and that they were "very attractive"—presumably by Caucasian definition. Reverend Johnson's comment is supported by Ludlow Werner.
[15] *Amsterdam News,* September 15, 1934.
[16] *Age,* September 22, 1934.
[17] *Ibid.,* October 6, 1934.
[18] *Ibid.,* September 22, 1934.
[19] *Ibid.,* October 27, 1934.

Johns of the New York *Age* defended the League against the charge of color discrimination, Moore contending that the rebel committee's insistence upon jobs for dark-skinned girls was itself color prejudice and to comply with this demand would be to "discriminate."[20] Vere Johns defended the accord with Blumstein's with his usual vigor, entitling one column, "When Fools and Liars Run Amuck," in reference to the rebel group.[21] He became increasingly more belligerent, and even accused the Committee's leaders of being racketeers whose only interest was in lining their own pockets.[22] Later Johns contended that people like Kemp and Reed suffered from "Blackophobia" — a disease which prevented them from seeing any virtue in light-skinned Negroes.[23]

Despite continuous assault from the New York *Age* and later the *Amsterdam News,* the accusation of color prejudice proved very effective, since it activated a dormant but powerful cleavage within Negro society. Lighter-skinned Negroes had formed a separate class since slavery, and for many decades a great barrier existed between mulattoes and darker Negroes. In fact special social clubs were formed to maintain the division. This internal hostility was declining by 1934, to be sure, but the large West Indian population (almost forty percent of Harlem) — which came from a social system emphasizing intra-Negro color divisions as the basis of social position — encouraged it.

The accusation also proved effective in gaining support because it was probably true. Reed had claimed that the light-skinned leaders of the Citizen's League for Fair Play had intentionally picked "high-yellow" girls to work at Blumstein's. Reverend Johnson (in a 1966 interview with the author) denied the charge, declaring that the committee had no part in selecting the girls, and that William Blumstein was wholly responsible. Under persistent questioning, however, he admitted that some members unofficially may have given Blumstein a list of names, but only as individuals, not as League members.

It is an unavoidable conclusion that some Leaguers actually selected girls, since Blumstein had no way of obtaining acceptable help on short notice. Certainly the League did have a stake in getting the best and most "attractive" examples of Negro Womanhood into Blumstein's as a model for other stores.[24] It is likely that Leaguers would suggest girls

20 *Ibid.*, September 15, 1934.
21 *Ibid.*, September 22, 1934.
22 *Ibid.*, October 27, 1934.
23 *Ibid.*, September 29, 1934.
24 Interview with Ludlow Werner.

who met their standard of "high quality." Confirming this assumption, Vere Johns recently stated that after Blumstein's capitulated and asked for the League's terms, "we had the terms, *and we had the bodies* [italics mine]. Bright and early on the Monday following, thirty-five neat, attractive Negro girls . . . took their places behind Blumstein's counters."[25] The choice of such girls may have been a sincere effort on the part of some League leaders to "put their best foot forward": nothing more than that. But their concept of the "best foot" was a person so light as to be only nominally Negro.[26]

William Blumstein, to be sure, played some part in actually choosing the girls, if only that he undoubtedly had to approve the selections. Furthermore, the *Amsterdam News* reported that he would not accept anyone who had picketed his store.[27] It is significant, however, that Blumstein's position in no way clashed with that of those League members who favored the advancement of upper-class Negro girls — a group which had never actively participated in the picketing.

The accusation of Kemp and Reed, therefore, appears accurate, but their actual motive in shattering the Citizen's League over the color question still remains obscure. On the face of it, there is good reason for assuming their sincerity: both men were very sensitive to color discrimination. Arthur Reed was a West Indian immigrant and a follower of Marcus Garvey. Kemp, a dark-skinned Georgian, was identified with the West Indians and had been a loyal Garveyite.[28] Both the social situation in the West Indies and the propaganda of Garvey's Back-To-Africa movement intensified hostility between dark and light-skinned Negroes. Such antagonism could conceivably have been heightened by the Blumstein accord.

Yet this thinking is not persuasive, especially in the case of Arthur Reed who, even today, is a forceful and logical thinker. Though nationalistic and race-oriented, his viewpoint is sophisticated. It emphasizes the effect of impersonal economic forces on social conditions rather than conspiracy or "prejudice." In all likelihood, then, his attack on the conservative Citizen's League derived from a desire to transform it into a radically nationalistic vehicle.

---

[25] See Vere Johns article in the *Star*, December 1965.
[26] Interview with Reverend Johnson. After saying that the girls were not easily distinguishable as Negroes, he added, "I have never had issue with him [Blumstein] on that [picking the girls]. They were attractive."
[27] Reverend Johnson says he never knew of this statement. Interview, March 1966.
[28] Interview with Ludlow Werner, April 1966.

Color discrimination by League leaders served as proof, which Reed and Kemp could use, to demonstrate that they, not an upper-class elite, should control the jobs campaign. Once the movement took a more radical turn, Reed planned to agitate for "all the jobs" in Harlem, instead of the token number the League demanded.[29] Outside of this rather limited aim, the ultimate objectives of Reed and Kemp were vague. At best, they had an amorphous idea that white-collar employment would somehow lead to the formation of Negro businesses and of a black economy, but their idea lacked substance. Having no real ideology, they were forced into a superficial "crusade" for dark Negroes in order to attract a following.

Their picketing committee (still officially part of the Citizen's League) began its drive by approaching the A. S. Beck Shoe Store on 125th Street and demanding the hiring of Negro sales personnel. Beck's then sought an injunction against the League as well as Arthur Reed (and his African Patriotic League), Ira Kemp, and others. The complaint specified that the picketers were not a labor union, that there was no labor dispute, that they had used violence against customers, and that they were inciting a race riot.[30] The court judgment constituted a major legal-historical precedent. Presiding Judge Rosenman stated:

> The controversy here is not a labor dispute. The defendants do not constitute a labor union or a labor organization of any kind. . . . It is solely a racial dispute. . . . It is purely a dispute of one race opposed to another. . . . If they were permitted, there is substantial danger that a race riot and race reprisals might result in this and other communities. They would serve as a precedent for similar activity in the interests of various racial and religious groups.[31]

The decision could be interpreted to mean that a racial group denied job opportunities and union membership because of its color was forbidden to unite on the basis of race to protect itself.

The picketing committee, sometime before this decision, had challenged another store on 125th Street. Its new campaign aroused more hostility against the picketers than had any earlier action. When the Orkin Dress Shop opened it employed fifty percent colored sales personnel. The picketing committee demanded that the level be raised to seventy-five percent and that the committee's own people be hired —

---

[29] Interview with Arthur Reed, April 1966.
[30] Charles Lionel Franklin, *The Negro Labor Unionist of New York* (New York, 1936), 132-33.
[31] New York *Law Journal*, November 1, 1934, p. 1578.

even though it meant firing blacks presently employed.[32] This demand alienated many who were otherwise sympathetic to the rebel cause.[33] They agreed with the *Amsterdam News* when it charged that the picketeers were nothing more than racketeers attempting to get skilled Negroes fired and their own henchmen hired.[34]

Boycott motives are clear enough. One irate reader, probably a picketer, defined the issue in the *Amsterdam News*: Reed, Kemp, and others were incensed by the fact that light-skinned Negroes were receiving jobs, while black ones did all the picketing.[35] A few days earlier, in the New York *Age,* the same writer declared that the forced discharge of the Orkin Girls was not "inhuman," because they never picketed in aid of the movement. While, she admitted, they had been hired before the picketing began, Orkin's had only employed them as a result of the original Blumstein campaign.[36]

The rest of the story can be pieced together from articles in the New York *Age.* In order to forstall a future boycott, Orkin's went to Philip M. Jenkins, of the Harlem YWCA, it being one of the places to go if one wanted to avoid employing dark-skinned blacks, and obtained a list of upper-class "high yellow" girls. The Rebel Picketing Committee charged "foul play" and proceeded to boycott the store.[37]

Whatever their purpose in boycotting Orkin's, Reed and Kemp were frustrated by the Beck case ruling of November 1934.[34] Within nine months of this decision Sufi Hamid also found himself forced out of the jobs campaign and, at least for a while, it appeared that Harlem's radicals had been completely defeated. The cessation of picketing along 125th Street was greeted with pronounced relief not only by the white merchants, but by the inactive Citizen's League for Fair Play as well. Men like Reverend Johnson and Fred Moore had been shocked by the forces their movement had unleashed and many League's leaders were eager to disassociate themselves from the boycott campaign.

---

[32] *Age*, October 20, 1934, reported that twenty-three girls were fired as a result of the boycott.

[33] *Amsterdam News*, October 29, 1934.

[34] *Ibid.,* October 20, 1934.

[35] *Ibid.,* November 3, 1934.

[36] *Age*, October 27, 1934.

[37] *Ibid.,* October 20, 1934. James Brown told the present author that white merchants often contacted the Urban League or the YWCA because both groups showed a preference for light-skinned Negroes. (The Harlem Urban League was so conservative that its Executive Secretary James H. Hubert, had actually opposed the Citizen's League for Fair Play *Age*, August 4, 1934).

[38] *Age*, November 17, 1934, announced that two men had been sent to jail for violation of Judge Rosenman's injunction.

9

While the white-dominated courts, using the injunction, ended Harlem agitation, they did not eliminate the agitators. Rather, Reed and Kemp began to evaluate the reasons for their failure in the Beck case. The main reason, they believed, was that the Rebel Picketing Committee lacked status as a recognized labor union. The significance of a union in obtaining white-collar employment and, ultimately, in creating a black economy, was not clear to them — perhaps partially because Marcus Garvey had vehemently opposed labor unions — but they would nevertheless organize one if the court required it. For a year and a half, beginning late in 1934, attorney (later Judge) Vernon C. Reddick fought for a union charter for the picketing committee.[39] During the interim, though unable to picket, Kemp and Reed continued to expound the doctrine of "Don't Buy Where You Can't Work" from their street-corner platforms.

While 1935 saw a cessation of boycott activity, Reed and Kemp did not remain unoccupied. Italy's Ethiopian campaign created unprecedented racial self-awareness among Harlemites, and both men used the opportunity to spread the gospel of black business. Reed had for years fostered a movement to drive the Italians out of Harlem's ice and push-cart business but with little success until the Ethiopian war. Now he was able to organize hundreds of Negro push-cartmen, supplying each with his first load of vegetables or cake of ice. He mounted a nightly campaign from his stepladder, exhorting his listeners to patronize only colored salesmen. Reed, however, did not organize a union since each push-cart was supposedly the basis of a small, independent business. But the enterprise failed because black push-cartmen were unreliable compared with the Italians.[40]

Kemp, meanwhile, instituted a fiery campaign against the Bella Restaurant in Harlem. He accused the establishment of housing prostitutes, gangsters, and other undesirables who degraded and demoralized Harlemites. His charges served as both a nationalistic attack on the hated Italians and as a means of popularizing the idea of black business in Harlem.[41]

Finally, in 1936, Ira Kemp obtained a charter for the Harlem Labor Union, Incorporated, (H.L.U.), and received permission to work in an

---

[39] Harlem Labor Union pamphlet: "Facts You Should Know About the Harlem Labor Union, A ten year campaign of work and sweat and results," by Colombus Austin, Sr., Public Relations Director, 1946.
[40] (Baltimore) *Afro-American*, July 25, 1936.
[41] Writer's Program, "Activities of Ira Kemp and Trade Unionism," by Ellis Williams.

area bounded by 125th Street on the north and 110th Street on the south.[42] The organization owed its creation to the example set by one of Sufi's organizations, the Afro-American Federation of Labor, as well as to the Beck decision. Indeed, Claude McKay maintains that the H.L.U. was formed out of the ruins of Sufi's group.[43] The H.L.U. itself claims descent, at least spiritually, from Sufi's campaign:[44] and, interestingly enough, Francis Minor, the so-called "Hermann Goering" of Sufi's organization, became an H.L.U. President.[45]

Beginning with only seven members, the H.L.U. compensated for its lack of size with the enthusiasm of youth. Its members, with two exceptions, were in their late teens or early twenties. Most were West Indians and almost all of them were followers of Marcus Garvey and his philosophy of a self-sustained black economy.[46]

No one in the newly chartered organization possessed a clear idea of the purpose of a trade union. "We didn't know so much about labor unions," James Brown, one of the first members, recalled, "but since we weren't allowed to picket when we weren't a union . . . we became one. . . . We wanted to get them [Negroes] jobs — but once we succeeded we wanted to keep them there — and so we became a real union."[47] Since Ira Kemp, the union's actual founder and first president died soon after its formation, Arthur Reed actually developed H.L.U. strategy. It involved aggressive picketing of stores along 125th Street, including impromptu sit-ins (a procedure which, though effective, continually sent them to jail)[48] when employers refused to cooperate. Merchant hostility and adverse judicial decisions notwithstanding, the union successfully organized employees of pawnshops, grocery stores, meat markets, and

---

[42] Interview with Miriam Skeete, bookkeeper of the H.L.U. in 1941 and secretary from 1945 to the present. She stated that the charter was later expanded to permit unrestricted activity in New York.

[43] Claude McKay, "Labor Steps Out in Harlem," *Nation*, CXLV (October 16, 1937), 400.

[44] Austin H.L.U. pamphlet (broadside) [n.d.]

[45] Interview with James Brown, March 1966; Roi Ottley, *New World A-Coming: Inside Black America*, (Boston, 1943), 118.

[46] Interview with James Brown, March 1966. It is difficult to assess the influence of Garveyism upon the events of 1934-1937. Most of the radicals, whether a part of the Citizen's League for Fair Play, Sufi's Negro Industrial and Clerical Alliance, the African Patriotic League, the Rebel Picketing Committee, or the Harlem Labor Union, were followers or ex-followers of Marcus Garvey. In fact, the reason for their interest in self-help movements was the spirit of Negro nationalism which Garvey had instilled in them. Garvey's ideas, however, had little *direct* relevance to the events of these years, because 1.) the connection between Negro white-collar employment in white-owned stores and the establishment of Negro businesses was not obvious; and 2.) Garvey's hostility to labor unions made his ideas useless for those desiring to promote unionism.

[47] Interview with James Brown, March 1966.

[48] *Ibid.*

11

shoe stores, as well as other establishments, by 1938.[49]

Arthur Reed helped promote H.L.U. interests not only by his activities as Union President but also as the head of the African Patriotic League, the H.L.U.'s political mouthpiece.[50] He delivered nightly soapbox talks on prominent politico-economic subjects, such as the notorious "Bronx Slave Market," where black women congregated while they waited to be "inspected" and picked for a day's domestic labor at 10 to 15 cents an hour. Reed's power as an orator helped keep Harlem aware of the conditions that made labor organization so important.

The practical experience derived from organizing the H.L.U. had a striking effect upon the thinking of those involved. Kemp and his associates, to repeat, applied for a union charter before they had come to appreciate its significance — except insofar as it could neutralize the court decision which made union status a legal *sine qua non* for conducting the boycott. But it did not take the reluctant unionists long to discover the practical necessity of labor organization in their fight for permanent job opportunities for Negroes. Nor did it take them long to realize the potential power which resided in the black community if that power could be channeled into an all-Negro union. Consequently, with these discoveries, Kemp, Reed, and Brown began to see the H.L.U. itself as a substantial contribution to Negro self-help, rather than merely as a device to legitimize their boycott activities.

The ghetto would benefit, as they ultimately saw it, from three functions of the H.L.U.: 1) it would obtain and then maintain white-collar jobs for blacks; 2) it would help create a supply of competent Negro sales people by conducting classes in "the art of selling"; 3) it would pave the way for the creation of Negro business since a good sales clerk would ultimately become an independent entrepreneur.[51] Once reaching this conclusion about the possibilities for their organization, it was not surprising that H.L.U. members preached the new gospel of black labor unionism to Harlemites.

Unfortunately, after all this initial activity, the plans of the H.L.U. leadership received a permanent setback. The District Attorney of New York County called the union's leaders to his office and demanded that they resign. According to Brown, the H.L.U. had "stepped on too many toes," frightened too many people by its aggressive tactics, and thus pro-

---

[49] Austin, H.L.U. pamphlet (broadside), and interview with James Brown, March 1966.
[50] The organization he had founded in 1933.
[51] At this point a definite connection between Garveyism, unionism, and the Jobs-For-Negroes campaign was established.

voked counter-action. It was opposed not only by the white merchants and the Negro elite, but also by the American Federation of Labor, the newly formed Congress of Industrial Organization, and the Communists![52] The leadership did indeed resign and a steering committee of junior members took over in the interim.[53]

The union, according to the present Secretary, existed in name only during the period immediately preceding 1941.[54] At that time, an entirely new group of men obtained control and made substantial changes in an organization which, in its new form, continues to exist. The H.L.U. founders had "excelled in rough, pioneering tactics of picketing and boycotting," but they lacked "organizational ability and a clear concept of the labor movement in its relationship to the Negro minority."[55] As a result, the new leaders were forced to construct an entirely different organizational basis for the union. They hired a certified public accountant, systematized the records, and instituted bookkeeping reorganization.

* * *

The Boycott of 1934 in sum was an outstanding event in Harlem history, one which radically altered the atmosphere of that community. The movement demonstrated for the first time the latent power residing within the black ghetto. It shattered the apathy and self-abnegation which had convinced Harlem of the futility of dynamic self-help. The militancy which the Citizen's League for Fair Play stimulated was expanded and heightened by the activities of Sufi's organization, the Negro Industrial and Clerical Alliance, Reed's and Kemp's Rebel Picketing Committee and, later, the Harlem Labor Union. The activities of these organizations reinforced the conviction among Negroes that they could meet the standards of white-collar employment.

The successors of the Citizen's League also provided publicity for the idea of labor unionism. Sufii, Reed, and Kemp enabled thousands of people to understand the urgent need for trade unionism among blacks. While they did not convince many that race should be the major basis of labor organization, they did make Harlemites more responsive to the appeals of progressive white unions.

---

[52] Claude McKay, "Labor Steps Out . . ."
[53] It is impossible to discover the actual charges against the leadership. No legal action was brought against them probably because they resigned.
[54] Interview with Miriam Skeete, March 1966.
[55] McKay, *Harlem: Negro Metropolis*, 299.

Raymond Wolters

The New Deal and the Negro

"The test of our progress is not whether we add more to the abundance of those who have much; it is whether we provide enough for those who have too little."—Franklin D. Roosevelt

DURING THE GRAY YEARS OF THE GREAT DEPRESSION, AMERICA'S twelve million Negroes were the most disadvantaged major group in American society—"the first fired and the last hired." Government studies indicating the "color or race" of families receiving relief reported that blacks were "added to the relief rolls twice as frequently [in proportion to their number in the total 1930 population] by loss of private employment as whites, and are removed through finding places in private employment only half as frequently."[1] Black people naturally hoped that the programs of Franklin D. Roosevelt's New Deal would be constructed in such a way as to assist their recovery. They were encouraged by the president's 1932 campaign promise that Negroes would be included "absolutely and impartially" in his new deal for the forgotten man.[2]

President Roosevelt's program was so diverse and multifaceted that it is difficult to generalize about its impact on Negroes. Some New Deal programs were clearly advantageous, others less so, and some aggravated the condition of black people. Yet on the whole, the New Deal was as notable for its lost and rejected opportunities as for its actual achievements. Its recovery program was limited and cautious, of more benefit to organized workers and to those who had fallen from relative affluence than to those at the very bottom of society. Despite its deficiencies, however, the New Deal offered Negroes more in material benefits and recognition than had any administration since the era of Reconstruction. In gratitude for

14

these limited but real benefits, many Negroes in the 1930s began to vote for the Democratic party for the first time. This major realignment in black partisan identification—the breaking loose from traditional loyalty to the Republican party and the subsequent and tenacious loyalty to the urban Democratic coalition—was one of the most important developments in the political history of the decade, but it is not evidence that the Roosevelt administration fulfilled the promise of its egalitarian rhetoric. It is, rather, testimony to the fact that Negroes had come to expect little from governments in Washington or elsewhere and recognized that the New Deal, with all its shortcomings, was better for them than the existing Republican alternative.

More than half of the nation's Negro population lived in rural areas during the 1930s, but less than 20 percent of the black farmers owned the land they worked. Most were employed as tenants and wage hands with yearly incomes of less than $200, and any attempt to describe how Negroes were affected by the Roosevelt administration's agricultural policies must focus on the extent to which these impoverished, landless farmers shared the benefits of the various programs. The most important of these programs, that of the Agricultural Adjustment Administration (AAA), was essentially an attempt to increase farm purchasing power by sponsoring acreage and production control. It was thought that crop reduction would lead to higher farm prices, and thus the AAA was authorized to disburse government benefit payments to farmers who voluntarily promised to cultivate only a portion of their acreage. All farmers—owners, tenants, blacks, and whites—had suffered as a result of disastrously depreciated crop prices during the depression, and it was assumed that they all would profit from a general rehabilitation of the rural economy. The purpose of the AAA, then, was not to redistribute income within agriculture but to increase general farm prices and farm income through crop reduction.

The New Deal's agricultural administrators feared that given the system of caste and class relations in the cotton South, where the great majority of black farmers were employed, landowners would not support the government's crop reduction program unless they were assured that it posed no threat to the traditional dependence of tenants. Cully Cobb, the head of the AAA's cotton section, was a Tennessee farm boy who was educated at Mississippi A. and M. College, and his two assistants, E. A. Miller and W. B. Camp, were also recruited from southern agricultural colleges. They knew that many southern landlords would oppose any

15

government program that gave tenants, especially black tenants, an independent source of income, and they saw to it that the AAA's cotton contracts were drafted in such a way as to take account of southern traditions. These contracts provided that landlords would receive four and one-half cents from the government for each pound of cotton not grown, of which the tenant's share was to be only one-half cent, a considerably smaller portion than the fifty-fifty division the AAA was distributing to tenants producing other crops and a ratio that suggests a great deal about the caste and class biases of those who controlled the AAA's cotton program. Cobb and his assistants also knew that many planters would object to direct payment of government money to tenants and thus all government money was distributed to landlords, who were instructed to act as trustees for their tenants' one-ninth share—a procedure that was contrary to the traditional method of handling government funds and one that offered virtually limitless opportunities for graft and deception.

The AAA delegated primary responsibility for the adjudication of any disputes that arose in the course of the reduction program to local authorities chosen in elections at the county and community levels. Negroes were allowed, even encouraged, to vote for members of these local committees; but they were not permitted to participate in the nomination of candidates, and throughout the South not a single black farmer served on a county committee. Eighty percent of the committeemen were white landowners, and most of the remainder were white cash renters. If a tenant believed his landlord had given him an unfair acreage allotment or had failed to distribute his share of the government money, he was required to present his case before the county committee. Since the committees were composed of the landlord's own friends and associates, such complaints were rarely decided in favor of the tenant and often resulted in further harassment for the complainant. Mordecai Ezekiel, an adviser in the office of Secretary of Agriculture Henry A. Wallace, correctly assessed the situation when he noted that "there can be no question that farm owners, constituting less than half of those engaged in agriculture, have been the dominant element in the preparation and administration of AAA programs. . . . In certain commodities, notably cotton, this has resulted in their receiving the lion's share of the benefits."[4]

To compound the difficulties of tenant farmers, the cotton section, fearful of even seeming to threaten the existing plantation system, never took effective steps to ensure that tenants would receive their allotted small share of the government benefit payments. Cully Cobb and his associates knew that in most cases the landlord did not forward the government money to the tenant but simply credited the money to the tenant's account at the company store. But they steadfastly rejected suggestions that landlords be required to fill out detailed forms specifying the price and quantity of goods they had advanced to tenants, arguing that such procedures would lead to a "colossal and expensive task" of administration and would provoke a "negative reaction" among planters.[5] The practice of distributing all money through the landlords naturally invited fraud, and one of the AAA's own studies acknowledged that "there have been a considerable number of cases in which tenant farmers have not received the full amount specified by the cotton contract . . . Whether the tenant received anything at all . . . depended upon the charitableness of the landlord."[6] Yet the prevailing view within the administration was that the cotton reduction programs had succeeded in raising the price of cotton from 6 cents a pound in 1932 to 12 cents in 1935, and, as Assistant Secretary of Agriculture Paul Appleby noted, "this doubling in value of the South's chief crop and that particular crop in which colored people are most interested . . . has had a far-reaching favorable effect."[7]

In addition to failing to protect the interests of tenants and sharecroppers, the AAA adopted policies that encouraged evictions. Put in the most simple terms, it was impossible to reduce cotton acreage by 40 percent without also reducing the need for labor in the cotton fields. The leaders of the AAA recognized that crop reduction might cause substantial unemployment among farm tenants; hence, special provisions were written into paragraph 7 of the 1934-35 cotton contracts requiring that landowners "maintain on this farm the normal number of tenants and other employees" and that all tenants be permitted "to continue in the occupancy of their houses on this farm, rent free." Yet Cully Cobb and his colleagues in the cotton section believed that these stringent requirements would antagonize many southern planters and jeopardize the chances for voluntary cooperation. Consequently, they proposed that the qualifying words *"insofar as possible"* be affixed to the requirement that landlords "maintain . . . the normal number of tenants." They also knew that it would be extremely difficult to force a landlord to keep an undesirable tenant, and therefore they proposed that tenants be permitted to "continue in the occupancy of their houses . . . *unless any such tenant shall so conduct himself as to become a nuisance or a menace to the welfare of the producer."* The AAA's legal division objected to these proposed qualifications, pointing out that the additional phrases were vague, left the landlord with the prerogative of determining what was "possible" and who was a "nuisance," and made it impossible to go to court and force a recalcitrant landlord to honor the protective sanctions of paragraph 7.[8] Nevertheless, Secretary Wallace and AAA administrator Chester Davis supported the cotton section on this issue, and the cotton contracts, as finally drafted, expressed nothing but the AAA's hope that tenants would not be evicted.[9] The result was predictable. Beginning in 1934, observers throughout the South reported that many landlords were evicting tenants and thereby reducing their acreage in the easiest and most economical manner. The full extent of tenant displacement became clear when the 1940 census revealed that there were 192,000 fewer black and 150,000 fewer white tenants than there had been in 1930.[10]

Admittedly, the AAA cotton reduction program was not the only cause of tenant displacement during the 1930s. The availability of relief, the mechanization of agriculture, and the movement of population from city to countryside during the depression were other factors that also undermined the tenant's position. Moreover, it should be remembered that there was considerable displacement prior to 1933 when low cotton prices forced the curtailment of the labor force. Yet the AAA cotton reduction program must be charged with responsibility for a significant amount of displacement. As Gunnar Myrdal has written:

> Landlords have been made to reduce drastically the acreage for their main labor-requiring crops. They have been given a large part of the power over the local administration of this program. They have a strong economic incentive to reduce their tenant labor force, a large part of which consists of politically and legally impotent Negroes. Yet they have been asked not to make any reduction. It would certainly not be compatible with usual human behavior if this request generally had been fulfilled. Under the circumstances, there is no reason at all to be surprised about the wholesale decline in tenancy. Indeed, it would be surprising if it had not happened.[11]

When it became apparent that black tenant farmers were not receiving a fair share of the government benefit payments and that some previous difficulties had been aggravated by the AAA, the established Negro betterment organizations moved into action. The NAACP proposed that federal officials accept responsibility for distributing larger payments directly to tenant farmers and recommended the appointment of qualified Negroes to administrative posts in all phases of agricultural administration.[12] Most of the NAACP's suggestions were not adopted,

18

however, and the association then turned to publicizing "the oppression suffered by the Negro—America's real 'forgotten man'—under the New Deal." It condemned the "shameless and unrebuked stealing of government checks made out to sharecroppers and tenant farmers," and chastised the federal government for "ignoring . . . complaints against maladministration, fraud and dishonesty."[13] Walter White, the secretary of the organization, protested strongly against the eviction of black sharecroppers and personally urged President Roosevelt "to instruct AAA to hold up all payments until [the] present situation is straightened out."[14] Benefit payments never were suspended, however, and attorney John P. Davis of the Washington-based Negro lobby, the Joint Committee on National Recovery, reflected a growing disenchantment with the Roosevelt administration when he complained that the government had "failed absolutely to protect the equities of the tenant . . . and made it an easy matter for the cotton producer to defraud and cheat his tenants. . . . Yet the administration in Washington—like Pontius Pilate—washes its hands of the whole matter and leaves it to the consciences of the white plantation owners of the South to see that justice is done."[15] The delegates to the NAACP's twenty-fifth annual conference in 1934 officially declared that the "nearly six million Negroes dependent upon agriculture have found no remedy for their intolerable condition in this [AAA] program."[16]

The response of the Roosevelt administration to the growing criticism of its cotton reduction program was essentially twofold. First, beginning in 1936 the cotton contracts were rewritten so that tenants would receive at least one-quarter of the benefit payment directly from the government, and this amount was raised to one-half in 1938. Yet increasing the tenant's share of the government money gave landlords a greater economic incentive for evicting tenants, a danger that was particularly great because the 1936-39 cotton contracts failed to improve the inadequate security provisions that had been written into paragraph 7 of the earlier contracts. Thus, it is not surprising that tenant displacement continued *at an accelerated rate* after 1935; the orders to increase the tenant's share of the benefit payment evidently prompted many landlords to resort to wholesale eviction.[17]

A second indication of the administration's growing concern for landless farmers occurred in 1937, when the president threw his support behind Senator John Bankhead's proposal to create a Farm Security Administration (FSA) that would provide very liberal tenant purchase loans (3 percent annual interest with a forty-year period for amortization) and additional funds for rural rehabilitation, relief, and resettlement. Despite the fact that

19

the FSA's programs, like those of the AAA, were administered locally, about 23 percent of its benefits in the South were distributed among Negroes—a figure that corresponds closely with the black percentage of the southern rural population. Although one could argue, as Walter White and others did, that even this share was inadequate because the Negro's needs were so much greater and because Negroes made up 40 percent of the South's nonlandowning farmers, it is nevertheless a tribute to the fair-mindedness of the FSA's administrators that Negroes received as large a share of farm security benefits as they did.[18]

The agitation of groups such as the NAACP was partially responsible for the sensitivity of FSA's officials to the special problems of black tenants. Equally important was the fact that Will W. Alexander was chosen as the first administrator of the FSA. Unlike his counterparts in the AAA, Alexander had strong convictions concerning the need for interracial justice and cooperation. He had served as executive director of the Committee on Interracial Cooperation, as a trustee for five southern Negro colleges, as president of New Orleans's predominantly black Dillard University from 1931 to 1935, and as deputy administrator of the Resettlement Administration in 1936-37.[19] During his service with Resettlement, Alexander was constantly plagued by the special problems of black tenants; and to keep himself informed, he appointed a Negro farm specialist, Joseph H. B. Evans, to serve as his administrative assistant. (By way of contrast, Rexford Tugwell was "unable to see what advantage there could be to Negro farmers in the appointment of a special assistant" in the Department of Agriculture, and Henry Wallace claimed that such an appointment would be "patronizing" or even "discriminatory.")[20] Alexander took Evans with him when he moved from Resettlement to Farm Security, and during the next few years other advisers on Negro problems were added to the FSA's central office staff in Washington. Moreover, by 1941 each of the three southern regional directors had a black assistant to advise him concerning the special problems of black tenants. Negroes shared in the FSA benefits to the extent they did only because the Washington and regional offices exerted great pressure on local authorities to grant benefits to needy farmers regardless of race.

Of course, the FSA was not without its shortcomings, the most important being the economic limitations that sharply restricted the scope of its operations. While 192,000 black farm tenants were displaced during the 1930s, the egalitarian but financially starved FSA was able to provide tenant purchase and resettlement loans to only 3,400 Negroes. At this rate,

20

it would have required several centuries to provide farms for all the needy tenants, and there was a grain of truth in the view expressed by Congressman William Lemke of North Dakota: "If ever a mountain labored to produce a mouse this bill is it. We have heard a lot of lip service that we are going to make farm tenants farm owners. In the light of that lip service this bill is a joke and a camouflage."[21] In addition, the FSA cautiously refused to challenge the southern caste system. The FSA countenanced segregation when it decided that applicants for rehabilitation communities would have to be selected "according to the sociological pattern of the community";[22] it bowed to white supremacy when it appointed only 72 Negroes to its staff of more than 7,000 southern farm and home supervisors;[23] and it generally worked with carefully selected tenants who were likely to make a good showing on loan collection records rather than with the most impoverished and needy.[24] Yet these compromises were just that, compromises undertaken to preserve the life of a small program which, however limited, distributed more than 20 percent of its benefits to black farmers. Unlike the leaders of the AAA, who assumed that there was no need for special attention to the problems of black farmers since prosperity was supposed to trickle down to the tenants after the plantation economy had been revived, the FSA made as many special efforts to ensure the distribution of benefits among Negroes as were consistent with institutional survival.

The AAA's dismal neglect of black tenants invites criticism, but has often been excused on the ground that political circumstances restricted the practical operations of the New Deal in the South. Bernard Sternsher, for example, has claimed that critics of the New Deal have not dealt adequately, "in some instances hardly at all, with the question of what the New Deal *could have been*. . . . To say that [Roosevelt] should have been something other than what he was is like saying that if Charlemagne had been more imaginative he would have discovered America in 792."[25] Among the forces constraining the administration, none was more important than southern domination of key congressional committees. Most of these southerners were willing to support the New Deal; they were loyal to the Democratic party, and their sectional economy was desperately in need of federal aid. But most of them also shared the conventional racial attitudes of their section, and President Roosevelt believed he would jeopardize the essential support of these southerners if his administration made any direct efforts to alter the dependent condition of black tenants. When Walter White complained, as he did on several occasions, that the

21

president "did not go as far as he had the power to go," Roosevelt replied that he had "to get legislation for the entire country passed by Congress. If I antagonize the Southerners who dominate Congressional committees through seniority, I'd never be able to get bills passed."[26] Consequently, according to Frank Freidel, Roosevelt had "to modify or water down the New Deal in its practical operation in the South."[27]

Granting that political considerations required caution in race relations, FSA's success in dealing with black tenants suggests that the AAA could have done much more through bold administrative action. Perfunctory criticism doubtless would have emanated from the cotton South if the AAA had appointed qualified Negroes to advisory posts or had protected landless farmers by refusing to release payments to evicting landlords, but this desperately impoverished section simply could not have afforded to refuse cooperation with a program that brought so many benefits.[28] The men in the AAA believed that southern poverty could be alleviated without forcing a modification of either the tenancy system or white supremacy. Blacks, on the other hand, insisted that economic recovery could not be achieved in the South unless special programs were inaugurated to protect black tenants by substantially altering the equilibrium in the tenancy system. The New Dealers insisted that they were not responsible for tenancy, but they never came to grips with the thrust of the Negro argument: that the system of tenancy made black poverty inevitable and that the existence of widespread Negro poverty sooner or later would contradict and undermine white prosperity. Negro leaders believed that during the depression tenancy would have collapsed under the weight of its own inefficiency if the federal government had not rescued it with benefit payments. They insisted that, as NAACP Assistant Secretary Roy Wilkins put it, "now, while the Government is pouring millions of dollars into the South, is the time for it to insist upon the correction of some of the evils of the plantation system as a condition of government aid."[28] Unfortunately, this argument had little impact on the New Deal's most prominent agricultural officials, who consistently maintained that their goal was to revive the plantation system, not to reform landlord-tenant relations. Like some modern historians, New Dealers denied that farm tenancy and farm poverty were inextricably intertwined and insisted that there were legitimate reasons for refusing to make race relations a paramount issue.[29]

Although members of the Roosevelt administration generally agreed that the economy was badly imbalanced because mass purchasing power

22

was insufficient to consume the products of the nation's factories and fields, they were of three minds (with many nuances) when it came to prescribing programs for industrial recovery.

One small group believed that the balance between production and consumption could best be restored by vigorous trust-busting that would destroy oligopolies and force lower prices. However, this antimonopoly approach had little impact on the black community. Although the administration's occasional forays in antitrust prosecution had some effect on the economy at large and on the general price level, there is no way to determine the extent to which Negroes as such were affected.[30]

A second group of New Dealers, with quite different assumptions, insisted that the depression was caused by excessive competition that destroyed reasonable profits, undermined business confidence, and reduced the rate of investment in job-creating enterprises. The solution, according to this view, lay in government-sponsored trade associations that would prohibit unfair competitive practices and establish fair minimum prices that would ensure profits and thus revive investment. These associationist advocates of "fair" competition had a beneficial effect on the black community in that they humanized the competitive struggle and encouraged the spread of labor standards that had existed previously only in the most advanced industrial states. In the past, "rugged individualism" had all too often led to "ragged individualism" for black workers; and in the long run, Negroes stood to benefit a great deal from the surrender of laissez faire and the stabilizing of industry on a basis of fair labor standards.

Unfortunately, many businessmen used cooperation as an excuse for raising prices more than was necessary to offset the cost of shorter hours and higher wages, and some took advantage of cooperation to make arrangements whereby short-run losses were minimized by restricting production. This combination of high prices and diminished production naturally subverted the plan for increasing purchasing power. High prices reduced everyone's purchasing power, and low production quotas led to work stoppage and unemployment. Although the New Dealers were aware of these dangers, they felt there was no alternative but to hope that businessmen would see that their own self-interest demanded that they agree to establish fair wages and hours without at the same time raising prices unduly or restricting production. Hugh Johnson, the administrator of the New Deal's industrial recovery program, appealed to businessmen to "keep prices down, for God's sake, keep prices down." He warned that if no control were placed "on undue price increases so that prices will not move up one bit faster than is justified by higher costs, the consuming public is going to suffer, the higher wages won't do any good, and the whole bright chance will just turn out to be a ghastly failure and another shattered hope."[31] Yet Johnson's plea was generally ignored, and by 1934 members of the Roosevelt administration were sadly acknowledging that "in case after case the price charged to the consumer has gone up . . . more than the increasing purchasing power paid out in production."[32] Insofar as New Deal-sponsored cooperation encouraged higher prices and restricted production, it was a burden for everyone —white and black.

A third group of reformers thought that purchasing power could be increased most effectively by prescribing higher minimum wages, encouraging the development of trade unions, financing employment on public works projects, and dispensing relief. These reformers joined with the cooperationists to produce a hybrid system of industrial cooperation under the supervision of the government's National Recovery Administration (NRA). Declaring that the economy would be invigorated by "increas[ing] the consumption of industrial and agricultural products by increasing purchasing power," the first title of the enabling legislation authorized the NRA to license businesses that were complying with nationally approved standards (minimum wages, maximum hours, recognition of the workers' right to collective bargaining, fair prices); and only those firms would be permitted to engage in interstate commerce or to display the NRA's symbol of compliance, the Blue Eagle. A second title provided for the establishment of a Public Works Administration (PWA) with an appropriation of $3.3 billion to finance construction of "a comprehensive program of public works."[33] Negroes naturally hoped that the new program would revive the economy, and initially most of them supported the NRA. *Opportunity*, the journal of the National Urban League, claimed that "a minimum wage . . . and maximum hours of work . . . will be of immeasurable benefit to the Negro worker who above all others has borne the cruel weight of prolonged unemployment and its resulting misery and want."[34] Yet even at the outset of the New Deal a few perceptive black critics recognized that though the new program might ameliorate the perilous condition of the general population, it would not necessarily improve the position of black workers, because Negroes were affected by the factor of race as well as that of economic condition. It was not long before many black spokesmen were criticizing discrimination in public works programs and claiming that higher minimum wages led to the displacement of black workers who had been employed only because their labor was cheaper.

The pressure of unemployed whites desperately searching for any sort of work naturally increased during the depression, and even before the NRA, white workers were being substituted in jobs customarily held by blacks. Nevertheless, most Negro spokesmen opposed proposals to establish a lower NRA wage scale for black workers. They knew that some blacks would lose their jobs if such a differential scale were not established, but they feared that any racial differential would become the entering wedge of a drive to classify Negroes as inferiors who deserved only substandard benefits. Some blacks also opposed differentials because they thought that workers could improve their position only if they submerged racial differences and joined together in biracial trade unions. Robert Weaver, soon to become a special assistant in the Department of the Interior, believed it would be better to keep the two races on a parity than to create so wide a difference in pay that antagonisms would be aroused; he objected to a racial differential primarily because "it would destroy any possibility of ever forming a strong and effective labor movement in the nation."[35] And Robert Russa Moton, the principal emeritus of Tuskegee Institute, maintained that it would be better for Negroes to lose their jobs than to be "put down by organized labor . . . as a group of strikebreakers and 'scabs.' "[36] Southern businessmen naturally saw things differently. Contending that black labor was less efficient than white, that it cost less to live in the South, and that the whole sociological condition of predominantly agricultural areas would be upset by paying high NRA wages to a few Negroes employed in industry, they appealed for lower minimum wages for the South, and particularly for southern Negroes. But in every case, the NRA rejected southern requests for racial differentials.[37]

While rejecting appeals for explicitly racial wage scales, the NRA permitted a complicated series of occupational and geographical classifications that enabled employers to pay white workers more than blacks.[38] Several NRA codes provided that minimum wage scales would cover only certain positions in the industry—positions generally held by whites. Thus, most of the thirteen thousand Negroes employed in cotton textile mills were classified as "cleaners" and "outside employees," categories specifically exluded from NRA coverage; in foundries there were two classifications of molders, with the black "molder's helper" receiving a lower wage than the white "molder"; and black workers in cotton oil mills were said to be processing farm products and were classified as agricultural laborers beyond the pale of the NRA, even though they were working in industrial factories with vast machinery. In addition, more than one hundred NRA codes established geographical classifications that permitted the payment of lower wages in the South than in other sections of the country. Negro leaders noted, however, that the NRA's geographical classifications were extremely inconsistent and concluded that "the one common denominator in all these variations is the presence or absence of Negro labor. Where most workers in a given territory are Negro, that section is called South and inflicted with low wage rates. Where Negroes are negligible, the procedure is reversed."[39]

Given the social and economic conditions prevailing in the South, the NRA's implicitly discriminatory classifications should not be censured. Black workers certainly would have suffered if the government had forced the payment of equal wages at a time when there was a tremendous surplus of unemployed white workers. The NRA faced an insoluble dilemma: on the one hand, it would be criticized for displacing Negroes if it pushed black wages too high; on the other, it was criticized for allowing any differentials at all. Perhaps its solution to the problem—permitting classifications that applied disproportionately to blacks but refusing to allow a specifically racial differential—was the best arrangement that could be made under the difficult circumstances.

The NRA's general emphasis on minimum wages was more blameworthy. In the South, most factory jobs were restricted to whites, but thousands of Negroes nevertheless were employed by small marginal enterprises that had little capital and obsolete machinery and could compete with more modernized concerns only because they paid less for their labor. Given their antiquated assembly lines, these marginal concerns were plagued by low productivity. By specifying minimum wages per man-hour rather than per unit of production, the NRA placed these inefficient firms at a severe competitive disadvantage. In effect, it forced small enterprises to choose between modernizing and going out of business. Most New Dealers agreed with President Roosevelt that "no business which depends for existence on paying less than living wages to workers has any right to continue in this country."[40] They knew that the NRA's minimum wage laws implied economic death for thousands of marginal enterprises, but they were convinced that "such economic surgery is necessary in a competitive economy in order to preserve the health of the larger body."[41] These sentiments were on a high moral plane, but this should not obscure

26

the fact that either the bankruptcy or the modernization of marginal firms endangered a disproportionate number of Negro jobs.

In Greensboro, Georgia, for example, twenty Negroes were employed by a cotton textile mill. Before the NRA, the daily wage of workers at the mill was about 75 cents for a ten-hour day; afterward, wages ranged from $2 to $2.40 for an eight-hour day. The machinery in this mill was obsolete, and the firm had been able to compete with modernized mills only because its labor costs were so low. With the coming of the NRA, the mill had only two viable alternatives: to evade the NRA's stipulations by taking advantage of the classification system and other loopholes, or to install more productive machinery and pay code wages to fewer workers. Late in 1933, the mill made the second choice. After the new machines were installed, the management calculated that the mill could produce the same amount of goods with twenty fewer workers, and the Negroes were released. Economic factors had dictated the installation of improved machinery; racial attitudes dictated the displacement of Negro employees first.[42]

Similarly, in Virginia, North Carolina, and Kentucky tobacco manufacturing was a major endeavor that since colonial days had depended overwhelmingly on black labor. As a result of the NRA, the average work week in tobacco stemmeries declined from 55 hours to 40, while wages were rising from an average 19.4 cents per hour in 1933 to 32.5 cents in 1935 (a rate that would be doubled by 1940 in response to the subsequent Fair Labor Standards Act). Faced with rising wages, the tobacco companies installed stemming machines and commenced a mechanization program that halved black employment by 1940 while the number of white workmen was increased by more than 40 percent.[43] Thus, although it can be argued that in the long run black workers profited from the NRA-encouraged spread of better labor standards, the immediate impact of minimum wage legislation was harmful. Insofar as the new standards were enforced, efficient, modernized, lily-white firms were given a competitive advantage that enabled them to bankrupt the marginal concerns that employed most Negroes. Under the circumstances, Negroes were fortunate that the NRA was riddled with so many loopholes and classifications, and encumbered with such inadequate enforcement machinery, that most marginal businesses were beyond the effective reach of the Blue Eagle and continued to employ black workers at substandard rates.

In the United States of 1930, twenty-three of every two hundred persons gainfully employed were Negroes. Of these twenty-three, nine were engaged in some form of agricultural work, six were employed in industry, six earned their living as household employees, and the remaining two were engaged in trade, the professions, or public service. A consideration of the manner in which these workers were affected by the NRA must take account of the fact that there were no codes of fair competition, and consequently no government-sponsored increases in wages, for workers engaged in agriculture, domestic service, or the professions. Moreover, as just noted, black workers employed in jobs supposedly covered by the NRA often had to submit to a complicated system of classifications that, in total effect, resembled a racial differential, or run the risk of displacement by unemployed whites. For most black people, then, the NRA meant an increase in the cost of living without a corresponding increase in wages, and they must have sympathized with the *Norfolk Journal and Guide*'s contention that the NRA was defective because it did not reach down

> to the large body of farm and mill laborers or domestic servants. . . . As commodity prices rise—as part of the NRA plan—these people will have to pay more for their bread and meat and clothes and rent. . . . With all costs of living going up the living standards of Negro wage earners will necessarily be forced down. . . . Recovery cannot be accomplished by bestowing all of the benefits of NRA upon white workers and crucifying Negro workers on an economic cross, merely because it has become customary . . . to take advantage.[44]

During the two years of the NRA's existence, Negroes repeatedly insisted that some of the racial problems of the industrial recovery program could be solved if the government would appoint qualified Negroes to key positions in the administration. Within the entire NRA bureaucracy, however, there was only one Negro professional worker, Miss Mabel Byrd, a graduate of the universities of Chicago and Oregon and a specialist in labor relations. Miss Byrd hoped to be sent to the South to study the problems of black labor under the NRA, but her research trip was canceled when high officials decided they would be "playing with fire to send a northern Negro to the South, and certainly one trained in Chicago."[45] Hugh Johnson believed that it would be simply "preposterous" to have a study of Negro labor made by a northern Negro, and Miss Byrd was effectively shut out of the NRA's decision-making process.[46] She was ignored as much as possible, excluded from staff meetings, and late in 1933 informed that there was no work for her and that she would be relieved of her duties. This dismissal left the NRA without anyone specifi-

28

cally concerned with Negro problems and emphasized the recovery administration's indifference to the plight of the black worker. Indeed, as the NRA began its second year of operations, there was not a single Negro employed with a rank equal to that of a clerk, and the Negro press suggested that the initials "NRA" in reality stood for "Negro Removal Act."[47]

The NAACP condemned the recovery administration for its refusal "to name qualified Negro experts to positions of authority" and concluded that "the result of this discrimination has been the impoverishment of hundreds of thousands of black workers and a complete failure in remedying the serious condition of unemployment among Negro workers."[48] Some Negroes, such as T. Arnold Hill, the industrial secretary of the Urban League, admitted that because black industrial workers had been abused for generations the NRA was not responsible for all the Negro's disadvantages. But this was "cold comfort to the hard pressed Negro worker who is looking around today for some means of relief from his present intolerable situation." According to Hill, "Whether [the Negro's] plight began three years ago or three centuries ago, the fact is that [he] remains the most forgotten man in a program planned to deal new cards to the millions of workers neglected and exploited in the shuffle between capital and labor." It was Hill's view that "a government which is honest in its claim of a New Deal, and which wishes to improve the lot of the forgotten man, should protect those who are least protected." But, he concluded, "this has not been done. On the contrary, the will of those who have kept Negroes in economic disfranchisement has been permitted to prevail, and the government has looked on in silence and at times with approval. Consequently, the Negro worker has good reason to feel that his government has betrayed him under the New Deal."[49]

Although the NRA's minimum wage codes were ineffective in terms of stimulating recovery from the depression and failed to have disastrous consequences for marginal black workers only because they were generally evaded, spending for public works offered the government the opportunity to pump purchasing power into the economy without jeopardizing any existing jobs. Yet definite measures were needed to ensure that black people would benefit from public works programs, and, because each New Deal administrative agency established its own procedure for handling Negro problems, much depended on the extent to which the dominant personalities in the Public Works Administration were sensitive to the special problems of Negroes. In this regard, Negroes clearly benefited from President Roosevelt's decision to appoint his secretary of the interior, Harold Ickes, to the post of public works administrator. Ickes was particularly concerned with race problems, and had served as the president of the Chicago branch of the NAACP. He promptly appointed Clark Foreman (white) and Robert Weaver (black) as special assistants to keep him informed on race matters, and local committees in charge of public works in particular areas were encouraged to have Negro members to keep them posted on any special problems that developed. Given this commitment to working with and for Negroes, the PWA provided tremendous benefits for black workers, who, with an unemployment rate more than double the national average, stood to benefit disproportionately from the creation of employment on nondiscriminatory public works projects.[50]

The PWA had a dual purpose: building useful projects and providing employment for those in need of it. With regard to the first of these, most of the work was for projects that would benefit the entire population—roads, dams, post offices, government buildings—and there is no way to determine how Negroes fared as a group. All that can be said, as Ickes observed, is that "they, like the rest of the American population, now have much better facilities in many lines than existed before." Ickes insisted, however, that the PWA did not discriminate "against any project submitted by or for the benefit of Negroes"; and insofar as the color of its beneficiaries can be determined, blacks fared well under the PWA.[51] During President Roosevelt's first administration, the PWA spent more than $13,000,000 for Negro schools and hospitals, a greater infusion of federal funds than had occurred in the seventy preceding years since Emancipation. By 1940, one-third of the 140,000 dwelling units constructed by the PWA and the United States Housing Authority, which succeeded the housing division of the PWA, were inhabited by Negroes. One hundred and thirty-three of the government's 367 housing projects were for the exclusive occupancy of Negroes, and 40 more were for the joint occupancy of blacks and whites. Although many Negroes had reservations about using government money to finance segregated facilities, most knew that it would be foolish to refuse such aid; and they gratefully accepted segregated projects as better than nothing at all. Negroes received 58.7 percent of the federally subsidized housing in the South, and this again suggests that determined federal administrators could overcome much despite the constraints of sectional race prejudice.[53]

The second of the PWA's major purposes—giving employment to the unemployed—presented greater problems for black workers. Due to the exclusion of Negroes from many trade unions and the widespread belief that whites should be given favorable consideration in the allocation of scarce jobs, there was blatant discrimination in many government construction programs. As the PWA began operations, for example, only 11 Negroes were included among the more than four thousand workers employed at the $166,000,000 project at Boulder Dam.[54] Administrator Ickes was determined to prevent discrimination, and to this end he officially ordered that there be "no discrimination exercised against any person because of color or religious affiliation."[55] Yet this ruling established no criteria for determining the existence of discrimination, and many contractors managed to comply by accepting token integration. Several Negroes complained that in their areas, as Roy Wilkins described the situation in New York, "we have discovered some surprising attitudes on the part of construction firms who have erected post offices, court houses, parcel post buildings, etc. To illustrate what they consider 'no discrimination' we found that out of 122 bricklayers on a parcel post building, one was a Negro. The firm handling this contract claims that it was not discriminating."[56] To prevent discrimination effectively it was necessary to find some criterion that could be used to indicate when discrimination existed. Late in 1933, the PWA's housing division decided to include a quota clause in its contracts requiring that skilled black workers receive a portion of the payroll corresponding to at least one-half their percentage in the local labor force. Where it was considered necessary, similar contractual provisions were included to protect unskilled black labor. The advantage of this procedure, according to Robert Weaver, was that it did "not correct an abuse after the project is completed—as is usually the case when Negroes' rights are being protected—but it set up a criterion which is *prima facie* evidence of discrimination. If the contractor does not live up to this requirement, it is accepted— until disproved—that he is discriminating against colored workers. Instead of Government's having to establish the existence of discrimination, it is the contractor's obligation to establish the absence of discrimination."[57]

By and large, this technique proved to be an effective solution to a difficult problem. It was later adopted by the successor to the PWA's housing division, the United States Housing Authority; and as of December 1940, $2,250,000, or 5.8 percent of the total payroll to skilled workers, had been paid to black workers. Weaver could proudly note that "this represented a portion of the total skilled payroll larger than the proportion of Negro artisans reported in the occupational census of 1930."

31

Of course, this method of defining and enforcing nondiscrimination did not solve the problem of Negro unemployment. The objective of the minimum percentage quotas was to retain past occupational advances for Negroes in the 1930s—a period when there was intense competition for every job and when the rate of black unemployment was more than twice as great as that for whites. The clauses, Weaver acknowledged, were "a device to regain lost ground; they were not designed to open new types of employment." Much remained to be done with regard to opening new jobs and upgrading Negro skills, but Weaver was convinced that "it would have been most unrealistic to have attempted to secure significant occupational gains for a minority group in a period when there was mass unemployment."[58]

Beginning in the spring of 1935, certain functions of the PWA, along with some responsibilities of the Federal Emergency Relief Administration (FERA), were taken over by the Works Progress Administration (WPA).[59] Fortunately for Negroes, Harry Hopkins, the director of the WPA, was sensitive to their special problems and appointed a Washington teacher, Alfred E. Smith, as an administrative assistant to coordinate the activities of a staff of Negro advisers: James Atkins, a professor of English from Tennessee A & I State College, served in the adult education division as a specialist in education among Negroes; literary critic Sterling Brown worked as an editor of Negro material in the Federal Writers Project; T. Arnold Hill of the Urban League served as a consultant on white-collar workers; social worker Forrester B. Washington operated as director of Negro work in the FERA; and John W. Whitten was appointed to the post of junior race relations officer. In addition, several of Hopkins's white assistants, led by Aubrey Williams, a top aide in the FERA, were also greatly concerned with the special difficulties of Negroes and did what they could to help resolve problems. The WPA's central administration repeatedly exerted pressure on local authorities to give jobs to needy workers regardless of race.[60]

Largely as a result of these determined efforts, the share of FERA and WPA benefits going to Negroes exceeded their proportion of the general population. The FERA's first relief census reported that more than two million Negroes were on relief in 1933, a percentage of the black population (17.8) that was nearly double the percentage of whites on relief (9.5).[61] By 1935, the number of Negroes on relief had risen to 3,500,000, almost 30 percent of the black population, and an additional 200,000 blacks were working on WPA projects.[62] Altogether, then, almost 40 percent of the nation's black people were either on relief or were receiving support from the WPA. Of course, even this was an unsatisfactory measure of participation because Negro needs were so much greater. The FERA and the WPA constructed hundreds of badly needed Negro schools and recreation centers and provided hundreds of thousands of relief grants and jobs for black workers; but when matched against the needs of the day, all this amounted to little more than the initiation of a mild beginning. Yet it was only because of the fair-mindedness of the central administrations in Washington and their willingness to exert pressure on local authorities that blacks received as large a share of the benefits as they did.

The over-all statistics should not obscure the fact that welfare and work relief practices varied widely, with the Negro's chance for securing government assistance depending on geographical location and the personnel in the local relief offices. Blacks generally were well represented in the North and in the urban areas of the South, but found it difficult to receive government assistance in the rural South, where many landlords insisted that precautions be taken to ensure that relief would not compete with even the most menial employment. Thus, the average monthly expense for Negro relief in Georgia's rural Green County in 1934 was only $2.30, and in Macon County only $1.19.[63] The evicted rural black was in the impossible position of having to seek relief as the only means of staying alive, and yet having his landlord demand that any assistance be kept to a minimum lest relief spoil the tenant or wage hand, if and when regular farm work again became available.

In line with this conviction that government welfare benefits should not be so attractive as to "ruin" those on relief rolls for private employment, most employers in all sections of the country, and especially in the South, insisted that wages for work relief be kept below the prevailing rates in the private labor market. As a result, the WPA was forced to abandon its original thirty-cent-hourly minimum wage and instead established a scale that in 1935 ranged from a low of $19 a month for 130 hours of unskilled work in the rural South to $94 for skilled technical work in the urban North. As in the case of the NRA's classifications, these occupational and geographical categories affected a disproportionately large number of black workers. John P. Davis noted that the $19 rate would cover "71.5 percent of the [southern] Negro working population but only 26 percent of the white working population."[64] Walter White warned that race prejudice would cause black workers in the South to be "uniformly classed as unskilled" and charged the administration with surrendering "to the demands of Governor Eugene Talmadge [of Georgia] and Southern officials."[65] But federal authorities thought it would be foolish to alienate southern support by paying government relief workers more than their counterparts in private enterprise. Indeed, government officials were so concerned with placating local powers that they acquiesced in the release of black workers from federal jobs at harvest time, thus forcing them to take low-paying, seasonal jobs in the fields. Yet in fairness to the work relief program, it must be emphasized that though the WPA was willing to compromise with local forces, it never accepted the $2 and $3 weekly wages that prevailed in large areas of the South and often made life more tolerable for rural workers than it had ever been before.

Negroes also complained of many specific abuses in the relief and work relief programs—so many that it would require a volume to describe and categorize all the charges. The NAACP, for example, charged that black women on work relief in South Carolina were forced to do road work and that female construction workers in Jackson, Mississippi, were supervised by armed guards.[66] The *Chicago Defender* alleged that only three Negro workers were employed in the construction of WPA's black Wendell Phillips High School in Chicago,[67] and other Negro newspapers repeatedly printed similar allegations. The National Urban League charged that there was definite discrimination against Negro employees on the Triborough Bridge project in New York City, on the Inter-City Viaduct in Kansas City, and on all public works in St. Louis.[68] The files of the NAACP and the Urban League are replete with similar charges, and Mary White Ovington, the treasurer of the NAACP, summed up the feelings of most Negroes when she wrote that "as to the Washington work relief, . . . it varies according to the white people chosen to administer it, but always there is discrimination." Government officials such as Aubrey Williams were forced to acknowledge that "most of the contentions are true."[69]

Yet it must again be emphasized that, in spite of its local shortcomings, the FERA-WPA progam of relief and work relief was of enormous importance in helping Negroes survive the depression. Although federal control of relief has often been criticized, it is clear that blacks were served best by federal, as opposed to state or local, control; and many Negroes must have come to believe, with Professor Rayford Logan of Atlanta University, that the black man benefited from the New Deal "in just the proportion that the federal government exercises direct control over [its] many ramifications."[70] Indeed, while the locally controlled AAA cotton reduction program was shoring up the plantation system by displacing labor and subsidizing landowners, the New Deal's relief and work relief programs were providing an unprecedented number of jobs for Negroes, especially in urban areas. Thus, as Donald Hughes Grubbs noted recently, "both the 'push' and the 'pull' forces impelling black urbanization were intensified as an aim or byproduct of national policy."[71]

The Negro's encounter with the New Deal's twin programs for youth, the Civilian Conservation Corps (CCC) and the National Youth Administration (NYA), underscored two important lessons suggested by the experience with the more comprehensive relief programs: the distribution of significant benefits, in spite of inequity and discrimination, to black youths who were represented proportionately in terms of their percentage of the general population but underrepresented in terms of actual need; and the crucial influence, for good or ill, that officials in Washington could bring to bear on local authorities. The CCC was organized in 1933 to help relieve poverty and provide training for young men by employing them in conservation work under joint civilian and military supervision at salaries of about $25 a month. Unfortunately for Negroes, the civilian director of the corps, Robert Fechner, a white Tennessean and a prominent official in the racially exclusionist International Association of Machinists, had so absorbed southern mores that he was determined to prohibit racial mixing and was extremely reluctant to press for either the acceptance of Negroes or the appointment of blacks as supervisors in the segregated colored camps. As a result, the benefits of the CCC in the South were limited at the outset almost wholly to whites; less than 3 percent of the first 250,000 corpsmen were black. The state director of selection in Georgia, John de la Perriere, explained that "there are few negro families who . . . need an income as great as $25 a month in cash"; and, moreover, "at this time of the farming period in the state, it is vitally important that negroes remain in the counties for chopping cotton and for planting other produce."[72] After much pressure from the NAACP and officials in the Departments of Labor and Interior, southern Negroes gradually were admitted to the CCC, and the percentage of blacks increased each year until by 1936 the Negro enrollment had come up to the proportion of Negroes in the total youth population. Altogether, almost 200,000 of the 2,500,000 men who served in the corps during its nine-year life span were black.[73]

Given the customs of the era and the army's traditional Jim Crow organization, it was inevitable that the southern corpsmen would be segregated by race; but the CCC's central administration required segregation wherever there were enough blacks to form a colored company, even in states where companies originally had been integrated and where in at least one instance the governor, Philip LaFollette of Wisconsin, specifically requested that camps in his state be integrated.[74] Accepting the conventional southern view of race relations, director Fechner believed it would be dangerous to allow any but the right type of whites to exercise authority in Negro camps, and the CCC officially prohibited black officials in any position of authority other than that of educational adviser.[75] The education was kept to a minimum and slanted toward preparing blacks for menial jobs.

Thus, although blacks were belatedly and grudgingly permitted to join the CCC, they were segregated in units with limited opportunities for training and advancement and never received the measure of relief to which their economic privation entitled them. Yet despite the missed opportunities and compromised ideals, the CCC did provide relief for 200,000 black youths; and "in doing so it fed many of them better than ever before, provided them with living conditions far superior to their home environments, and gave them valuable academic and vocational training." Despite all the special problems, as one black corpsman noted, "as a job and as an experience, for a man who has no work, I can heartily recommend it."[76] "The failure of CCC," John Salmond has judiciously concluded, "was not so much one of performance as of potential. Much had been accomplished, but much more could conceivably have been done."[77]

Established in 1935, the National Youth Administration set up two programs that were of great assistance to young men and women: a Student Work Program that provided part-time work at a small stipend for youngsters who otherwise could not attend school, and an Out-of-School Work Program for unemployed youths between the ages of 18 and 24. Fortunately for Negroes, Aubrey Williams, the Alabama-born grandson of a planter who had freed a thousand slaves, was appointed as executive director of the NYA, and Williams was prepared to use his considerable skill and influence to help Negroes receive a fair share of the NYA's appropriations. With the support of President Roosevelt, who wanted to avoid a repetition of the CCC's discrimination, Williams named Mordecai W. Johnson, the president of Howard University, to a position on the NYA's advisory committee and, more importantly, appointed Mary McLeod Bethune, the founder of Bethune-Cookman College and president of the National Council of Negro Women, as head of a specially created Division of Negro Affairs. Mrs. Bethune and her black staff, in turn, persuaded most state directors to appoint additional blacks as administrative assistants and committeemen, and eventually more Negroes were employed in administrative positions in the NYA than in any other New Deal program. Although the actual NYA projects were sponsored by people from the local communities, a situation that often complicated the work of these black officials, Mrs. Bethune and her staff enjoyed considerable success in their efforts to ensure a fair deal for black youth. From the outset, Negroes received about 10 percent of NYA's appropriations, with their share increasing to almost 20 percent in the early 1940s as a growing number of whites found jobs in the reviving economy.[78]

At the same time, there were limits to what the NYA accomplished for blacks. Unwilling to jeopardize the existence of the agency's southern operations, Williams and Mrs. Bethune accepted segregated projects, though they never followed the CCC's example of forcing segregation on unwilling localities. In addition, knowing that many whites were thoroughly convinced that blacks should be trained only for "Negro jobs," the NYA accepted a disproportionate amount of servile work; and consequently, as Mrs. Bethune observed, many blacks concluded that "all they can get is cooking, sweeping, and agriculture."[79] Yet these jobs were better than nothing at all, and wherever the local authorities were willing to cooperate, the NYA sponsored projects that held out a larger promise. In Texas, for example, the state administration headed by Lyndon B. Johnson operated fifteen Freshman College Centers that offered special college prep courses each year to about four hundred black high school graduates who were planning to go on to college.[80] The most important weakness of the NYA was not racial discrimination or insensitivity but the very limited scope of its operations. Despite the disproportionately high rates of unemployment for the nation's youth, and particularly black youth, it was not until 1940 that as many as 300,000 young people were served by the Out-of-School Work Program, while the larger student program distributed checks to only a third of a million students each school month from 1935 to 1939, and half a million in 1940 and 1941.[81] Negroes received a fair share of these valuable benefits, but the National Youth Administration was able to help only a minority of those who needed its assistance.

Of all the New Deal's many programs, none had a greater effect on the nation than the social security program, inaugurated in the summer of 1935. This program marked a decisive turning point in American development, a rejection of the older exaltation of individual responsibility and self-help and an acceptance of the government's responsibility for providing social security for the aged, the unemployed, the infirm, and the dependent. Since black people were numbered disproportionately among the socially insecure, they eventually profited from all aspects of the government's social security program. Although blacks were assisted by the welfare provisions from the outset, however, the old-age and unemployment insurance provisions initially covered only 10 percent of the black work force; and thus, ironically, for a few years more blacks felt the impact of social insurance in the form of higher consumer prices (as employers passed on the cost of social insurance for whites) than benefited directly from old-age pension or unemployment checks.

Although they endorsed the principle of social insurance, most Negro leaders objected to three specific aspects in the Roosevelt administration's program. In the first place, they warned that the decision to give the states responsibility for administering the unemployment and welfare programs would lead inevitably to discrimination against southern blacks. George Edmund Haynes of the Race Relations Department of the Federal Council of Churches testified before committees in both the Senate and House of Representatives, reminding congressmen that several locally administered federal programs had been plagued by "repeated, widespread and continued discrimination on account of race or color" and appealing vainly "for a clause in this economic security bill against racial discrimination."[82]

Second, Negroes called attention to the fact that agricultural workers were explicitly excluded from coverage by the program, and most domestic servants were implicitly barred by provisions that extended coverage only to those who worked for employers with at least eight employees. Noting that 65 percent of the nation's black workers were classified in these two categories (and at least another 25 percent of the Negro population was unemployed and thus beyond the pale of social security), the NAACP's Charles H. Houston concluded that "from the Negro's point of view" the administration's Wagner-Lewis social insurance program "looks like a sieve with the holes just big enough for the majority of Negroes to fall through."[83] The association's journal, the *Crisis*, complained that "just as Mr. Roosevelt threw the Negro textile workers to the wolves in order to get the [NRA] Cotton Textile Code adopted in 1933, by exempting them from its provisions, so he and his advisers are preparing to dump overboard the majority of Negro workers in this security legislation program by exemption from pensions and job insurance all farmers, domestics, and casual labor."[84] The *Norfolk Journal and Guide* used the same analogy when it concluded that "like NRA, this new economic panacea seems to be intended to bring security to certain people, but not to all."[85]

Third, Negroes objected to the provision that employee contributions for old-age insurance would be supplemented by taxes on the employer's payroll, and unemployment compensation would be financed entirely by payroll taxes. Such taxes, Negroes contended, were essentially indirect sales taxes that employers would pass on to consumers in the form of higher prices, causing greatest discomfort among the low-waged domestics and agricultural wage hands who would be "doubly exploited" because they did not receive any benefits from the new program but still had to pay higher prices for the necessities of life. Writing in the *Crisis*, Abraham Epstein called for the program to be financed by the federal treasury and pointed out that the refusal to finance the program through progressive taxes had the effect of placing the entire cost of social security on the workers and their employers and exempted the well-to-do from responsibilities they had shared since the establishment of the Elizabethan poor-law system. "No other nation," Epstein insisted, "has ever put into operation an old age insurance plan without placing at least some of the burden on the government in order to make the higher income groups bear their accustomed share."[86]

For these reasons, among others, the administration's Wagner-Lewis social security bill was, as William Leuchtenburg has written, "in many respects . . . an astonishingly inept and conservative piece of legislation."[87] Not surprisingly, most black leaders opposed the administration's bill and supported Representative Ernest Lundeen's proposals to provide generous unemployment and old-age benefits for all workers, with federal subsidies financed by taxes levied on inheritances, gifts, and individual and corporate income in excess of $5,000 a year, and with a firm prohibition of discrimination and uniform minimum standards of administration to be enforced throughout the country.[88]

But though regressive financing, local administration, and the exclusion of black workers were real weaknesses in the social security program, it does not follow that Negroes would have benefited from a more careful and fair drafting of the legislation. Unfortunately, most black workers were trapped by a "Negro wage scale" that in all but a relatively few cases ranged from $100 to $500 a year. These wages were simply too small to permit the slow accumulation of reserves that is the essence of *insurance*. As Charles Houston pointed out, the average monthly pension for the 10 percent of the black population that would someday be eligible for old-age annuities would be only $4.50, or $54 a year.[89] What Negroes needed was not insurance but recognition by the state of its responsibility to cover the overhead social costs of capitalistic production. That is, poor people, black and white, were in no position to provide for their own security during the depression, but depended on their more prosperous fellow citizens to accept responsibility for financing security for those who were elderly, sick, or unemployed.[90] In a word, they needed *welfare*, which the Lundeen bill proposed in the guise of social *insurance*. Given the opposition of the administration, though, the Lundeen proposal had no chance of passage, and the Wagner-Lewis bill was enacted into law.

Despite frequent discrimination and limited funding, the welfare provisions of the Wagner-Lewis program provided immediate benefits for many indigent, infirm, and dependent Negroes; and, in the wake of agitation and negotiation with federal officials over the course of the next four decades, the provisions for unemployment and old-age insurance were modified so as to provide greater coverage for blacks. By emphasizing the need for social insurance, however, the Roosevelt administration misrepresented the needs of the nation's poorest citizens. Although the New Deal provided an unprecedented amount of welfare through FERA, WPA, and other agencies, its welfare programs were always considered temporary expedients to tide the unemployed over until recovery had been achieved. Social insurance, on the other hand, was a permanent program; but because it was insurance, it meant little to those at the bottom of the economic ladder. Some advocates of the Wagner-Lewis program frankly admitted that though social insurance would do little for the indigent and nothing for race relations, it was nevertheless a desirable step forward. But others justified the program with exaggerated claims that it would bring a New Deal to the forgotten man. In retrospect, it would seem that this rhetoric had the effect of deflating discontent by offering hope to the indigent while offering real benefits to the lower middle class, recently fallen from relative affluence and with frustrations and aspirations that threatened to become disruptive. Thus, the administration protected the essentials of the established system, but in so doing it fell well short of its egalitarian promises. Here, at least, in the words of Howard Zinn, "what the New Deal did was to refurbish middle-class America, which had taken a dizzying fall in the depression, . . . and to give just enough to the lowest classes . . . to create an aura of good will. . . . The New Dealers moved in an atmosphere thick with suggestions, but they accepted only enough of these to get the traditional social mechanism moving again, plus just enough more to give a taste of what a truly far-reaching reconstruction might be."[91]

The gulf between egalitarian rhetoric and discriminatory practice was particularly wide in the Tennessee Valley, where Congress, at the president's suggestion, created the Tennessee Valley Authority (TVA) to pioneer the development of regional multipurpose projects. The TVA was authorized to conduct a wide variety of operations: the construction of dams, the supervision of flood control and irrigation, the production of hydroelectric power and fertilizer. But the TVA was concerned with more than simply the production and sale of power and fertilizer. As Arthur E. Morgan, the chairman of the authority, explained, "TVA is not primarily a dam-building job, a fertilizer job or a power-transmission job. . . . We need something more than all these."[92] It was an experiment in comprehensive social planning. "The President," Morgan claimed, "sees the Valley Authority as a means for displacing haphazard, unplanned and unintegrated social and industrial development by introducing increasing elements of order, design and forethought."[93] Morgan's ambitious hopes for regional planning were only partially fulfilled, but historians nevertheless have generally concluded that the TVA was "an eloquent symbol of the time,"[94] "the most spectacularly successful of the New Deal agencies."[95]

Despite the TVA's general obeisance to planning and the need to improve social as well as physical conditions, it was clear to the 250,000 black residents of the valley that the TVA envisioned a lily-white reconstruction. To be sure, on paper the authority prohibited racial discrimination and promised blacks a proportionate share of jobs, but it practiced discrimination in housing, employment, and training. Because many TVA projects were in remote areas where housing was not available, it was necessary for the TVA to build dormitories and camps for the construction workers and villages for the permanent work force. Yet the work camps were segregated, with blacks given inferior accommodations, and Negroes were barred altogether from the "model village" at Norris that TVA spokesmen proudly heralded as an ideal American community that would serve as a "yardstick" for other villages and point the way to new residential possibilities throughout the valley. Black spokesmen naturally were indignant, and Walter White pointed out that "in using Federal funds to establish 'lily-white' communities," the TVA went beyond segregation to exclusion.[96] But John Neely, Jr., the secretary of the authority's board of directors, candidly explained to John P. Davis, "You can raise all the 'rumpus' you like. We just aren't going to mix Negroes and white folks together in any village in TVA."[97]

As for jobs, the TVA claimed that Negroes constituted about 10 percent of the work force—a figure roughly equivalent to their proportion of the total population of the valley—but it admitted that the Negro percentage of the payroll was lower because blacks were concentrated in unskilled construction work. As a matter of fact, the TVA seemed incapable of thinking of blacks in any capacity except that of unskilled and semiskilled laborers. After making a firsthand investigation in 1938, Thurgood Marshall of the NAACP reported that "not a single Negro has a white collar job in the entire TVA set up except for about five Negroes in the training division," and "absolutely no Negro is included in the apprenticeship program"; he concluded that TVA's policy was to "freeze Negro workers into unskilled categories forever."[98] Similarly noting the practically complete exclusion of blacks except as laborers, Charles Houston reported, "There is not even a Negro messenger, a Negro file clerk in the entire TVA organization";[99] and Robert Weaver charged that TVA had "a jim-crow labor policy, and none of the benefits of separation."[100] TVA Personnel Director Gordon R. Clapp claimed that the authority was simply "showing reasonable regard and respect for [the] traditional and reasonable approach of a particular locality," and especially for the views of labor unions that objected to the training and employment of skilled Negroes even in the construction of Jim Crow dormitories and villages.[101] Spokesmen for the NAACP, however, insisted "that TVA is a Federal agency and that TVA jobs are Federal jobs, and as such do not belong exclusively to any one element of citizens regardless whether organized or unorganized."[102]

Claiming that the TVA was "a symbol of the failure of the government to hire Negroes in any capacity except unskilled and semiskilled"[103] and knowing that the valley was one of the few places in the South where protest might be effective, the NAACP made the Tennessee Valley Authority the focal point of a public campaign for more jobs for Negroes. Beginning in 1934, John P. Davis, Charles H. Houston, and Thurgood Marshall were sent to the valley to conduct investigations for the NAACP, and Robert Weaver made a similar probe for the Department of the Interior; and in 1938, Congress established a Joint Investigation Committee under the chairmanship of Senator Victor A. Donahey of Ohio.[104] These inspections confirmed reports about discrimination in housing, employment, and training and pointed additionally to such unfortunate practices as excluding blacks from the recreational areas developed by the TVA and the National Park Service near Norris Dam, employing Negroes in skilled work without comparable pay, and refusing to discipline foremen who harassed and abused black workers. To correct these conditions, Robert Weaver urged the TVA to appoint a director of Negro work and black administrative assistants with responsibility for training and employing skilled black workers and foremen, emphasized the need to make white personnel and staff members recognize that the authority's proclamations against discrimination were going to be enforced, and suggested that the TVA would do well to follow the example of the PWA's housing division and establish objective quotas to determine the existence of discrimination against skilled black workers. Chairman Morgan and the TVA refused to adopt any of these suggestions, however, and by 1938, most Negroes believed that discrimination was a firmly established policy. The majority report of the Joint Congressional Investigating Committee concluded, "On paper the Authority policy toward Negroes is one of no discrimination and a proportionate share of jobs. In practice the Authority has not felt able to enforce this policy as fully as could be desired. . . . The Authority cannot solve the race problem in a year or in ten years, but it can and should do more for Negroes than it is doing."[105]

TVA officials initially claimed that their discriminatory policies were the result of oversight, but that explanation hardly sufficed after the NAACP and other organizations repeatedly brought attention to the authority's unfair race policies. Then, beginning in 1934, the TVA claimed that it could not risk jeopardizing the existence of its entire program by violating the traditional customs of the South. Chairman Morgan, beset by fervent criticism from rugged individualists and staunch defenders of the property rights of competing private enterprises, would do nothing for Negroes that might further antagonize the public and endanger the TVA's daring experiment in regional planning. Instead, he attempted to justify the TVA's neglect of blacks, claiming that they would not be happy in integrated communities, that they would be served best by a cautious policy of "inching along" without arousing racist suspicions that the TVA was violating Tennessee's segregation statutes. He warned that the TVA's black critics were only "provoking . . . anti-Negro sentiment to a more determined attack."[106]

Blacks insisted, however, that local statutes did not apply to federal territory, and that the TVA was a federal agency and as such differed from private employers and was required to conform to national policy and the egalitarian clauses of the Constitution. Moreover, Charles Houston discovered evidence indicating that, far from following local customs, the TVA was injecting a policy of discrimination unknown in the area. Mixed crews and black foremen were frequently employed by nonunion enterprises in the valley, but the TVA's decision to employ union labor while avoiding any semblance of a pro-Negro position had the effect of increasing segregation and black servility "beyond the usual sectional pattern."[107] Similarly, Walter White pointed out that Norris was the only community of its size in the entire valley that completely excluded Negroes, and he condemned "the timidity of those entrusted with the responsibility of directing the policies of TVA."[108]

Beyond timidity, the authority, like many other New Deal agencies, was guilty of indifference and, paradoxically, insufficient planning. The TVA never developed a program for Negro participation because it considered the status of blacks as a matter of only marginal importance. The authority was concerned essentially with promoting the economic recovery of the Valley, and its officials openly claimed that they had "[no] special responsibility to attempt to revise or reconstruct the attitude of this area toward the race question."[109] Consequently the TVA never developed a comprehensive plan to include Negroes, but instead dealt with each race problem as a special case. Negro interests were sacrificed whenever they conflicted with the claims of better-organized and more powerful white groups.

The fear that any challenge to white racism would alienate the South and thus endanger the administration's entire program for economic recovery also dissuaded President Roosevelt from endorsing the major civil rights proposal of his time, the NAACP-sponsored anti-lynching bill. The president was no doubt appalled by the more than one hundred lynchings that occurred during the first five years of the depression, but he refused to create problems for himself by challenging white supremacy and patiently postponed a firm public condemnation of lynching until after two white men were victimized in San Jose, California. Moreover, he never put the anti-lynching bill on his list of "must" legislation and was not willing to speak out against the filibusters and threats of filibusters that prevented the proposal from coming to a vote in the Senate. The president wanted the support of northern blacks, but he did not want to anger the southern congressional delegations, which, despite some misgivings, always remained an important element in the New Deal coalition, voting for its domestic bills and, as the threat of war approached, for the president's foreign policy and defense program.[110] Roosevelt did not oppose those who were working for Negro rights, and on one occasion he told Walter White to "go ahead; you do everything you can do. Whatever you can get done is okay with me, but I just can't do it."[111] He even authorized his wife to "say anything you want [in favor of the anti-lynching bill]. I can always say, 'Well, that is my wife; I can't do anything about her.'"[112] But the president himself would do nothing, explaining, "If I come out for the anti-lynching bill now, [the southerners] will block every bill I ask Congress to pass to keep America from collapsing. I just can't take that risk."[113]

Negroes complained about the silence of "the Sphinx" in the White House, claiming that "the utterly shameless filibuster could not have withstood the pressure of public opinion had [the president] spoken out against it."[114] Yet this criticism missed the mark. Regardless of what the president had done, there was no real chance of cloture being voted and the anti-lynching bill passed. Indeed, there is considerable evidence suggesting that the leaders of the NAACP themselves recognized there was no realistic possibility of securing the legislation; they launched the anti-lynching campaign to keep the name of their organization before the public, to raise funds, and, most importantly, to outmaneuver militant black critics who were demanding that the association deemphasize agitation, courtroom activities, and congressional lobbying and devote more of its attention to the economic problems that plagued the masses of Negroes.[115]

Although the success of Will Alexander's FSA, Harold Ickes's PWA, and Aubrey Williams's NYA demonstrates that bold administrative action could moderate the restrictions of race prejudice and suggests that other New Dealers were using the threat of alienating racists to excuse their own lack of interest in altering prevailing forms of segregation and discrimination, it does not follow that President Roosevelt exaggerated the problems that would have ensued if he had thrown the influence of his office behind a bill considered anathema by the great majority of southern politicians. The fact is that presidents, working in the full glare of publicity and symbolically representing "all the people," do not enjoy as much latitude as administrators who work in relative obscurity and of necessity must specify the multiplicity of conditions under which government funds will be disbursed or curtailed. If President Roosevelt's record in race matters is to be faulted, it is not for failing to endorse a historically premature civil rights bill but for refusing to consider enlightened and fair racial attitudes an important prerequisite for all his administrative officers. The president

45

failed to recognize that the special problems of black farmers and work-ingmen demanded special attention from sensitive administrators, and evidently accepted the facile belief that Negroes would benefit automatic-ally from the New Deal—not because they were singled out for special consideration but because they preeminently belonged to the under-privileged class that the government's recovery programs were designed to assist. Refusing to consider race a matter of vital importance, the president acquiesced in the Negro policies of his various administrators—malign neglect in all too many cases. Many blacks certainly must have wondered if the president, in his inner heart, really was interested in challenging white supremacy, and must have concluded with Roy Wilkins that "it will be found in the record of Franklin Roosevelt that he was no special friend of the Negro."[116]

Beyond this lay the more fundamental and basic deficiencies of "broker leadership." The New Deal was essentially an attempt to solve the nation's economic problems democratically, but such a "democratic" system usu-ally gives the greatest benefits to those who are well organized and politically influential. Since blacks were neither, they inevitably gained little. There were some administrators who were aware of the special problems of Negroes, and they were able to do something for blacks; but other officials were not particularly sensitive, and some were hostile. Essentially, the history of "The New Deal and the Negro" is a chronicle of the manner in which the concern or indifference of individual adminis-trators modified or reinforced an underlying disregard for those without power.

Despite the New Deal's checkered record—an amalgam of concern and assistance, on the one hand, with indifference and neglect, on the other —black voters during the depression abandoned their traditional allegiance to the party of Lincoln. By the end of the 1930s, Negroes were the most favorably disposed of all major social groups toward Franklin D. Roosevelt and the New Deal.[117] There can be no doubt that the benefits accruing as a result of the Roosevelt administration's relief and work relief programs were largely responsible for a major shift in black voting pat-terns. Many Negroes would not have survived the depression without relief, and the distress of the entire black community was alleviated by the administration's programs. Indeed, the impact of relief was so great that contemporary critics of the right and more recent historians of the left have concluded that Negroes were "politically purchased by relief."[118] But though considerations of immediate self-interest were undoubtedly influential with impoverished blacks (as they are with the great majority of all people), it is an extreme oversimplification to suggest, as Dorothy Thompson once did, that "the Negro vote which has traditionally been Republican, partly because of memories of the Civil War, but also because the Republicans paid more for it, has gone largely Democratic because the Democrats are able for the first time to compete—not with cash at the polls but with relief and WPA jobs."[119] Relief was one important factor, but only one, in a complex equation of components that produced the important transformation in black partisan identification.

One of the additional factors that influenced Negro voting behavior was a growing dissatisfaction with the Republican party. During the 1920s, many officials in this party of Emancipation had come to assume that Negro devotion was unalterable and could be renewed simply by reminding blacks of the oppression suffered by Negroes in the Democratic South and by occasional egalitarian speeches and the distribution of patronage to black politicians. Even these meager benefits were curtailed after the GOP's unprecedented southern success in 1928, when Herbert Hoover carried five states that had formerly belonged to the Confederacy, and Republican strategists evidently concluded that the party could permanently attract a large number of southern whites if it dissociated itself from the cause of Negro rights. Thus, President Hoover proceeded in such a manner as to earn Walter White's condemnation as "the man in the lily-White House."[120] Though fifty-seven Negroes were lynched during Hoover's presidency, the chief executive resolutely refused to condemn this form of mob violence.[121] Instead, he insisted on nominating for the Supreme Court a southern judge who had publicly called for the disfranchisement of Negroes;[122] he acquiesced in the segregation of "Gold Star" mothers sent to Europre at government expense to visit the graves of sons killed in World War I;[123] he kept political contacts with blacks to a minimum and refused to be photographed with Negroes until the last month of his second campaign for the presidency;[124] he threw his influence behind the lily-white Republican organizations in the South by consenting to the punishment of dishonest black politicians and allowing dishonest whites to flourish;[125] he sharply reduced the number of first-class appointments for Negroes;[126] and, finally, since blacks were in such desperate economic straits, President Hoover's resistance to federal relief hurt them more than any other group. This record naturally disheartened Negroes, and, except in a few cities where local Republican machines remained solicitous to please blacks, most Negro leaders concluded that the race had

47

allowed the GOP to monopolize its vote for too long and that in the future Negroes should become more independent politically and should support the party that would best serve their immediate interests. The Republican *Chicago Defender* editorialized, "It is now apparent that we have had our political eggs in one basket too long. It is true that tradition has inclined the average Colored voter toward the Republican party, but changing conditions are forcing the thoughtful Colored man and woman to seek protection within the ranks of all parties. . . . The managers of the Democratic party now have an unparalleled opportunity—if they will grasp it. It is their privilege to profit by the blunders of the Republicans."[127]

One Democrat who was eager to take advantage of the opportunity was Joseph Guffey of Pennsylvania. In 1932, upon hearing Robert L. Vann, the Negro editor of the *Pittsburgh Courier*, condemn Republican neglect and indifference and urge blacks to "go home and turn Lincoln's picture to the wall," Guffey envisioned millions of Negroes voting the Democratic ticket and persuaded the reluctant James A. Farley and Louis McHenry Howe to establish the first really effective Negro division of the Democratic campaign committee. Vann was then brought to New York as the division's manager-in-chief, and after the campaign Guffey persuaded President Roosevelt to appoint Vann as assistant to the attorney general, a position once held by a black football star from Harvard and one that Guffey calculated as the best Washington job ever given to a Negro by the Republicans. At the same time, Guffey introduced a special agreement in Pennsylvania whereby Negroes were entitled to 10 percent of the Democratic patronage, "no more and no less." Guffey also insisted that public relief be distributed equitably and threw his support behind a civil rights bill making it a criminal offense for a Pennsylvania hotel, restaurant, or theater to refuse accommodations to Negroes.[128] Guffey was using patronage, public money, and civil rights legislation to court the Negro vote; and in the process, he was making Pennsylvania something of a test case of a strategy designed to lure Negroes into the Democratic coalition. Black voters, concentrated in overwhelmingly Republican Pittsburgh and Philadelphia, cast more of their ballots for Roosevelt in 1932 than for any previous Democratic candidate for the presidency; but the Negro trend toward the Democrats was less pronounced than that of the whites, and Hoover managed to carry every black ward in Philadelphia and one of the two Negro wards in Pittsburgh. Yet as Guffey continued to court black voters, the Democratic trend emerged more clearly; and Negroes contributed significantly to the upsets that sent Guffey to the United States

Senate and his running mate, George H. Earle, to the governorship. Throughout the remainder of the decade, President Roosevelt and his supporters made their best Pennsylvania showings in the black wards of Pittsburgh and Philadelphia, where they generally received about 80 percent of the vote.[129] Thus, Guffey's vision became a shining reality, and Guffey himself became one of the first of the new style of political bosses—liberal in rhetoric and policy and, unlike his conservative predecessors who served big business and raised slush funds in the offices of large corporations, dependent on grants from the federal treasury to support his multitude of clients.

Guffey's experience suggests the crucial importance of local political machines in facilitating or retarding the transformation of Negro partisan identification. Like other citizens, Negroes wanted the recognition and patronage that accompany political victory, and the Negro underworld depended on the sufferance and protection of the ruling machines. (With individual numbers syndicates employing as many as 1,500 policy writers in Chicago and New York, this consideration was of no small importance.) Thus, the transfer of Negro political allegiance to the Democrats was effected most conspicuously in northern cities where the Democrats gained power and where there was a minimum of discrimination in the practical operation of New Deal programs. This was true not only of Guffey's Pennsylvania but also of "Boss" Tom Pendergast's Kansas City and the New York of Jimmie Walker, where Tammany Hall cultivated blacks throughout the 1920s and where many Negroes voted the Democratic ticket in municipal and state elections long before the advent of the New Deal.[130] Conversely, in Chicago, where the local Democrats had traditionally been hostile to the aspirations of blacks and where the Republican machine headed by William Hale "Big Bill" Thompson was extremely eager to please black voters, Negroes lagged well behind whites in shifting to the Democratic party; it was not until 1940 (after a newly ascendant local Democratic machine headed by Mayor Edward J. Kelly had demonstrated its willingness to deal fairly with blacks) that FDR captured a majority of Chicago's Negro vote.[131] But whatever the local variations, the basic trend was consistent: despite tremendous economic deprivation and widespread disillusionment with the Republican party, blacks initially lagged behind whites in shifting to the Democratic party; but in 1936 and thereafter, Negroes became increasingly Democratic while whites were beginning to return to the GOP. The trend in national elections was unmistakably Democratic, even in Des Moines, where Negroes voted overwhelmingly

Republican in "off" or non-presidential years,[132] and in St. Louis, where blacks voted first against the Republicans and then against the Democrats in local elections.[133] Local factors could not stay the basic swing of the political pendulum, though they could influence the width of the arcs.[134]

There is some question, however, as to whether the Democrats were mobilizing the support of blacks who had formerly been Republicans or were organizing those who had not previously participated in the political process. There are, it is true, occasional critical elections in which a considerable number of voters break decisively with their past partisan identifications and form new and durable electoral groupings.[135] The depression witnessed the emergence of new political coalitions, and mobile Negroes fleeing the rural South and then encountering the contrast between the neglect of some Republicans and the concern of many northern Democrats were more likely than other groups to alter their traditional political allegiance.[136] Nevertheless, a growing body of political analysis suggests that most voters enter the electorate with a marked preference for one or the other of the major parties, and this partisan identification increases as the voters grow older.[137] Thus, it is interesting to note that John A. Morsell, a student of black voting behavior in New York during the depression, has concluded that "most of the Negro votes which went Democratic in the thirties had not been Republican before; they had not been in existence before." During the 1920s, many Harlem Negroes expressed their political dissatisfaction by staying away from the polls. With the depression and the New Deal, however, there was a politicization of the masses, a surging participation in politics on the part of young people in the process of establishing their partisan identification and among previously apathetic citizens. The number of votes cast in Harlem increased by 50 percent during the depression, while the total population increased by only 1 percent, and these new voters were overwhelmingly Democratic. By 1936, when Franklin D. Roosevelt's *plurality* in black Harlem exceeded the largest Republican *totals* of the 1920s, Negroes were securely ensconced in the New Deal coalition. But it seems likely that most of these black Democrats were not erstwhile Republicans who had turned Lincoln's picture to the wall but younger people and other new voters in the process of forming their political allegiance.[138] (That these new Democrats would adhere ever more tenaciously to their party as they grew older should occasion no surprise. The elaborate data collected by the Survey Research Center at the University of Michigan have demonstrated that once voters establish a prevailing disposition, they are only marginally affected by the immediate issues and candidates in an election.)

Granting the significance of Negro disillusionment with the GOP, the emergence of egalitarian Democratic machines, and the opportunity created by the migration- and depression-induced surge of new voters to the polls, there was still an area of discretion within which the personality and policies of President Roosevelt could exercise great influence. Roosevelt possessed, as Leslie Fishel has noted, a "consummate ability to personalize his understanding of human exploitation and underprivilege." His voice "exuded warmth and a personal inflection which brought him close to his listeners. His own physical affliction and the way he bore it earned him deserved admiration and gave encouragement to those who had afflictions of their own."[139] Yet FDR's personal charm had a negligible impact on the black community during the election campaign of 1932. Negroes recalled that Roosevelt had served as assistant secretary of the navy in the segregationist Wilson administration and had uncomplainingly signed and forwarded orders Jim Crowing the rest rooms in the buildings of the navy department.[140] As a candidate for the vice-presidency in 1920, he had boasted of having written a constitution for Haiti ("and if I do say it, I think it is a pretty good constitution") that placed this black Caribbean republic under the control of American financial interests and the United States Marines.[141] Negroes were far from reassured by FDR's periodic vacations at his "second home," a "segregated mud hole" at Warm Springs, Georgia, and they looked askance at his delight in "listening to the singing of Negro musicians dressed like old-time plantation hands."[142] They positively feared that, if anything should happen to Roosevelt, his running mate, John Nance Garner of Uvalde, Texas, would preside over a resurgence of Jim Crow discrimination in the nation's capital.[143] Although a majority of black leaders endorsed Roosevelt in 1932 on the ground that "a vote for Roosevelt means merely a protest against Hoover,"[144] about three-fifths of the black electorate remained loyal to the Republican party.[145]

In 1936, however, the Democrats captured about 75 percent of the Negro vote, ballots that were cast almost entirely in cities where there was relatively little discrimination and where the benefits of the New Deal were most apparent. By this date, moreover, many blacks had begun to react positively to Franklin D. Roosevelt as a human being. Despite discrimination in the implementation of New Deal programs and the administration's cautious fear of alienating the white South, the president did speak out forcefully against the crime of lynching,[146] even while he refused to use his influence in an effort to break the southern filibuster that prevented a vote on anti-lynching legislation. In notable contrast with President Hoover, Roosevelt frequently conferred with black leaders and graciously received Stenio Vincent, the black president of Haiti.[147] He had, moreover, appointed some Negroes to advisory positions in the New Deal, not just politicians brought in as patronage appointees but professional men employed for the express purpose of securing relief from flagrant discrimination and integrating Negroes into the administration's recovery program.[148]

Equally important, in terms of the blacks' increasingly favorable impression of the president, were the activities of the first lady, Eleanor Roosevelt. At the very outset of the New Deal, Mrs. Roosevelt arranged a special conference with black leaders to discuss the integration of Negroes into the New Deal's subsistence homestead program,[149] and thereafter she repeatedly manifested her concern for the special problems of blacks. She acted as an intermediary between Walter White and the president during negotiations over anti-lynching legislation and clearly indicated that her sympathies were with the NAACP.[150] While attending the Southern Conference on Human Welfare in Birmingham, Alabama, she conspicuously took a seat on the "Colored" side of the segregated auditorium and refused to move to the "White" side. When police threatened to cancel the meeting, she reluctantly moved her chair to the middle of the aisle separating the two sections and refused to move again.[151] When the Daughters of the American Revolution refused to permit the gifted black contralto, Marian Anderson, to give a concert in Constitution Hall, Mrs. Roosevelt publicly resigned her membership in the DAR and immediately set about making arrangements to hold the concert at the Lincoln Memorial.[152] Throughout her years in the White House, she broke with previous tradition by holding receptions for black leaders and student groups.

The impact of Mrs. Roosevelt's personal conduct and example is difficult to determine, but impressionistic evidence indicates that it was considerable. Roy Wilkins claimed that Franklin Roosevelt was a friend of the Negro "only insofar as he refused to exclude the Negro from his general policies that applied to the whole country," but Mrs. Roosevelt was a true champion of the race. "The personal touches and the personal fight against discrimination were Mrs. Roosevelt's. That attached to Roosevelt also—he couldn't hardly get away from it—and he reaped the political benefit from it."[153] The *Pittsburgh Courier* later recalled that "though her husband as President was given credit for sympathizing with the plight and aspirations of Negroes, it has since become apparent that it was she who made him conscious of the social injustices existing in the country."[154]

While New Deal benefits trickled down to the black community and while President and Mrs. Roosevelt assumed an increasingly egalitarian posture, the Democrats of 1936 organized an ambitious campaign for the Negro vote. Openly acknowledging that blacks held the "balance of power" in Pennsylvania, Ohio, Indiana, Michigan, and Illinois, campaign manager James A. Farley established two amply staffed Colored Democratic Divisions—under the general supervision of Robert L. Vann, with the Negro attorney Julian Rainey in charge of eastern operations and the first Negro Democratic congressman, Arthur W. Mitchell of Chicago, at the helm in the West.[155] These organizations waged an extremely effective campaign: they publicized the New Deal's benefits; secured an official endorsement from the Bishops' Council of the African Methodist Episcopal Church and testimonials from blacks as diverse as heavyweight boxing champion Joe Louis and Tuskegee Principal Frederick Douglass Patterson;[156] held dances, such as one at Philadelphia's Convention Hall that was free of charge to those who stopped by Democratic headquarters to pick up their tickets, and monster rallies, such as one gathering of 20,000 blacks at New York's Madison Square Garden where the Colored Committee ceremoniously unveiled a colossal painting of FDR standing to a height of twenty feet, his hands outstretched in benediction over a kneeling group of Negroes with the spirit of Abraham Lincoln hovering in the background.[157] Catching the spirit of the campaign, President Roosevelt himself addressed the assembled black students and faculty of Howard University and proclaimed that "among American citizens there should be no forgotten men and no forgotten races."[158]

Yet it would be a mistake to conclude that black voters were simply seduced by Democratic rhetoric.[159] They could not fail to observe widespread discrimination and had firsthand knowledge of the limited nature of the Roosevelt administration's recovery program. To reinforce this awareness, the Colored Divisions of the Republican party spent twice as much as their Democratic counterparts pointing out the deficiencies of the New Deal and enlisting the support of such celebrities as Mamie Smith and the Beale Street Boys, J. Finley Wilson of the Negro Elks, and Olympic sprint champion Jesse Owens.[160] Francis E. Rivers, a black graduate of Yale and the director of colored Republican operations in the East, sounded the keynote of the 1936 campaign when he declared that dependence on relief would inevitably lead to "political and economic serfdom." There could be no lasting solution to the Negro's economic problems, Rivers insisted, until black people were reemployed and integrated into the productive life of the nation, and he complained that the New Deal's AAA and NRA programs had actually reinforced the trend toward Negro displacement.[161] Continuing with this theme, Governor Alfred M. Landon of Kansas, the Republican nominee for the presidency, charged that the New Deal was using "relief rolls as modern reservations on which the great colored race is to be confined forever as a ward of the Federal Government, . . . excluded from the productive life of the country." Landon predicted that this policy would prove to be "not only disastrous to a great people, but of alarming consequence to our entire economic and social life."[162] Other black Republicans presciently warned that continued dependence on government largesse might destroy self-respect and independence and paralyze the will to work. In 1935, for example, Professor Newell D. Eason of Shaw University predicted that relief would pauperize the race by inculcating a certain contempt for work and a willingness "to cling to the minimum existence which seems to be guaranteed by the relief agency." Noting that relief grants often approximated the meager wages for which blacks had labored so industriously in the past, Eason thought it was understandable that "normal attitudes toward work are not being preserved," but he warned that in the long run black people would suffer most from any erosion of the traditional work ethic.[163]

In retrospect we can see that there was some merit to the Republican critique of the New Deal, but most Negroes of the depression decade could not afford the luxury of considering the long-range ramifications of the dole. They were in desperate and immediate need of welfare and government employment, and for most, as Lillian P. Davis noted, this relief was not just "a pittance to drag them through . . . but a godsend of plenty such as in all their lives for generations back they have never known before."[164] The *Baltimore Afro-American* spoke for most Negroes when it claimed that though "relief and WPA are not ideal, they are better than the Hoover bread lines and they'll have to do until the real thing comes along."[165] The *Pittsburgh Courier* reflected the prevailing Negro mood when it editorialized that as a result of the New Deal

armies of unemployed Negro workers have been kept from the near-starvation level on which they lived under President Hoover. . . . Armies of unemployed Negro workers have found work on the various PWA, CWA, WPA,

THE NEW DEAL AND THE NEGRO 211

CCC, FERA, and other projects. . . . Critics will point to discrimination against colored sharecroppers, against Negro skilled and unskilled labor. . . . This is all true. It would be useless to deny it even if there were any inclination to do so, which there is not. . . . But what administration within the memory of man has done a better job in that direction considering the very imperfect human material with which it had to work? The answer, of course, is none.[166]

1. Federal Emergency Relief Administration, *Unemployment Relief Census* (Washington, 1933), report 2, p. 26.

2. *Baltimore Afro-American*, 24 Sept. 1932.

3. For a detailed and extensively documented discussion of the impact of the New Deal's agricultural recovery program on black farmers, see Raymond Wolters, *Negroes and the Great Depression: The Problem of Economic Recovery* (Westport, Conn., 1970), pp.3–79.

4. Mordecai Ezekiel to Henry Wallace, Memorandum, 5 Feb. 1936, Records of the Department of Agriculture, R.G. 16 (National Archives).

5. Jerome Frank to D. P. Trent, Memorandum, 5 Nov. 1934; Cully Cobb to Chester Davis, Memorandum, 26 Oct. 1934, Records of the Agricultural Adjustment Administration, R.G. 145 (National Archives).

6. Calvin B. Hoover, "Human Problems in Acreage Reduction in the South," 1935 typescript in AAA Records.

7. Paul Appleby to Walter White, 6 Mar. 1935, AAA Records.

8. Oscar Johnston to Chester Davis, Memorandum, 26 Jan. 1935; Alger Hiss to Jerome Frank, Memorandum, 26 Jan. 1935, AAA Records (italics added).

9. David Eugene Conrad, *The Forgotten Farmers: The Story of Sharecroppers in the New Deal* (Urbana, Ill., 1965), pp. 57–59.

10. The census data on this point have been conveniently summarized by Gunnar Myrdal, *An American Dilemma* (New York, 1944), p. 253.

11. Ibid., p. 258.

12. John P. Davis to Henry Wallace, 23 Apr. 1934; White to Wallace, 21 Feb. 1935, Agriculture Department Records.

13. NAACP Press Release, 1 July 1934; Resolutions of the 25th (1934), 26th (1935), and 27th (1936) Annual Conferences of the NAACP, NAACP Files (Library of Congress).

14. White to Franklin D. Roosevelt, Telegram, 18 Feb. 1935, OF 2538, Roosevelt Papers (Franklin D. Roosevelt Library).

15. John P. Davis, Speech to the 25th (1934) Annual Conference of the NAACP, NAACP Files.

16. Resolutions of the 25th (1934) Annual Conference of the NAACP, NAACP Files.

17. Wolters, *Negroes and the Great Depression*, pp. 58–60; Myrdal, *American Dilemma*, pp. 253, 257; Louis Cantor, *A Prologue to the Protest Movement: The Missouri Sharecropper Roadside Demonstration of 1939* (Durham, N.C., 1969), pp. 42–43.

18. Richard Sterner, *The Negro's Share* (New York, 1943), pp. 295–309.

19. For Alexander's career, see Wilma Dykeman and James Stokeley, *Seeds of Southern Change: The Life of Will Alexander* (Chicago, 1962). For a full discussion of "The Negro in the New Deal Resettlement Program," see Donald Holley's article in *Agricultural History* 45 (1971): 179–93.

20. Rexford G. Tugwell to Fred Hildrebrandt, 4 Aug. 1933; Tugwell to W. F. Reden, 7 July 1933; Wallace to Hildrebrandt, 28 Aug. 1933, Agriculture Department Records.

21. U.S. Cong., House, *Congressional Record*, 75th Cong., 1st sess., 1937, 81, pt. 6:6438.

22. Paul K. Conkin, *Tomorrow a New World: The New Deal Community Program* (Ithaca, N.Y., 1959), p. 200.

23. Wolters, *Negroes and the Great Depression*, p. 77n.

24. Sidney Baldwin, *Poverty and Politics: The Rise and Decline of the Farm Security Administration* (Chapel Hill, N.C., 1968), pp. 193–294, and especially pp. 217 and 255.

25. Bernard Sternsher, ed., *The Negro in Depression and War: Prelude to Revolution, 1930–1945* (Chicago, 1969), pp. 46–47.

26. Allan Morrison, "The Secret Papers of FDR," *Negro Digest* 9 (1951): 9; Walter White, "Roosevelt and the Negro," typescript, no date, NAACP Files.

27. Frank Freidel, *F. D. R. and the South* (Baton Rouge, La., 1965) p. 36.

28. Roy Wilkins to Oscar Chapman, 21 May 1934, NAACP Files.

29. Jerold Auerbach, "New Deal, Old Deal, or Raw Deal: Some Thoughts on New Left Historiography," *Journal of Southern History* 35 (1969): 21–22. A few New Deal officials could not accept these priorities, but they were either isolated or, as in the famous purge of 1935, forced to resign from the agricultural administrations.

30. For an extended analysis of the rationale behind the New Deal's industrial recovery program, see Ellis W. Hawley, *The New Deal and the Problem of Monopoly* (Princeton, N.J., 1966), pp. 3–146.

31. Arthur M. Schlesinger, Jr., *The Coming of the New Deal* (Boston, 1959), p. 131; Charles L. Dearing and Associates, *The ABC of the NRA* (Washington, 1934), p. 32n.

32. Gardiner Means, "The Consumer and the New Deal," *Annals of the American Academy of Political and Social Science* 173 (1934): 11.

33. U.S., *Statutes at Large*, 48, pt. 1: 195.

34. *Opportunity* 11 (1933): 199.

35. Robert C. Weaver, "A Wage Differential Based on Race," *Crisis* 41 (1934): 238.

36. *Pittsburgh Courier*, 30 Sept. 1933.

37. Wolters, *Negroes and the Great Depression*, pp. 98–113.

38. Ibid., pp. 124–35.

39. John P. Davis, Speech to the 25th (1934) Annual Conference of the NAACP, NAACP Files; Allan A. Banks, Jr., "Wage Differentials and the Negro Under the NRA," (M.A. thesis, Howard University, 1938). For example, in the fertilizer industry, where 90 percent of the workers were black, seventeen states were classified as southern and given wage rates 40 percent below those elsewhere in the country; yet in cotton textiles, where very few Negroes were covered by the codes, only eleven states were classified as southern and the wage rate was only 8 percent below that paid outside of the South. Evidence such as this convinced Roy Wilkins that the differentials, "while not labeled on the basis of color, have nevertheless operated almost exclusively on that basis." Roy Wilkins to Oscar Chapman, 21 May 1934, NAACP Files.

40. Samuel I. Rosenman, ed., *The Public Papers and Addresses of Franklin D. Roosevelt*, 13 vols. (New York, 1938–50), 2:251.

41. Joel Berrall to R. L. Houston, Memorandum, 10 Sept. 1934, Records of the National Recovery Administration, R.G. 9 (National Archives).

42. Arthur F. Raper, *Preface to Peasantry* (Chapel Hill, N.C., 1934), p. 241.

43. Herbert Northrup, *The Negro in the Tobacco Industry* (Philadelphia, 1970), pp. 26–29.

44. *Norfolk Journal and Guide*, 12 Aug. 1933.

45. Minutes of the 18 Sept. 1933 meeting of the Special Industrial Recovery Board, as published in the *Chicago Defender*, 23 Dec. 1933.

46. Horace R. Cayton and George S. Mitchell, *Black Workers and the New Unions* (Chapel Hill, N.C., 1939), p. 102n.

47. Wolters, *Negroes and the Great Depression*, pp. 135–48; William Pickens, "NRA—'Negro Removal Act'?", *World Tomorrow* 16 (1933): 539–40.

48. Resolutions of the 25th (1934) Annual Conference of the NAACP, NAACP Files.

49. T. Arnold Hill, "The Plight of the Negro Industrial Worker," *Journal of Negro Education* 5 (1936): 40.

50. Wolters, *Negroes and Great Depression*, pp. 193–203.

51. Ickes, Message to the 26th (1935) Annual Conference of the NAACP, NAACP Files.

52. Harold Ickes to George McGill, 13 Nov. 1934, Records of the Department of Interior, R.G.48 (National Archives): Sterner, *The Negro's Share*, p. 319.

53. Sterner, *The Negro's Share*, p. 319. Unfortunately, two other New Deal housing agencies—the Home Owners' Loan Corporation and the Federal Housing Administration—encouraged segregation. Organized on the basis of ordinary business principles and consequently concerned with protecting real estate values, the HOLC and the FHA prohibited all influences that were thought to endanger property values. Although the FHA *Manual* was careful not to refer to Negroes as an adverse influence, the discussion of natural physical protection contained the statement that "protection from adverse influences . . . includes prevention of the infiltration of business and industrial uses, lower class occupancy, and inharmonious racial groups." It recommended a number of deed restrictions, including "g. Prohibition of the occupancy of properties except by the race for which they are intended." FHA, *Underwriting Manual* (Washington, 1938), pp. 932, 935, 980.

54. William Pickens to White, Memorandum, 21 Sept. 1936; Wilkins to Charles West, 18 May 1936; Wilkins to Chapman, 21 May 1934, NAACP Files.

55. Ickes, Message to the 26th (1935) Annual Conference of the NAACP, NAACP Files.

56. Wilkins to Harry Hopkins, 30 Nov. 1934, Records of the Works Progress Administration, R.G. 69 (National Archives).

57. Robert C. Weaver, "An Experiment in Negro Labor," *Opportunity* 14 (1936): 298.

58. Robert C. Weaver, *Negro Labor: A National Problem* (New York, 1946), pp. 12–13.

59. For a discussion of the Negro policies of the FERA, see Sterner, *The Negro's Share*, pp. 218–38.

60. Alfred E. Smith, "New Deal Gives Negro Square Deal," in *WPA and the Negro*, 1937 pamphlet, Department of the Interior Records; Ralph J. Bunche, "The Political Status of the Negro," typescript, Carnegie-Myrdal Manuscripts (135th Street Branch, New York Public Library), pp. 1393–98.

61. Federal Emergency Relief Administration, *Unemployment Relief Census*, 1933, report 2.

62. Sterner, *The Negro's Share*, pp. 239–53.

63. Raper, *Preface to Peasantry*, p. 260.

64. John P. Davis, "Report of the Executive Secretary," 1 June 1935, typescript, Records of the Department of Labor, R.G. 183 (National Archives).

65. White to Roosevelt, Telegram, 21 May 1935, NAACP Files; "U.S. Adopts the Georgia Plan," *Crisis* 42 (1935): 17.

66. *Norfolk Journal and Guide*, 6 May 1933.

67. *Chicago Defender*, 16 Feb. 1935.

68. National Urban League, "The Negro Working People and National Recovery," typescript, 4 Jan. 1937; St. Louis Branch of the Urban League, "Report on Local Labor Conditions, 1934," typescript, NAACP Files; *Opportunity* 14 (1936): 316.

69. Mary White Ovington to Wilkins, 6 Mar. 1934, NAACP Files; Aubrey Williams to Hopkins, 30 Nov. 1934, WPA Records.

70. Rayford W. Logan, "The Negro and the National Recovery Program," *Sphinx*, March 1934, p. 10.

71. Donald Hughes Grubbs, "Tenant Farmers and the Second Reconstruction," paper presented to the Southern Historical Association, November 1971, pp. 9–10.

72. W. Frank Persons to John de la Perriere, Memorandum of Telephone Conversation, 19 May 1933; Persons to Frances Perkins, 1 June 1933, Records of the Civilian Conservation Corps, R.G. 35 (National Archives).

73. John A. Salmond, "The Civilian Conservation Corps and the Negro," *Journal of American History* 42 (1965): 75–88.

74. Philip La Follette to Robert Fechner, 19 Dec. 1938, CCC Records.

75. President Roosevelt was undoubtedly embarrassed by this racist refusal to appoint Negroes to administrative positions in the CCC, and he issued an executive order revoking Fechner's ban. Yet a de facto prohibition remained in effect, and the president evidently decided it would not be politically expedient to make a major issue of this point.

76. Luther C. Wandall, "A Negro in the CCC," *Crisis* 42 (1935): 254.

77. Salmond, "The Civilian Conservation Corps and the Negro," p. 88.

78. Allen F. Kifer, "The Negro Under the New Deal" (Ph.D. diss., University of Wisconsin, 1961), pp. 261–69.

79. Mrs. Bethune, as quoted by Kifer, "The Negro Under the New Deal," p. 133.

80. Kifer, "The Negro Under the New Deal," pp. 127–28.

81. Ibid., pp. 82–83.

82. George Edmund Haynes, "Lily-White Social Security," *Crisis* 42 (1935): 85–86.

83. "Statement of Charles H. Houston," prepared for Hearing of the Senate Finance Committee, 74th Cong., 1st sess., typescript, 9 Feb. 1935, NAACP Files.

84. "Social Security—for White Folks," *Crisis* 42 (1935): 80.

85. *Norfolk Journal and Guide*, 9 Feb. 1935.

86. Abraham Epstein, "The Social Security Act," *Crisis* 42 (1935): 333–34, 338, 347.

87. William E. Leuchtenburg, *Franklin D. Roosevelt and the New Deal, 1932–1940* (New York, 1963), p. 132.

88. Wilkins to White, Memorandum, 2 Feb. 1935, NAACP Files; T. Arnold Hill, "A Statement of Opinion on H.R. 2827 (Lundeen Bill)," 1935 typescript in Urban League Files (Library of Congress).

89. "Statement of Charles H. Houston."

90. Frank G. Davis, "The Effects of the Social Security Act upon the Status of the Negro" (Ph.D. diss., State University of Iowa, 1938), passim.

91. Howard Zinn, ed., *New Deal Thought* (Indianapolis, 1966), pp. xvi-xvii.

92. Schlesinger, *Coming of the New Deal*, p. 327.

93. John P. Davis and Charles H. Houston, "TVA: Lily-White Reconstruction," *Crisis* 41 (1934): 290.

94. Schlesinger, *Coming of the New Deal*, p. 334.

95. Leuchtenburg, *Franklin D. Roosevelt and the New Deal*, p. 165.

96. Walter White, Foreword to John P. Davis, "The Negro and TVA," typescript, 1935, NAACP Files.

97. Davis, "The Negro and TVA," p. 16.

98. Thurgood Marshall, Memorandum for Press Release, 11 Aug. 1938, NAACP Files.

99. Charles H. Houston, "Abstract of Proposed Testimony before Joint Congressional Investigating Committee," typescript, August 1938, p. 5, NAACP Files; Testimony of Charles H. Houston, U.S. Cong., Joint Committee of the Investigation of the Tennessee Valley Authority, Hearings pursuant to Public Resolution No. 83, 75th Cong., 3d sess., 1935, pt. 6, pp. 2347–90.

100. Robert C. Weaver to Arthur E. Morgan, 12 Feb. 1935, NAACP Files.

101. *Knoxville News-Sentinel*, 31 Aug. 1938.

102. Houston, "Abstract of Proposed Testimony," p. 7.

103. Charles H. Houston, Memorandum for the Files, 25 Aug. 1938, NAACP Files.

104. Davis and Houston, "TVA: Lily-White Reconstruction," pp. 290–91; 311; Davis, "The Negro and TVA," passim; Thurgood Marshall to Sylvia R. Frank, 10 Oct. 1938; Weaver to Morgan, 12 Nov. 1935, NAACP Files.

105. U.S. Cong., Joint Committee on the Investigation of the Tennessee Valley Authority, *Report pursuant to Public Resolution No. 83*, 76th Cong., 1st sess., Sen. Doc. 56, pt. 1, pp. 56–58.

106. John P. Davis, "The Plight of the Negro in the Tennessee Valley," *Crisis* 42 (1935): 315.

107. Houston, "Abstract of Proposed Testimony," p. 6.

108. White, Forword to Davis, "The Negro and TVA."

109. *Knoxville News-Sentinel*, 31 Aug. 1938.

110. Freidel, *F. D. R. and the South*, pp. 71–102.

111. Walter White, "Roosevelt and the Negro," typescript, n.d., NAACP Files.

112. Tamara Hareven, *Eleanor Roosevelt: An American Conscience* (Chicago, 1968), p. 123.

113. Walter White, *A Man Called White: The Autobiography of Walter White* (New York, 1948), p. 169–70.

114. White to Roosevelt, 6 May 1935, OF6-Q, Roosevelt Papers; *Norfolk Journal and Guide*, 2 Mar. 1935.

115. Wolters, *Negroes and the Great Depression*, pp. 302–52, 365–66.

116. Roy Wilkins, interview in the Columbia University Oral History Project, pp. 98–99.

117. On this point, see the public opinion survey in *Fortune* 18 (July 1938): 37.

118. Paul K. Conkin, *The New Deal* (New York, 1967), p. 75.

119. Dorothy Thompson, column, *New York Herald Tribune*, 11 Aug. 1936. The relation between the Roosevelt vote and the percentage of Negroes on relief was positive but not close. In Chicago, for example, about 60 percent of the black population was on relief, but Roosevelt's share of the vote was 24 percent in 1932, 49 percent in 1936, and 53 percent in 1940. Obviously, then, at least 10 percent of the Negroes on relief were voting Republican; and Harold F. Gosnell of the University of Chicago, perhaps the most eminent black political scientist of the 1930s, was "inclined to the view that a much larger proportion of the Negroes on relief actually voted Republican." One of Gosnell's able graduate students, Elmer Henderson, calculated that "about 16 percent of the variation in the Negro vote as between census tracts could be explained by variations in the ratios of those on relief." See Gosnell, "The Negro Vote in Northern Cities," *National Municipal Review* 30 (1941): 264–67, 278; and Henderson, "A Study of the Basic Factors Involved in the Change in the Party Alignment of Negroes in Chicago, 1932–1938" (M.A. thesis, University of Chicago, 1939).

120. White, *A Man Called White*, pp. 102–19. Richard B. Sherman has written a thorough account of black voters and the Republican party: *The Republican Party and Black America from McKinley to Hoover* (Charlottesville, Va., 1973).

121. *Chicago Defender*, 9 Dec. 1933.

122. Richard L. Watson, Jr., "The Defeat of Judge Parker: A Study in Pressure Groups and Politics," *Mississippi Valley Historical Review* 50 (1963): 213–34.

123. White to W. J. Rice, 29 Sept. 1932, NAACP Files.

124. *Norfolk Journal and Guide*, 22 Oct. 1932.

125. W. E. B. Du Bois, "Mr. Hoover and the South," *Crisis* 36 (1929): 131–32; Du Bois, "Mr. Hoover and the Negro," *Crisis* 38 (1931): 207–8.

126. Du Bois, "Mr. Hoover and the Negro," pp. 207–8; *New York Times*, 23 May 1932.

127. *Chicago Defender*, 11, 25 June 1932.

128. On Guffey, see Joseph Alsop and Robert Kintner, "The Guffey: Biography of a Boss, New Style," *Saturday Evening Post*, 26 Mar. 1938, pp. 5–7, 98–102. On Vann, see James H. Brewer, "Robert Lee Vann, Democrat or Republican: An Advocate of Loose Leaf Politics," *Negro History Bulletin* 21 (1958): 100–103.

129. On Negro voting in Philadelphia and Pittsburgh, see James Erroll Miller, "The Negro in Pennsylvania Politics with Special Reference to Philadelphia since 1932" (Ph.D. diss., University of Pennsylvania, 1945); Ruth Louise Simmons, "The Negro in Recent Pittsburgh Politics" (M.A. thesis, University of Pittsburgh, 1945); and James E. Allen, "The Negro and the 1940 Presidential Election" (M.A. thesis, Howard University, 1943), appendices 7 and 8.

130. For New York, see Earl Brown, "The Negro Vote," *Opportunity* 6 (1936): 302–4; and John Albert Morsell, "The Political Behavior of Negroes in New York City" (Ph.D. diss., Columbia University, 1951).

131. Among the many good studies of Negro politics in Chicago, see especially the works of Harold F. Gosnell and Elmer Henderson cited in note 119 above, as well as Gosnell, *Negro Politicians: The Rise of Negro Politics in Chicago* (Chicago, 1935); St. Clair Drake and Horace R. Cayton, *Black Metropolis* (New York, 1945), chap. 13; and Rita Werner Gordon, "The Change in the Political Alignment of Chicago's Negroes during the New Deal," *Journal of American History* 56 (1969): 584–603.

132. For the situation in Des Moines, see James Braddie Morris, Jr., "Voting Behavior in Four Negro Precincts in Iowa since 1924" (M.A. thesis, State University of Iowa, 1946).

133. For St. Louis, see Howard Fisher, "The Negro in St. Louis Politics, 1932–1940" (M.A. thesis, St. Louis University, 1951).

134. Samuel Lubell has written a brief but perceptive general account of the impact of the "Roosevelt revolution" on black voters, *White and Black: Test of a Nation* (New York, 1964), chap. 4.

135. On this point, see V.O. Key's seminal article, "A Theory of Critical Elections," *Journal of Politics* 17 (1955): 3–18.

136. The migration of Negroes from the rural South to the urban North also led to an erosion of parental control and family stability. This increasing family disorganization was reflected, as is well known, in higher rates of desertion, divorce, illegitimacy, and juvenile delinquency, and also in a growing political independence as young blacks were socialized outside the old (Republican) family traditions. On this point, see E. Franklin Frazier, *The Negro Family in the United States* (Chicago, 1939); and Henderson, "A Study of the Basic Factors," p. 47.

137. See, for example, Angus Campbell, Philip E. Converse, Warren E. Miller, and Donald E. Stokes, *The American Voter* (New York, 1960), especially pp. 120–67.

138. Morsell, "The Political Behavior of Negroes in New York City," pp. 53–61, 74.

139. Leslie H. Fishel, Jr., "The Negro in the New Deal Era," *Wisconsin Magazine of History* 48 (1964–65): 111.

140. *Chicago Defender*, 15 Oct. 1932.

141. White to Roosevelt, 28 Sept. 1932, PPF 1336, Roosevelt Papers; White, letter to editor, *New York Times*, 23 May 1932; *Chicago Defender*, 10 Sept. 1933.

142. White to Eleanor Roosevelt, 20 Oct. 1936, PPF 96, Roosevelt Papers; Freidel, *F. D. R. and the South*, p. 64.

143. *Chicago Defender*, 3 Sept., 5 Nov. 1932; *Norfolk Journal and Guide*, 5 Nov. 1932.

144. *Baltimore Afro-American*, 22 Oct. 1932.

145. Charles H. Martin, "Negro Leaders, the Republican Party, and the Election of 1932," *Phylon* 32 (1971): 85–93.

146. W. E. B. Du Bois, "Roosevelt," *Crisis* 41 (1934): 20.

147. *Norfolk Journal and Guide*, 28 Apr. 1934.

148. There are two good master's theses that tell the story of the New Deal's Negro advisers: William J. Davis, "The Role of the Adviser on Negro Affairs and the Racial Specialists in National Administration" (M.A. thesis, Howard University, 1940), and Jane Motz, "The Black Cabinet: Negroes in the Administration of Franklin D. Roosevelt" (M.A. thesis, University of Delaware, 1964).

149. Conkin, *Tomorrow a New World*, p. 200.

150. White, *A Man Called White*, pp. 166–70.

151. Hareven, *Eleanor Roosevelt*, p. 118.

152. Hareven, *Eleanor Roosevelt*, p. 119; Harold L. Ickes, *The Secret Diary of Harold L. Ickes: The Inside Struggle* (New York, 1954), pp. 612–15.

153. Roy Wilkins, interview in the Columbia University Oral History Project, pp. 51–52.

154. *Pittsburgh Courier*, 17 Nov. 1962. Joseph P. Lash has written a detailed account of Eleanor Roosevelt's relations with Negroes, *Eleanor and Franklin* (New York, 1971), pp. 512–35.

155. *New York Times*, 1 Aug. 1936; "Campaigning for the Negro Vote," *Newsweek*, 12 Sept. 1936, 18–19.

156. *New York Times*, 22 June 1936.

157. Miller, "The Negro in Pennsylvania Politics," pp. 243–44, 201; Allen, "The Negro and the 1940 Presidential Election," pp. 67, 70–72.

158. Rosenman, ed., *The Public Papers and Addresses of Franklin D. Roosevelt*, 5:537–39.

159. It seems to me that Barton Bernstein has made this error in his generally scintillating essay, "The New Deal: The Conservative Achievements of Liberal Reform," in Bernstein, ed., *Towards a New Past: Dissenting Essays in American History* (New York, 1968), p. 281.

160. *Baltimore Afro-American*, 7 Nov. 1936; Ralph D. Casey, "Republican Propaganda in the 1936 Campaign," *Public Opinion Quarterly* 1 (April 1937): 27–44.

161. *New York Times*, 7 Aug. 1936; William N. Jones, "Day by Day," *Baltimore Afro-American*, 24 Oct. 1936.

162. *New York Times*, 6 Oct. 1936; *Baltimore Afro-American*, 10 Oct. 1936.

163. Newell D. Eason, "Attitudes of Negro Families on Relief," *Opportunity* 13 (1935): 367–69, 379.

164. Lillian P. Davis, "Relief and the Sharecropper," *Survey Graphic* 25 (Jan. 1936): 22.

165. *Baltimore Afro-American*, 24 Oct. 1936.

166. *Pittsburgh Courier*, 11 Jan. 1936.

Franklin Roosevelt: Ambiguous Symbol for Disabled Americans

JOHN DUFFY

PRESIDENT Franklin D. Roosevelt provides an ambiguous symbol for disabled people. In spite of his work on behalf of Warm Springs, the rehabilitation institute in Georgia he helped to found, Roosevelt, by his failure to act to reduce physical barriers, retarded the social and economic progress of his fellow disabled Americans. Instead of assisting disabled people to overcome the physical barriers and consequently the social prejudices they faced, he hid the reality of his disability and presented himself to the public as a man who was recovering from or who had recovered from an illness, a myth perpetuated by his biographers.

When Roosevelt took office, the nation faced an economic depression affecting all Americans, including the disabled. The Roosevelt administration promised to take action to help all Americans in their efforts to overcome the barriers to their economic and social well-being. Roosevelt, because of his special knowledge of the problems faced by disabled Americans, combined with his powers as President of the United States, was in an unique position to enable disabled Americans to share in the progress which his government helped other Americans to achieve. He failed to use that knowledge and power to benefit other handicapped Americans.

What manner of man was Roosevelt? He is given credit, and justly so, for the establishment of a major rehabilitation and treatment center at Warm Springs. He was properly proud of his role as "doctor" Roosevelt when Warm Springs was being established. Theo Lippman, in *The Squire of Warm Springs*, describes how Roosevelt used his position to promote the treatment and research done at Warm Springs. At Warm Springs there was an "FDR Special Fund" to help the needy. Most of the others distributed the funds, but sometimes he ordered that certain disabled people be helped. Some disabled people did not have to go through the admissions office or be placed on a waiting list. The stories of political favoritism surrounding the funds and Roosevelt's actions were probably exaggerated. It is true Roosevelt's work on behalf of Warm Springs aided some handicapped people.

Roosevelt presented himself to the public as a man who had recovered from an illness, arguing that what was done in his case could be done for others. At Rochester, New York, on October 22, 1928, FDR said he was interested in the care of disabled children. He went on to say he was a good example of what could be done. He was on his feet because of proper care. What private wealth did for him, state funds could do for others, and the cost of restoring cripples to useful roles would be comparatively cheap. Rexford Tugwell, in *The Democratic Roosevelt*, while noting FDR's use of humor to deal with rumors about his health, argues also that Roosevelt made his speech at Rochester on October 22 to promote the extension of welfare services for the disabled. Theo Lippman, in *The Squire of Warm Springs*, takes a different view. The point of FDR's speech at Rochester, Lippman argues, was to present himself as a "recovered cripple." FDR continued to promote that image after he became governor, saying that society has a moral obligation to help cripples, and it was wasteful to allow them to remain unproductive.

Roosevelt also expressed the contradictory view that private, not public funds, should be used to deal with the handicapped. In a speech to the Banker's Club on June 4, 1929, inviting its members to contribute to his pet project, Warm Springs, he said there were 50,000 cripples in New York. Very few of them, he continued, received adequate medical treatment. He did not intend that the state do a great deal about it; it was not a governmental function. Neither the state nor the national government could look after the needs of the nation's 350,000 cripples. It had to be done by private charity, but the state would make a complete census and would investigate the possibility of developing spas.

Both as private citizen and public official, Roosevelt had to deal with functional problems—problems of disabled people, particularly people in wheelchairs—such as transportation and access to and within buildings. In his private life he learned quickly about some of the difficulties of moving about. His wealth and social position enabled him to overcome many problems, including those of transportation and access. The lack of mobility made household duties cumbersome. Many such duties were handled for him by a secretary, Missy LeHand. When FDR was staying at Val-Kil Cottage, he crawled along the sand to exercise when no one was watching. When he was exercising with Dr. McDonald, FDR had to crawl along the sand to go to the outhouse, and when he needed to use the bathroom, his son helped him. Frank Freidel reports that FDR was not able to walk up the many steps to his law office at 52 Wall Street in New York City, and he did not want to be carried in public; furthermore, he could get up the single step at the Fidelity and Deposit Company, his business office, only with difficulty, and he arranged to be whisked unobtrusively in and out of the building in a wheelchair after falling in the lobby on his crutches. His wealth and social position enabled him to avoid the humiliation of being carried into one building and enabled him to get help to enter the other. FDR's home in Hyde Park was equipped with an elevator and internal ramps to enable him to use a wheelchair. When FDR purchased a boat in Florida, he knew he needed a boat so designed that he could crawl back on deck from his fishing skiff. He also needed a boat in which he did not have to go down a ladder to reach the cabin. In addition to owning a boat which enabled him to exercise and swim in warm water, FDR, when he was at Warm Springs, had Tim Bradshaw, a blacksmith, equip his model T Ford with levers and pulleys so he could drive around Warm Springs. Almon Jones, who helped make much of the special equipment used by President Roosevelt, confirms that Roosevelt also had his 1938 Ford equipped with hand controls.

Governor Roosevelt was helped with many of the functional problems in public life. His lunch was brought to him because it was hard for a cripple to go to lunch. There was an elevator in the governor's Executive Mansion, which was fortunate because Eleanor assigned him a bedroom on the second floor. After Roosevelt became Governor of New York, Earl Miller, Al Smith's former body guard, became a state trooper and aide to Roosevelt. Miller lifted Roosevelt into and out of places where he could not lift himself. When Governor Roosevelt visited some of New York's state prisons, mental institutions, and hospitals, Eleanor entered the facilities to inspect them because it was difficult for FDR to do so.

When FDR became President, he frequently used the wheelchair for short distances on specially constructed permanent and portable ramps. For inaugurations he drove to the Capitol and went under the main stairway to the Rotunda. At the Rotunda door, the ramps enabled him to be pushed to the elevator which took him to the office of the Sergeant-at-Arms for the Senate. He waited there until the preparations for the inaugural were complete. Then he went to the inauguration stand in a wheelchair with a board wall marking the passageway to the Rotunda. At the last door, he rose from his chair and walked the 35 feet to the inaugural stand. In addition to the elevator in the Capitol, there was one in the White House—a small, squeaky one—which FDR first used to go to his second floor study to swear in his Cabinet.

FDR regularly used his wheelchair at the White House. The second floor of the White House is cut by a large east-wall hall with steps at the higher eastern end. A ramp with a rubber mat was made for the President's wheelchair. His valet pushed him in an armless wheelchair from the bedroom to the Oval Office where the President swung himself into an office chair to work. For his radio talks, FDR was wheeled to his doctor's office where his throat was sprayed, and then he was pushed to the Oval Office to give his speech. FDR was pushed to his pool when he wanted to use it. After using it, he was lifted into his wheelchair. At the end of the day, at about 6 in the evening, the President was wheeled to Dr. McIntire's office for his sinus checkups.

Early in his presidency, FDR approved plans for the expansion of the Executive Office. FDR told Eric Augler, the architect, he needed the room because he was disabled. In public FDR said the White House needed to be renovated to meet governmental requirements. He assured the public that the artistry of the Founding Fathers would be retained.

The Secret Service helped FDR with many of his functional problems. They built chutes to enable FDR to leave the White House in case of fire. When FDR went to vote, as he did in 1942, Secret Service agents carried FDR up the steps of the election hall. Then FDR stood in his braces and walked into the hall to vote. When he had to enter a car, FDR turned his back to it. He was then lifted by Secret Service men into the jump seat, and then he pulled himself into a rear seat. The procedure was performed so easily that thousands of people never realized his condition.

When FDR travelled, special aids, as well as manual assistance, were provided for him. Elevators were built into the President's special railroad car. Jones states, in a letter to the author, that he helped to construct "a series of railings throughout the President's railroad Pullman car which was named the Ferdinand Magellan. These railings allowed the President to swing himself about and to travel throughout the car. This car was, from all outward appearances a standard Pullman car. . . ." In fact,

The President was most sensitive about public information concerning his disability and would allow no photographs to be made of him while he was being transported or loaded or in any was assisted. For that reason, we constructed an elevator on the rear of the train car which would allow the President to be loaded onto the train in his wheelchair very rapidly. The elevator was equipped with sensors that would detect the top platform and the corner platform and shut off the elevator lift mechanism so as to bring the President to a level position either at the top or bottom of the elevator. All of this equipment, when it was constructed, had to be made so that a person casually seeing the train in passing would not note any difference between it and another standard Pullman car. So these items of assistance had to be constructed in somewhat of a camouflage manner.

On his way to board *Amberjack II*, a Presidential yacht, in June 1933, Roosevelt came by train from Washington, D.C. to New Haven. To accommodate the Presidential party, the fence and gates separating the track from the Rotunda were taken down. The doors connecting the station and the Rotunda were removed, making an opening from the street to the waiting room. In an isolated part of the station, the President was put in a black car. After the Democratic National Convention in 1944, special ramps were put on the cruiser *Baltimore*, docked at San Diego, so the President could be pushed on board and go from the deck to the captain's quarters while enroute to Hawaii. FDR used a ramp and assistance to go from the *Potomac* to the *Augusta* in August, 1941, and during the Atlantic Charter Conference, FDR saw as much of the *Prince of Wales* as possible from a wheelchair. The Presidential Plane had a folding electric elevator between the outside skin and the floor for FDR's use, and when he took extended sea voyages, the ship was equipped with special elevators between at least two decks.

Roosevelt experienced both failure and success in dealing with problems of access and transportation. The failures and frustrations he faced are common to all people similarly disabled. His successes, however, were due largely to his high social and economic position. He did not have to go to a law or business office. He had hand controls on his car at least 20 years before they became available to the general public. He was able to obtain all kinds of personal assistance to move about. He had special devices built for his use when he needed them to deal with a functional problem.

Roosevelt must have known that many of these same aids could have helped thousands, if not millions, of disabled Americans. There is no evidence that he acted upon that knowledge. In fact, he hid knowledge about advances in technology for the disabled from them. One of the most common types of wheelchairs in use at that time was of rigid wood and wicker construction. Roosevelt had created for his own use, according to Jones, a collapsible, portable wheelchair made of stainless steel and leather.

It is true that if he had been candid about his disability at the beginning of his career, he would probably have had no career. In a series of letters to his friend Louis Wehle, Roosevelt made it clear that being seen with a disability would be fatal to anyone's political aspirations. But even after he became President, he failed to act directly or through subordinates to change the public view of disability or sponsor legislation to help remove physical and functional barriers which were, and still largely are, preventing the vast majority of disabled Americans from leading creative and productive lives.

Roosevelt and his alter-ego, Louis M. Howe, hid the reality and manipulated the image of the former's condition to enable FDR to obtain and retain political office. In 1912, when FDR experienced a bout with typhoid fever, Howe presented him to the public as a selfless public servant working from his sick bed against his doctor's orders. When FDR contracted polio in 1921, Howe at first said nothing, then said FDR was recovering from an illness, and finally admitted he had polio but stated FDR would experience no lasting injury. When Howe realized FDR was not going to recover soon, he laid down the rule that FDR was not to be carried in public. If FDR were to be seen as an invalid, it would ruin his political prospects. By joining various organizations, FDR kept his name before the public in the 20s. Eleanor served the same purpose, and she also kept the public from knowing about his disability. In his correspondence, FDR described his condition as one which was improving. He only permitted his condition to be seen under controlled positive conditions, avoiding any situation where the severity or permanence of his disability would become a matter of public knowledge. When running for public office, he campaigned hard and obtained the cooperation of the press in order to present himself to the public as a vigorous and healthy man—which he was—while, at the same time, hiding his disability. Once in office, he continued to be careful of his public image, presenting himself as a "recovered cripple," and he used a variety of special aids—some of which he had used as a wealthy private citizen—to deal with his functional problems.

During his lifetime, Roosevelt became a positive symbol for disabled Americans both because of his work for Warm Springs and his image as a "recovered cripple." Disabled Americans, like other Americans, did not know the full story. Even after his death, Roosevelt remains a positive symbol for disabled

Americans because both they and nondisabled Americans still do not believe how well Howe and Roosevelt deceived them.

When Howe released the story that FDR had polio but would not be permanently injured, he defined FDR's condition either intentionally or accidentally, in effect, as an illness rather than a disability. This public perception of FDR's condition was a boon to both Howe and Roosevelt because they both proceeded to describe Roosevelt's condition as an ailment from which he appeared to be recovering or had recovered rather than as a disability, which is a condition that results in a permanent impairment or loss of an important human function, or is a condition wherein one is perceived to have a permanently injured or lost function. It is true that Roosevelt's condition began as a disease but when he was presenting his condition to the public it was no longer a disease. The disease had run its course. It was a disability but he could not define it as such so he described it as an illness.

Howe's action had another important consequence. The vast majority of FDR's biographers make no distinction between illness and disability; they use the terms interchangeably, and they accept the view, which I do not, that FDR was concerned about the public perception of his health. Certainly questions about his condition were posed in terms of health, but I believe he and Howe defined the question in those terms so that is how the public and his biographers saw the question. A man regaining his health or who has recovered from an illness presents an acceptable public image; a cripple does not.

FDR and Howe defined the former's condition in terms of health in order to hide his disability. Even those biographers who make a distinction between

illness and disability fail to realize the significance of
that distinction. Theo Lippman was the first of FDR's
biographers to write that FDR hid his disability,
which, according to Lippman, Roosevelt did to dispel
public concern about his health. I believe Lippman's
view is wrong.

Several of Roosevelt's biographers argue he overcame his illness by means of the power of his spirit.
Eleanor Roosevelt, in *My Days*, writes that FDR did
not have a soft philosophy because he recovered from
invalidism to physical strength and activity. Mrs.
Roosevelt knew and admitted her husband did not
recover complete use of his legs; clearly she means
FDR spiritually overcame his illness and returned to
active life. Frances Perkins puts the matter directly in
The Roosevelt I Knew. She writes that FDR was
spiritually transformed by his battle with pain.

Modern scholars do not accept the unprovable
metaphysical explanation for FDR's success. They
argue he did not do a great deal of reading or writing
and that his political and economic views had been
shaped and developed by his political experiences
during the Wilson era. Elliott Roosevelt and James
Brough characterize as a myth the idea that polio
changed his character. He did not identify himself
with other cripples as one might expect if his views
had become more democratic. James Roosevelt, who
was a young man when his father contracted polio and
who accompanied him on many of his political trips,
also writes in *My Parents* that his father's disability
did not alter his character.

James M. Burns provides a more detailed analysis
in *The Lion and the Fox*. He describes as a legend the
view that polio transformed FDR into a more humane
person. The qualities he needed to overcome polio

were already within him. At best it gave him an opportunity to strengthen those qualities. Polio did not, for example, give him patience. He had already acquired that ability while maneuvering and battling with the politicians of Tammany Hall and New York State. He was already cocky and brought that optimism to his fight against polio. His progressivism was formed in the Wilson period. He never considered retiring from politics both because he was a man not given to meditation and because he was enjoying the political game. His condition had one important advantage: it allowed him to avoid political campaigning until Smith requested his help in 1928, although Howe did not want him to run even then. The 20s were bad times for Democrats.

Frank Freidel, in *The Ordeal*, believes polio increased Roosevelt's power of self-control and made it easier for FDR to make decisions. Roosevelt did not worry about things he could not change. Freidel believes the delay imposed by the disability afforded Roosevelt the opportunity to play the role of distant elder statesman, keeping on friendly terms with all sections of the party, until he was ready to play a more active political role.

John Gunther, viewing *Roosevelt in Retrospect*, states FDR developed his upper body to compensate for the weakness in his legs. In a fit of perverse logic, Gunther argues FDR's illness made him healthy and robust. Alfred Rollins, in *Roosevelt and Howe*, succinctly describes the few advantages Roosevelt acquired by contracting polio. The disability removed him from close public association with Democratic party failures. His illness did not affect his ideas but did influence the timing of his career.

The idea that FDR was spiritually transformed by

his illness is, I believe, a dubious view. FDR's sons (James and Elliott), who were closely associated with Roosevelt's political campaigns, particularly the early ones, deny the reality of such a transformation. Many modern scholars have severely criticized the idea, but they, as the preceding discussion on the views of Gunther and Rollins indicates, still confuse the terms "illness" and "disability." If the terms are interchangeable—and they are not—modern scholars do not explain how FDR could have been disabled yet could have recovered from his illness. They regard Roosevelt, in Lippman's phrase, as a "recovered cripple."

Louis Wehle, a friend and biographer of Roosevelt, who had long been interested in his political career, asked Ray Howard of the Scripps-Howard newspaper chain to counteract the rumors about FDR's health which were circulating during FDR's first campaign for the governorship of New York. The New York *World Telegram* published several articles about FDR's condition. Yet the rumors persisted. Wehle arranged for an interview to be given to Kents Speed of the New York *Sun* to enable him to write about FDR's health. FDR talked to Speed while the former was in his wheelchair. Under a headline describing FDR as "Roosevelt, Titan of Energy, Runs Multifarious Enterprises," the Speed article referred to a "list of activities he's heading [which] reads like a business directory—requiring use of legs by exercises," and finally, it mentioned FDR was "Built Like a Harvard Guard."

Kenneth Davis, in *FDR*, refers to FDR as ill and states that, as soon as everyone knew of the gravity of the illness, Howe became concerned about the effect of public awareness on Roosevelt's career. Davis relates Howe released stories saying FDR was ill but would recover. He notes that no mention was made in these stories of polio or paralysis, but he fails to make anything of the fact.

James Burns, in *The Lion and the Fox*, takes a curiously ambiguous view of Roosevelt's condition. He argues Roosevelt deceived himself into thinking a cure was possible, which he sought for seven years before finally admitting he would never walk again. Yet Burns also sees FDR's condition as one of illness. He notes that after FDR decided to run for Goveror of New York in 1928, Republicans charged the crippled FDR was being sacrificed for Smith's benefit. FDR stated he would continue Smith's programs, but he knew his best reply to Republican charges was a vigorous campaign by train and by car. He kidded people about the hard campaign he was conducting, saying it was too bad a sick man must campaign so hard. Burns also notes that FDR instructed his staff not to send out any mail that mentioned disability or health during the 1932 Presidential campaign. FDR wanted, Burns reports, to conduct a vigorous campaign in order to attack Hoover, show his physical vitality, and crush the whispering campaign against his health. Burns does not question Roosevelt's presentation of his problem as one of health.

Frank Freidel accepts Roosevelt's presentation of his condition as one of illness. Freidel notes without adverse comment that the novelist Thomas Wolfe reflected the view of many of Roosevelt's contemporaries in *Of Time and the River* that his illness ended his career. He would not get better. His disease forced him to retire. In order to counteract such a view, FDR liked to appear well in public. Freidel notes that a Republican paper called Roosevelt the

Boy Scout of Democracy, which pleased FDR because it would not have written about him if it had thought he was terribly ill. Freidel mentions two letters in which FDR told friends he was improving, and Freidel notes also that FDR told the same thing to James Cox, his former Presidential running mate.

During the Coolidge Presidency, FDR sought to advance the party and his own interests. He believed he could do that by helping Smith. During this period, he kept telling people what he would do when he could walk without braces. He told people he planned to resume an active political role in the future, but he avoided the nomination because he would be forced to take sides on controversial issues. He would, Freidel notes, also lose the immunity from attack and the glamour provided by illness. FDR said he could not run then, but his legs would be in such great shape within two years that he would be able to walk without braces. He went on to state he preferred executive work to being a member of an uninteresting social club. Howe told FDR to make the party delegates believe he was still too ill to run for political office for two more years. "Look pale, worn, and weak," Howe advised Roosevelt.

Freidel fails to note what a curious condition FDR had. He was improving when he made public statements, but in order to avoid a nomination to an office where it would be difficult to hide his disability, he became suddenly ill again. Howe and Roosevelt were willing to manipulate the image of his health in any fashion which would promote his political prospects and hide his disability.

In 1928 FDR conducted a vigorous campaign for Governor and displayed a masterful use of humor to counteract the image of invalidism. He said in a speech in Yonkers that if he were able to campaign for a year he could throw away his canes. Republicans who had been portraying FDR as dangerously ill changed their tactics for fear of arousing public sympathy for him. He told the press he was not in condition to run for Governor, but he was counting on his friends to walk into the Governor's chair. On his upstate tours, FDR created an image of himself as vigorous and healthy by standing erect in locked braces in his cars, often causing his audiences to laugh and inviting them to look at him and decide about his health. But Freidel notes that FDR sought primarily to keep his audiences' attention on issues other than his condition.

Theo Lippman, in *The Squire of Warm Springs*, takes a different view from that of FDR's other biographers, who believed Roosevelt was trying to respond to Republican charges directly by means of hard campaigning and humor. Lippman believes FDR's humor was designed to distract people from the fact that he could not walk because he was worried about public knowledge of his health. He was not concerned about it in private. Indeed, he was playful about being carried in private, but when he ran for Governor of New York in 1928, Roosevelt drafted a reply to Republican doubts about his health in which he admitted to having a disability which he believed would go away. He never used that reply. Lippman also points out FDR went beyond trying to distract people about his health. In order to dispel public concern about his health, FDR hid his crippled legs. A healthy man who cannot walk, cannot lead, but he who is unhealthy and can walk can give confidence.

Roosevelt portrayed himself as recovering or recovered while hiding from public view any evidence of a permanent disability. Lippman argues he hid the disability to silence public concern about his health, but Lippman's account makes it clear Roosevelt declined to clarify the distinction between the terms. Roosevelt knew he was fine. Even before engaging in vigorous campaigns for the governorship, he had led an active life, traveling to Florida and Georgia. As long as the public believed his condition was an illness, he could persuade them he was improving or was in good health, but a disability is a permanent condition which presents an image of helplessness. Lippman's point that a healthy man who cannot walk cannot lead is true only if he is seen as disabled. Disability, not health, is the real problem. Lippman's other point, that an unhealthy man can give confidence, is at least paradoxical if not contradictory. If a person is unhealthy, he will have to recover if he is going to inspire confidence for any appreciable length of time.

In *Triumph Over Disability*, a work written in 1981, Richard Goldberg presents the same old points. He argues polio changed FDR and helped him to become President. The onset of polio, Goldberg believes, was a time of spiritual struggle for Roosevelt. According to Goldberg, FDR had paralytic polio, an incurable disease, and Louis Howe was sick and suffering from chronic bronchial asthma. To say both men had the named conditions is true. To say both men were ill is ridiculous in view of their long and active careers.

The evidence that FDR had a disability, not a disease, is to be found in Goldberg's own work. Roosevelt had his last visit with Dr. Lovett between May and June of 1923. At that time, his condition was characterized as follows: his arms are normal; his face and neck are normal; his bladder, bowel, and sexual functions are normal; his back is normal; his abdominal muscles range from poor to fair; he is paralyzed from the waist down; he has poor ability to bend from the hip; there is a loss of motion in his right quadriceps and none in his left; there is no hamstring motion; and there is no toe motion. To meet these problems, FDR developed new functional techniques. As Almon Jones states:

> Much of what we were involved with was preserving the illusion that the President did have some function in his lower extremities. It may be noted that the President was often seen to be walking with his son, Elliott. They were always arm in arm with Elliott giving support to the President. In order for the President to do this, he used a walking stick and had a specially designed set of stainless steel braces which were made by me and were of all-welded construction. Because he lacked control over his ankle joint I made them spring loaded so that he would not drag his foot as it was swinging through stride. The spring loaded braces did give the impression of function by flexing the foot and make it appear that the President had some flexion function in his ankle joint.

> There is another interesting apparatus which we designed and contracted for the President and that was the platform from which he spoke in the rear of the train. As I said, we were involved in creating illusions and we constructed the microphone stand such that when the President came to speak, a post-like saddle was slid out from under the microphone stand and a harness-type arrangement was quickly clipped into either side of the microphone platform, thus giving the illusion that the President was standing. He would be able to move from the left and right and lean to give emphatic statements, all the while, sitting astride this saddle and tied to the microphone platform with a harness.

Goldberg, like FDR's other biographers, states FDR gave the impression of being well, but he describes FDR's political activity at this time—inaccurately I believe—as nothing more than a facade. But his polio gave him a chance to become acquainted with other sufferers and to broaden his awareness of other social problems, a point not accepted by Roosevelt's major biographers. Despite the fact that FDR liked to give the appearance of being well or on the road to recovery, it was Dr. Draper's opinion that Roosevelt had achieved the limit of his recovery in the summer of 1923, and he informed Dr. Lovett in February 1924 he believed that FDR would make no further appreciable progress. What is strange is that in spite of the clinical evidence and the medical opinion that FDR's condition was a permanent disability, capable of improvement only by retraining of other muscles to take over the functions of the damaged ones, Goldberg still accepts without question FDR's opinion expressed in 1928 that he believed he could learn to walk without canes or crutches.

Hugh Gregory Gallagher's recent work entitled *FDR's Splendid Deception* contributes little of value to this topic. Gallagher re-states information already known from other sources, such as the pains the Secret Service took to hide Roosevelt's disability and the voluntary silence of the newspapers. Gallagher argues that FDR changed the way Americans viewed the handicapped, but Gallagher does not say how Roosevelt accomplished that while keeping his disability hidden. He makes no attempt to clarify the difference between illness and disability. Gallagher refers to Roosevelt as one who was "confined to a wheelchair" and as a "polio." The use of such prejudicial language by one who, because of his disability ought to know better, destroys what little value the book may have for someone unfamiliar with Roosevelt. In my view the book presents Roosevelt not as a human being who dealt successfully with his handicap but as an object, a condition, a cause for pity. Gallagher reinforces some of the worst myths about disability and in doing so damns all disabled people.

As I have mentioned before, it would have been fatal to Roosevelt's political ambition to have been perceived as permanently disabled. Yet, even after he obtained the Presidency, he still did not use his power and special knowledge to benefit the disabled. He could not have proposed such comprehensive legislation as the Rehabilitation Act of 1973, which forbids discrimination in federally funded programs. Such legislation could only have been advocated in an age concerned with civil rights. But he might have proposed legislation to eliminate physical and functional barriers that prevented persons with disabilities from using public housing, public buildings, trains and buses.

Roosevelt's administration was pragmatic. It was open to new ideas and new programs. That was a chief reason for his success, yet he was not open to change for disabled people. Imagine how much the problem of accessibility to and within buildings could have been reduced or eliminated if work on the problem had begun in the Roosevelt presidency instead of only in the last decade. President Roosevelt had a special elevator which lifted him on and off his train. Imagine how much more accessible public transportation would be if Roosevelt had either directly or indirectly obtained passage of legislation mandating that similar devices be installed on all buses and trains. Roosevelt did not support directly or indirectly the passage of progressive legislation in either instance. Nor did he attempt privately to influence members of the business community to advocate or adopt such changes for humanitarian reasons. Had such legislation passed,

Roosevelt would have made it possible for persons with disabilities to participate more fully in the life of the nation. That would have enabled citizens with disabilities and citizens without disabilities to know each other better. That fact would not have done away with social and economic inequalities, nor would it have eliminated prejudice. It would have made it possible for greater progress towards ending these evils.

Roosevelt could have done all this without endangering his position. He could have acted indirectly through friends and supporters. It was the age of radio, and no member of the public could see his disability, but they could be charmed by the power of his voice to support the improvement of disabled people. By the time he gained the presidency, Roosevelt had the press in his pocket at least where this subject was concerned. In fact, after the first presidential election not even the Republican opponents made an issue of his condition until the rumors about his fading health at the time of the 1944 elections. Even if he had directly advocated legislation of the kind that I suggested, I believe he would have run no risks. One does not have to belong to a special group to advocate legislation that would benefit them. Consider the case of U.S. Senator Lowell Weicker of Connecticut. He is undoubtedly the foremost legislative champion of the rights of persons with disabilities. Today no one calls him a cripple or questions his health. If Roosevelt had done the same he would have run the same risk—none. If he was asked why he supported such legislation, he could have said with perfect candor that it was because of his previous experience with the problems faced by people who have polio.

From all that has been said before, it is, I believe, clear that Roosevelt had knowledge and power that he could have used during his Presidency to benefit the disabled. He used that power only to benefit Warm Springs. While President, he never attempted either directly or indirectly to promote legislation to benefit citizens with disabilities or to use his private influence to assist them. His failure to do so means that the disabled community is living in a society which is full of physical barriers instead of living in a society which is largely free of them. If he had acted, we would be living with greater understanding and less prejudice between citizens with disabilities and those without them.

It may be argued that Roosevelt should not be blamed for his failure to act because the legislation might not have received congressional approval and his voice in public or in private might have gone unheeded. That seems improbable considering the many legislative accomplishments of his presidency and his personal charm in private conversation. Yet even if the record indicated that he had attempted it and failed, he could then be justly regarded as a proponent of the rights of disabled citizens. Instead his reputation as a friend of the disabled is based largely on a myth. It is a myth begun by Louis Howe and Roosevelt for the purpose of enabling him to obtain and retain political office. They knew that public knowledge of his permanent disability would be fatal to Roosevelt's political ambition. Roosevelt was presented to the public as one who is recovering or has recovered from an illness—one who has triumphed over his condition. This myth perpetuated by FDR's biographers sustains Roosevelt's reputation as a friend of the disabled. The reality of his actions and his omissions show him to be an ambiguous symbol at best for persons with disabilities.

SELECT BIBLIOGRAPHY

Bellush, Bernard. *Franklin D. Roosevelt as Governor of New York*. New York, 1958.

Bishop, Jim. *FDR's Last Year, April 1944-April 1945*. New York, 1974.

Burns, James. *Roosevelt: the Lion and the Fox*. New York, 1956.

_____. *Roosevelt: The Soldier of Freedom*. New York, 1970.

_____. *FDR: The Beckoning of Destiny, 1882-1928, A History*. New York, 1972.

Davis, Kenneth. *Invincible Summer: An Intimate Portrait of the Roosevelts Based on the Recollection of Marian Dickerman*. New York, 1974.

Feidel, Frank. *Franklin D. Roosevelt Launching the New Deal*. Boston, 1970.

_____. *Franklin D. Roosevelt: The Ordeal*. Boston, 1954.

_____. *Franklin Roosevelt: The Triumph*. Boston, 1956.

Gallagher, Hugh. *FDR's Splendid Deception*. New York, 1985.

Goldberg, Richard. *The Making of Franklin D. Roosevelt: Triumph Over Disability*. Cambridge, Massachusetts, 1981.

Gunther, John. *Roosevelt in Retrospect: A Profile of History*. New York, 1950.

Lash, Joseph. *Eleanor and Franklin: The Story of Their Relationship Based on Eleanor Roosevelt's Private Diaries*. New York, 1971.

Lippman, Theo. *The Squire of Warm Springs: FDR in Georgia, 1924-1945*. Chicago, 1977.

Looker, Erol. *This Man Roosevelt*. New York, 1932.

Perkins, Frances. *The Roosevelt I Knew*. New York, 1945.

Reilly, Michael. *Reilly of the White House*. New York, 1947.

Rollins, Alfred. *Roosevelt and Howe*. New York, 1962.

Roosevelt, Eleanor. *My Days*. New York, 1938.

Roosevelt, Elliott and James Brogh. *A Rendezvous with Destiny: The Roosevelts of the White House*. New York, 1975.

_____. *An Untold Story: The Roosevelts of Hyde Park*. New York, 1973.

Roosevelt, James. *My Parents: A Differing View*. Chicago, 1976.

_____. *Franklin D. Roosevelt on Conservation, 1911-1945*. Compiled and edited by Edgar B. Nixon. Vol. I. General Services Administration, National Archives and Record Services, Franklin D. Roosevelt Library. Hyde Park, 1957.

Rosenman, Samuel. *Working With Roosevelt*. New York, 1952.

Schlesinger, Arthur, Jr. *The Crisis of the Old Order*. Boston, 1957.

Sherwood, Robert. *Roosevelt and Hopkins: An Intimate History*. New York, 1948.

Smith, A. Merriman. *Thank You Mr. President: A White House Notebook*. New York, 1946.

Starling, Edmond and Thomas Sugone. *Starling of the White House: The Story of the Man Whose Secret Service Detail Guarded Five Presidents From Woodrow Wilson to Franklin Roosevelt as told to Thomas Sugone*. New York, 1946.

Tugwell, Rexford. *The Democratic Roosevelt*. Garden City, New York, 1957.

Wehle, Louis. *Hidden Threads of History: Wilson Through Roosevelt*. New York, 1963.

THE CONSOLIDATED TENANTS LEAGUE OF HARLEM:
BLACK SELF - HELP VS. WHITE, LIBERAL INTERVENTION
IN GHETTO HOUSING, 1934 - 1944 [1]

Joel Schwartz

Harlem community groups, particularly those inspired by Marcus Garvey's economic nationalism, often dreamed of black-run housing ventures that would incorporate ghetto realtors, apartment managers, and building tradesmen. But bold dreams usually ran up against the power of white realtors and white-controlled government agencies, not to mention the intentions of white liberals awakening to the Harlem "problem." Harlem's Consolidated Tenants League, which flourished during the 1930s, illustrates the limits of black ventures in a field that whites were not ready to penetrate. Operating as a protection service for dues-paying members, the Consolidated would confront landlords and bargain for lower rents in the city courts. Although liberals regarded such efforts as faintly extortionate, they still chose to patronize the League, along with other Harlem groups, as instruments of their own housing and city planning agenda. Their recognition brought the Consolidated to periphery of New York's housing-reform circles, only to shut it out with their redevelopment programs in the 1940s. A product of the Jim Crow, Depression ghetto, the Tenants League never survived the full embrace of benevolent interracialism.

In August, 1934, a few weeks after the Harlem West Indies Federation had celebrated the centennial of island emancipation, the event's temporary chairman, Donelan J. Phillips, a young accountant and graduate of New York University, led some neighbors on a rent strike. His landlord, the Central Hanover Bank, had done what property owners often did on the West Harlem race frontier known as "Sugar Hill"—curtailed elevator and doorman service and hiked the rents for the new black tenants. At the same time, a few blocks north on Edgecombe Avenue, an acquaintance of Phillips, Vernal J.

Joel Schwartz is a faculty member of the History Department at Montclair State College (Upper Montclair, New Jersey).

Afro-Americans in New York Life and History (January 1986)
P.O. Box 1663
Buffalo, New York 14216

Williams, had also organized a rent-witholding action, complete with tenant pickets, against another arrogant landlord. A thirty-eight year old Jamaican, Williams had graduated from NYU Law School, was an ex-counsel to Marcus Garvey's Universal Negro Improvement Association, and was still prominent in Garveyite quarters. He had been a founder of the Harlem Lawyer's Association and was known as one of Harlem's most adroit trial lawyers.[2]   But like many Harlemites, Phillips and Williams had been driven to extra-legal acts. With hard times, tenants had doubled-up, sheltered extra boarders, and tried to force landlords to accept rent "concessions." Because landlords rarely gave written leases, however, they could post arbitrary rent hikes or thirty-day vacate notices and rely on the courts' "summary proceedings" to evict "trouble-makers." In Central Harlem, pitiful sidewalk evictions were exploited by the Communists' Unemployed Council into occasional intimidation of the courts and eviction marshalls.   But middle-class Sugar Hill searched for respectable protection and found a model in the summer, 1934, boycotts against Jim Crow practices in the stores along 125th Street. Black indignation, white-collar professionalism, and consumer agitation—all these ingredients were present when Phillips and Williams incorporated their Consolidated Tenants League and on October 5, 1934, elected Julius A. Archibald, a thirty-four year old Trinidad-born graduate of NYU Law School as president. While the letterhead boasted "Moderate Rent and Better Housing Conditions," the immediate goal was "mutual protection" against landlord reprisals.[3]

At first the Consolidated had little more than a letterhead, Phillips' apartment, and a small group of former Garveyite professionals who were attracted to its speculative possibilities. The League advertised that modest fees could retain its skilled "legal staff," along with its collective strength. But that winter, only a score, mostly women, regularly attended the bi-monthly meetings at the 135th Street YMCA, to hear an opening prayer and Phillips' harangues against landlords. With only seven active buildings by March, 1935, the League was clearly struggling to "sell" mutual protection to a Harlem wary of paid, self-improvement schemes. The officers toyed with getting insurance agents to canvass for recruits while on their collection rounds. They scouted among West Indies lodges and local churches, and sought out political endorsements. But membership continued to lag and finance remained scanty. In February, 1935, the treasurer suggested that $15 might be raised each month if men contributed $.50 and women $.25. Fearing the half-dollar might drive some away, they eventually agreed on collecting a nickle a week from each.[4]

The League might have remained frustrated on this narrow stage were it not for the Harlem Riot of March 19, 1935, which gave the

Consolidated's rent bargaining at Graham Court unexpected significance. The Graham Court Apartments (1925 Seventh Avenue at 117th Street) was a square-block, multi-elevator landmark known for its large interior court and spacious apartments. With hard times, Edbro Realty had subdivided the apartments, shut down services, and in 1933, opened the building to blacks with the customary rent increases. One demand in September, 1934, touched off a tenant protest led by Dr. Cyril H. Dolly, a Trinidad-born opthamologist at Harlem Hospital. Dolly managed to arrange a meeting with Tenement House Commissioner Langdon W. Post, who "commended their action and told them that only by bringing mass pressure to bear, could housing be made a live political issue—which . . . would force the appointment of an arbitration committee." [5] These tactics convinced Edbro to cancel the increase, but it soon reneged and handed thirty-day notices to the leaders. The Consolidated responded with pickets and dispatched fifty tenants to support Dolly at his eviction trial on March 20. By then, the Seventh District Court on West 151st Street was in utter chaos, jammed with police, reporters, and blacks being booked on charges from the riot the day before. Amid the uproar, the case was thrown out on a technicality, and the Consolidated made the downtown newspapers. Phillips warned reporters that if landlords did not end their blacklists, he would call tenants out on general strike and camp 10,000 in the streets.[6]

The next day, the Consolidated voted that one of its officers should rightly be part of the city's urgent post-riot inquiry, the Mayor's Committee on Conditions in Harlem. Convinced that Fiorello H. LaGuardia's nominees—upper class whites with a handful of Urban League blacks—could not grasp the "deeply rooted" socio-economic causes behind the upheaval, the Tenants League called for the addition of Socialist Frank R. Crosswaith, activist minister Reverend Adam Clayton Powell, Jr., Dr. Dolly, and Tenants League vice-president Mrs. Minnie L. Green. The Mayor's Office politely rebuffed them, but still invited "J. Phillip Donelan" and his associates to submit their views.[7] They soon dominated hearings held by the sub-committee on housing, chaired by white attorney Morris L. Ernst. They supplied victimized tenants, whose lurid details of rent extortion had an indelible impact on the sympathetic Ernst and the Mayor's Committee's venture into the taboo area of Harlem real estate exploitation. A draft report predictably found "great complaint and considerable distress in practices surrounding evictions" and proposed giving statutory power to judges to issue stays and to require marshalls to post "decent notice" of their intent. But virtually borrowing Williams' testimony on the subject, it also called for laws that would have enabled tenants to offer the "proof of landlord's promise to repair," and to allow rents to be paid into court-administered accounts until violations had been corrected.[8]

With understandable exaggeration, Phillips described the League's progress to an admiring young interviewer from the Mayor's Committee. He was the only paid officer, he said, of a voluntary "clearing house" for five-thousand members in Harlem and the Bronx. He claimed that the League had already organized one hundred buildings in Harlem alone. Dollar-a-month fees bought an imposing array of services provided by standing committees. Vernal Williams' "Legal Section" took care of a continuing stream of dispossesses and thirty-day notices. The "Labor Section" kept a file of unemployed union men in the building trades, although Phillips conceded that it had found jobs for very few. Mrs. Green's "Social Service Section" provided emergency aid for the evicted and claimed that it had helped some families secure Home Relief and new lodgings. All this may have been plausible to the Mayor's Committee, particularly to Ernst, an old Socialist familiar with Harlem Communists' diatribes and perhaps anxious to recognize the Tenants League as a conservative rival.[9]

Certainly, black Communists had heated up Harlem's politics, forcing many organizations, including the Consolidated, to the left. As a veteran Garveyite, Williams was suspicious of such radicals, but like many Harlemites, he could not remain immune to their blandishments. As he admitted at a League meeting, "If the doctrine of the Communists is equal housing and good housing it is our doctrine . . . go to 6 Negro lawyers and ask them the name of the Scottsboro boys . . . try it some time and see if you can find one who knows . . . ask any I.L.D. or communist. They can tell you."[10] While the Unemployed Council had effectively exploited the evictions crisis, the Consolidated's stilted handbill tried to harvest mass excitement:

TENANTS: STOP! LISTEN! THINK!!!

Join the Consolidated Tenants' League, some of whose objects are:
(a) To take steps as soon as possible to reduce rents by calling a MASS RENT STRIKE
(b) To effect better housing conditions by compelling landlords to make their houses fit for human beings to live in.[11]

Practical cooperation made sense, as arranged by Robert T. Bess, the Consolidated's general organizer, who had been ejected from a Mayor's Committee hearing in June for heckling a Home Relief bureaucrat. While the Tenants League bitterly denounced Bess' treatment as proof of LaGuardia's indifference to "the common problems of the masses," Harlem Communists exploited the attempt to "gag" Bess and organized a Conference Against Discriminatory Practices at the Abyssinian Baptist Church.[12] They embarked on joint demonstrations. When the Consolidated learned that the Kinghaven Apartments (441 West 153rd Street) had opened to blacks but with jacked-up rents, it threw pickets around the entrance. The Communists' League of Struggle for Negro Rights took places in the jeering line, establishing a united front against what Phillips called "the traitorous deeds of the strike breakers." Williams later reciprocated, lending his legal skills to several Communist eviction contests. The *Daily Worker* published appreciative notices of the Consolidated's work and the Unemployed Council continued to reinforce Tenants League pickets that summer.[13]

Despite these flirtations, the Consolidated remained bourgeois and Garveyite. Some even branded its dues and protection a "racket," pointing to the alleged paid boycotts staged by ultra-nationalist Sufi Abdul Hamid the previous autumn. Obviously stung, Phillips collected endorsements from the Baptist Ministerial Conference, including one from a pastor who lauded "a fine experiment in self-determination."[14] But his vindication was a May 23, 1935, rally that became an outpouring of community support. League leaflets helped to assure a good turnout, as some 1,500 crowded into a nearby school auditorium, ushered by teenage girls wearing blue armbands stamped with a gold "C.T.L." Phillips held center stage, describing the League's campaign against landlord greed. Then Williams recounted his struggles in the courts against "landlord judges" and asked the crowd to bring him their dispossesses. He told them not to worry; the League would "take care" of legal fees.[15] Organizer Bess also proved more an impetuous black nationalist than a left ideologue. At a Tenants League meeting during the Ethiopian crisis, members had argued that blacks should harass Italian shopkeepers out of Harlem. Merril C. Work of the Unemployed Council attacked this "incorrect" proposition:

> We must not fall into this [race divisive] trap set by Capitalists . . . got to unite all Negroes and then all exploited and working people so the Wall Streeters will never live to enjoy the fruits of the next war . . . at the last meeting of the League Against War and Fascism, the Italian ice men gave Twenty five ($25) dollars.[16]

Bess retorted: "Where did they get it? Where do they make their living? In Harlem!!!" While some outsiders feared the Tenants League's ideological alignment with the Unemployed Council, others knew better. Harlem Assemblyman LaMar Perkins, who had succeed Vernal Williams as UNIA general counsel, amiably warned his League friends to continue to steer clear of "politics and rackets."[17]

Fierce professional and social resentments, which contemporaries only partly identified as West Indian "pushiness," kept the Consolidated going. Racism had pent up men like Phillips and Williams on Sugar Hill and forced them to make a living on divorces and custody suits, debt collection, and fraternal accounts. Law partners like Julius A. Archibald and Hutson L. Lovell found with the Consolidated another means to scrounge some income and perhaps gain some leverage on the city's political, and patronage, system. The League also won the support of Dr. Lucien M. Brown, a prominent West Indian who was among the first blacks to integrate the medical staff of Harlem Hospital and a persistent gadfly against its discriminatory practices. (His younger colleague, Dr. Dolly, had also spoken out against the hospital's racism.)[18]   Two-thirds of the Consolidated's building "units" came from Harlem's bourgeois periphery along St. Nicholas and Edgecombe Avenues, particularly facing Colonial Park, and within a one-block radius of Graham Court. Both neighborhoods had undergone dizzying racial turnover in the previous years, encouraged by landlords who slashed services to remove whites and then greatly increased rents for apartments shown to blacks on a take-it-or-leave-it basis.[19]

A Mayor's Committee observer caught some of their anger at a League meeting in August, 1935.[20]   Earl Miller, a World War I veteran who "walked across the desert four years for the British government to kill Germans," advised his friends:

> Keep all you know to yourself. Don't tell the landlord nothing; tell the Consolidated Tenant's League everything, that's cooperation. . . . What do you do? When the Rent is due you tell the landlord I got mine, but my partner didn't get her part. . . . If you got 100 people in your apartment it's none of his business. And look out, pretty soon he is going to put on the screws. . . if you live up to the C.T.L you have plenty jobs. Why don't you go down to 125th Street and ask Mr. Porter for jobs? When you give him Forty dollars rent, certain amount of it goes for salaries? Ask him why he doesn't hire a colored office girl and Negro lawyers on his legal staff.

Another, Earl Williams, recalled that the "Belclair Market, a colored organization, almost closed its doors last year . . . shameful . . . did not receive the cooperation of Negro housewives . . . C.T.L. will soon be able to bargain with landlords in an unprecedented manner." Vernal Williams, splendid in a borsolino and spats, gestured with his silver-tipped cane and admitted, "I guess I'm married to the League."[21] He had only intended to collect some dispossesses, but he went on to recount his day in court and a judge who reprimanded him about a landlord's complaint:

> I asked what the Court proposed to do? He said: "Investigate." I said, "I'm going to write a letter to the chief justice." I'm going to put it into the records of the C.T.L. later . . . pardon the first person, But I am one of the Negro lawyers in Harlem who fights on facts, don't go to friends on the bench or hang around Court. I go into the courts and fights on the merits of a case like a gentleman. I said, I am not impressed by the complaint, but that it comes from your office. I am one black man who will fight . . . unless a Negro is a Buffoon, a comedian or a tap dancer to entertain white people, they are after him to kill him . . . hereafter, complaints will not be coming about me but from me about the Justice who interprets the law for the landlords and disregards the tenants . . . As long as I can keep a Lawyer's license you will find me in court fighting in the future as in the past. . . . The Justice is going to make an investigation (scornfully). Well, I am going to ask the Appellate Division of the Supreme Court to make an investigation . . . I said to him, I get a large number of these cases because I am

regarded as a specialist in this kind of work and people know it and they further
know that no landlord can bother with me.

Race pride set the Consolidated on a collision course with the city's
housing liberals who proceeded at their own pace with plans for
Harlem. Tenement House Commissioner Langdon W. Post was a
zealous technocrat, who pledged scientific management of the city's
vast slums and took this gospel personally into the neighborhoods.[22]
By mid-1935, the Tenants League had requested that the Tenement
House Department inspect its members' buildings for Multiple
Dwelling Law violations and thus provide affidavits for Williams'
legal defenses based on neglect of services. In 1936, League requests
had become routine, indeed, part of its organizational plan. It could
provide tenants who feared their landlords with a cloak of anonymity
when they made complaints and could forward these by the
hundreds. But League practice soon ran up against Post's own
preference for systematic inspection. As he petulantly complained to
Mayor LaGuardia regarding one request to check a firetrap on West
133rd Street ("in no worse condition than thousands of others," he
snapped), "We are covering the City as rapidly as possible with our
cycle inspection, but I do not feel that it would be desirable to disrupt
this cycle in order to make wholesale inspections in particular
localities which happen to be complained of."[23] It was one thing for
the Tenement House Department to reach out for Harlem to confirm
its initiative; it was quite another for Harlemites to presume to
redirect priorities predetermined by professional city managers.

Not surprisingly, the Tenants League and city housing officials
took sharply divergent views over credit for Harlem's first public
housing project. In 1934, the New York City Housing Authority
under Commissioner Post's chairmanship had begun to pick over sites
for slum clearance. In Harlem, as elsewhere, the task went to the
Authority's survey staff, which used unemployed whites on loan from
federal work-relief agencies, thus shutting out blacks from any
substantial contribution.[24] Yet to pry construction subsidies from
the New Deal, the Housing Authority needed to politicize local
support, which the Consolidated, fresh from Graham Court and the
Mayor's Committee, was eager to supply. Counting on this citizens'
pressure. Chairman Post during spring, 1935, presented a
$150,000,000 city-housing package to the Public Works Authority.
But Harlemites became exasperated when Post talked only about a
single Manhattan project vaguely slated for "midtown." The
Consolidated sent off a flurry of letters to the Authority, the Mayor,
and President Roosevelt demanding that Harlem be given top
priority for new public housing. In mid-May, when Chairman Post
still failed to make a commitment, the League announced a
neighborhood rally at which Chairman Post, Reverend Powell, and
other local leaders were expected to speak and Phillips was to unveil

plans for a rent strike by 30,000! While some 1,500 attended, most of the guests, including Chairman Post, never appeared, perhaps unnerved by the strike talk. The evening's resolutions stopped far short of the apocalypse, with modest demands for improved tenement inspections and the appointment of more black inspectors. But a few days later, the League boasted its new influence, when Mayor LaGuardia pointedly made a commitment to a West Harlem site, then in talks with federal officials proclaimed that the project would "take preference over all others in New York City." [25]

The League was enraged a few weeks later, however, when Interior Secretary Harold L. Ickes made the PWA subsidy for the housing site, determined for Macombs Place and 151st Street, contingent on fair value for the acreage. But the owner, the Rockefeller Estate, was demanding too much for the Macombs site and wanted to unload with it the financially-troubled Paul Lawrence Dunbar Houses. While the League helped organize a "joint community protest" against the LaGuardia Administration's alleged complicity in Ickes' decision, it also took the quarrel into the streets. "TENANTS OF HARLEM, WAKE UP!!!" read its leaflets. "$7,000,000 from the Federal Government is knocking at your door to build houses to rent from $5 to $7 a room, per month, but the monied interests won't sell the land." [26] At a July 11 League meeting, Phillips called for "mass" action against the Housing Authority, then urged members to march with the Unemployed Council at City Hall. At the same time, Bess was busy with the Unemployed Council, haranguing and leafletting, trying to focus community resentment against evictions, the meager rent allowances from the Home Relief Bureau and the shortage of low-rent housing. [27] The mood was far less patient at the Consolidated's mass rally later in July to demand that the city force the Rockefellers to relinquish their land. Phillips and Williams had aroused the crowd, as did Bess who pointed to what his pickets had won at Kinghaven and at other League "fights." This time Chairman Post was present, and on the defensive: "Said he was afraid the League had heard him promise action so many times and he had not been to Harlem for such a long time, perhaps they felt he was stalling." He promised that the project would go through. "We won't get the land without a fight," he said, "but we'll get it." Then he ended with a pledge that left the crowd on its feet: "The Macomb's project would be for the 1,800,000 people who have always had to take leavings." The League later boasted how its Harlem mobilization had forced the city to proceed with site condemnation and Secretary Ickes to release PWA funds for the new Harlem River Houses. [28]

Phillips' interest in the project became virtually proprietary when he and Mrs. Minnie Green were appointed to the Housing Authority's Harlem Advisory Committee on tenant selection. He promised that the League would "insure that only people of the low income group would be eligible for renting."[29] Phillips may also have anticipated an arrangement in Harlem similar to the First Houses project on the Lower East Side, where the Authority asked settlement house leaders on the advisory committee to go through the financial and moral credentials of some 9,000 applicants. But the Housing Authority had foreclosed that possibility by appointing a Cooperating Committee on Management dominated by the city's social work establishment. The most prominent black appointee, Roscoe C. Bruce, had managed the Dunbar Houses (and his martinet policies had already been contested by Vernal Williams in court).[30] The Cooperating Committee referred technical questions, including tenant-selection criteria, to its staff of white social workers, headed by the Housing Authority's Catherine F. Lansing, who also chaired the Harlem Advisory Committee.[31] Sensing his limited role, Phillips announced a week after his appointment that the Harlem Advisory Committee "was not up to requirements." At a League meeting, he bitterly reviewed the members, starting with the kindergarten worker who ran the Utopia Children's House and the executive secretary of the Brooklyn Urban League: "Mrs. Daisy Reed—we can't count on her; Mr. Robert Elzy, who knows anything about him?" Merrill Work of the Unemployed Council said Elzy spoke for the "business men of Brooklyn . . . he's a tool of the Rockefeller Fund." Mrs. Harriet Shadd Butcher of the Russell Sage Foundation, according to Phillips, "doesn't contribute a thing to community life . . . probably not known to ten people in this room." Another cracked that the New York Urban League's secretary, James Hubert, "has done nothing but suggest that we return to Bermuda or to the South. It is a known fact that the Urban League is segregated." The meeting was in no mood to disagree with Merrill Work's shrewd comment: "It must be publically recognized that the Consolidated Tenants League is responsible for New Low Cost Housing . . . Mayor at a meeting 2 nights ago said: 'we gave . . . we . . . we . . .' you want to let the entire world know that the C.T.L. did.' "[32] The meeting demanded that the Housing Authority accept their nominees for the committee, but Chairman Post responded with a "sharp" dismissal.[33]

They may also have resented the ineluctable institutional necessities which downtown experts could so glibly cite. Pressed by the Housing Authority—and haunted by the financial difficulties at Dunbar—the Harlem Advisory Committee felt compelled to reserve the Macombs project for blacks with proven records of rent payment. In late November, 1935, Mrs. Green agreed with the Tenant Selection Committee's adoption of a "point" system which, according to historian Larry A. Greene, provided 63 out of a possible 100 points to applicants presenting middle-class income and social traits. Citing the need to maintain project "morale," the Committee allocated extra

points to those without records in the Domestic Relations or Criminal
Courts. But Mrs. Green surprisingly acceded to a provision that
awarded applicants who had never been involved in summary
proceedings for non-payment of rent. Institutional rationales also
frustrated attempts to integrate the project's construction force. A
Tenants League rally in October resolved that at least 75 per cent of
the work gangs, skilled and unskilled, be made up of Harlem blacks.
Backed by this mass prodding, the Harlem Advisory Committee
demanded that a black be appointed to the Housing Authority
executive staff to coordinate a program of open-housing opportunity
and fair employment. But as historian Larry Greene found, the
Tenants League's resolution was dismissed by the project manager,
who "refused" to hire additional blacks. He reminded the League
how on his personal recommendation, skilled blacks on the site had
increased from 3 to 10 percent.[34]

The Consolidated's resentments could apparently be mollified with
another welcome into the vestibule of downtown decision-making. On
August 28, 1935, in response to prodding from the Mayor's
Committee, a new Mayor's Committee on City Planning claimed that
it "has not had in view any specific investigation of conditions in
Harlem," although it had already embarked on neighborhood surveys
in other areas of the city.[35] In an about-face a week later, the
Mayor's Committee sent the Consolidated a letter asking for
recommendations of individuals to advise on a proposed study of
Harlem. Phillips ultimatley chaired an advisory committee that
oversaw preparation of the *West Harlem Community Study*
(completed in 1937), although Phillips' group had little impact on the
Columbia University-run squad of WPA investigators. While aiming
for "a range of possibilities within which its [Harlem's] future may be
worked out," the *Community Study* concluded that "No solution
seems possible short of wide demolition . . . and complete
reconstruction of whole sections." Compared to the Planning
Committee's grand visions for white, middle-class Forest Hills, or
even its modest hopes white, working-class East Harlem, the West
Harlem survey eminently signaled the Mayor's Office's inclination to
let the black ghetto fend for itself.[36]

Still, the political currents of the late 1930s had sent the
Consolidated in conservative directions. The liberals' meager
patronage served to encourage this tendency, as did the Communists'
new Popular Front "line" which eschewed disruptive confrontation.
In March, 1936, the Consolidated decisively shrank back from mass
action when a strike by Local 32-B, Building Service Employees
Union, paralyzed large, elevator apartments in midtown Manhattan
and inspired white, middle-class radicals to withhold rent via a new
City-Wide Tenants Council. When 32-B extended its strike to
Harlem, effecting several Tenants League units, some firebrands saw

the chance to send around organizers and wring rent concessions. "This is the psychological moment to tie up the rents," exclaimed an ̣₋ₑr Phillips. But Vernal Williams smothered the fervor by warning members "not to loose ourselves" in the CWTC's enthusiasm.[37] His anti-Communism aroused, the veteran Garveyite absolutely refused to "accept outside domination," least of all by the white, middle-class "progressives" who controlled the CWTC.[38]

This retreat reinforced Williams' preference for litigation, even in the unreceptive environs of the city courts. When evicted for non-payment, Harlemites naturally argued that they should not be charged high rents for uninhabitable rooms, an argument that judges regularly denied. Decisions usually cited the property-law doctrine of "constructive eviction," which held that a tenant's only way to avoid his contracted rent was to quit the premises that a lack of services had made uninhabitable, or the more venerable dogma that rent payment was an obligation entirely separate from the landlord's obligation to provide services. Most judges refused to countenance a collective withholding, following the City Corporation Counsel's disdain of "such thing known to law as a 'Rent Strike.' "[39] Nevertheless, Williams constantly pursued the legal route, particularly on his home grounds, Manhattan's Seventh and Tenth District Courts (the latter created in 1930 by Assemblyman LaMar Perkins), veritable "people's courts" never immune to ghetto realities.[40] While the Consolidated's attorneys often complained about "landlord judges," they could name a sympathetic few and recall better days in court, as on June 4, 1936, when Phillips reviewed how "the judges of the Seventh District Court changed their attitudes towards the League's attorneys".[41] Furthermore, in 1930 Assemblyman Perkins had added some new statutory weapons. One defined a Multiple Dwelling Law or Health Department citation as a possible constructive eviction on which judges might stay non-payment proceedings. Another provided a six-month "hardship" stay where tenants faced evictions for failure to pay a rent *increase*. Both required tenants to deposit their usual rents into court escrow accounts, and, of course, were often sabotaged by conservative or indifferent judges.[42] Understandably, Williams pursued a more sweeping goal of laws that would have granted tenants in non-payment proceedings the right to cite landlords' breach of promise to make repairs or their failure to remove Tenement House violations. He wanted laws that would have legitimized "partial" constructive evictions—Harlem's slum reality—into practical rent-bargaining.[43]

Phillips and his associates yearned for the kind of bargaining with large institutional landlords that would have established their reputation as responsible mediators for a reliable Harlem clientele. They projected a business-like mien, even when they held in reserve threats to picket and seek jury trials.[44] Their first struggles had provided some basis for this hope. They had successfully used publicity against Graham Court and Kinghaven, in each case holding out the olive branch of compromise. At Kinghaven, Phillips played the magnanimous broker, willing to treat with management to settle mutual differences. But such approaches remained an illusion. When embarrassing publicity faded, Graham Court's management again pursued evictions, and the judge agreed. The League, it turned out, had no way to reach Edbro Realty, as evidenced by frustrated members who proposed picketing the judge's home. The Kinghaven campaign dragged on through October, 1935, as the League's strength ebbed. Nevertheless, Phillips and his friends kept up their pretence, sustained by the few instances when their offers to negotiate were taken seriously. During a July, 1937, rent strike at 312 Manhattan Avenue, the tenant committee had brought in Phillips to bargain with the owner, the Greenwood Cemetery Association. With both sides adamant, Phillips sought out local churches who had influence with the cemetery trustees. When the landlords persisted with plans to evict, the Seventh District judge mediated a compromise which stayed rent increases as long as Tenement House violations still remained. Later, when the building was sold, Phillips "extended the hand of greeting to the new landlord and said he hoped we could count on the new landlord's cooperation in developing a friendlier spirit in the house."[45]

With few real clientage relationships, the Consolidated's legal staff necessarily slogged on in the Harlem courts, fashioning Fabian defenses out of the intricacies of summary proceedings. Williams usually began by challenging defective precepts, and constantly admonished his clients to "know how to calculate the days of a notice of dispossess" or the legal ways that it had to be served.[46] Much of the time he tried to hold the judge's attention on Harlem's grim tenements, "the social circumstances, and the high rents faced by Harlemites."[47] Williams also tried to apply to Harlem's non-payment cases the argument that Depression conditions could bring about the *de facto* modification of terms of a lease where there was "consideration," i.e., corroborative evidence. While judges looked for witnessed oral agreements or receipted payments for lower rent, Williams tried to present the "evidence" of reduced services like broken elevators, peeling plaster, no hot water, for "agreements" to reduce rent.[48] Whether Williams had any more success with this ploy than with any other remains unclear. In November, 1937, the League claimed to have saved its members $30,000 rent for that month alone. Associates estimated that the Consolidated's attorneys handled 7,000 tenant cases in the courts (and settled another 4,000 outside) between 1936-1941.[49] The League certainly had an impact on Harlem's standard leases, as landlords began to phase out monthly tenancies for written agreements, which contained waivers of tenant rights to jury trials in non-payment proceedings. This new militancy inevitably entered the courts. Judge James S. Watson, the first black elected to the Seventh District Court, testified at 1936 Housing Authority hearings that while 90 percent of dispossess cases were for non-payment, most stemmed from "dissatisfaction with the condition of the premises or with services rather than by inability to pay." [50] By 1939, complaints to the Tenement House Department had become a palpable force. As a department clerk explained to a Charity Organization Society researcher:

> there is a very strong tenants' union, with thousands of members, who had taken their complaints directly to the Mayor. He intimated that there was the reason why pressure had been brought to bear on these landlords with the result that many of the buildings in Harlem had already been fire-retarded and had legal fire-escapes. [51]

For a brief time, such accomplishments brought the Consolidated on the threshold of the city's reform establishment. Invited to join the new Citizen's Housing Council, Phillips sat on sub-committees dealing with Old Law housing and tenant relationships beside realtors like James Felt, the millionaire property owner in West Harlem. Such encounters must have held a certain poignance for the Harlem accountant: in the board room of a major philanthropic agency thrashing out policy with a benvolent realtor, who had never granted the Tenants League recognition where it counted—in West Harlem apartments. The Consolidated was also summoned whenever the views of black leaders were needed to fill out a housing-reform campaign. In late 1936, Phillips and Williams appeared before Housing Authority hearings investigating high rents, where they advocated changes in the statutory six-month stays to make Harlem's overcrowding presumptive evidence of hardship. They appeared before the 1937 Temporary State Commission on the Condition of the Colored Population to demand a special rent-control zone in Harlem and struck a responsive chord among housing liberals. Later in 1938, the Consolidated joined with the City-Wide Tenants Council, settlement headworkers, and liberal reformers to lobby for the Minkoff Rent Control Law. It was Williams' favorite kind of legislation, allowing judges to stay summary proceedings for non-payment of a rent increase in any Old Law tenement that failed to conform to the MDL; and Williams, backed by the CWTC, successfully pursued the law's constitutionality all the way to the U.S. Circuit Court. [52]

Yet real recognition continued to elude the League. Although the League constantly admonished the Housing Authority for a second low-rent project in Harlem, one larger than the Harlem River Houses which it deemed "entirely inadequate" to meet the ghetto's dire needs, the Housing Authority staff chalked up such interest to its own public-relations efforts in black neighborhoods. When the League in conjunction with the CWTC planned an October 7, 1939,

"Tenants Day Parade" and mass rally and needed a speaker from the Authority, a staff member commented that she considered this organization "the most militant in Harlem—but are a representative group, and helpful in our relations with tenants, and not objectionable in any way."[53] If the Housing Authority maintained any ambiguity about the Tenants League's function, it was dispelled during a half-hour interview which James H. Hubert of the Urban League, Roy Wilkins, and Donelan Phillips had with Monsignor E. Roberts Moore and Mary K. Simkhovitch on November 6, 1939. Time and again the visitors attempted to obtain hard statements about Housing Authority decisions on racial quotas and assignments in projects, and repeatedly and firmly the steely lady bountiful from Greenwich House, Mrs. Simkhovitch, turned them aside. Appointed to advise on policy, Phillips and the others were given the chance to appear to advise on decisions already carried out in their names.[54]

Ironically, World War II would provide the Consolidated with its ultimate prominence and ensured its eventual decline. In late 1941, liberal stewards of black welfare formed the City-Wide Citizens Committee on Harlem, which viewed the impending "People's War" as the moral force that would compel broad improvements in black lives. Phillips and Williams were invited on the CWCCH housing sub-committee, although whites like Charles Abrams, James Felt, and Algernon D. Black of the Ethical Culture Society steered its emphasis to outside intervention for building-code enforcement, new public housing, and zoned rent control.[55] But the Consolidated also joined the mass Harlem agitation led by the Communist-dominated National Negro Congress and Rev. Powell's Abyssinian Baptist Church, who vowed to collect 100,000 signatures on petitions for mandatory rent controls in the ghetto. Both campaigns, however, were abruptly superceded by the November, 1942, order from the federal Office of Price Administration to hold down *city-wide* rents through voluntary means. This policy was to be carried out chiefly by "fair rent" committees of prominent realtors, including that for North Manhattan (and Harlem) organized by Felt. Phillips bitterly complained to a *New York Times* reporter that the OPA's "discriminatory order," which handed controls enforcement to landlords, had "snatched" rent relief from a suffering community.[56]

The OPA order merely intensified the campaign for Harlem controls waged by two separate camps, and the Consolidated was lured into both. Behind the scenes, Phillips worked with the CWCCH sub-committee's lobby with OPA officials, guided by Abrams' tactical assessment that "pressure should come principally from Harlem and that our Committee should urge it."[57] The sub-committee urged immediate OPA controls for the entire city, focusing on the low-rent category, and an OPA Harlem office as convenient to residents as the Seventh District Court. But the Consolidated also participated in the streeet-corner rallies of Reverend Powell's Citizens' Committee for Lower Rent in Harlem. Making his Consolidated an arm of OPA voluntarism, Phillips had never been busier. Using his CWCCH connections, he conferred with OPA attorneys. Citing these OPA briefings, he negotiated with landlords and referred examples of rent-gouging to the OPA as well as to Powell's group.[58] His work in the liberal camp reached a high point with a May, 1943, radio symposium with Charles Abrams, where Phillips pleaded that Harlem needed special, mandatory controls. But such appeals could not dent the OPA's staunch reliance on voluntarism or rally faint-hearted liberals to overcome that reliance, as divisions on the Citizens' Housing Council indicated. In July, 1943, Phillips argued heatedly that 11,000 Harlem tenants were at the mercy of wanton rent increases. Felt blandly replied that he had done his own checking "with an agent in Harlem who represents about 3,000 buildings," and was satisfied that rents had not been raised.[59]

This complacency was finally shattered on 125th Street, with the August 1, 1943, looting known as the Harlem Riot. The OPA rushed in extra attorneys, opened a 135th Street office, and tried to reassure local consumer leagues and the Harlem Civil Defense Council. But its voluntary efforts were undermined, and subsequent rumors that rents would spiral with the October renewal of leases gave voluntarism the coup de grace. On November 1, 1943, New York City became a "War Rental Area." The OPA "froze" rents at the March 1, 1943, level and required landlords to obtain OPA certificates of eviction before trying to dispossess. OPA registrars recorded March 1 rents and services of hundreds of thousands of apartments, while tenants were exhorted to be vigilant about their rights.[60]

At first the new regime proved a boon for the Consolidated, trying to familiarize Harlemites with the strange new argot of "prevailing" rents, "comparable" services, and the landlord's appeal for a "hardship increase." As the OPA's self-appointed mediator and propagandist, the League never handled so many cases or enrolled so many new units: 12 in December, and 21 in January, each with 8 to 10 tenants. Harlemites quickly swamped the 135th Street office with desperate pleas about rents, but also about hot water and building repairs, regarding the OPA as a one-stop housing office. The sheer scope of its operation soon undercut the Consolidated's efforts. The narrow grounds for OPA certificates of eviction reduced fears of thirty-day notices and much of the work of the Magistrates' Courts. Harlem was deluged with OPA leaflet advice: "WHEN IN DOUBT ASK THE RENT DIRECTOR," which the Tenants League, along with other groups, feverishly distributed.[61] The League also discovered that unlike the accessible district court judges, OPA rent decisions involved a remote administrative process. Proximity to the 135th Street OPA office counted for little. Phillips found that to expedite his cases he needed the intervention of Abrams and other liberals with the OPA downtown. [62]

By then, liberals, satisfied with Harlem's rent amelioration, had turned to other concerns, like new public housing and ventures in philanthropy proposed by James Felt. Based on his experience in West Harlem, Felt brought to the CWCCH an idea for a non-profit housing corporation that would operate Harlem tenements on progressive principles reminiscent of the English, Octavia Hill Association. Economies of scale would cut maintenance costs of the adjoining buildings without sacrificing operating standards. An interracial board of trustees would oversee an all-black staff of rent-collectors and social visitors. The Abrams sub-committee solicited the interest of Phillips and Williams in the scheme for an "Urban Housing Management Association, Inc.," which Felt readied in the weeks following the riot. But he intended it as an Urban League operation, with a board of directors chosen from Urban League officials and Harlem's social-work establishment. The plan had no place for the tenant advocates.[63]

All around Harlem; the Consolidated had become overshadowed by large downtown institutions which had awakened to Harlem's housing problems. In 1943, the Metropolitan Life Insurance Company, shaken by outcries against its all-white, 8,755-unit Stuyvesant Town planned for the Lower East Side, tried to make amends with "interracial" Riverton, planned for 135th Street and Fifth Avenue. Although affronted by Metropolitan's arrogance, Phillips broke with white liberals and welcomed Riverton's much-needed 1,232 middle-income units. As for Jim Crowism, Phillips characteristically remarked, "Negroes have their own insurance policies and can make demands on" the Metropolitan. Nevertheless, Riverton would soon render passe the Consolidated's traditional housing services. Its rent schedules were fixed and well-publicized, its waiting list was subcontracted to a Metropolitan subsidiary, and Riverton management went to Felt's protege at the UHMA, Clifford L. Alexander, Sr. [64] While busy tending the three UHMA tenements on West 136th Street, Felt was also collaborating with city planner William Lescaze on a Harlem redevelopment idea that envisioned the wholesale removal of existing slums and their replacement by monolith "superbuildings" on superblocks surrounded by arterial highways.[65] Much the same grandiosity would characterize the postwar resumption of Housing Authority slum clearance, but with the Consolidated cut loose from any special relationship with the Authority. Now politically entrenched and having systematized tenant-selection as a city-wide process with hundreds of thousands of names on IBM punch cards, the Authority could let the Harlem Advisory Committee lapse and dispense with any further citizen involvement for the next ghetto project, the James Weldon Johnson Houses. The Consolidated became one among many community groups scrambling to do the Authority's bidding, lucky enough if it could distribute project brochures and otherwise extend the Authority's "story" to the neighborhood. Little wonder that Tenants League units soon drifted away, its membership shrunk, and the few remaining members began to question what special services their League dues really bought. [66]

The Consolidated was a product of the Jim Crow ghetto which had imprisoned an extraordinary array of ambitious professionals and turned many to the logic of Garveyite self-help. It could never overcome the suspicions by outside whites that such assertive action was a "racket," and remained vulnerable to their intrusive rationales, whether the Communist-organized "united front from below," or the liberals' city-wide commissions and housing renewal authorities. Neither had much patience for young black professionals forced to play their trades on limited ghetto resources. [67] Years later, of course, the Tenants League might have found a more legitimate function in the housing field. In the 1960s, the heyday of Jesse Gray's Harlem rent strikes, the War on Poverty's Community Action Program, and the emerging fascination with Black Power, the Consolidated might have served as the prototype for a local community corporation that rehabilitated or managed housing. It might have found sponsorship and funding from the Ford Foundation or the New York Episcopal Archdiocese. Its accountants and lawyers might have been hailed as the cadre for Harlem's economic bootstraps, for Black Capitalism, or a ghetto housing venture. But much would have depended upon those outside judgments of "legitimacy."

NOTES

1 Research for this article began, in part, in conjunction with the Tenants Movement Research Project (TMRP) of the Center for Policy Research in New York, funded by the Research Foundation of the City University of New York and the Center for Metropolitan Studies, National Institute of Mental Health. The author expresses appreciation to TMRP director Dr. Ronald Lawson. The conclusions expressed here do not necessarily reflect the views of the TMRP or its director.

2 Clipping, (Kingston) **Daily Gleaner**, August 17, 1934, Vertical File, "West Indians in U.S.," Schomburg Center for Research in Black Culture (Schomburg); "Brief Outline of Consolidated Tenants League," Works Progress Administration, Federal Writer's Project, Box 5, Schomburg; John McLoughlin interview with Donelan J. Phillips, April 10, 1976; **Amsterdam News**, May 18, 1935, p. 3; **New York Times**, March 21, 1935, p. 2; February 9, 1952, p. 13; Vernal J. Williams to C. Cardoze, December 15, 1940; and to Alfred L. King, January 15, 1941, Universal Negro Improvement Association Papers, Box 10, Schomburg.

3 New York State Temporary Commission on the Condition of the Urban Colored Population (NYSTCCUCP), Hearings, (9 vols., typescript, 1937), VII, 1245, Schomburg; Betty Friedman, "A Brief Survey of Blacklisting" (typscript, 1938), in Citizens' Housing Council, Committee on Housing Management, Minutes, Citizens' Housing and Planning Council Library; **New York Times**, January 30, 1932, p. 32; February 9, 1932, p. 2; September 18, 1932, p. 16; January 15, 1933, p. 22; May 28, 1933, XI, p. 2; Larry A. Greene, "Harlem in the Great Depression, 1928-1936" (unpublished Ph. D. dissertation, Columbia University, 1979), p.252; Consolidated Tenants League, Minutes (CTL Minutes), April 4, 1935, TMRP files. See also Margaret Reynolds' interviews and reports for the Mayor's Committee on Conditions in Harlem in Fiorello H. LaGuardia Papers (FHLP), Municipal Archives and Records Center.

4 CTL Minutes, February 21, March 14, 25, April 11, 18, May 9, 16, and December 5, 1935.

5 Lassalle Best, "Brief History of Graham Court," WPA Writer's Project, Box 5; Reynolds interview with Dr. Cyril H. Dolly, no date, FHLP, Box 668.

6 CTL Minutes, March 7, 14, and 21, 1935; **New York Times**, March 21, 1935, p. 2.

7 CTL Minutes, March 20, 1935; Resolutions of the Consolidated Tenants League, March 22, 1935, and Eunice H. Carter to J. Phillip Donelan, April 4, 1935, FHLP, Box 667; Mark D. Naison, "The Communist Party in Harlem" (unpublished Ph. D. dissertation, Columbia University, 1976), pp. 324-325.

8 Handwritten history of housing subcommittee, no date, and "Preliminary Report on the Subject of Housing," April 8, 1935, both in FHLP, Box 667; **New York Age**, May 25, 1935, p. 2.

9 Margaret Reynolds interview with Donelan J. Phillips, no date, FHLP, Box 668.

10 Margaret Reynolds, Report of CTL Meeting, August 15, 1935, **ibid.** For the Communists' tenant work, see James W. Ford and Louis Sass, "Development of Work in Harlem Section," **Communist**, XIV (April, 1935), pp. 313, 319; and Naison, "The Communist Party in Harlem," pp. 23-24, 31-38, 71-72, 119.

11 Handbill, FHLP, Box 667.

12 Ethelbert D. Anderson to Dr. Charles Roberts, June 21, 1935, and to LaGuardia, June 20, 1935; handbill, "Monster Mass Meeting, July 1st," all in FHLP, Box 667.

13 CTL Minutes, July 25, 1935; clippings, **Daily Worker**, October 9 and 27, 1935; clippings, **Negro Liberator**, August 1 and 8, 1935, FHLP, Box 667.

14 CTL Minutes, May 2 and 9, 1935; Naison, "The Communist Party in Harlem," p. 247.

15 Margaret Reynolds, Report of CTL Meeting, May 23, 1935, FHLP, Box 668; **Amsterdam News**, June 1, 1935, p. 14.

16 Margaret Reynolds, Report of CTL Meeting, August 22, 1935, FHLP, Box 668.

17 **Ibid;** CTL Minutes, August 29, 1935.

18 Greene, "Harlem in the Great Depression," pp. 93-96, 317-318, 338, 343-345; and Harlem directories and guides in Vertical Files, Schomburg. Tenants League leaders fit the classic socio-economic profiles of Carter G. Woodson, Jr., **The Negro Professional Man and the Community** (Association for the Study of Negro Life and History, Inc., 1934), Chaps. VI-VIII, XIII-XVI; and E. Franklin Frazier, "Negro Harlem: An Ecological Study," **American Journal of Sociology**, XLIII (July, 1937), 72-88.

19 These conclusions are based on CTL building units and members' addresses plotted on maps of the **Landbook of the Borough of Manhattan, City of New York** (Philadelphia: G.W. Bromley & Co., 1934) and **Maps and Charts Prepared by the Slum Clearance Committee of New York** (New York: Slum Clearance Committee of New York, 1934).

20 Margaret Reynolds, Report of CTL Meeting, August 15, 1935, FHLP, Box 668.

21 Joel Schwartz interview with Hope R. Stevens, August 3, 1981.

22 Joel Schwartz interview with Arthur C. Holden, March 3, 1981; Langdon W. Post to Ralph Walker, February 9, 1934, Arthur C. Holden Papers (ACHP), Box 66, Cornell University Library.

23 CTL Minutes, 1935-1936, passim; Louis B. Bryan, "Housing Conditions," p. 24, WPA Writer's Project, Box 4; Post to LaGuardia, April 2, 1937, FHLP, Box 668.

24 Holden to Julian Levi, December 12, 1932, ACHP, Box 58; Schwartz interview with Holden, March 3, 1981; New York Times, May 5, 1935, p. 1. The Housing Authority's Technical Division had blueprints well underway on the Harlem River Houses long before it thought to take on a black technician in an advisory capacity. New York Times, July 4, 1935, p. 17; August 21, 1935, p. 38. As black architect Vertner Tandy complained to the Consolidated Tenants League, the project's white architects have "worked on plans 18 months . . . practically completed . . . if a Negro came in now, it would be only the tail end of the work as plans are finished and approved . . . can you imagine it, not even a single Negro draughtsman on a ($) 4,000,000 project." Margaret Reynolds, Report of CTL Meeting, August 15, 1935, FHLP, Box 668.

25 New York Times, February 12, 1935, p. 1; May 2, p. 7; May 5, 1935, p. 1; Langdon W. Post, The Challenge of Housing (New York: Farrar & Rinehart, 1938), pp. 157-159; Amsterdam News, May 18, 1935, p. 1, and June 1, 1935, p. 14; New York Times, May 23, 1935, p. 27, and June 11, 1935, p. 33.

26 Post to LaGuardia, June 27, 1935, FHLP, Box 761; CTLPresident to James Allen, July 6, 1935; Handbills, "Tenants of Harlem;" "Tenants! City Hall Rally, July 13, 1935"; clipping, Amsterdam News, July 27, 1935; all in FHLP, Box 667.

27 Margaret Reynolds, Report of CTL Meeting, July 11, 1935, FHLP, Box 668, Handbill, "Joint Manifesto," FHLP, Box 667.

28 Clipping, Amsterdam News, July 27, 1935, FHLP, Box 667; Margaret Re nolds, Report of CTL Mass Meeting, July 18, 1935, FHLP, Box 668.

29 New York Times, August 21, 1935, p. 38; CTL Minutes, August 8 and 15, 1935.

30 Post, Challenge of Housing, pp. 187-188; May Lumsden, "First Families," Survey Graphic, XXV (February, 1936), 103-105; New York City Housing Authority, Community Facilities and Activities in New York City Public Housing Projects (New York City Housing Authority, January, 1946). Williams had successfully defended a Dunbar tenant who had been evicted for owing back rent and was then hounded by Bruce at his place of work. Williams' victory made the front page of the Amsterdam News on March 31, 1935.

31 Harriet Townsend to Edith E. Wood, no date, Edith Elmer Wood Papers, Box 63, Avery Library, Columbia University; May Lumsden, "Procedures for Selection of Tenants, Harlem River Houses," February 1, 1937, FHLP, Box 761.

32 CTL Minutes, August 22, 1935; Margaret Reynolds, Report of CTL Meeting, August 22, 1935, FHLP, box 668

33 CTL Minutes, August 22, September 5, 1935.

34 Amsterdam News, October 12, 1935, p. 1; "Recommendations of the Harlem Housing Committee," in binder marked "Management Training Course," Box 45, New York City Housing Authority Records, Williamsburg (NYCHA Records); Greene, "Harlem in the Great Depression," pp. 281-284.

35 Lawrence M. Orton to Charles H. Roberts, August 28, 1935, FHLP, Box 667.

36 CTL Minutes, September 5, November 14, 1935; Mayor's Committee on City Planning, West Harlem Community Study (Mayor's Committee on City Planning as a Partial Report on Project No. 165-197-6037 Conducted Under the Auspices of the Works Project Administration, 1937), pp. 29-31, 39.

37 New York Times, March 3, 1936, p. 2; March 9, 1936, p. 12; March 10, 1936,

p. 20; CTL Minutes, March 5, 12, and 19, 1936.

38 Bryan, "Housing Conditions," p. 24.

39 **Real Estate News**, December, 1931, pp. 410, 422; March, 1933, p. 83; Naison, "The Communist Party in Harlem," pp. 255-256; Thomas F. Keogh, **Landlord and Tenant and others in Summary Proceedings for the Recovery of the possession of real property** (New York: Baker, Voorhis & Co., 1932), pp. 302-309, 384-412.

40 Committee for the Centralization of Magistrates' Courts in Manhattan, **Brief in Support of Centralizing the Magistrates' Courts in Manhattan** (February 11, 1929).

41 CTL Minutes, December 19, 1935, and June 4, 1936.

42 For Section 1436a of the Civil Practice Act, see William B. Rudell, "Concerted Rent-Withholding on the New York City Housing Front," (unpublished paper, Yale Law School, 1965), p. 37, copy in TMRP; and for Section 1436a, sub 2, see **J.E. & A. Realty Corp.** v. **Coulter** (Mun. Ct., Bronx, 1938), 169 Misc. 871, 3 NYS 2nd 811.

43 CTL Minutes, February 28, 1935; **Report to His Honor, Fiorello H. LaGuardia, Mayor of the City of New York, by the New York City Housing Authority, Pursuant to Article Five of the State Housing Law, on its Investigation and Public Hearings on Living and Housing Conditions in the City of New York, January 25th, 1937** [NYCHA Report], pp. 76-78; NYSTCCUCP, Hearings, VII, 1247-1249.

44 NUSTCCUCP, Hearings, VII, 1246.

45 Clippings, **Negro Liberator**, August 1 and 15, 1935, FHLP Box 667; CTL Minutes, June 13, July 25, and August 15, 1935; NYSTCCUCP, Hearings, VII, 1275.

46 CTL Minutes, March 7, April 4, October 3, 1935.

47 ibid., June 6, 1935.

48 Schwartz interview with Stevens, August 3, 1981; R.A.Lockwood, "Necessity and Nature of Consideration Supporting Landlord's Reduction of Rent," **American Law Review**, 3rd Series, XXX, 1259-1298.

49 Bryan, "Housing Conditions," p. 23; Schwartz interview with Stevens, August 3, 1981; Rudell, "Concerted Rent Withholding," p. 63.

50 NYSTCCUCP, Hearings, VII, 1245; **NYCHA Report**, pp. 51-52.

51 Hortense Goldstone, "A Study of Fifty Municipal Term Court Cases of the Division of Housing of the Department of Housing and Buildings," (unpublished M.A. essay, New York School of Social Work, 1939), p. 15.

52 Citizens' Housing Council, Executive Committee, Minutes, 1937-1939, **passim**; CHC Committee on Housing Management, Minutes, 1937-1939, **passim**, CHPC Library; **NYCHA Report**, pp. 76-78; correspondence in United Neighborhood Houses Papers (UNHP), Folder 110, Social Welfare History Archives, University of Minnesota; Rudell, "Concerted Rent Withholding," pp. 72-75.

53 Resolution adopted at Mass Meeting of CTL, June 13, 1938; Earl Miller to Alfred Rheinstein, July 20, 1938; Richard Barclay to same, September 12, 1939, with unsigned Housing Authority Memo, September 15, 1939; all in NYCHA Records, Box 31.

54 Transcript of meeting, November 6, 1939, in Binder marked "Management Training Course," NYCHA Records, Box 31.

55 Draft Statement by Functional Committee: Housing (early 1942), and Ruth Farbman to Charles Abrams, December 5, 1941, both in Reel 11, Charles Abrams Papers (CAP), Cornell University Library.

56 **New York Times**, May 3, 1942, IV, p. 1; May 17, 1942, IX, p. 1; June 17, 1942, p. 17.

57 **Ibid.**, September 3, 1942, p. 17; September 7, 1942, p. 21; September 20, 1942, IX, p. 1; October 4, 1942, IX, p. 1; October 13, 1942, p. 25; CWCCH, Board of Directors, Minutes, November 2, 1942, Reel 11, CAP.

58 Report on Rent Control Issued as a Supplement to the Housing Report of the City-Wide Citizens' Committee on Harlem, December, 1942, Reel 11, CAP; CTL Minutes, July 1, 10, 15, 24, and 29, 1943.

59 Transcript, WEO Symposium, May 26, 1943, Reel 11, CAP; CHC Minutes, July 27, 1943, ACHP, Box 68.

60 **New York Times**, August 3, 1943, p. 11; August 7, 1943, p. 13; Samuel Poses to Edward L. Coffey, August 5, 1943, Office of Price Administration, Enforcement Branch, Box 1207, Record Group 188, National Archives (OPA Enforcement); Joseph Platzker Memorandum, September 21, 1943, FHLP, Box 153.

61 CTL Minutes, September 30, October 28, December 2, 9, 1943; March 2, April 13, September 7, 1944; Leigh Athearn to Thomas I. Emerson, October 5, 1943, OPA Enforcement, Box 1207; Tom Tippett to Walter Hort, April 12, 1944, OPA Enforcement, Box 1208; Mildred A. Gutwillig, Latest Information on Rent Control Enforcement, December 20, 1943, Folder 103, UNHP; Ivan D. Carson, Memo, September 22, 1942, revised April 8, 1944, OPA Enforcement, Box 1207.

62 CWCCH, Housing Committee, Minutes, February 2, 1944, Algernon D. Black Papers (ADBP), Box 8, Columbia University Library.

63 Franklin O. Nichols to Charles Abrams, January 3, 1941; James Felt to Abrams, February 16, 1942; Goode A. Harney to Abrams, November 4, 1943, all in Reel 11, CAP; "Urban Housing Management Association, Inc." (Confidential Draft, New York Urban League, 1943), ACHP, Box 71.

64 Arthur Simon, **Stuyvesant Town** (New York: New York University Press, 1970), pp. 15-41; Informal Meeting on the Riverton Project, October 25, 1944, AGBP, Box 8; **New York Times**, July 2, 1946, p. 41; October 30, 1946, p. 35; August 31, 1947, VIII, p. 1.

65 While boasting a concern for "human needs," Lescaze's and Felt's work looked more like an attempt to clear human obstacles out of the way of the traffic generated by Robert Moses' Triborough Bridge. William Lescaze and James Felt, "A Plan for Harlem's Redevelopment," **Architectural Forum**, LXXX (April, 1944), 145-152.

66 New York City Housing Authority, **13th Annual Report** (New York City Housing Authority, 1947); **16th Annual Report for 1949**, p. 12; **17th Annual Report, 1950**, p. 8; CTL Minutes, July 8, 1948; March 24, 1949; McLoughlin interview with Phillips, October 1, 1975; John McLoughlin interview with Theodore Anderson, January 8, 1976.

67 Nor has there been much patience from analysts who are convinced that such assertiveness was a reactionary relic or at best a crude prerequisite for the mass collectivism of the 1930s. See, Naison, "The Communist Party in Harlem;" William Muraskin, "The Harlem Boycott of 1934; Black Nationalism and the Rise of Labor Union Consciousness," **Labor History**, XIII (Summer, 1972), 361-373; Martin Kilson, "Political Change in the Negro Ghetto. 1900-1960s," in Nathan Huggins, et al., eds., **Key Issues in the Afro-American Experience** (2 vols.; New York: Harcourt, Brace Jovanovich, 1971), II, 167-192.

Chicago street scene, 1933

Black Chicago Political Realignment During the Great Depression and New Deal

CHRISTOPHER ROBERT REED

During the 1930s, the character of politics in Chicago's Republican Black Belt began to undergo a steady transformation. The emergence of the Democratic Kelly-Nash machine and the advent of the New Deal—the twentieth century's most comprehensive, national program of social and economic reconstruction—produced a truly adversarial relationship between the two major parties.

At the start of the Great Depression, Chicago blacks predominantly held membership in a party that lacked the power, imagination, or will to offer relevant programs and policies to meet the challenge of the economic crisis. Harold F. Gosnell described the Republican organization as "completely bankrupt, financially and morally."[1] Nevertheless, black loyalty to the "Party of Lincoln" was remarkably durable, posing the last formidable threat to Democratic hegemony over all Chicago. While the Republican party was in demise throughout white neighborhoods, its decline in the

Christopher Robert Reed is assistant professor in the Black Studies Program at the University of Illinois-Chicago. He received the Ph.D. in American history from Kent State University. His area of specialization is twentieth-century urban history, and he is now completing a history of the Chicago branch of the N.A.A.C.P.

212

Black Belt was slowed by economic circumstances, racial ideology, and local affiliations at the ward level.[2]

The Democratic party's movement toward dominance in Chicago, Cook County, and Illinois coincided with, and grew from, the New Deal. Roosevelt's socially ameliorative programs in the areas of relief, employment, and housing contributed significantly to the movement, along with two factors endemic to Chicago. By 1933, the Democratic party had experienced its fourth year of political success in the county and state and was in nearly complete control in Chicago.[3] Then, the death of Mayor Anton J. Cermak two days after Roosevelt's inauguration brought Edward J. Kelly into prominence as mayor. In concert with Patrick J. Nash, the Cook County Democratic Central Committee chairman, Kelly formed a part of the leadership known as the Kelly-Nash machine. That fusing of forces and events in 1933 initiated Democratic hegemony in the political life of the city not only for the Depression decade but for fifty years after that. Republicanism would live, but mainly on Chicago's black South Side, and with a constantly diminishing influence over political and economic matters in that racial enclave.

By consistent identification with the programs and funding of the New Deal—promising new services, opportunities, favors, and hope—the Kelly-Nash machine and the Democratic organization not only accumulated power but garnered prestige. The popularity of Mayor Edward Kelly was especially significant in the Black Belt and must be ranked as one of the key factors in understanding why black support for the Democratic party continually expanded, albeit slowly, throughout the decade.

Initially, Kelly's ascension to power was opposed by black political leaders in Chicago and Springfield. Staunchly Republican and reflecting the black electorate's aversion to Democrats along both political and ideological lines, black legislators from Chicago at first voted to stall the passage of a bill in the general assembly that would have enabled the Chicago City Council to bypass an election and instead choose a temporary mayor after Cermak's death. But once the power of the Democratic party prevailed in Springfield, Chicago's two black Republican aldermen, William L. Dawson and Robert R. Jackson, dropped their opposition and voted for Kelly. By the end of Kelly's first term in office, he was the recipient of praise from the voice of black Republicanism, the *Chicago Defender.* What was evolving was a relationship of frequent cooperation between two opposing powers: Democrats who controlled the city, and the only remnant of organized viable Republicanism extant in Chicago, the blacks of the Second and Third Wards.[4]

On taking office, Kelly continuously courted the black electorate—in one instance by restoring to the Civil Service lists those blacks removed by Cermak. Kelly prepared for his first elective campaign by having Louis B. Anderson, former Second Ward alderman, approach black Republicans for

[1]Gosnell, *Machine Politics: Chicago Model* (1937; rpt. Chicago: Phoenix Books, 1967), p. 18.

[2]*Ibid.*, pp. 97, 120–22, 158–59; Gosnell, "The Negro Vote in Northern Cities," *National Municipal Review,* 30 (1941), 264–67, 278; Elmer W. Henderson, "A Study of the Basic Factors Involved in the Change in Party Alignment of Negroes in Chicago, 1932–1938," Thesis University of Chicago 1939; Edward T. Clayton, *The Negro Politician: His Success and Failure* (Chicago: Johnson Pub. Co., 1964), pp. 52–56; Rita Werner Gordon, "The Change in the Political Alignment of Chicago's Negroes During the New Deal," *Journal of American History,* 56 (1969), 584–603; Roger Biles, "Big Red in Bronzeville': Mayor Ed Kelly Reels in the Black Vote," *Chicago History,* n.s. 10 (1981), 99–111; Charles R. Branham, "The Transformation of Black Political Leadership in Chicago, 1865–1942," Diss. University of Chicago 1981; Christopher R. Reed, "A Study of Black Politics and Protest in Depression-decade Chicago, 1930–1939," Diss. Kent State University 1982; John M. Allswang, "The Chicago Negro Voter and the Democratic Consensus: A Case Study, 1918–1936," *Journal of the Illinois State Historical Society,* 60 (1967), 145–75.

Gosnell, *Machine Politics,* p. 9.

[4]Reed, pp. 207–12, 216–20.

support. The Mayor was presented as a fair and powerful leader who was already assured victory. In that vein, Anderson told blacks, "In Edward J. Kelly as mayor you have another Bill Thompson."[5] The reference was meaningful to blacks because opportunities available to them were always minimal until their votes helped elect Republican William Hale "Big Bill" Thompson in 1915.

What black Chicagoans saw in Kelly was a fellow South Sider from the partially black Fourth Ward, a white politician who personally advanced the civil rights program of the *Chicago Defender* at the 1932 Democratic convention and a leader who was not afraid of incurring the wrath of his fellow whites when speaking out for justice. Kelly had once boldly challenged South Side blacks to disdain voluntary segregation and actively pursue their law-given rights throughout the city. He condemned racism in a Far South Side school as being against the public policy of both the city and the nation. (That act was to cost him a large

number of votes in 1935 in the virtually all-white ward in which the school was located, but that loss was submerged in his landslide victory.)[6]

The skills of Kelly the politician matched those of Kelly the egalitarian. Before the aldermanic primary of 1935, sensing the effect that an overwhelming mandate would have both for himself and his party, Kelly declared that he would not slate Democrats against the Republican incumbents running in the Second and Third Wards, Dawson and Jackson. Praising their records and the support they had given in the city council, he applied a bit of simple and convincing political logic in his move: In an ostensibly nonpartisan aldermanic election, he was quite justified in allowing Republican

---

[5]*Chicago Defender*, Jan. 26, 1935, p. 3, cols. 1-2.
[6]*Defender*, March 30, 1935, p. 3, cols. 1-2, p. 4, cols. 7-8. For a report of Kelly's statement of the situation at Morgan Park High School, see *ibid.*, Oct. 6 (p. 1, col. 1, p. 3, col. 4), Oct. 13 (p. 1, cols. 1-2, 4-5, p. 3, cols. 3-4), 1934.

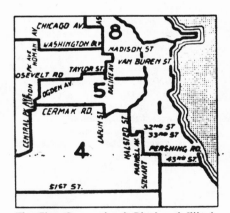

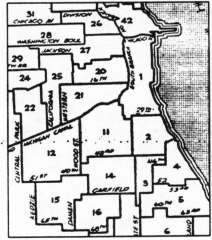

The First Congressional District of Illinois (shown above) included all of Ward One and portions of Wards Two, Four, and Eleven (shown at right).

successes if candidates had an exemplary record of public service. Dawson and Jackson, in turn, pledged to support the Mayor's bid for election irrespective of whom their party ran in the April general election. Dawson pledged more than twenty thousand votes in the Second Ward, and Jackson promised, "My Republican friends in this ward [the Third] will do for Mayor Kelly what they used to do for former Mayor Thompson." The symbol of black Chicago Republicanism, Oscar DePriest, stayed out of the city during part of the campaign, thereby avoiding the label of being a political "turncoat."[7]

The leadership of the *Defender*, always politically calculating, explained that Kelly's retention in office would "in a large sense promote our political advancement in the city of Chicago." A. N. Fields of the *Defender* noted: "You must know that the Republican party will not again come to life under its present leadership. The reasons are obvious. Those who are trying to revive the party are using the same opiate that they used in putting it to sleep. Black men and women who vote for Edward J. Kelly next Tuesday are not voting against the Republican party because there is no Republican party in Chicago. . . . It simply doesn't exist anymore."[8] By 1935, Republicans could not even challenge Kelly with a respectable adversary. Harold Gosnell observed that "five

years earlier, a man with Kelly's record would have been regarded as an easy mark for the Republican organization."[9]

The election results demonstrated conclusively the extent of Kelly's appeal. He was a landslide victor, and the enormity of his victory would have been impressive even without the black contribution from the Second, Third, and Fourth Wards. Blacks delivered on their promises in all wards and, in effect, had indicated that they were no longer enamored with Republicanism to the detriment of their own interests. Kelly received 80.5 percent of their vote—nearly matching the 82.7 percent garnered citywide from white wards. In all, Kelly received 800,000 votes to his opponent's 167,000.[10]

There were charges that the impressive Democratic showing in black wards resulted from threats by Democratic precinct captains to remove from the relief rolls any voter who failed to cast a ballot for Kelly, a charge that was repeated with each election. "Whether these rumors are true or not," the *Defender* claimed, the frequency of straight-party Democratic tickets in municipal elections throughout the Black Belt was most suspicious.[11]

As the years progressed, Kelly's reputation among blacks grew to a point that he was credited with bestowing favors he did not, could not, or would not as long as most blacks were Republicans. In reality, his appointment of blacks to office after 1935 and until the end of the decade never matched Thompson's totals but easily exceeded Cermak's. In addition, Kelly vacillated in supporting the completion of long-overdue, federally sponsored housing such as the Ida B. Wells project. He steadfastly refused to appoint a black to the school board until late in 1939, and he did not support wholeheartedly the black aspiration to reclaim a lost judgeship.[12]

Concomitant with the rise of the Kelly-Nash machine, a few blacks began to rise within the Democratic organization.

---

[7]*Ibid.*, Feb. 23 (p. 2, cols. 1–2), March 23 (p. 3, cols. 1–2), March 30 (p. 6, col. 6), 1935; *News Bulletin of the Third Ward Republican Club,* 1936, p. 2, copy in Arthur W. Mitchell Papers, Chicago Historical Society (hereafter cited as Mitchell Papers).

[8]*Defender,* Feb. 16 (p. 3, cols. 4–5), March 30 (p. 1, cols. 1 ff.), 1935.

[9]Gosnell, *Machine Politics,* p. 18.

[10]Allswang, pp. 172–74; Gordon, p. 602.

[11]*Defender,* April 13 (p. 1, cols. 1–2, p. 10, cols. 7–8), Aug. 4 (p. 3, cols. 1–2), Sept. 8 (p. 3, cols. 1–2), 1934; *ibid.,* Nov. 12, 1938, p. 7, cols. 2–3.

[12]Henderson, p. 78. On black efforts to secure a seat on the school board, see *Defender,* Oct. 7 (p. 1, col. 5), Oct. 21 (p. 1, col. 5), 1939.

Shrewdly aware of the new political opportunities, they began to make demands upon party leaders for greater representation. The argument was always the same: If the party wanted to build a citywide organization, it could do so only by slating blacks for offices; and if it wanted to crush the Second and Third Ward Republican organizations, that could be accomplished only by attracting more blacks into the party.

The Democrats' first overtures to blacks had occurred during the Cermak administration. In 1931 Edward M. "Mike" Sneed was named Third Ward committeeman—a masterstroke that paid handsome dividends. After 1933, the benefits of New Deal patronage jobs and privileges for the underworld elements of the ward enabled Sneed to lay the foundation for a solid ward organization. Another example of the type of reward that Democrats were willing to bestow on blacks was the appointment in 1933 of Earl B. Dickerson to the post of Assistant Attorney General for the northern district of Illinois.[13] Dickerson's appointment was spurred by two factors: He had been a longtime Democratic loyalist, and he was filling a position normally held by a black man. But the Dickerson and Sneed appointments marked the limit to which Democrats would extend themselves until blacks proved their loyalty at the polls. The party stood to lose white support if blacks were rewarded too quickly without having proven decisively in attitude and substantially in electoral support that they had divested themselves of their Republican connections.

Democrats elected only two other black officials before 1939 in their efforts to win control of the Black Belt, but the two were highly significant. In 1934, Arthur W. Mitchell assumed the national mantle of black political leadership when he defeated Oscar DePriest to become the first Democratic black congressman. Throughout the decade he was the lone black man to sit in the United States House of Representatives. In

1938, William Wallace captured the Illinois Senate seat of William E. King. Yet, neither man could match the Republicans in the manner in which they used personal amiability and emphasis on racial ideology to build party loyalty.

Alabama native Mitchell, for example, an attorney and former college president who worked briefly for the Hoover administration, was unpopular among both Republicans and Democrats because of his personal eccentricities. Filled with paradoxical traits that were revealed in almost every instance of his behavior, Mitchell seemed to lack any special instinct, attribute, or strategy as he advanced politically. Yet, more than any other black politician, he symbolized the impact of the Depression on Black Belt politics.[14] With the advent of the New Deal as a remedy to the economic crisis, the emphasis on race began to subside somewhat, allowing a man such as Mitchell to rise in prominence. His politics, racial ideology, and personality were out of harmony with the racially-charged milieu of his constituents (who had traditionally not only resisted close cooperation with southern whites but also viewed the Democratic party as the incarnation of racial terrorism), but Mitchell enjoyed a successful political career because he was both an heir to and product of the New Deal.

Mitchell's three consecutive terms were directly attributable to the success of the Roosevelt victory wagon, and he drew his strongest support not from the black Republican Second Ward, but rather from the First

[13]*Defender*, Feb. 18, 1933, p. 5, col. 1. See also Mitchell to Dickerson, Feb. 14, 1933, and Dickerson to Mitchell, Feb. 15, 1933, both in Mitchell Papers.

[14]Reed, pp. 220–31.

[15]Mitchell to Williams, Aug. 28, 1934, Mitchell Papers.

[16]Mitchell to Pearl Silberman, March 21, 1935, and Mitchell to R. H. Folger, March 13, 1937, both *ibid*. In contrast, a typical letter to blacks displaying his caustic tone is Mitchell to Rev. W. J. G. McLin, April 11, 1935, *ibid*.

Works Progress Administration projects, such as this Chicago sewer, provided valuable city improvements as well as employment for the party faithful.

and Eleventh Wards, both of which were Democratic, pro-New Deal, and predominantly white.

Mitchell measured racial progress to a great extent by the material changes brought by the New Deal. He expressed those views in a letter to Rev. Lacey Kirk Williams, head of the most powerful black Baptist group in America: "I believe that no people have suffered as much from discrimination, injustice and prejudice as our Race. I think that I understand much that is necessary to be done to bring about better conditions, and I pledge myself to work to the end that the New Deal will mean as much, if not more, to our people than to any other group."[15]

Beyond the material promise that the New Deal held, Mitchell found inspiration, motivation, and direction in the ideology of Booker T. Washington, whom he had

worked for as a youth and to whom he proved a devout follower. Mitchell's strategy for racial progress followed Washington's program to near total duplication, in that he avoided confrontations—especially verbal ones—with whites. Unlike DePriest, who had been brazen and, on occasion, belligerent when dealing with whites, Mitchell appeared to be unusually obsequious. (A major exception to that rule involved whites who would be readily identifiable as wealthy First District Republicans, whom he freely attacked as "economic royalists.")[16] Upon taking his congressional seat in 1935, Mitchell immediately disclaimed any affinity with black racial aspirations by saying: "I would work harder for my people than any other Congressman, but I would not keep thinking about the fact that I was colored. . . . I am not a Negro agitator, but a member of

Franklin D. Roosevelt at the October, 1937, dedication of the Outer Park Drive bridge. Built with federal money, the project was regarded as one of the outstanding accomplishments of Mayor Edward Kelly's administration.

the Congress of the United States. I am not the exclusive property of one class and race, but the agent of all the people."[17]

Ward-level politics dramatically illustrated the start of change in the Black Belt. Although the source of political power in Chicago emanated from City Hall through Roosevelt's programs, the locus of black political power—where the spoils of the New Deal were divided by black Democrats and coveted by black Republicans—was still the South Side's Second and Third Wards of Mitchell's First Congressional District. There, black Republicans held steadfastly to their party ideology, traditions, and allegiance, despite a virtual lack of patronage and privileges.

In the Second Ward, power rested in the hands of Joseph "Joe" Tittinger, a politician of German and French ancestry who since 1932 had worked in a hostile political environment to build his party from its weak, minority status to one that could operate at parity with the Republicans. By the summer of 1933, Tittinger's activities were reinforced by patronage jobs created by the new alphabet agencies, including the CWA

(Civil Works Administration), FERA (Federal Emergency Relief Administration), and PWA (Public Works Administration). Under the guidelines formulated by the Kelly-Nash organization, Tittinger, as committeeman, controlled all patronage appointments in the ward. Even Congressman Mitchell, considered a protégé of Tittinger's, continually deferred to him.[18]

As the decade progressed, Tittinger's tenure became more controversial and precarious. Blacks composed ninety percent of the Second Ward's fledgling Democratic organization, and as early as 1933, the *Chicago*

[17]*Kansas City* (Mo.) *Times*, Dec. 7, 1934 (clipping), and Mitchell to Fred R. Moore, June 1, 1935, *ibid.*; Chicago Branch [NAACP] to Leonard Schuetz, Jan. 29, 1936, Branch Files, Papers of the National Association for the Advancement of Colored People, Library of Congress, Washington, D.C.; *Defender*, Nov. 10 (p. 1, cols. 1–2, p. 2, cols. 3–4), Nov. 17 (p. 14, col. 2), Dec. 1 (p. 14, col. 2), 1934.

[18]Mitchell to Mary Lee Colbert, Dec. 10, 1934, Mitchell to Laurine Beckwith, Jan. 8, 1935, and Tittinger to Claude Holman, Feb. 14, 1935, all in Mitchell Papers; Gene DeLon Jones, "The Local Political Significance of New Deal Relief Legislation in Chicago: 1933–1940," Diss. Northwestern University 1970, pp. 131–32, 149–52.

Defender had urged them to rid themselves of Tittinger's "mediocre white leadership" in favor of the "intelligent members of their own race" who had earned their respect and confidence. Edgar Brown, outspoken leader of the New Deal Organization, described Tittinger's power as "unbelievable." "A foreigner invades our neighborhood and starts using gang methods to inflict his will upon a defenseless people," he declared. "The bourbon South has come to 35th and Michigan."[19] Three popular black Democrats did file to run against Tittinger for the committeemanship in 1934, but two of them withdrew before the election; when the votes were in, Tittinger had won again. That challenge was the only serious one before Tittinger's removal by Kelly in 1939.[20]

Christopher C. Wimbish, a former Republican assistant state's attorney who became a New Deal Democrat, summarized the situation of blacks in Tittinger's ward:

I feel perfectly justified, regardless of politics, to address myself to the colored citizens of the Second Ward. You are bone of my bone, and flesh of my flesh. With you I must either rise or sink. . . . Many of you left the South because you desired to exercise the right of suffrage. The fact that you reside in the Second Ward and that your political opportunities and privileges are controlled by one not of your group should be proof positive to you that you are still being denied the proper exercise of your rights of suffrage.[21]

Opposition to Tittinger also remained strong because of his apparent negligence in

rewarding loyal party workers with patronage jobs. In February, 1935, it was reported that thirty—or about one third—of his precinct captains were out of work; it was later found that one white captain was holding seven jobs while thirty-seven black captains were jobless. Rev. Junius C. Austin of the Pilgrim Baptist Church complained to Congressman Mitchell about the plight of black loyalists:

I am in quandary as to what to do right now. I am receiving the taunts and jeers, even in my congregation, from those who feel that my fight for this administration was not after all appreciated. . . . I shall not call attention to my service. It should be well known. I have not been able to secure any patronage for my people here; not even those of my church who have taken the civil service examination and have high ratings.[22]

There was substantial proof that Tittinger's interest in his constituents was superseded by his connections to criminal elements, both black and white. The *Defender* repeated charges that he had "insistently and continuously served certain well-known interests that are not in harmony with the program of the Democratic party . . . and [are] inimical to the progress of the majority of the voters of the Second Ward." Tittinger was accused of foregoing patronage possibilities in "return for gambling and vice privileges." Reformer Christopher Wimbish told his Second Ward neighbors, "For the most part the entire ward is farmed out for vice and racket privileges for the enrichment not of you, but of white people."[23]

Nevertheless, throughout Tittinger's tenure in office, he was supported by numerous blacks, including Congressman Mitchell. Mayor Kelly campaigned on Tittinger's behalf and extended the machine's full support throughout the 1934 election. In addition, some of Tittinger's black defenders maintained that the element of race had been injected into the elections as a substitute for political achievement by his critics. Tittinger had done as much as could be expected

[19]*Defender*, Sept. 2, 1933, p. 3, cols. 4–5, and March 17, 1934, p. 2, col. 5. Chicago committeemen were generally chosen from the racial or national groups of ward constituents; see Gosnell. *Machine Politics*, p. 44.

[20]*Defender*, March 10 (p. 4, cols. 1–2), March 17 (p. 2, cols. 5–6), March 26 (p. 5, cols. 1–2), 1934.

Wimbish, "To the Citizens of the Second Ward, *The Truth*, March 12, 1938, p. 1, Christopher C. Wimbish Papers, Chicago Historical Society.

[22]Austin to Mitchell, Jan. 12, 1937, Mitchell Papers.

[23]*Defender*, Aug. 26, 1933, p. 2, col. 4; *ibid.*, March 26, 1934, p. 5, cols. 1–2; Wimbish, p. 3.

from a fledgling ward organization, they claimed. Although many Second Ward blacks voted Democratic in the presidential election of 1936, they did so because of federal relief and job projects. They were not, however, true Democrats with a solid party affiliation.[24]

Democrats in the Third Ward also diligently worked to build a viable political base while engaging in intense factional strife. Committeeman Edward M. Sneed, who was selected to fill an unexpired term in 1931 and ran for reelection in 1932, always faced primary challenges. Many of his other problems paralleled Tittinger's. Despite the fact that Sneed was black, he was not able to escape the charge of racial insensitivity. Critics accused him of allowing "twenty people of the opposite group [to] hold jobs which are charged to and belong to the peo-

ple of the ward."[25] However, in 1938, the *Defender*, now a partisan voice of the Democratic party, hailed him as "a fighter for racial rights."[26]

Sneed was a local power when contrasted to ward Republicans, but he exercised little power in the service of his black constituents. Opponents complained that too much employment was given to whites who did not live in the ward, that too many black party workers were underemployed on city and federal jobs, and that no sizeable dent had been made in the labor woes of the ward's unemployed masses. His supporters

[24]Reed, p. 236.
[25]*Defender*, Feb. 17, 1934, p. 6, col. 3.
[26]*Ibid.*, Feb. 26, 1938, p. 4, cols. 2–3.

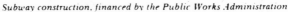

Subway construction, financed by the Public Works Administration

countered that "much mention [ought to be made of] the committeeman's untiring efforts in obtaining patronage jobs for some 130 deserving people of his organization; of his causing thousands in his district to receive prompt and proper aid from the various relief agencies; and his making possible the employment of over 200 others in business places of the community."[27] In 1938, Sneed took credit for recommending and placing more than four thousand persons.[28]

Throughout his terms in office, Sneed, like Tittinger, dodged accusations of associating with gambling and vice elements, black as well as white. As a city vehicle commissioner, he got into squabbles with taxi interests on the South Side and violent confrontations with competing businesses. The major opposition to his retention in office in 1938 was generated by his associations with underworld figures and the Kelly-Nash machine.[29]

Sneed did deliver the votes needed to challenge Republicans in the ward, however. Early in his tenure he remarked on the potential power that blacks had at their disposal if they voted as a unified Democratic bloc. In 1934 he pledged that he would work not only for victory but for "rolling up a record Democratic vote" in order to win "higher standing and more power with the central

committee" and "greater benefits of local government for the district."[30]

Meanwhile, the black Republican organization under DePriest, King, and Dawson attempted to hold the line while the political world as they knew it was collapsing around them. Republicans found that they could sustain themselves only on the hope that the 1936 presidential election might bring a return to the halcyon milieu of pre-Depression days. But the electorate of Chicago's Second Ward gave FDR an unprecedented 47.8 percent of their votes. In contrast, the vote throughout the rest of the congressional district reached 63.7 percent and throughout the state was 67.6 percent.[31] The growing black Democratic vote clearly indicated that the New Deal was winning friends. If there was one bright spot to Republicans, it was to be found in the party's entrenched status in the Black Belt, where a preponderance of votes and not a close near-majority typified victory.

Writing in 1937, Harold Gosnell postulated that patronage was the "cement" that united the party organization. While that was true in a general sense, the ingredient that held the black Republican organization intact while the rest of the citywide organization stumbled was the element of race. Because of race consciousness, black Republican leaders had the ability to extract maximum benefits from the siege mentality that had dominated the thinking and mood of the South Side. From 1931 to 1933, blacks perceived themselves as being exploited by a hostile Mayor Cermak. Given the dire economic conditions in the Black Belt, to them it also appeared to be a program of racial debilitation.[32]

The spoils of power had all but disappeared for black Republicans, but internecine warfare based on personality marked political life throughout the 1930s. As chief *Defender* political observer A. N. Fields observed in 1934, "When there is no food for the subjects, the king must start a war."[33]

[27]*Ibid.*, Feb. 17 (p. 2, col. 1), March 17 (p. 3, cols. 7–8), 1934.

[28]*Ibid.*, Feb. 28, 1938, p. 4, cols. 2–3.

[29]Mitchell to Kelly, April 15, 1935, and Mitchell to George B. Weiss, Jan. 28, 1939, Mitchell Papers; "Reports on Democratic Ward Committeemen," 1936, copies in Harold F. Gosnell Papers, a part of the Robert Merriam Papers, Box XCVIII, University of Chicago Libraries.

[30]*Defender*, Feb. 26, 1938, p. 4, cols. 2–3.

[31]*Chicago Daily News*, Nov. 4, 1936, p. 6, col. 7. Not even when FDR received 56 percent of the Second Ward vote in 1940 could the Democratic party be said to be in control of the ward. In the Black Belt, a preponderance of votes cast—in the range of 80 to 90 percent—was the only indication of political hegemony.

[32]Gosnell, *Machine Politics*, p. 39.

[33]*Defender*, April 14, 1935, p. 1, cols. 1–2.

The Second Ward, Chicago's "banner Republican Ward"—alleged to be "the strongest Republican ward in the country" throughout the period of the New Deal—retained its status as the linchpin of black Republicanism into the 1940s.[34] Moreover, it was the key to the black vote of the First Congressional District, coveted prize of Democratic politicians even after the Democrats captured the congressional seat in 1934 without it.

In the days of GOP control of the city, the Second Ward committeeman had immense power, but with the New Deal the instruments of power were denied the committeeman, State Representative William E. King. Even with that disadvantage, however, King proved to be a strong leader, aggressively plotting a course attempting to substitute party loyalty and future victories for actual power in dealing with his constituents. He prevented Democrats from capturing more than two key offices, congressman in 1934 and state senator in 1938. The price that Republicans paid was warfare so intense in 1934 that King was hard-pressed to hold his committeemanship in the spring election. He did win, but only over the opposition of Alderman William L. Dawson, who had the support of DePriest. King consolidated his power by running against and defeating the only black state senator, fellow Republican Adelbert Roberts, who had run with the backing of DePriest. The *Defender* observed that King's victory meant "the reorganization of Republican politics in the Second Ward and First congressional district. . . . Congressman Oscar DePriest put his money on the wrong horse."[35]

In the Third Ward, DePriest ruled as committeeman even after his loss to Mitchell in the congressional contest of 1934. Within a year, the ward was jolted with intense factionalism. Alderman Jackson disavowed his allegiance to DePriest, allegedly over the latter's refusal to make him second in command of ward affairs. Jackson withdrew

from the regular Republican organization, taking with him members of the Third Ward Republican Club, including its president, Irvin C. Mollison, and fifty precinct captains. Jackson justified his formation of a competing organization by accusing DePriest of opportunism, political inconsistency, and a tendency toward "bossism." In the committeeman election of 1936, DePriest withstood the Jackson challenge by a comfortable margin of sixteen hundred votes.[36] Still an alderman, Jackson remained active in the political field and emerged in 1938 with his political troops to help Dawson in the Second Ward.

Major changes in Republican resistance to Democratic advances in the Black Belt occurred in 1939. Democrats held the power to dictate the outcome not only of their own party's primary but also, if they chose, of the Republicans'. Second Ward Alderman Dawson sought reelection for another four-year term, and his primary challenger was Committeeman William King, the Republican leader who, as one local wag in the *Defender* put it, had "nothing to COMMIT."[37] Meanwhile, Democratic leadership at City Hall was said to be considering entering the Republican race with full support for Dawson or not running a candidate of its own. Tittinger was disposed to support Dawson; in contrast, the two key black elements in the ward, Congressman Mitchell and the precinct captains, were opposed to either strategy as a betrayal of their hard work in promoting the Democratic party.[38]

[34]Draft of speech, undated but evidently a version of one given by Mitchell on March 2, 1939, before the United States House of Representatives, Mitchell Papers; Barnett to John Hamilton, Dec. 1, 1937, Claude A. Barnett Papers, Chicago Historical Society (hereafter cited as Barnett Papers).

[35]*Defender*, April 14, 1934, p. 1, cols. 1-2, p. 10, cols. 7-8.

[36]*Ibid.*, Nov. 9, 1935, p. 5, col. 1, and April 18, 1936, p. 2, col. 1.

[37]*Ibid.*, March 11, 1939.

[38]Corneal Davis to Mitchell, Jan. 4, 1939, and James McLendon to Mitchell, Jan. 16, 1939, Mitchell Papers.

In the primary, Dawson campaigned on his record in the area of housing—advocating fair rents, decent housing, and an end to evictions. On the negative side, the Dawson camp engaged in ad hominem attacks, accusing King of seeking a political office simply because he lacked one.[39]

After considerable negotiation, the Democrats chose Earl B. Dickerson as their candidate. Dickerson won immediate support of precinct captains but was slow in gaining support of the machine. While an adherent to the principles of the New Deal, Dickerson was intellectually inclined, somewhat independent in behavior, and in the eyes of many, a maverick undeserving of full party support. His uncompromising commitment to civic improvement and racial advancement also made him an anomaly among the Black Belt's political leadership. Mitchell, acting as Dickerson's patron, displayed an unusual amount of political honesty when he wrote to Dickerson: "Without a doubt you are by far the ablest man running for alderman. I think there is no comparison between your ability, your statesmanship and that of the others whose names will be on the ticket."[40]

Opposing Dickerson in the primary was Corneal Davis, a black aspirant who had allied with the independent, anti-Kelly-Nash faction headed in the city at large by white States' Attorney Thomas Courtney

WILLIAM E. KING

and in the ward by Christopher C. Wimbish. When the moment of political truth came in the primary, Dickerson easily trounced Davis by a margin of 7,500 votes, and King defeated Dawson in a close race decided by a margin of only 644 votes.[41]

The stage was set for the Second Ward general election. Mitchell urged Dickerson: "You must allow no grass to grow under your feet. . . . You have made a splendid fight, and you have done a mighty fine job in eliminating Dawson. You must now finish the job by eliminating King."[42] Dickerson drew unexpected support from the Courtney-Wimbish faction and from the Dawson faction of the Republican party. The fragile nature of the new circle of unity troubled Mitchell, who was suspicious both of Dawson's ability to deliver Republican votes and of Tittinger's new willingness to support Dickerson.[43]

Farther south in the Black Belt, the political activities of the Third Ward virtually

[39]*Defender*, Feb. 18 (p. 2, cols. 2–3), March 4 (p. 2, col. 5), 1939; Davis to Mitchell, Jan. 4, 1939, and Edison A. Love to Mitchell, Jan. 8, 1939, Mitchell Papers.

[40]McLendon to Mitchell, Jan. 18, 1939; Henry Woods to Mitchell, Jan. 24, 1939; Mitchell to Dickerson, Feb. 22, 1939, all in Mitchell Papers. See also Footnote 38.

[41]*Defender*, Feb. 18 (p. 2, cols. 2–3), March 4 (p. 2, col. 6), 1939.

[42]Mitchell to Dickerson, March 3, 1939, Mitchell Papers.

[43]Mitchell to McLendon, March 24, 1939; Mitchell to Dickerson, March 27, 1939; Mitchell to Tittinger, March 27, 1939; Dickerson to Mitchell (telegram), March 28, 1939; Tittinger to Mitchell, March 28, 1939, all *ibid.*

duplicated the Machiavellian activities that were occurring in the Second Ward. DePriest challenged Robert Jackson for the City Council post Jackson had held for twenty-one years. Already a victim of three consecutive, major defeats in the decade, DePriest was reduced to fighting for the scraps of political recognition. Appropriately, he was an ally to another fallen Republican, William Thompson, who was making his fifth bid for the mayor's office. Jackson was another pathetic figure who desperately tried to hold on to the only trapping that gave meaning to his political life. Running on his record of having been elected to his aldermanic post without defeat since 1918, he could claim very little else in the way of major accomplishments.[44]

The Democratic primary centered around candidates supporting or opposing the Kelly-Nash organization. The Sneed camp, after considering running no candidate at all, chose an outstanding one—Benjamin A. Grant, deputy coroner and graduate of both the University of Chicago and the John Marshall Law School. Grant's support from within the party almost guaranteed success from the start as Sneed got him the support of the entire Kelly-Nash organization, including Congressman Mitchell.

Opposing him was John A. Lewis, who had been considered one of Sneed's "closest advisors and supporters" and the president of the Third Ward Regular Democratic Organization before allying with the good-government faction of Courtney and Governor Henry Horner. Grant ran on a rather bland program that avoided the issues of municipal corruption and staggering unemployment. Lewis spoke candidly on the dilemma of being "a loyal and conscientious Democratic worker" in Kelly's Chicago, summing up poignantly the impact of the Depression and New Deal on Chicago's Black Belt:

For six years I have suffered the humiliation and injury of seeing our ward given only privileges that destroy good citizenship and decent community life. I have seen the moral foundation of women and children insidiously undermined. All this under the false cry of economic necessity. I have realized that the future economic and social progress of my people and community cannot be built under a system of political exploitation such as is encouraged by the present administration.[45]

The Third Ward primaries produced a close Republican contest—DePriest defeated Jackson by 1,200 votes—but a Democratic rout. Grant trounced Lewis by 8,500 votes and went on to defeat DePriest in April by 4,000 votes.[46]

In the Second Ward, where Dickerson had pitted the successes of the New Deal against the effete rhetoric of Republican opposition, Dickerson beat King decisively by more than two thousand votes. Alderman Dickerson proved himself politically astute as he quickly attributed his success to the Roosevelt movement. "In view of the fact that my campaign was based on the New Deal, I feel that my victory was a victory for the New Deal," he said. "While my opponent was slinging mud of a vicious sort, I stuck to the issues and told the people that I would do all that I could in the event of my election to carry forth the principles of the New Deal."[47]

The elections sealed the fate of Joe Tittinger as committeeman of the Second Ward. Tittinger had always faced criticism within the ward, but there was no strong contender for his post until William L. Dawson dramatically announced his conversion to the Democratic party. Only Dawson could bridge the gap between the parties. His efficacy as a vote getter for Earl Dickerson had made a good impression on the Kelly-Nash

[44]*Defender*, April 8, 1939, p. 1, col. 2, p. 2, col. 1.
[45]*Ibid.*, Jan. 21, 1939, p. 1, col. 3.
[46]*Ibid.*, March 4 (p. 7, cols. 7–8), April 8 (p. 2, col. 1, p. 12, col. 1), 1939.
[47]*Ibid.*, April, 8, 1939, p. 1, col. 2; Dickerson to Mitchell, April 7, 1939, Mitchell Papers.

hierarchy. Conversely, at one point Tittinger had opposed Dickerson's nomination. The presence of Dickerson and Tittinger in the same ward generated friction. Dickerson was a product of the district, and Tittinger was not. Dickerson was a noted attorney, active civic leader, and holder of a high Democratic state post; Tittinger possessed authority without prestige.

After Dickerson's victory, an open revolt broke out among Second Ward precinct captains over the issue of unemployment within their ranks. Forty-three—or almost half—of the captains were out of work at a time when most felt that there was work available. One captain was quoted as saying, "Hungry, unfed warriors cannot win fights." He complained that too many patronage jobs went to whites who were not captains and had not contributed to the party's success and that certain trucking jobs on federal projects had been given away to white drivers from outside the Second Ward. At one meeting Tittinger was soundly booed when he attempted to explain that he had delivered as many jobs as he could.[18]

Tittinger's performance in turning out the vote was criticized by party chairman Patrick Nash. After the poor showing of Democratic judicial candidates in April, Nash warned him personally, "If you don't deliver, you had better resign."[49] Precinct captains cautioned that Tittinger's recklessness increased the likelihood that Republicans would return to power in 1940. (While that possibility was actually remote, the captains' complaints and lower-than-expected

William L. Dawson's 1939 conversion to the Democratic party was dramatic proof of political realignment in Chicago's so-called "Black Belt."

voter turnouts did seem to influence the Democratic leadership at City Hall.) Mitchell, in the meantime, tried to bolster Tittinger's standing with party leaders during the summer with letters extolling his contributions to the party and accusing Dickerson and Dawson of fomenting dissension.[50]

The reality of the situation set in as preparations began for the Mayor's Christmas Fund. Dawson and Dickerson were appointed by Kelly to head the ward effort.[51] Within days, Dawson received patronage within the Second Ward without the consent or knowledge of Tittinger.[52] Pro-Tittinger precinct captains and Mitchell rallied to the Committeeman's cause, but by November, 1939, Dawson had officially replaced him. Some captains, apprehensive about what was transpiring, refused to report to Dawson for their instructions.[53] One political critic wrote, "Some of them wanted a Negro Committeeman and they have one now and

[18]*Defender*, June 17, 1939, p. 1. col. 3.
[19]Thomas J. Price to Mitchell, May 27, 1939, Mitchell Papers.
[50]*Metropolitan Post* (Chicago), Nov. 11, 1939 (clipping), and James P. Durden to Mitchell, Jan. 2, 1940 (incorrectly dated 1939), Mitchell Papers.
[51]*Defender*, Oct. 28, 1939, p. 1, cols. 2–3.
[52]Mitchell to Nash (telegram), Oct. 30, 1939, Mitchell Papers.
[53]Frederick Larkins to Mitchell, Nov. 6, 1939, and Durden to Mitchell, Dec. 23, 1939, *ibid.*

still they are not satisfied."[54] What many had wanted, however, was an improvement over Tittinger's leadership. To some, the elevation of Dawson brought none, and their previous dissatisfaction and opposition to Tittinger was merely transferred to Dawson.

The conversion of William L. Dawson to the Democratic party was a significant event in Chicago politics. He developed a close identification with the masses of the Black Belt, much as DePriest had done, becoming an outspoken champion of the rights of blacks. It was during that period that W. E. B. DuBois praised him on the basis of his reported statement, "I am not playing Party politics but race politics."[55] Dawson's private and public statements along with his political actions tend to support that assertion. His highly respected Republican contemporary Claude A. Barnett called him a "fighter [for his people], but level-headed."[56] On his responsibility as a racially-oriented politician, Dawson said quite pointedly: "I believe that only a black man can speak [on] what is in the hearts of black people. . . . I have seen these people who are unemployed. Thousands of them live here on the south side. Anybody who says they are lazy or shiftless or don't want to work simply distorts the facts. I have hundreds of them in my organization. Why must they be insulted by every peanut politician who wants to curry favor with reaction? I have seen some of these people take jobs at 10 cents an hour in order to buy bread and feed their children."[57]

Dawson's switch in party affiliation was not unusual for the times and, in fact, was quite consistent with political and economic realities. One contemporary likened his conversion to the Democratic party to that of Saul on the road to Damascus, in that it was a genuine transformation in political allegiance.[58] As the hard times of the Great Depression were relieved by the economic upswing related to the nation's involvement in the European war, Dawson's image appears to have changed. When he made his move to national prominence in 1942, he became the third in a line of complex individuals who served the Black Belt in the United States House of Representatives. Dawson the congressman differed from Dawson the local politician—at least in terms of outward appearances in his dealings with whites. He was no longer the local, selfless, activist politician, but the mature, cautious politician who instructed blacks that "party should come first and race second."[59]

The realignment in political affiliation from the Republican to the Democratic party was slow in coming to Chicago's Black Belt community and was not complete until after the decade of the Great Depression. Importantly, the rate of change was directly linked to the Democratic organization that the Kelly-Nash machine produced in the Black Belt. That change also illustrates the impact of the largesse of the New Deal under the influence of the Kelly-Nash machine, which, in meeting the exigencies of the Depression, weakened the once-solid bond between racial ideology and political affiliation.

[54]*Metropolitan Post*, Nov. 11, 1939 (clipping), *ibid.*

[55]W. E. B. Du Bois, *Dusk of Dawn: An Essay Toward an Autobiography of the Race Concept* (1940; rpt. New York: Schocken Books, 1968), p. 203.

[56]Barnett to Hamilton, May 12, 1938, Mitchell Papers; Barnett to Joseph W. Martin, June 18, 1938, Barnett Papers.

[57]William L. Patterson, "Dawson for Congress: A Progressive Negro Candidate," *Midwest Daily Record*, June 18, 1938 (clipping), Mitchell Papers.

[58]Author's interview with Hon. Sidney A. Jones, Jr., Chicago, Oct. 25, 1978.

[59]Clayton, p. 68; James Q. Wilson, "Two Negro Politicians: An Interpretation," *Midwest Journal of Political Science*, 4 (1960), 355-56.

COMMUNIST UNIONS AND THE BLACK COMMUNITY: THE CASE OF THE TRANSPORT WORKERS UNION, 1934-1944

By AUGUST MEIER and ELLIOTT RUDWICK*

Recent years have witnessed a growing and increasingly sophisticated scholarly interest in analyzing the role that Communists have played in the blacks' struggle for full equality. Where the older literature portrayed the ideologically egalitarian Communists as having manipulated the race issue to follow the shift in strategies of the Comintern, the more modern research consists of case studies of how Communists actually operated in specific, diverse situations. Little attention has thus far been given to a systematic examination of how Communist-led trade unions dealt with white racism, but the complexity of the subject is illustrated in Donald Critchlow's pioneering comparison of the policies of two such organizations during World War II—the United Electrical Radio and Machine Workers (UE) and the National Maritime Union (NMU). He concluded that the UE, operating in an industry employing few black workers, confined itself principally to verbal support of Negro protest causes, while the

* We wish to thank the labor journalist Tom Brooks, and William Kirrane, Educational Director of the Transport Workers Union for their assistance in helping us obtain access to the TWU Archives in New York City. Unfortunately we were able to consult only the files of New York Local #100; the records of the Philadelphia local for the period under consideration do not survive, and we were unable to gain permission to consult Michael Quill's files. Broadly speaking, we found that as in the case of most other CIO unions, surviving union records have only skimpy information on the relationship with black workers, and examination of the subject therefore depends chiefly upon careful research in the black press and relevant white journals, as well as in the archives of both the racial advancement organizations and interested federal agencies. We also wish to thank Professors Mark Naison of Fordham University and Eugene Genovese of the University of Rochester for their helpful suggestions.

0023-656x|82|2302–165 $01.00
© 1982 Tamiment Institute

NMU, which had a substantial black membership and a Negro Communist as secretary-treasurer, worked far harder at advancing the job interests of blacks. Yet even this union often found the prejudices of both white employers and many white workers serious enough to inhibit its efforts at promoting fully-egalitarian practices in the industry. Interestingly enough, vigorously anti-Communist black community leaders recognized the sincerity of the NMU and refrained from attacking the union in instances when it felt unable to fight the discriminatory practices of the shipping companies.[1]

In light of Critchlow's suggestive comparison, our essay examines the Transport Workers Union (TWU), another CIO affiliate which was run by a Communist-dominated leadership in the 1930s and early 1940s, and which in many circles had the reputation of being a staunch defender of the Negroes' cause. Since this reputation grew out of certain dramatic incidents in New York and Philadelphia—where the TWU had its largest local

---

[1] Donald T. Critchlow, "Communist Unions and Racism: A Comparative Study of the United Electrical, Radio and Machine Workers and the National Maritime Union to the Black Question During World War II," *Labor History*, 17 (1976), 230-44. See also the able discussion in Mark Naison's forthcoming *Communists in Harlem During the Depression*, University of Illinois Press.

Critchlow's analysis of the NMU is effectively supported by documents in the NAACP Archives. The NAACP, concerned about discrimination in the hiring of personnel for government ships under the Maritime Commission, conferred on the matter with the black NMU vice president Ferdinand Smith and other union officials: "Mr. Smith told Mr. [Thurgood] Marshall that the Union was faced with severe problems of organization as well as a split in the labor movement between the C.I.O. and A.F. of L., that it had a bloc in the Union which was actively supporting every type of disruptive action within Union ranks, and that taking these things as a whole, Union officials had their hands full. He made it clear that the Union leadership stood 100% opposed to any kind of discrimination against its 10% Negro membership, and was fighting to break it up. However, he said that the Union was also faced with keeping its ranks together, despite all of these problems, that it was aware of its large southern membership which had not yet been educated to taking Negro members into full equality, which means not only the right to work with white seamen . . . but [to] eat and sleep in the same room with these white seamen. He was firm in his statement that while the Union leadership was going to fight the discrimination problem wherever possible, no intelligent person could defend the Union's fighting the problem to the extent of breaking up the Union over the issue." Thus the very survival of the union took higher priority than guaranteeing equality for black workers; the NAACP, convinced of the NMU leadership's sincerity, continued to press them, but refrained from an open attack, given the rivalry between the NMU and the racist AFL International Seamens Union. George Murphy, Jr., "Memorandum," Nov. 16, 1938, NAACP Papers, Library of Congress, Group I, Container C-284; Thurgood Marshall to William H. Hastie, April 19, 1940, NAACP Papers. (Hereafter the form for citing the various NAACP groupings will be I, C-322; II, A-11, etc. The Marshall to Hastie memorandum, consulted before the post-1939 materials were fully processed, was at that time located in a 1941 file labelled "Labor Unions: Dean Hastie.")

memberships—we will analyze the way that the union actually confronted job bias in the transit industry in these two cities. In the course of this inquiry we will be interested in examining two questions: the extent to which its actions were shaped by pressures from black community organizations and the larger question of whether a Communist-led union like the TWU was able to solve black grievances more effectively than other CIO unions at the time.

* * * * *

Established by Communist functionaries in 1934, the TWU affiliated with the CIO in the spring of 1937. Whether TWU president Michael J. Quill himself actually ever belonged to the Party is disputed, but the union's founders and Quill's chief lieutenants were all Communists. Quill's earlier and much-advertised connection with the Irish Revolutionary Movement made him ideally suited to the difficult task of welding a predominantly Communist leadership to an overwhelmingly Irish-Catholic membership, especially in the face of strong opposition from New York's Church hierarchy.[2] By the end of 1937 the TWU had signed up all the major surface, elevated, and subway networks in New York except for the city-owned Eighth Avenue or Independent (IND) subway system.[3]

On New York's two privately-owned elevated and subway systems—the Interborough Rapid Transit (IRT) and the Brooklyn-Manhattan Transit (BMT), blacks constituted about eight per cent of the work force, but were restricted to menial positions as porters and elevator operators. The Fifth Avenue Coach and New York City Omnibus companies, which not only enjoyed heavy

[2] L. H. Whittemore, *The Man Who Ran the Subways: The Story of Mike Quill* (New York, 1968), Ch. I and *passim*; *Party Organizer* 8 (Mar. 1935), 23: A. H. Raskin, "Presenting the Phenomenon Called Quill," *New York Times Magazine*, Mar. 5, 1950. For discussion of whether Quill was a Communist see Max M. Kampelman, *The Communist Party vs. the C.I.O.* (New York, 1971; reprint of 1957 book), 149-51. *PM*, the New York liberal daily tabloid, Mar. 13, 1941, had material on Quill's life and the union's Irish membership. For text of CIO charter see mimeographed "Minutes of the Proceedings of the TWU First Biennial Convention, October 1937," 2 (copy at University of California, Berkeley, Library). On Catholic Church's active opposition see TWU Executive Board Minutes, Aug. 2, 1937, TWU Archives, TWU National Office, New York City.
[3] "Minutes of the Proceedings of the TWU First Biennial Convention," session of Oct. 7, p. 2, and *PM*, April 30, 1941.

black patronage but maintained garages and terminals in Harlem, each employed a scant half-dozen blacks, all in the lowest categories.[4] Only on the civil service-controlled IND subway were conditions different, and even there few blacks were promoted to the better jobs until Negro civic and political pressures broke down the barriers after the 1935 Harlem riot.[5] Blacks had no leverage whatever on the privately-owned lines, where management's rampant discrimination had the support of rank-and-file white employees, making it exceedingly difficult for the Communist union leaders to confront the issue.[6] Yet the TWU leaders' declaration of a deep commitment to equal opportunity only increased black resentment over the failure to end job bias in the transit industry, and provided a focus for attacks against them from anti-Communist race-advancement organizations.

In New York, black dissatisfaction with the TWU became most salient in connection with the IRT subway system and the Manhattan bus companies. Actually when the TWU in its infancy was organizing IRT workers and broached the subject of job equality for blacks, it quickly met deeply imbedded resistance. The union's original 1934 constitution specified the inclusion of all workers "regardless of race, creed, color, or nationality," and the union's official organ, *Transport Workers Bulletin*, early made a forthright appeal for equal rights and interracial unity in the face of capitalist divide-and-conquer tactics.[7] Yet in 1935 Communist party members trying to organize an IRT maintenance shop in Harlem lamented their inability to raise the question of Negro rights except in the most general terms, and when the

---

4 See testimony of company officials in "New York [State] Temporary Commission on the Condition of the Urban Colored Population, Public Hearings, New York, 1937," (Albany, NY mimeographed, [1938], copy at New York State Library), 1420-40, 1546-65, 1374-81 and 1391-1403. On galling presence of terminals in Harlem see number of sources especially *New York Amsterdam News*, Dec. 25, 1937 (hereafter cited as *Amsterdam News*).
5 *New York Age*, June 8, 1935, Jan. 2, 1937 (hereafter cited as *Age*).
6 Speaking at the 1943 TWU convention Quill said: "At one time we had a battle right in this [Transport Workers'] hall on the question of the transit companies giving to our fellow Negro workers equal opportunities. Some of our members came in and said, 'I am satisfied to work with the Negro brothers as long as he [sic] remains a porter.' We had a fine bout with them then, and we said that until the time that our Negro workers became more than porters . . . the Transport Workers Union would be divided and beaten." *Proceedings of the Fourth Biennial Convention, Transport Workers Union of America . . . October 20th to 23rd, 1943* [New York, 1943], 25.
7 *1934-1963: TWU and the Fight for Civil Rights* (TWU pamphlet, New York: 1963), 9; *Transport Workers Bulletin*, Nov. 1934; see also *Ibid.*, Mar. 1935,

union staged its first annual ball an enormous amount of educational effort was required to persuade whites to allow an integrated affair.[8] As late as October 1936, the TWU's executive board had to fight off a last-ditch attempt by some members to insert a "white clause" in the organization's ritual.[9] Amidst these racial tensions the *Bulletin* felt constrained to virtually ignore the subject of blacks in the union.

A few blacks were among the TWU's early members, and one porter, Clarence King, by 1936 was serving on the union's first executive board.[10] Moreover the Ladies Auxiliary pointedly included black women, and the interracial office staff once successfully sued a restaurant owner who refused to serve the mixed group.[11] And as the TWU intensified its IRT organizing drive in late 1936, it made special efforts to attract black workers. One leaflet concluded: "Above all, the porters must assist in discontinuing the discriminatory policy of the Company which relegates the Colored employees to perpetual serfdom. . . . Positions and promotions should be governed by an employee's ability." [12] The response was generally positive, and in the NLRB elections held the following May most of the black IRT workers joined the whites to help provide the TWU's landslide victory.[13]

In the union's first IRT contract the blacks did benefit from a new minimum wage which granted an average 10 per cent increase for the whites, but an average 25 per cent increase for the lower-paid porters.[14] Yet the city's race-advancement organiza-

---

8 Louis Sass, "Concentration on Transport," *Party Organizer*, 8 (Mar. 1935), 26; *Transport Workers Bulletin*, April-May, 1935.

9 Minutes, TWU Joint Executive Committee, Oct. 6, 1936, TWU Archives.

10 Minutes, TWU Executive Board, Feb. 4, 1936 to Aug. 2, 1937, *passim*. When the union expanded into other cities King, though he did not serve on the International Executive Board, continued on the Executive Board of the largest Local, #100 in New York. See references in *Transport Workers Bulletin* and biennial convention minutes through 1941, *passim*.

11 *Transport Workers Bulletin*, Oct. 15, 1935; and "Minutes of the Proceedings of the TWU First Binnial Convention," evening session, Oct. 7, 1937, 38-40; *Daily Worker*, Oct., 29, 1937 (hereafter cited as *Worker*).

12 Mimeographed leaflet, "To the I.R.T. Porters," issued by Special Committee to Organize IRT Porters [Mar. 1937], in NAACP Papers, Group I, Container C-322.

13 Roy Wilkins to Austin Hogan, Feb. 16, 1939, NAACP Papers, I, C-414.

14 [Charles H. Houston], "Memo from Conference with Mr. Bath," July 3, 1938; NAACP Papers, I, C-414. See also "Minutes of the Proceedings of the TWU First Biennial Convention," first session, 6. This is confirmed by the technical terms of the agreement itself—see "Memorandum of Agreement Between Thomas B. [sic] Murray, Jr., as receiver of the Interborough Rapid Transit Co., and the Transport Workers Union of America . . . ," [July 1937], TWU Archives.

tions received disquieting reports that in the negotiations the TWU had quietly dropped its demand for non-discrimination in promotions when management balked. This information came from Rupert Bath, an elevator operator who years earlier had fully qualified himself to be a generator cleaner, but was denied a promotion. Disillusioned with the union's action he had turned for help to the NAACP and Urban League. But Michael Quill did not even answer the NAACP's telegram of protest.[15]

Quill may have been reluctant to deal with an organization like the NAACP, given the history of bitter relationships between the Association and the Communist Party ever since the Scottsboro Case. In any event, the fruits of what NAACP Assistant Secretary Roy Wilkins termed this "faint-hearted" stand[16] were soon apparent. In the summer of 1937 after the IRT announced openings for 75 station agents but summarily rejected all the black applicants,[17] Bath and his associates again found Quill unresponsive and appealed once more to the Urban League and NAACP. But even an urgent statement from Charles Houston, the Association's pro-CIO chief counsel, who appealed to Quill on the basis of what he knew was a principle that the Communists valued highly—interracial working class solidarity—received no reply. Instead TWU leaders responded with convention resolutions denouncing "reactionary" employers and the AFL for race discrimination and endorsing the Communist-oriented National Negro Congress.[18]

---

15 Charles H. Houston to Thomas E. Murray, Oct. 3, 1937; Houston to George Keegan, May 3, 1938: [Houston], "Memo from Conference with Mr. Bath," July 3, 1938; Wilkins to Quill, telegram, March 30, 1937; Wilkins to Austin Hogan, Feb. 17, 1939, assailing Quill for his failure, all in NAACP Papers, I, C-414. The TWU executive board minutes also have some references to the IRT negotiations (see esp. Minutes Nov. 16, 1936, Aug. 2, 1937, TWU Archives), but nothing on the black workers' demands.

16 Wilkins to Hogan, Feb. 17, 1939, NAACP Papers, I, C-414. For the best discussion of the relationships between the NAACP and the Communists over the Scottsboro case see especially Dan T. Carter, Scottsboro: A Tragedy of the American South, (Baton Rouge, 1969), passim. Evidence of the bitterness and continuing conflict between the two organizations is to be found in many sections of the NAACP Papers.

17 Houston to A. L. Merritt, Oct. 3, 1937; Wilkins to Quill, Oct. 5, 1937; Houston to Quill, Oct. 3, 1937, all in NAACP Papers, I, C-414.

18 Amsterdam News, Oct. 9, 1937; extensive correspondence October 1937, in NAACP Papers, I, C-414, esp. Houston to Quill, Oct. 3, 1937; for Quill not replying to Houston see Houston to Committee of One Thousand for Michael J. Quill, Oct. 23, 1937, Ibid; "Minutes of the Proceedings of the TWU First Biennial Convention," Oct. 7 afternoon session, 29-30, 61-62, and Oct. 8 morning session, 37. See also report of convention in Worker, Oct. 9, 1937.

The race-advancement organizations were not impressed, and with Quill running for a seat on the city council, they placed him in an awkward position with an open letter to his most prominent backers appealing for help.[19] Quill and his lieutenants now finally sat down with the Urban League and NAACP leaders, and convinced them that he had indeed taken up Bath's grievance with the IRT's general manager. When the latter promised to promote Bath if white fellow workers approved, TWU officials "after a bitter fight" secured their unanimous consent, only to find that the IRT executive had changed his mind and refused to discuss the subject. Quill prevailed upon the two organizations to take the initiative and they attempted to force management's hand by exposure through a series of public hearings being conducted by the New York State Temporary Commission on the Condition of the Urban Colored Population. But this tactic fizzled when transit spokesmen blandly denied practicing job discrimination.[20]

On the other hand, the hearings led to a development that would ultimately have profound effects on the TWU's relationship to the black community, for they prompted Adam Clayton Powell, Jr., pastor of the Abyssinian Baptist Church, to create the Greater New York Coordinating Committee for Employment, as an instrument to fight discrimination by the utilities. At the time, the future congressman was friendly with Communist leaders in Harlem, and it seemed that the Coordinating Committee criticized Quill only when prodded by a rival, the Harlem Labor Union (HLU), which was a black nationalist offshoot of the Garvey Movement.[21] Appearing at the Coordinating Committee's first mass rally in April 1938, HLU President Arthur Kemp, known for his open hostility to both AFL and CIO, angrily denounced the TWU as the sole reason for the absence of black bus drivers in the city. Powell, on the defensive, was prompted

---

[19] Houston to the Committee of One Thousand for Michael J. Quill, Oct. 27, 1937; NAACP Papers, I, C-414.

[20] Walter White, Secretary's Report to the November 1937 Meeting of the NAACP Executive Board, NAACP national office, New York; Houston, "Memorandum on Meeting at Transport Workers Union Headquarters, Saturday, Oct. 31, 1937," NAACP Papers I, C-414; citations to public hearings of the New York Temporary Commission on the Urban Colored Population in note 4 above.

[21] The Harlem Labor Union, which had emerged during the early 1930s, as one of several competing organizations using picketing and boycotts to secure jobs in Harlem's white-owned stores, was not a true labor union. Indeed many New York Negro leaders regarded the HLU as little more than a "racketeering" group that forced merchants to hire its own members.

to make his own public attack on Quill, and in his weekly column in the Harlem newspaper, *Amsterdam News*, he wrote: "Strangely, Negroes must fight labor as well as capital for work. . . . Take the TWU of which the loudly liberal Michael Quill is president. Not a Negro driver rolls a bus on the thoroughfares of New York City. This is strictly the union's fault." [22]

As never before Harlem was stirred over the issue of transit jobs. For its part, the NAACP again pressed both the union and the IRT on behalf of Bath. [23] Powell's Committee, now armed with a pledge of support from the embarrassed TWU president, called another mass meeting attended by all elements in the community—a fact underscored by the participation of the NAACP's Secretary, Walter White, who feared competition from Powell as well as Communist influence on him. Quill himself personally addressed the gathering, guaranteeing TWU help in the struggle against the IRT. Blacks he maintained, "don't have to fight our union . . . . we are fighting for the equal conditions for all." [24]

Quill had thus again placed the entire blame on management; but for the first time his union had publicly endorsed the NAACP's struggle with the transit companies. For reasons that cannot now be ascertained, Powell and his associates decided to let the NAACP continue managing the battle with the IRT. The company, threatened by Houston with a possible lawsuit under the state's civil rights legislation, finally promised in June to "experiment" with appointing a few blacks as platform men and station agents. [25] Then, with the IRT dragging its feet on implementing this agreement, Bath prevailed upon Austin Hogan, president of the TWU's New York Local 100 to accompany him to the corporation's general manager. The latter assured them that six would now be promoted, though they would have lower seniority than the 250 whites just hired for these jobs. However,

22 *Amsterdam News*, April 30, 1938.
23 See Houston to George Keegan and Thomas E. Murray, Jr., both May 3, 1938, and Keegan to Houston, May 12, 1938, all in NAACP Papers I, C-414, and also in the TWU Archives.
24 *Worker*, May 18, 1938; *Amsterdam News*, May 21, 1938.
25 Murray to Houston, June 10, 1938, and NAACP press release, June 17, 1938, both in NAACP Papers I, C-414. It is also possible that additional NAACP pressure on Quill (see Houston to Quill, Jan. 4, 1938, TWU Archives) had led the union president to make his own further representation to the company, that produced the June 10 understanding between Houston and Murray.

because the TWU leaders failed to object to this kind of arrangement which virtually guaranteed that the blacks would be demoted in the autumn, Bath turned again to Houston. The NAACP's attorney, after making bitter complaints, finally secured assurances from both Hogan and the IRT that the promotions would be carried out in "good faith."[26]

Hogan's representation and Houston's persistence had thus finally paid off in management's appointment of the six as station agents and platform men, but many white union members became absolutely enraged. Hogan confided to Houston that he was "under fire" for sticking to "union principle."[27] For weeks afterwards union meetings were punctuated with "open opposition from the floor" to giving Negroes "white men's jobs."[28] In the face of this uproar the TWU leaders adopted a two-pronged strategy. On the one hand, fearful that a clique of white workers would cause major disruption, they continued to promote black union members and to urge race-advancement organizations to bear the main responsibility for pressing management.[29] On the other hand they prevailed upon Local 100's Joint Executive Committee to "unanimously endorse" a resolution portraying the controversy as "a test for every member of our union" to demonstrate "that we really treasure this union and its firm unity and are not willing to cast its future to the winds at the instigation of those who are using the weapon of prejudice and foul play to weaken the TWU."[30] Although the angry whites simmered down, and although Hogan had assured Houston of the union's commitment to oppose the demotion of the six blacks, they were nevertheless back at their old jobs by autumn. Quill and his colleagues again did not intervene. In fact only a heated

---

[26] [Houston], Memorandum, "Conference with Rupert Bath, July 11, 1938"; Houston to Murray, July 12, 1938; Houston to Adam Clayton Powell, to Hogan, to Quill, all July 13, 1938 in NAACP Papers I, C-414.

[27] Age, Aug. 1, 1938; [George B. Murphy], "Memorandum," Aug. 3, 1938, and Houston, "Memorandum re Interborough Rapid Transit Co., Case," Aug. 1, 1938, both in NAACP Papers I, C-414.

[28] Wilkins to White, Mar. 18, 1940, NAACP Papers, II, A-343; see also T. Arnold Hill to Houston, Aug. 5, 1938, Ibid, I, C-414.

[29] [Murphy], "Memorandum," Aug. 3, 1938; Houston "Memorandum re Interborough Rapid Transit Co., Case," Aug. 1, 1938, both in NAACP Papers, I, C-414.

[30] Quotations in NAACP press release, Aug. 29, 1938, NAACP Papers, I, C-414, and carried in Age and Amsterdam News of Sept. 23, 1938. We were unable to find this statement, entitled "Fair Play, Justice and Our Unity," in the Transport Workers Bulletin; it probably appeared in a local edition of this journal that has not survived.

exchange of letters between the NAACP and the IRT got the blacks restored to their higher positions.[31]

Scarcely had the matter been resolved, however, when it became evident that a new action by the union itself would have the effect of demoting the blacks once more. Faced with a crisis posed by the demolition of the IRT's Sixth Avenue Elevated Line, and the agitation of the dismissed employees for a new system-wide seniority policy throughout the IRT, the union awarded the Sixth Avenue members preference over both the newly-hired whites and the recently-upgraded blacks.[32] TWU leaders were caught on the horns of a serious dilemma. On the one hand they were ideologically committed to equal racial opportunity; on the other, they were faced with the very delicate question of seniority rights, a matter that was central to the union's appeal to the white workers in the first place. Accordingly, the union leaders, unable to solve the blacks' grievances, once again did not respond to NAACP protests.[33] Thereupon the Association's infuriated Assistant Secretary wrote Hogan, "We maintain that the union has exhibited color prejudice," and "has consented to flagrant discrimination," even though "in conference with you and Mr. Michael Quill, we have been led to believe . . . that the TWU would stand four-square for non-discriminatory treatment." Finally, referring to the legislation currently being debated at Albany (and supported by Harlem Assemblymen) proposing to ban unions on the IRT and BMT when the lines passed to municipal ownership in the near future,[34] the NAACP executive warned that "colored people generally in New York City cannot be depended upon" to support the TWU in its demand for a collective bargaining contract with the city. While the NAACP believed in "the principles of organized labor. . . . We cannot conscientiously urge unionization . . . in the face of mistreatment

[31] Wilkins to Murray, Nov. 3, 16, 1938; Murray to Wilkins, Nov. 15, 30, 1938; Wilkins to Houston, Dec. 2, 1938, all in NAACP Papers I, C-414; and for transfer of men back to platform jobs see NAACP, *Annual Report for 1938* (New York, 1939), 15.

[32] On delicacy of the issue see discussion in *Proceedings of the Second Biennial Convention of the Transport Workers Union . . . September 20-23, 1939,* (New York [1939]), 126-27.

[33] Wilkins to Quill, and to Hogan. both Jan. 31, 1938, NAACP Papers, I, C-414.

[34] See *Age* and *Amsterdam News,* both Mar. 25, 1939, for support black assemblymen gave this bill, which the governor signed in June (*Amsterdam News,* July 1, 1939). On TWU resistance to the Wicks bill see TWU International Executive Board Minutes, Jan. 27, 1939, TWU Archives.

and betrayal by union leaders." Wilkins followed up this letter with a press release accusing the TWU of duplicity against its black members. "Pained" by Wilkins' sharp tone, Hogan finally responded. Declaring that in the face of many resentful white members the union had waged "a continual battle" on behalf of blacks, and employing the old argument about the porters' big wage increase in the first IRT contract, he blamed as usual the "reactionary employer" for all the turmoil. "Your indiscriminate use of terms 'mistreatment,' 'discrimination,' 'failure,' 'faint-heartedness,' and 'betrayal by union'" was "wholly unwarranted."[35]

Thus pressed, the union evidently did intervene on behalf of the six blacks, who retained their new jobs; over the following year several more were added and a few were even promoted to trainmen.[36] While this was at least minimal progress, the situation on the bus lines and the BMT had not changed at all. Further, in sharp contrast to all these privately-owned transit systems covered by union contracts, by 1940 the non-union municipal subway system had five hundred Negro civil service employees, who comprised ten percent of the labor force and held such positions as motormen, power maintainers, station agents, shop men, draftsmen, shop foremen, and assistant station supervisors.[37]

Accordingly, just as Wilkins had warned, when the city took steps to acquire the IRT and BMT lines, the TWU found few black allies in its battle with Mayor Fiorello LaGuardia, who wanted to prevent transit strikes by excluding the union and placing the new city employees under civil service. The NAACP vigorously backed the mayor. Wilkins publicly declared in his *Amsterdam News* column, "Messrs Quill and Hogan . . . may shout as loudly as they please. . . . But until they get their union straight with Negroes, they cannot expect much sympathy from the Negro public." The union perceiving the need for a rebuttal, circulated a black porter's statement that appeared simultaneously in the black press and the *Daily Worker*: "The TWU has done

[35] Wilkins to Hogan, Feb. 13, 1939; NAACP press release, Feb. 17, 1939; Hogan to Wilkins, Feb. 23, 1939, all in NAACP Papers, I, C-414.
[36] Wilkins column in *Amsterdam News*, Mar. 16, 1940; *Amsterdam News*, April 6, 1940; *Transport Bulletin*, April 1940.
[37] *Amsterdam News*, April 6, 1940.

a great job in a situation which is admittedly difficult. .... We
who are on the inside looking out know what the leadership of
this union and most of its members have gone through in the
battle for equal opportunity."[38]

LaGuardia, compromising with the TWU by agreeing to maintain the existing contracts until their expiration, assured black
leaders that no discrimination would be tolerated.[39] Yet job opportunities on the old IRT and BMT lines did not improve
under city ownership. The TWU blamed the mayor and the
Board of Transportation, but blacks generally thought otherwise,
and in 1941 when Quill threatened a strike if LaGuardia would
not renew the contracts, the New York *Age* actually proposed
using black strikebreakers.[40]

By then the problem of job bias on the bus lines had again
come to the fore. As far back as 1934 the Communists had been
interested in this issue and their League of Struggle for Negro
Rights had led an unsuccessful picketing and boycott of the Fifth
Avenue Coach Company.[41] Subsequently sporadic initiative on
the matter came from the black nationalists of the Harlem Labor
Union.[42] Then in 1941 when the TWU inconvenienced Harlemites during a strike against the Fifth Avenue and New York City
Omnibus companies, fresh attention was focused on the way
that blacks were frozen out of bus jobs.

This TWU strike had received public support from only one
black advancement group, the National Negro Congress—by
now an openly Communist-front organization—which expressed
solidarity with the white strikers and gratitude for the union's
past efforts against discrimination.[43] Support from this quarter
notwithstanding, the annoyances arising from the eleven day

[38] White to Fiorello LaGuardia and John L. Lewis, Mar. 16, 1940, and White to
LaGuardia, Mar. 21, 1940, both in NAACP Papers, II, A-343; Wilkins column
in *Amsterdam News*, Mar. 16, 1940; *Amsterdam News*, Mar. 23, 1940; *Worker*,
Mar. 23, 1940.
[39] *CIO News*, April 8, 1940; NAACP press release, April 5, 1940, NAACP Papers,
II A-343.
[40] *Amsterdam News*, Mar. 29, 1941; Wilkins column in *Ibid.*, April 19, 1941; *New
York Weekly Transport Bulletin*, Feb. 1, 1941; *Age*, April 19, 1941.
[41] See account in August Meier and Elliott Rudwick, "The Origins of Nonviolent Direct Action in Afro-American Protest: A Note on Historical Discontinuities,"
in Meier and Rudwick, *Along the Color Line* (Urbana, 1976), 320.
[42] See esp. *Amsterdam News*, Oct. 28, Dec. 16, 23, 1939; *Age*, Dec. 2, 1939.
[43] *New York Weekly Transport Bulletin*, Mar. 22, 1941; William Gaulden, secretary of National Negro Congress State Committee to Quill Mar. 13, 1941, and
Hope Stevens, *et al.* to John A. Ritchie, Mar. 13, 1941, both in Fiorello La-
Guardia Papers, New York City Municipal Archives and Records Center, Box

strike only deepened Harlem's irritation with the TWU. Not surprisingly, Wilkins' weekly newspaper column greeted the strike announcement acidly: "There weren't any cheers from 350,000 Negro New Yorkers, however, for nary a black bus driver can be found anywhere. . . . The union will find that if they want the support of Negro public opinion, they had better stop talking so much labor theory and give black men some jobs."[44]

Moreover the TWU's victory actually led to renewed militant black activism against the union. Even before the strike ended on March 21, the Harlem Labor Union placed picket lines at several bus stops and was scheduling a gigantic torchlight parade and mass meeting. Powell, acting on behalf of the Coordinating Committee, rushed to embrace the angry campaign.[45] The well-attended HLU demonstration, the picketing of the TWU's head-quarters, and the fact that the National Negro Congress quickly joined the protest's sponsors to form a United Bus Strike Committee, led Quill to confer with the black leaders on March 24. Characteristically he blamed the companies and dramatically "pledged 'all-out-aid'" to the Negroes. Later that same day *Transport Bulletin* editor Maurice Forge, representing Quill at a mass meeting at Powell's Church, emotionally repeated the promise to the overflow crowd. Powell concluded the meeting by dramatically announcing the decision to launch a bus boycott: ". . . . You stayed off the buses for 11 days so that white men might have a better standard of living. Now we are asking that you stay off the buses so that the black man can have a decent standard of living also. . . . By the grace of God and the power of the mass[es], one day a black boy is going to roll a bus up Seventh Avenue."[46]

830; letter from Hope Stevens *et al* in *Worker*, Mar. 14, 1941.
[44] Wilkins column in *Amsterdam News*, Mar. 15, 1941.
[45] *Amsterdam News*, Mar. 22, 1941; *Age*, April 5, 1941. In the account that follows, the contemporary evidence is so much at variance with the contradictory recollections in Adam Clayton Powell Jr.'s two autobiographies (*Marching Blacks* [New York, 1945], 102, and *Adam by Adam* [New York, 1971], 66), that we cannot agree with Dominic J. Capeci, Jr.'s description of this event which accepts Powell's claims that the boycott had been planned by himself and Quill before the strike. See Capeci, "From Harlem to Montgomery: The Bus Boycotts and Leadership of Adam Clayton Powell, Jr., and Martin Luther King, Jr.," *The Historian*, 41 (1979), 724-26, esp. note 20.
[46] *Amsterdam News*, Mar. 22, 1941; *Worker*, Mar. 26, 1941; *PM*, Mar. 25, 1941, and *Amsterdam News*, Mar. 29, 1941. On picketing of TWU headquarters, interview with Arnold P. Johnson, NYC, Dec. 30, 1979.

The boycott was an instantaneous success. At the principal bus stops "scores of earnest men and women pleaded with their kinsmen to walk rather than submit to unfair discrimination;"[47] the United Bus Strike Committee had soon organized over a hundred automobiles into a jitney service which travelled the principal Harlem thoroughfares;[48] white Communists joined the massive picket lines that daily marched at Harlem's street corners.[49] The liberal white daily *PM* marveled at the unity in the Harlem community, and an enormous crowd filled Powell's church for another enthusiastic rally at the end of the month.[50]

Throughout the entire dispute the black leaders—the Coordinating Committee's Executive Secretary Arnold P. Johnson; Roger Straughn, the new head of the Harlem Labor Union; and Manhattan NNC President, Hope Stevens; as well as Powell himself—conferred with Quill and John A. Ritchie, who headed both bus companies. As a result of this black pressure, together with the fact that the Communist Party was then strongly encouraging left-wing unions to give especially vigorous attention to the issue of job discrimination—[51] and perhaps anticipating that Ritchie would refuse to make any concessions whatever—Quill quickly announced that the TWU would favor a preferential hiring plan, with whites and blacks to be hired in equal numbers until blacks were reasonably represented in the bus company's work force. Armed with his offer the black committee's spokesmen faced Ritchie three days after the boycott began. The astute

47 Editorial in *Opportunity*, 19 (May 1941), 130-31.
48 Interview with Arnold P. Johnson, Dec. 30, 1979; *PM*, Mar. 25, April 1, 1941.
49 *PM*, April 1, 1941; *Worker*, April 2, 1941; *Amsterdam News*, April 5, 1941; interview with Arnold P. Johnson, Dec. 30, 1979.
50 *PM*, April 1, 1941.
51 Interview with Mark Naison, Nov. 15, 1980.
    There were probably several reasons for the CP's use of this strategy at that time. It has been argued that in this period when the Soviet Union-Nazi non-aggression pact was in effect, the Communists opposed FDR's interventionist leanings, and unlike its general posture after Hitler invaded Russia in June 1941, the Party was eager to dramatize war industry discrimination especially if this might lead to delays in American rearmament. On the other hand, it should also be pointed out that the Communists' arch-rival, A. Philip Randolph was at this time leading the agitation for defense jobs through his famous call for a March on Washington. See Wilson Record, *The Negro and the Communist Party* (Chapel Hill, 1951), ch. 5, *passim*; and Herbert Garfinkel, *When Negroes March: The March on Washington Movement in the Organizational Politics for FEPC* (Glencoe, IL, 1959), *passim*. Interestingly enough the Communists clearly tried to tie the Harlem bus boycott to its anti-intervention campaign in the spring of 1941; numerous Communist-front peace organizations ostentatiously lent their support to the black movement. (*Worker*, April 11, 1941.)

transit executive not only wished to get black passengers back on the busses but very likely also sought to humiliate Quill. In any event he topped the TWU leader with a counter-offer to set aside for blacks the next 180 driver and maintenance openings if the union agreed.[52] Ritchie was of course aware of the hundreds of unemployed white union men on the seniority roster, and he must have calculated that Quill would now be caught in the difficult dilemma between his affirmation of non-discrimination and the intense racism among his white rank-and-file.

In response to Ritchie's offer, Quill assured the black leaders of the union's "full moral support" and promised that he would do everything possible to see that 180 blacks were soon driving the busses and working in the maintenance shops.[53] Yet the anticipated TWU ratification was not forthcoming because of problems in selling the white workers any package that would remotely approach Ritchie's.[54] Meanwhile, union leaders maintained a skillful propaganda campaign; bus drivers circulated leaflets citing the TWU's numerous Negro "officers" and members "in whose behalf we are carrying on a vigorous campaign for greater opportunity." Simultaneously friends in left-wing and liberal circles, such as the *Daily Worker* and *PM*, were condemning the "deceitful" bus companies and praising the union for its anti-discrimination record. The *Worker*, after underscoring the union's principle of absolute color-blindness and reminding readers that management controlled all hiring, added: "Mass solidarity between organized bus workers and the Negro people is necessary to win ultimate success in the campaign. . . ."[55]

The black community and the union's leaders were not as fully united as *PM* and the *Daily Worker* believed. Actually the TWU was under two kinds of pressure from a divided Negro community. One came from friends in the NNC and the Coordinating Committee, and the other came from hostile critics. Despite the mass black enthusiasm for the bus boycott, the NAACP,

[52] *Amsterdam News*, April 5, 1941.
[53] *Worker*, April 2, 1941; *Amsterdam News*, April 5, 1941.
[54] A year later, recalling the anniversary of the boycott, Powell's new weekly, *The People's Voice*, stated cryptically: "The companies gave early indication of their willingness to hire Negroes, but certain questions of union rights developed to interfere with the conclusion of an agreement" until "these difficulties were finally ironed out." (*People's Voice*, May 2, 1942).
[55] Leaflet as printed in *New York Weekly Transport Bulletin*, April 5, 1941; *Worker*, April 2, 1941, and editorial April 7, 1941; *PM*, April 1, 1941.

the Urban League, and A. Philip Randolph remained aloof, undoubtedly because of their reluctance to work with Communists.[56]
Moreover the black press was anything but sympathetic toward
Quill and the TWU. The *Age* doubted that that the union could
ever bring itself to accept Ritchie's proposal, while Wilkins informed *Amsterdam News* readers that despite Quill's "big, bold
statements," the TWU nevertheless had better comprehend that
the bus boycott represented an angry and aroused Harlem. With
Ritchie having offered his attractive package, the NAACP official warned that the TWU would be well advised to waive the
seniority rights of the laid-off whites, or "it may regret it . . . for
the brother is in no mood for excuses."[57] With the boycott continuing at a high pitch of enthusiasm, even Powell—close as he
was to Quill's left-wing circle—at a mass meeting of 5,000 in
early April pointedly referred to the virtues of Ritchie's offer.[58]

In the following days of hectic conferring with the bus boycott
committee, the union gradually moved closer to Ritchie's position. As early as April 8, Powell announced that a legal document
was being drawn up providing for the employment of 70 black
mechanics and 100 bus drivers. But it still required another 11
days before Quill could manage to arrange an agreement that
his members could accept. The month-long boycott ended with
the signing of a most unusual contract for the period. The agreement, involving not only an employer and a labor union, but also
the United Negro Bus Association (as the victorious black coalition was renamed), provided: 1) the seniority rights of all but
91 furloughed white drivers would be waived; 2) when the 91
had been reemployed, the next 100 drivers to be hired would be
blacks;   3) the next 70 mechanics to be employed would also be
Negroes;   4) black and white workers would thereafter be hired
alternately until, in keeping with Manhattan's population ratio,
17% of the bus companies' employees were black.[59]

The Communists credited themselves and the TWU for the
victory. Writing in the *Worker* the noted black Communist leader

[56] See Frank Reeves to Wilkins, May 2, 1941, NAACP Papers II, A-143, regarding
    NAACP and Urban League, and *Worker*, April 27, 1941, regarding Randolph.
[57] *Age*, April 12, 1941; Wilkins column in *Amsterdam News*, April 12, 1941.
[58] *Worker*, April 11, 1941; *PM*, April 20, 1941; *Worker*, April 20, 1941; *The New
    York Times*, April 20, 1941 (hereafter cited as *Times*); *Amsterdam News*, April
    26, 1941.
[59] *PM*, April 20, 1941; *Times*, April 20, 1941; *Amsterdam News*, April 26, 1941.

Benjamin J. Davis, Jr., overlooked the widespread racism among the white rank-and-file which had long immobilized TWU officials like Quill and had undoubtedly delayed Quill's successful resolution of the boycott. Instead Davis wrote of a militantly equalitarian industrial CIO union that had "immediately recognized its stake in the Harlem campaign." He blamed the bus companies and a few bourgeois black leaders for slandering the TWU in holding it responsible for the discrimination. "Every reactionary effort to provoke division between the Negro people and the bus drivers," he declared, "was energetically put down by the solidarity of the Negro community and the organized bus drivers." For Davis the events had demonstrated the falsity of the view "that white workers will not work with Negro workers. It was the white transit workers who themselves supported, by signed agreement, the Negro workers in becoming drivers and maintenance men." Even though the boycott had actually been initiated by the black nationalist HLU, Davis emphasized that many black and white Communists had walked the picket lines, and he proclaimed that Harlem residents were well aware of how much the Communist Party had done to promote the unity and militancy needed for victory. Indeed because the Communists were so vigorously claiming credit, the United Negro Bus Association cancelled its planned victory celebration.[60]

Although the agreement did not produce the dramatic results at first anticipated, it did pave the way for ending the job barriers on the bus lines. Blacks quickly appeared in the ranks of the garage mechanics, and finally in January 1942 the first black bus drivers started on their initial runs with an official ceremony at City Hall. The impact of these developments was reported by the Harlem journalist Roi Ottley: "Every time they [Harlem blacks] board a bus today and see Negroes at the wheel, they swell with pride." By 1944 although the 17% goal had not yet been achieved, the other Manhattan bus lines had joined the list of surface-transport firms employing blacks, and the unionized municipal subways had progressed to the point where the New York transit system was employing the largest number of blacks in the country.[61]

[60] *Worker*, April 27, 1941; *Amsterdam News*, May 3, 1941.
[61] *Amsterdam News*, May 3, 1941, Jan. 17, Feb. 7, 1942; *People's Voice*, May 2,

Thus in the end a convergence of several factors had created a situation that appeared to validate the TWU's claims to being the champion of black worker interests. In early 1941 with the expansion of defense industries, Negroes were becoming increasingly agitated over job discrimination, while the Communists themselves were giving greater priority to the role that left-wing unions could play on behalf of equal job rights. Even more important was the pressure coming from an angry black community during this boycott. The Coordinating Committee's executive secretary, Arnold Johnson, who was an active participant in the negotiations with the union and management, recalls that with the leftist union leadership having dragged its feet, it was the forcefulness of the black pressure (combined with the specter of white unemployment in a protracted bus boycott) that gave Quill the leverage needed to convince his members.[62] Yet even these pressures would probably have been unavailing if the racist corporation management had not reversed itself—Ritchie had made it impossible for Quill and his Communist associates to continue assigning all blame to "reactionary capitalists." Undoubtedly it was a discriminatory employer's efforts to undermine the TWU that ironically gave the blacks the leverage needed to push Quill to implement his egalitarian principles and thus promote the union's reputation as an advocate of Negro rights.[63]

Three years later during the height of World War II, the TWU again found itself taking an ambiguous position when faced with

1942; Roi Ottley, 'New World A-Coming: Inside Black America (Boston, 1943), 229; Opportunity, 22 (Winter 1944), 65; People's Voice, Oct. 13, 1945; CIO News, Oct. 21, 1944.

[62] Interview with Arnold P. Johnson, Dec. 30, 1979.

[63] A somewhat different scenario, giving greater credit to the Communists in arranging the agreement is possible. Unfortunately it is difficult, if not impossible, at this point to reconstruct precisely the detailed course of events and the precise role of the Communists or the TWU leadership in bringing about the settlement. There is not even a reference to the bus boycott in the minutes of the TWU International Executive Board Meeting of Mar. 29-30, 1941 (TWU Archives); while the TWU officers' report to the 1941 biennial convention boasted of the victory in the union's bus strike (Proceedings of the Third Biennial Convention, Transport Workers Union of America . . . September 24th to 27th, 1941 (New York: [1941]), 62, but is completely silent on the union's cooperation in the bus boycott. (Paul Robeson, however, did address the convention. Ibid., 137-38.) On the other hand, Mark Naison has concluded on the basis of his interview data that the Communists indeed played a critical role, for only they and the National Negro Congress could have brought the union and the black community leaders together in an effective agreement. (Interview with Naison, Dec. 7, 1980. See also his forthcoming book on Communists in Harlem, cited above, Fn. 1). The inferences that we drew from our interviewing and our reading of the Communist and black press were that the highly effective boycott,

the challenge of advancing the rights of black transit workers. The occasion was the famous 1944 wildcat transit strike in Philadelphia. Once more the TWU leaders acted with care in the face of white worker prejudice, yet emerged from the confrontation with their union's reputation as a champion of black workers considerably enhanced.

According to the several published scholarly accounts of this strike the TWU vigorously backed the blacks' cause.[64] But none of these studies has dealt in detail with the TWU's interaction with black workers or community leaders. The analysis that follows, drawing upon hitherto unused materials in the black press and the NAACP papers, sheds new light on the subject and presents the union in a more ambiguous role.

This transit strike resulted from the attempt of the Philadelphia Transportation Company (PTC) to reverse the results of a collective bargaining election in which the TWU had defeated the Philadelphia Rapid Transit Employees Union (PRTEU)—essentially a continuation of the old company union. Both the PTC and the PRTEU, taking refuge behind a "custom clause" in their contract continuing earlier arrangements existing under the original company union, acted in collusion to restrict the 500 black employees (less than 5% of the total work force) to the maintenance department primarily as porters and unskilled laborers.[65] In 1943 rival unions—the AFL's Amalgamated Association of Street and Elec-

---

combined with Ritchie's offer, placed Quill in a difficult dilemma between his principles and his white worker constituency. How much his desire to implement his equalitarian ideology and please his Communist friends influenced his strategy is not entirely clear. In addition a riddle remains as to how he was able to sell the agreement to the white bus drivers. Possible answers to some of these questions may lie in Michael Quill's files in the TWU Archives, which are not at this point being made accessible to scholars. Interviews with two of the survivors among Quill's closest associates, attorney John O'Donnell, and Quill's cousin Josie Lynch, who worked for Local #100, while confirming the prejudices of the white workers, did not produce recollections of how he handled the bus boycott. (Interviews with Lynch, Oct. 10, 1980 and O'Donnell, Oct 5, 1980.)

[64] See treatments of strike in Nat Glazer and Frederick Hoffman, "Behind the Philadelphia Strike," *Politics*, 6 (Nov. 1944), 306-308; Robert C. Weaver, *Negro Labor: A National Problem* (New York, 1946), 155-70; Louis Ruchames, *Race, Jobs and Politics: The Story of FEPC*, ch. 7; Allan M. Winkler, "The Philadelphia Transit Strike of 1944," *Journal of American History*, 59 (1972), 73-89; Herbert Hill, *Black Labor and the American Legal System* (Washington 1977), ch. 11.

[65] Untitled document, n.d. in FEPC Archives, microfilm version, Reel 27 FR; "Summary of the Evidence with Opinion and Order on Hearings Held in Philadelphia, Pennsylvania, Dec. 8, 1943," issued Dec. 27, 1943, with accompanying documents in *Ibid.* See also Theodore Spaulding, "Philadelphia's Hate Strike," *Crisis*, 51 (1944), 281.

tric Railway and Motor Coach Employees of America, the independent Brotherhood of Railroad Trainmen, and the TWU—all renewed their attempts to replace the PRTEU.[66] These efforts came in the midst of increasing protests from black transit workers, the NAACP, and other black and interracial organizations against the job discrimination.[67] Finally at year's end, responding to this agitation, the President's Fair Employment Practices Committee directed the company and PRTEU to hire blacks as trolley motormen.[68]

PRTEU, quite correctly perceiving the TWU as its principal threat, decided to attack it as a friend of Communists and blacks. Scarcely had the FEPC's directive become known than signs appeared on carbarn bulletin boards proclaiming, "Protect Your Loved Ones: Get Rid of the Negro By Joining The White Crusade." At FEPC's public hearings in December PRTEU leaders denied that this agency had any authority over the union and predicted that any change in the status quo would produce a major strike crippling the war effort.[69] Once the FEPC order became

[66] For summary of complex interaction between the company and these unions see Joseph E. Weckler, *Negro Platform Workers* (Chicago, 1945), 3-6. For references in TWU sources to its early efforts at organizing Philadelphia transit workers see International Executive Board Minutes, Jan. 28, 1938, Jan. 27, June 28, 1939, TWU Archives and *Proceedings of the Fourth Biennial Convention, Transport Workers Union of America . . . October 20th to 23rd, 1943* (New York [1943]), 118-19.

[67] For summary discussions of these protests see Weckler, *Negro Platform Workers*, 7-8; Spaulding, "Philadelphia's Hate Strike," 281; and following documents: "Summary of Contacts, Negotiations, and Background in the Case of Philadelphia Transportation Company, Inc.," Oct. 4, 1943, FEPC Archives, reel 20; "Chronology of Events in Philadelphia Transport Case," Jan. 29, 1944, FEPC Archives, Reel 27 FR; and "Report on Fight for Equal Job Opportunities with the Philadelphia Transportation Company—NAACP," Oct. 28, 1943, NAACP Papers, II, A-447. See also correspondence of G. James Fleming, 1943, with union, company and fellow FEPC officials, 1943, *passim*, FEPC Archives, reel 20. For pressures from Philadelphia Branch NAACP see Philadelphia *Inquirer*, Dec. 6, 1942 (hereafter cited as *Inquirer*), clipping in Philadelphia NAACP Branch Papers, Temple University, Urban Archives, Temple University Library, Philadelphia; Carolyn M. Davenport to A. A. Mitten of PTC, Mar. 9, 1943, *Ibid.*, Reel 20. For examples of appeals of interracial civic groups see Jacob Billikopf, chairman of City-Wide Interracial Committee to Mayor Bernard Samuel, Oct. 30, 1943; Billikopf, circular letter, Nov. 22, 1943; and Minutes of the City-Wide Interracial Committee's Executive Committee, Nov. 5, 1943, all in Housing Association of Delaware Valley Papers in Temple University Urban Archives. See also material below regarding NAACP Political Action Committee.

[68] Malcolm Ross to PTC President Ralph T. Senter, Nov. 17, 1943, and attached undated "Directive to the Union," FEPC Archives, Reel 27 FR:

[69] Philadelphia *Tribune*, Dec. 4, 1943 (hereafter cited as *Tribune*); President's Committee on Fair Employment Practice, "In the Matter of the Philadelphia Rapid Transit Employees Union, Respondent Case No. 55," Transcript of Hearing, Dec. 8, 1943, FEPC Archives, Reel 27 FR; and "Statement of the PRT Employees' Union Concerning the Directive Order of the President's Committee

final, the PRTEU—backed by the company—flatly refused to comply.[70] They appealed to the House Special Committee to Investigate Executive Agencies headed by the Virginia arch-conservative Howard Smith, who swiftly scheduled hearings at which both PRTEU and company witnesses testified again that "serious interruption" of war industries[71] would result from implementing the enforcement order.

Fearful of the combustible situation, the TWU handled the racial issue cautiously in its organizing drive. A few months earlier at the union's national convention, Quill, who presented Adam Clayton Powell as a featured speaker, had mentioned the need of "conducting aggressive educational campaigns to the end of eliminating at least worker objections to fair employment practices." But his forthright remark was qualified by an explicit awareness that the issue might damage the union, and undoubtedly in an effort to deflect the hostility of white members, his emphasis was placed upon the importance of upgrading blacks to traditionally-white jobs as a means of combatting wartime manpower shortages.[72]

Nonetheless with all the TWU's competitors not only anti-Communist but to varying degree anti-black as well,[73] the TWU was radical in appealing at all to black workers to join. But it should be emphasized that Quill's union structured its approach to Negroes as unobtrusively as possible. As the black FEPC regional director G. James Fleming once expressed it, the TWU, fearing that it might be dragged down by the race question, believed that FEPC's involvement would give the PRTEU "a live issue."[74] During the organizing campaign the TWU sought to

---

on Fair Employment Practice," Dec. 8, 1943, *Ibid.*

[70] See PRTEU president Frank P. Carney to Malcolm Ross, Jan. 3, 1944, and Senter to Ross, Jan. 4, 1944, FEPC Archives, Reel 27 FR; *Inquirer*, Jan. 5, 1944; *Philadelphia Bulletin*, Jan. 6, 1944 (hereafter cited as *Bulletin*).

[71] *Inquirer*, Jan. 5, 1944; House of Representatives, "Report of Proceedings, Hearings Held Before Special Committee to Investigate Executive Agencies, Jan. 11, 1944," esp. 2029-2049, *passim*, copy in FEPC Archives, Reel. 17.

[72] *Proceedings of the Fourth Biennial Convention, Transport Workers Union*, 27-29, for Powell, and 133-34 for Quill.

[73] The by-laws of the Brotherhood of Railroad Trainmen restricted membership to white males; the Amalgamated's organizers openly spoke against the upgrading of Negroes. See Weckler, 12.

[74] Fleming to Ross, Mar. 15, 1944, FEPC Archives, Reel 20. Fleming, a native of the Virgin Islands, had been a leader of the Hampton Institute student strike during the 1920s, subsequently received his baccalaureate degree from the University of Wisconsin, and had served on the staff of the *Tribune* before joining the FEPC. (Interview with G. James Fleming, Sept. 14, 1980.)

obscure its ties to the black community. Thus in the drive's opening phase, TWU and NAACP branch leaders had agreed to cosponsor several meetings to recruit black workers for the union,
but the Association's involvement would be kept secret to avoid
alienating the whites.[75] A few months later when, despite serious
misgivings about working with Communist-oriented organizations, the Philadelphia NAACP allied with the local NNC for
a joint program of protest against PTC's job discrimination policy, the TWU discretely failed to associate itself with this effort.
The newly-formed NAACP Action Committee, headed by Arthur
Huff Fauset, the Philadelphia NNC president, quickly arranged
a series of mass meetings and demonstrations, including an interracial mass march past the PTC company offices in November
1943. Local officials from several CIO unions spoke on such
occasions and gave money, but in contrast with the TWU's overt
friendship with the New York NNC, the union in Philadelphia
avoided such activities.[76] In fact the TWU leadership went so far
as to discourage the NAACP from utilizing a legal strategy based
upon Pennsylvania's labor relations law which was empowered
to bar discriminatory unions from participating in collective
bargaining elections. Because the TWU advised that this action
could boomerang, the NAACP branch backed off.[77]

[75] Prentice Thomas to Walter White and Thurgood Marshall, May 29, 1943, NAACP
Papers, II, A-447.
[76] On Fauset and steps taken toward forming the NAACP Action Committee in
early Sept. 1943, see especially Fauset's column in *Tribune*, Dec. 18, 1943, and
"Action Notes," stamped Oct. 12, 1943, in FEPC Archives, Reel 27 FR. On
NAACP's persistent fears about working with Fauset and the Philadelphia NNC
because of Communist influence and domineering tactics, and the NAACP's
rivalry with the NNC front group known as the United Political Action Committee, see esp. Minutes of the Jan. 29, 1944 meeting of the Board of Directors
of the Philadelphia Branch NAACP, in Philadelphia NAACP Branch Papers.
On mass march of Nov. 8, 1943, see *Tribune*, Nov. 13, 1943; *People's Voice*,
Nov. 13, 1943; the following clippings in the Philadelphia Branch NAACP
Papers: Pittsburgh *Courier*, Philadelphia edition, Nov. 13, 1943; and Philadelphia *Afro-American*, Nov. 13, 1943; and "Action Committee PTC Employment,
11/8/43 Minutes," also in Philadelphia NAACP Branch Papers. For other activities of the NAACP Action Committee see *Tribune*, Oct. 2, 30, Nov. 13, Dec.
4, 18, 1943; Philadelphia Branch NAACP press release, Dec. 6, 1943, in NAACP
Papers, II, C-152; and Arthur Huff Fauset, "Liberals Caught Napping," *Congress View* (organ of National Negro Congress), 2 (Sept., 1944), copy in NAACP
Papers, II, A-447. On financial contributions of local unions in Philadelphia, see
Tribune, Oct. 30, 1943, Jan. 8, Feb. 19, 1944.
[77] Pittsburgh *Courier*, Philadelphia edition, Oct. 16, 1943, clipping in Philadelphia
Branch NAACP Papers; Thurgood Marshall, Memorandum for the files, Dec.
1, 1943, NAACP Papers, II A-447; *Inquirer*, Jan. 4, 1944; *Philadelphia Record*,
Jan. 6, 1944 (hereafter cited as *Record*); Fleming to David Ullman, Dec. 20,
1943, FEPC Archives, Reel 27 FR; Fleming to George Crockett, Jan. 6, 1944,

In the drive to determine who would be the collective bargaining agent, the Brotherhood of Railroad Trainmen dropped out
in January, but as the campaign intensified, the PRTEU's strategy was to depict the TWU as determined to force "Negro supremacy on the Company." [78] PRTEU's sound trucks toured the
city's carbarns blaring that a TWU victory would guarantee black
streetcar motormen and busdrivers ("A vote for the CIO is a vote
for niggers on the job"). Simultaneously the AFL hammered
away at the charge of domination by subversives, picturing the
election "as a fight to keep Communism out of the Labor Movement." [79]

For its part the TWU's strategy was to defuse these charges by
avoiding direct replies and emphasizing bread-and-butter issues.
Repeatedly the union promised higher wages and better working
conditions, while contending that the "red-baiting" and "race-
baiting" were "smoke-screens" to mask the real problems. Thus
in TWU newspaper advertisements featuring endorsements by
prominent Americans like Senator Robert Wagner and Bishop
Francis J. McConnell, the obvious intention was to counter not
the "race-baiting" but the "red-baiting." [80] Giving a virtuoso performance at a mass meeting Quill declared, "When we first came
to Philadelphia it was the Red issue . . . now it's the black issue.
From red to black, no matter what the issue, our only issue is
wages, hours, pay and working conditions." Typically TWU officials like international vice-president James Fitzsimon, who
directed the Philadelphia campaign, mentioned equal rights in
abstract terms while appealing to the workers' patriotism to ward
off PRTEU's prediction of a wildcat strike if blacks were upgraded. [81] Similarly CIO President Philip Murray, in a Philadel-

---

Ibid., Reel 20; "Minutes of the Regular Meeing of the Board of Directors,"
Philadelphia NAACP Branch, Feb. 25, 1944, in Philadelphia NAACP Branch
Papers.
[78] *PM*, Aug. 6, 1944.
[79] *Bulletin*, Mar. 1, 1944 (for quote); see also full page advertisements in *Bulletin*
and *Inquirer*, both Mar. 13, 1944. For discussion of campaign see also *Tribune*,
Mar. 25, 1944; *Transport Bulletin*, Jan.-Feb., and Mar.-April 1944; Douglas Mac-
Mahon, "The Real Philadelphia Story," *New Masses*, 42 (Aug. 1944), 21.
[80] *Transport Bulletin*, esp., Jan-Feb. 1944; union advertisements in Philadelphia *Bulletin*, Mar. 13, 1944 and in *Inquirer*, Mar. 1, 1944.
[81] *Record*, Jan. 6, 1944, clipping in FEPC Archives, Reel 20 (we have been unable
to locate this item in the edition of this paper on microfilm). See statement of
Fitzsimon at this same mass meeting quoted in *Tribune*, Jan. 8, 1944. A statement urging support for the union issued by its International Executive Board

phia appearance just prior to the March 1944 collective bargaining election, avoided subjects like FEPC and black upgrading, merely noting in passing the CIO's "guideposts everlastingly being equality of treatment, regardless of race, color, creed or nationality." [82]

Such low-keyed remarks nevertheless sharply contrasted with the race hatred expressed by the competing unions. Indeed, these TWU statements not only made it possible later for the organization's officials and friends to stress how courageous the Transport Workers had been to back a nondiscrimination policy, but they also led black activists to believe that the union would move agressively on their behalf once the election was won. [83]

Actually through the entire campaign the TWU kept the black leaders at arms length. When the Philadelphia *Tribune* urged the union to advertise in its pages, TWU officials declined because "it would prejudice their case" among the whites. The union even feared free publicity in the *Tribune* and asked the editor "not to over-emphasize the CIO's policy of 'no-discrimination' because such attention could boomerang to the PRTEU's benefit." [84] Assuming that the strategy was temporary the black leaders concurred. Thus in the *Tribune*'s pages the union's campaign went virtually unreported. Publisher E. Washington Rhodes' column did not mention the TWU and circumspectly confined himself to criticism of the PRTEU. Only in the very last issue prior to the balloting did the paper editorially endorse the Transport Workers. More significantly the NAACP's Action Committee had lapsed into silence. As Fauset explained afterwards: "The quiet of the past six weeks . . . was a strategic withdrawal [to avoid] race acrimony which might throw victory into the lap" of one of the anti-Negro unions. [85]

---

meeting in Philadelphia a month later, contained no reference to the racial issue. See TWU International Executive Board Minutes, Feb. 4-5, 1944, TWU Archives.

[82] *Transport Bulletin*, Mar.-April, 1944, and *Tribune*, Mar. 18, 1944. Interestingly neither the city's white dailies nor the *Worker*, in their accounts of his speech, even so much as mentioned this passage. *Bulletin* and *Inquirer*, Mar. 10, 1944, and *Worker*, Mar. 11, 1944.

[83] MacMahon, "The Real Philadelphia Story," 21; *Record*, Mar. 16, 1944; Weckler, *Negro Platform Workers*, 13; Glazer and Hoffman, "Behind the Philadelphia Strike," 306-308.

[84] This information revealed in *Tribune*, July 27, 1944.

[85] See esp. *Ibid.*, Feb. 19, 26, 1944, and Fauset column in *Ibid.*, Mar. 18, 1944; *Transport Bulletin*, Mar. 11, 1944.

On election day the TWU won handily, especially in the maintenance department where it garnered nearly two-thirds of the votes.[86] With the racist propaganda having failed to sway most whites, both union and black spokesmen mistakenly greeted the victory as a referendum on the race issue. Thus Maurice Forge, editor of the *Transport Bulletin*, exulted that the PTC workers had "rejected 'race-baiting' as un-American. . . . They exposed racism . . . as the devilish work of reactionary employers." Quill also praised the workers for seeing through the propaganda aimed at exploiting racial bigotry.[87] Black leaders reacted similarly. Not surprisingly Fauset as NNC head, proclaimed that the election results-meant that "together with the mighty hosts of labor . . . we will bring about the complete victory of the masses of the people by assuring the upgrading of Negroes in PTC." Even the *Tribune* ran a headline: "CIO VICTORY IN PTC ELECTION SHOWED AVERAGE AMERICAN DESIRES EQUALITY," while the editor concluded: "Decency and fairness loomed so large in the minds of average PTC workers that they would not permit the issue of race . . . to prevent them from voting for what they believed to be the best union." Summing it up, Fleming advised his FEPC superiors that since the PRTEU had made the race issue so salient, the TWU's "clear majority" indicated that with FEPC pressure the latter could become the real lever for substantial change in the company's job policies.[88]

The strategy that black leaders and FEPC officials favored was to press the TWU to demand a non-discriminatory clause in the new contract. Yet when FEPC chairman Malcolm Ross made a personal plea, Quill replied in generalities, as he had in New York during the 1930s: "You can be sure that we will do everything possible to keep the record of the Transport Workers Union . . . in its rightful place as far as the Negro question is concerned."[89] As contract negotiations dragged out through the spring, the NAACP and its action committee decided it would be best to sustain their low profile and desist from agitating the

---

[86] See *Inquirer* and *Bulletin*, both Mar. 15, 1944.
[87] Both quotations in *Transport Bulletin*, Mar.-April, 1944.
[88] Fauset column, *Tribune*, Mar. 18, 1944; *Tribune*, Mar. 25, 1944; Fleming to Ross, Mar. 15, 1944, FEPC Archives, Reel 20.
[89] Quill to Ross, April 20, 1944, responding to Ross to Quill, April 12, both in *Ibid.*, Reel 20.

issue.[90] Three months after the election the blacks still had no
guarantees of non-discrimination, and Fauset advised TWU
Vice-President Fitzsimon of the increasingly impatient mood in
the black community. The union official indicated that there
were "complications" which "require delicate handling," and to
the Negroes' consternation the contract presented on June 30 to
the union membership for ratification contained no protection
for blacks.[91]

In defending themselves to the disappointed black community,
TWU leaders argued simultaneously that the clause had been
both unobtainable and unnecessary. On the one hand Fitzsimon
told black leaders that union negotiators had argued forcefully
with a management that intransigently rejected such a non-discrimination clause. Yet the *Transport Bulletin* had also maintained that the company was on the verge of changing its racial
policy. Actually the union's explanations about the negotiations
were disingenuous.[92] *Tribune* editor Eustace Gay had learned
that PTC officials, expecting that the TWU would insist on such
a clause, were "most surprised" when the union negotiators failed
even to mention the subject. War Manpower Commission official
Robert C. Weaver whose access to the facts certainly placed him
in a position to know what had happened, reported that the TWU
had indeed declined to argue for a non-discrimination clause, on
the grounds that "since the union stand in favor of non-discriminatory hiring and up-grading was a matter of public knowledge,
there was no need to insert a specific clause on this issue in the
contract." [93]

Publisher Rhodes voiced the extreme disappointment that pervaded the black community when he bitterly declared, "I have
gone all out for organized labor, because I sincerely believe that
all workers—colored and white—have a cause in common. But
it certainly does not mean that those who own and operate the

[90] See following in Philadelphia NAACP Branch Papers. "Report of Chairman of
   Exec. Com. to Branch April 4, 1944"; Minutes of Special Board Meetings, April
   4, 11, 1944; and Minutes of Branch Executive Committee, April 28, 1944.
[91] Report in Fauset column, *Tribune*, July 22, 1944; *Transport Bulletin*, July 1944;
   Fleming to Ross, July 8, 1944, FEPC Archives, Reel 27 FR. For contract as
   finally signed on Aug. 9, see TWU press release, Aug. 10, 1944, in TWU Archives.
[92] *Tribune*, July 15, 22, 1944; *Transport Bulletin*, July 1944; see also Fauset's defense of TWU in *Tribune*, July 22, 1944.
[93] *Tribune*, July 8, 1944; Weaver, *Negro Labor*, p. 162.

Negro press must close their eyes to all weaknesses in unions. . . .
I am aware of all the difficulties involved, but I stand firm in the
position that the TWU should insist on a clause prohibiting discrimination against colored workers." [94] Not surprisingly the one
civic leader of consequence who defended the TWU was NNC
president Fauset, who echoed Fitzsimon's pleas about the "delicacy of the situation." [95]

Obviously since TWU officials knew how deeply blacks desired
that particular clause, the union's actions can only be explained by
its fear of alienating the white rank-and-file—especially because
the new contract contained a provision insisted on by management which gave disgruntled TWU members the right to resign
any time prior to August 23. [96] This provision clearly offered the
PTC, acting in collusion with the leaders of the defeated unions,
an opening to foment a racial crisis as the lever to destroy the
TWU in Philadelphia. At first, seemingly responding to the federal demand for the upgrading of some blacks, the Company
posted notices early in July announcing that henceforth Negro
men would be eligible for operating jobs on the streetcars. But
Fleming and his friends on the *Tribune* were skeptical about
PTC's real intentions." [97] This skepticism was well-founded, for
the notice had scarcely been put up when racist handbills appeared on company bulletin boards calling for "a white supremacy movement for the protection of our jobs." Moreover, somehow leaflets were widely circulated which read: "Your buddies
are in the Army fighting and dying to protect the life of you and
your family, and you are too yellow to protect their jobs until
they return. Call a strike and refuse to teach the Negroes; the
public is with you, the CIO sold you out." And PTC employees
found an anonymous letter in their mailboxes announcing that
"Your sons and buddies that are away fighting for the Country,
are being stabed [sic] in the back on the Home Front by the
National Association of Negroes and the F.E.P.C. . . ." [98]

Meanwhile with the rather obvious encouragement of PTC

[94] Rhodes column, *Tribune*, July 29, 1944.
[95] Fauset column, *Tribune*, July 22, 1944.
[96] Weaver, *Negro Labor*, 169.
[97] PTC Notice, July 7, 1944, copy in FEPC Archives, reel 27 FR: Fleming to Ross,
    July 27, 1944, *Ibid*; *Tribune*, July 15, 1944.
[98] *Record*, Aug 2, 1944; undated handbill, FEPC Archives, reel 27 FR; anonymous
    letter dated July 12 and printed in *PM*, Aug. 6, 1944.

officials, former top leaders in the PRTEU, the Amalgamated Association, and the Brotherhood of Railroad Trainmen,[99] were holding rallies on company property, threatening a strike if any blacks were upgraded to operating jobs.[100] On one occasion when Fitzsimon asked to speak, the angry workers defiantly booed him.[101] Early on the morning of August 1, with the handful of black operators scheduled to begin their trolley runs, the strike actually erupted. During the day the former PRTEU president, making rounds of the carbarns, told the strikers: "We don't want Negroes and we won't work with Negroes. . . . This is a white man's job and we intend to keep it that way." [102]

Fitzsimon and International Secretary-Treasurer MacMahon worked feverishly but fruitlessly to get the men back. TWU officers were consistently jeered when they appeared at the carbarns, and "a crowd of hooting, laughing strikers" pursued one TWU organizer shouting, "Take the Negroes off the cars and we'll go back to work." Fitzsimon and his associates seemed "as helpless to solve the situation as were the Army and Navy officers" who were also appealing to the men to return. Unforgettable to reporters for *PM*, circulating among the strikers, was the virulence of the race animosity expressed by the PTC workers, the intense "race hate" in their conversations, the anti-black speeches of strike leaders who maligned the race with crude allusions to "bed bugs," the audiences of strikers yelling, "put us in the army where we can fight beside white men." One correspondent, after spending several days in the city, concluded that "the race issue and the strike has split the CIO union wide open, with the leadership going 100 per cent against the strike, and the rank and file moving with the ex-company union leaders." As the TWU local's president recalled it at the next national convention: "We beat the company in an election. . . . [Then] in August on the colored issue they took the union right from under our feet. They threw our membership into turmoil, and we were holding a very questionable amount of members from the way it looked. . . ." [103]

[99] For role of these men see Ruchames, *Race, Jobs and Politics*, 111; Hill, *Black Labor and the American Legal System*, 295; *Record*, Aug. 7, 1944.
[100] Spaulding, "Philadelphia's Hate Strike," 283; Wecker, 13; *Tribune*, June 29, 1944.
[101] *Record*, Aug. 9, 1944 (referring to events of July 25).
[102] *Tribune*, Aug. 5, 1944; see also quote in *Bulletin*, Aug. 2, 1944.
[103] *Times*, Aug. 2, 1944; *Record*, Aug. 2, 1944; *PM*, Aug. 4 and 6, 1944; Statement

For their part, during the strike TWU leaders astutely minimized the component of racism among large segments of the
rank-and-file, and instead appealed to the strikers' patriotism and
concern with bread-and-butter issues. Fitzsimon and MacMahon
pointed out that the strikers were jeopardizing the concessions
made by the company in the still-unsigned contract; and they
urged the protesters as "loyal patriotic Americans" to keep in the
forefront the "interests for war production" rather than following
the "self-seeking leaders" of the rival unions.[104] Similarly on the
strike's second day when Quill personally arrived, his earliest
public statement stressed support for the government and "urged
all PTC employees, as soldiers on the home front, to respond to
the call of their Commander-in-Chief."[105] Even after President
Roosevelt sent in troops to quell the walkout, the union's officers
and shop stewards, while denouncing the collusion between the
company and strike leaders, still demurred from making racism
the issue, holding to the theory that the affair was a subversive
conspiracy blindly followed by a few anti-TWU "pawns."[106] Actually the strikers' overt racism was so pervasive that the local's
250 stewards—who were in virtually unanimous support of the
International union's opposition to the strike—nonetheless
doubted their ability to initiate the back-to-work movement. Two
such attempts by a handful of the stewards quickly ended in
failure.[107]

As Quill and his colleagues had hoped,[108] the fairly prompt
and decisive intervention of the federal government ended the

---

of Joseph R. Dougherty, in *Proceedings of the Fifth Biennial Convention of
the Transport Workers Union of America, CIO . . . Sept. 25-28, 1946* (New
York: [1946], 142.

[104] United States Office of War Information document, no title, Aug. 1, 1944, in
FEPC Archives Reel 27 FR and *Record*, Aug. 2, 1944.

[105] *Bulletin*, Aug. 3, 1944.

[106] *Inquirer*, Aug. 7, 1944; see also *Transport Bulletin*, Aug. 1944.

[107] *Bulletin, Inquirer* and *Times* all, Aug. 3, 1944; *PM*, Aug. 6, 1944. There are
also significant materials, dealing with the activities of the Urban League,
NAACP and other race advancement and interracial civic organizations during the strike. See esp., "Philadelphia Report on the Transportation Strike,
Aug. 1-6, 1944," NAACP Papers, II, C-152; "NAACP Action During the Philadelphia Transportation Company Strike," Aug. 19, 1944, *Ibid.*, II, A-252; various materials in Philadelphia NAACP Branch Papers, 1944; untitled report by
unidentified black Wharton Settlement House Worker (Aug. 1944), in Wharton
Settlement House Papers, Temple University Urban Archives; Wilkins, Memorandum to White, Aug. 9, 1944, NAACP Papers, II, A-497; local Philadelphia
dailies for Aug. 2-5, *passim*; *People's Voice*, Aug. 12, 1944.

[108] See *Bulletin*, Aug. 5, 1944, for strong statement by Quill calling for federal intervention.

wildcat walkout. Afterwards the company quickly signed the contract, and though in the short run some disgruntled strikers did resign from the TWU, by October the local had a larger membership than at the start of the crisis.[109] Nevertheless, the TWU evidently thought it best to avoid actions that might alienate the whites, and does not appear to have pressed the company to accelerate the upgrading of blacks. Although by November the number of blacks in the PTC work force had nearly doubled to 900, few were accepted in skilled jobs. As late as February 1945, six months after the strike, there were only about 20 Negro trolley operators.[110] On the other hand the union did encourage blacks to seek office in the local. Without overt white complaints a black was elected to one of the vice presidencies and three others were elevated to the executive board.[111]

In the strike's aftermath the TWU, not wishing to alienate white worker support, continued to play down the fact that the racial issue had been pivotal in the eruption, stressing instead the idea of a "reactionary" conspiracy against the union. Both Quill and MacMahon pointed out that the race issue had been "only a coverup" for the walkout's real purpose—the destruction of the TWU.[112] This interpretation was accepted at the time even by intellectuals like Nathan Glazer, who had been hostile to the TWU's Communist-domination but who nonetheless sympathized with the CIO.[113]

Of course, the TWU's destruction had been the goal of the company in collusion with the rival unions, but the fact is that they knew they could count on the widespread racism among the rank-and-file. These virulent attitudes not only led the men to strike in the first place but also accounted for so much else—the TWU's low profile in organizing the black Philadelphia transit

109 Weaver, *Negro Labor*, 169-170.
110 Fleming to Ross, Dec. 28, 1944, FEPC Archives, Reel 20; Fleming, "Interracial Feelings During and After the PTC Strike," Feb. 20, 1945, in NAACP Papers, II, A-447. Yet thirty-six blacks had been promoted to jobs in the maintenance department that the race had never previously held.
111 Fleming to Will Maslow, Nov. 20, 1944 and Fleming to Ross, Dec. 28, 1944, in FEPC Archives, reel 20; *Transport Bulletin*, Nov. 1944; *Tribune*, Oct. 21, 1944.
112 *Tribune*, Aug. 12, 1944. A similar tone characterized the TWU officers' report to the next biennial convention, which noted that "Our Union's reputation as an outstanding champion of equality for all races, religions, and creeds was at stake," yet essentially pictured the walkout as a "conspiracy" to discredit the TWU and "hurt the war effort." *Proceedings of the Fifth Biennial Convention of the Transport Workers Union*, 29. See also *Transport Bulletin*, Aug. 1944.
113 Glazer and Hoffman, "Behind the Philadelphia Strike," 306-308.

workers, the failure to press for a non-discrimination clause in the contract, and the kinds of appeals the TWU made in its unavailing efforts for a back-to-work movement.

The union's inability to publicly face the race problem within its ranks led E. Washington Rhodes, the *Tribune* publisher, to write an article in the Communist weekly, *New Masses*, which was intended as a gentle but firm rebuke of TWU's leaders. Rhodes declared that the central "issue" had indeed been "narrow race prejudice." The walkout had occurred because eight blacks had been promoted, and the strikers had explicitly promised to return if the eight were removed from the streetcars. Reminding his Communist readers of how deeply embedded racism was in American life he warned that the failure to challenge this racism more openly and to move vigorously against it would lead to further hate strikes and more ugly racial confrontations.[114]

* * * *

Thus the TWU's early history demonstrates that the response of a Communist-dominated union leadership to race discrimination in the job market was anything but simple. That leadership, regardless of its ideals, was dependent for survival in office on a white membership characterized by pervasive prejudices. Consequently a systematic assault on job bias was only briefly seriously considered. In both New York and Philadelphia, ideology was tempered by very practical concerns. As long as racist employers could exploit the anxieties of most white employees, TWU's Communist hierarchy felt severely circumscribed. Only with strong and effective pressures from the black community (backed by an employer's strategic change in policy) as in the Harlem bus boycott, or with the forceful presence of the federal government as in Philadelphia, could the TWU really begin to implement its principles and give effective support to advancing the interests of its black members.

Despite the complexities and inconsistencies in the early history of the TWU's actions on the race question, the union's publications portray a consistently heroic and successful struggle against employer racism. When Quill ran for reelection to the city council

---

[114] Rhodes, "Philadelphia's Shame," *New Masses*, 52 (Aug. 15, 1944), 21.

in 1945 the NNC stressed his boldness, crediting him with being a key person in settling the Harlem and Philadelphia crises to the satisfaction of blacks. In the following decades TWU tradition even came to claim that the union in New York had "succeeded in forcing the promotions of Negroes from porters to every classification in every department and on every transit line," and that in Philadelphia the TWU had unhesitatingly involved itself in a "serious clash on the civil rights question" because "we demanded the upgrading of Negro porters to mechanics, to streetcar operators, to all other positions for which our Negro membership could qualify."[115]

Public statements by the TWU and other CIO unions—Communist-dominated and not—fed this tendency toward wish-fulfillment among those who wanted to see in the industrial unions a genuine solution for the problems of the black working class. Yet as the noted radical intellectual Dwight McDonald had pointed out at the time of the Philadelphia strike, "racial prejudices have real grass roots among the American working class, including the most enlightened . . . part of it, the membership of the unions." He added that one could scarcely blame conservative labor leaders like those in the AFL for this situation because such attitudes also plagued the CIO unions where the top leadership often tried "to break down the racial prejudices of the ranks."[116] Thus the TWU was not alone. Other CIO unions—like the United Automobile Workers, which was not dominated by Communists—faced the problem of racist hate strikes during World War II when blacks were upgraded. Leaders of such unions treaded carefully and sought out government intervention to solve crises that they were simply unable to settle themselves. Like officials in other CIO unions who recognized the validity of their black members' grievances, Michael Quill and his colleagues were greatly inhibited by the prejudices endemic among their white constituents.

As Critchlow's 1976 article so suggestively revealed, despite agreement on the importance of interracial working class solidarity, the actual behavior of individual Communist-dominated

---

[115] *People's Voice*, Oct. 6, 1945; *1934-1963: TWU and the Fight for Civil Rights*, 11, 13.
[116] [Dwight McDonald], "Comment," *Politics*, 6 (Nov. 1944), 294.

unions was highly varied and depended upon the specific milieu in which they operated. Our study of the TWU indicates that such factors included the attitudes of employers, the outlook of the union's own constituency, the posture at critical junctures of federal manpower agencies, and pressures from the black community. However, where Critchlow stresses the proportion of blacks in a union as critical, we would conclude that in the TWU it was the racist attitudes of so many white workers that was really responsible for the way in which the Communist leadership acted. Our own research on the UAW, a union that was not dominated by Communist leadership and that operated in an industry where blacks played a far more important role, points to a similar conclusion. In addition our investigations of both the TWU and the UAW have shown the importance of examining the pressures from black community organizations as a factor in shaping the actual policies of these unions whose leadership was sympathetic to the aspirations of the black workers. Yet clearly further case studies of the complex interaction between the ideals of the union leadership, the attitudes of white workers, the policies of management, and pressures from both the black community and governmental agencies must be made before one can draw well-grounded generalizations about the behavior of Communist-dominated unions in regard to racial discrimination, or make valid comparisons between the policies of Communist-led and non-Communist CIO unions on this issue.

The Eastern Cherokee and the New Deal

By Charles J. Weeks*

With the election of Franklin D. Roosevelt and the launching of the New Deal, it appeared that the federal government's efforts to revive the nation's economy would include financial assistance to the poverty-stricken American Indians. Moreover, Roosevelt's appointment of John Collier, a longtime admirer of Indian culture, to the position of commissioner of Indian affairs suggested that the Indian was on the threshold of a new and progressive era.

Unfortunately, the dearth of studies on the Collier era has thus far made it extremely difficult to evaluate the impact of the New Deal upon American Indian culture. Most interpretations are concerned solely with national policy and neglect the actual implementation on the local level. Hence, this paper seeks to estimate the effectiveness of the New Deal's Indian program as it was applied to the Eastern Band of Cherokee Indians on the Qualla Boundary, a 63,000-acre reserve lying in Swain, Jackson, and Haywood counties in the Great Smoky Mountains of western North Carolina.[1] Because many of the problems of the Qualla reservation were quite similar to those encountered by other Indian groups, a study of the Eastern Cherokee may provide a starting point for an in-depth examination of the New Deal's effectiveness in addressing the concerns of Indians throughout the United States.[2]

---

* Dr. Weeks is an instructor in history at DeKalb College, Clarkston, Georgia. He expresses appreciation to Professors Joseph O. Baylen and Melvin W. Ecke of Georgia State University for their suggestions concerning the organization and substance of this paper.

[1] William S. Powell, *The North Carolina Gazetteer* (Chapel Hill: University of North Carolina Press, 1968), 399.

[2] For many years historians have paid little attention to the New Deal as it applied to the American Indians. Because of recent Indian activism, however, scholars are beginning to subject the Bureau of Indian Affairs under John Collier (who served as commissioner of Indian affairs from 1933 to 1945) to the same scrutiny that they previously devoted to other New Deal agencies. Not surprisingly, many of the same controversies that involved historians of the New Deal have also emerged in the evaluation of Roosevelt's Indian policy. Perhaps the most timely issue is whether Collier's program marked a radical reversal of previous policy or instead represented a conservative solution which merely attempted to arrest any further deterioration of the position of the Indians. Sociologists and anthropologists, meanwhile, have been unable to agree on whether it was advantageous or even possible to prevent Indian-white cultural assimilation.

Most evaluations of New Deal Indian policies have been extremely favorable to Collier. Both Angie Debo in *A History of the Indians of the United States* (Norman, Okla.: University of Oklahoma Press, 1970), 290-300, hereinafter cited as Debo, *Indians of the U.S.*, and Jennings C. Wise in *The Red Man in the New World Drama: A Politico-legal Study with a Pageantry of American Indian History*, edited and revised by Vine Deloria, Jr. (New York: Macmillan Company, 1971), 357-362, hereinafter cited as Wise, *Red Man in the New World Drama*, agree that the Collier program was a step toward meaningful reform. On the other hand, Alvin M. Josephy, Jr., in *The Indian Heritage of America* (New York: Alfred A. Knopf, 1968), 352, maintains that although the Indian New Deal was a significant reform, its basic long-term goal was cultural assimilation.

Although the Cherokee had inhabited the southern Allegheny mountains for centuries, the history of the Qualla Boundary may be said to have begun in the late 1820s when a group of white settlers attempted to wrest from the Cherokee those lands which they occupied in Georgia. The Indian Removal Bill enacted by Congress on May 28, 1830, was a result of efforts by Pres. Andrew Jackson and others to promote the emigration of various Indian tribes, including the Cherokee, from their original homelands in the southeastern United States to tracts west of the Mississippi River which had been set aside for permanent occupation. In 1837 federal troops under Gen. Winfield Scott forcibly rounded up the Cherokee, placed them in stockades, and prepared them for removal westward to Indian Territory (later Oklahoma).[3]

Scott was not totally successful, however, in removing the entire nation. Approximately 1,000 Indians, "principally of the mountain Cherokee of North Carolina, the most pure-blooded and most conservative of the nation," managed to elude Scott's forces and thus avoid the disastrous "trail of tears" to Indian Territory. During the following three decades, the Eastern Cherokee lived as fugitives in the mountains of western North Carolina. With the aid of Col. William H. Thomas, a white trader, the Cherokee ultimately were able to

William Holland Thomas, born in 1805 near Waynesville, Haywood County, and orphaned as a young boy, was adopted by the Cherokee chief, Yonaguska. Thomas became an Indian trader by profession and served several terms as a state senator. He purchased tracts in Swain and Jackson counties in behalf of the Cherokee, and these lands form the nucleus of Qualla Boundary. Photograph from the Barden Collection, Division of Archives and History.

acquire the use of specific tracts of land on or near the present site of the Qualla Boundary. Because North Carolina law did not then permit Indians to own land, Thomas purchased a number of tracts with funds which the federal government had paid to the Cherokee for the confiscation of their original landholdings in Georgia, and held it in his name for their use.[4]

[3] U.S. Department of the Interior, Bureau of Indian Affairs, *Indians of North Carolina* (Washington: Government Printing Office, 1966), 2-5, hereinafter cited as *Indians of North Carolina*; John Gulick, *Cherokees at the Crossroads* (Chapel Hill: University of North Carolina Press, 1960), 15-16, hereinafter cited as Gulick, *Cherokees*.

[4] For a detailed account of the career of Colonel Thomas see Mattie Russell, "William Holland Thomas: White Chief of the North Carolina Cherokees" (unpublished doctoral dissertation, Duke University, Durham, 1947).

With the illness and retirement of Thomas soon after the Civil War, the Cherokee drafted a constitution which provided for the election of a chief and a tribal council consisting of one representative from each tribal community. When Thomas's creditors attempted to lay claim to Cherokee land in 1874, Congress intervened to preserve the Indian holdings. To protect the tribe, the commissioner of Indian affairs was authorized to serve as trustee of the Cherokee lands in North Carolina. Then, in 1889, the North Carolina General Assembly granted the Eastern Band a charter which authorized the tribe to conduct business as a legally sanctioned corporation.[5]

By act of Congress in 1924 the title to Cherokee lands was transferred, in trust, to the United States, and members of the tribe became official wards of the federal government. This act authorized the secretary of the interior to "cause to be prepared a roll of the members of said [Eastern Cherokee] band, to contain the names of all living on the date of this Act. . . ."[6] After the completion of the census or "Baker roll," the tribal population nearly doubled, largely because thousands of persons with a small degree of Cherokee inheritance applied for membership in hope of obtaining an allotment of tribal land. The completed census contained 3,146 names, of which the Cherokee tribal council challenged 1,229 without success.[7]

The Cherokee had been relatively prosperous farmers as late as 1910, but the establishment of the logging industry in western North Carolina upset the delicate balance of their economy. Profit-hungry lumber companies rapidly denuded the area on and adjacent to the reservation of much of its best timber. The Indians neglected their farmlands while they worked for the lumber companies. But the timber boom was relatively brief in duration, and the Cherokee were soon reduced to subsistence farming.[8] Thus, as early as the 1920s the tribe's economic base had become unbalanced. The increased population remained dependent upon agriculture, but there was an inadequate amount of good land to go around. Consequently, many Cherokee found it necessary to purchase foodstuffs in order to survive; but with constriction of the local lumber industry, the Indians were severely limited in their efforts to earn money.[9]

The Great Depression which began in 1929 brought near disaster to the Eastern Cherokee. The deflation and shortage of money following the stock market crash drastically reduced the real income of the tribe's members. The deprivation of the Indians was often intense. On visiting a particularly wretched

    [5] *Private Laws of North Carolina*, 1889, c. 211. According to Cherokee tribal law, all land on the Qualla Boundary belonged to the Eastern Band. Consequently, no individual Cherokee "owned" his property outright.
    [6] 43 Stat. 376, c. 253 (1924). In 1900 the Eastern Cherokee numbered only 1,376. Chapman J. Milling, *Red Carolinians* (Chapel Hill: University of North Carolina Press, 1940), 372, hereinafter cited as Milling, *Red Carolinians*.
    [7] Gulick, *Cherokees*, 16; Milling, *Red Carolinians*, 372.
    [8] Harold W. Foght to John Collier, "Narrative Section of the Annual Statistical Report, 1935," October 19, 1935, in Records of the Bureau of Indian Affairs, Cherokee Agency, General and Statistical File, Record Group 75, 61A931, Federal Records Center, Atlanta, Georgia, hereinafter cited as RG 75, 61A931.
    [9] Gulick, *Cherokees*, 20-21; R. L. Spalsbury to Collier, May 17, 1933, in RG 75, 61A931.

These photographs were made on Qualla Boundary by a census taker in the mid-1920s. TOP, LEFT: home of a full-blooded Cherokee in a remote section of Qualla; TOP, RIGHT: home of a relatively prosperous mixed-blooded Cherokee. BOTTOM, LEFT: home of a full-blooded Cherokee family, described as very poor but industrious. Note the poor soil in the foreground. BOTTOM, RIGHT: home in one of the most remote areas of Qualla. The old woman on the porch was ninety-nine years of age when this picture was taken in 1922 or 1923 and was then the oldest member of the tribe. Photographs from Federal Records Center, Atlanta, supplied by the author.

Cherokee home in 1932, a census taker reported that the house "was worse than filthy; no furnishings, and not fit for a hog pen,—garbage knee deep about the house; offensive odor; human waste all about [the] house; flies in droves; sanitation uncared for; Webster does not list words that will describe this place. . . . I don't see how they live and they are not living, but just existing."[10]

Throughout their history the Cherokee had always assimilated white culture readily; this process continued unabated during the New Deal era. Unfortunately, the Cherokee also acquired many of the undesirable cultural traits of the neighboring whites. Harold W. Foght, who was appointed superintendent of the Qualla Boundary in 1933, observed that

The Cherokees . . . have a mixed culture status, their own and that of the mountain whites. They live in the same type of dwellings as do the mountain whites. They have the same shiftless ways; they chew and snuff the same kind of tobacco; and make and drink the same kind of bootleg! Like the whites, they are prone to neglect their work and "set around," so long as credit is available at the traders.

10 "Industrial Survey, 1932," in RG 75, 61A931. This same house was later rebuilt with funds made available in 1936 by the Indian Relief and Rehabilitation Project. Foght to Collier, December 2, 1936, in RG 75, 61A931.

Armstrong Cornsilk, his daughter and grandchildren. He was a veteran of Col. W. H. Thomas's Civil War legion. Cornsilk sometimes served as a Baptist minister. The census taker described this family as industrious and hardworking. Photograph from Federal Records Center, Atlanta, supplied by the author.

This appears to be particularly true of the middle age group and specifically so of our many white Indians.[11]

On the other hand, the Cherokee people were subjected to a social prejudice which did not affect the whites. While there were racial aspects to this discrimination, it was also political and economic in nature. Although all American Indians had been guaranteed American citizenship in 1924, until the early 1950s North Carolina Cherokee were being refused the right to vote or to attend public schools in Jackson and Swain counties. North Carolina laws did not then prevent persons from voting because of race, but a prospective voter was required to pass a literacy test "to the satisfaction of the [voting] registrar."[12] Even Indians better educated than the registrar consistently failed the test. The primary reason for this denial of the vote was that after 1924 the Cherokee were no longer subject to state and local taxation; this greatly reduced tax revenues in Jackson and Swain counties. Apparently the county officials felt that if the Indians did not pay taxes they could not vote.[13]

Meanwhile, Cherokee children were excluded from the public schools because North Carolina law forbade the mingling of whites and "persons of color." Consequently, the Bureau of Indian Affairs was forced to maintain a boarding school on the reservation during the 1930s.[14] The more talented young people who were able to leave the reservation to attend Indian or white schools and colleges found the obstacles of competition in the white world insurmountable because of cultural differences and racial discrimination. If they returned to the reservation, they often found that they had obtained training for occupations which did not exist there. The young frequently

---

[11] Foght to Dr. B. Youngblood (principal economist, U.S. Department of Agriculture), December 31, 1934, in RG 75, 61A931.

[12] Foght to Collier, November 12, 1936, in RG 75, 61A931.

[13] Milling, *Red Carolinians*, 374-376. In some instances exorbitant taxation by county officials was a device for foreclosing on Indian lands. To complicate matters further, the Cherokee tended to vote Republican in marginally Democratic counties.

[14] Foght to Collier, October 19, 1935, in RG 75, 61A931.

became discouraged and began to vegetate into total indifference and dissipation. The Cherokee's greatest handicap, however, was "the defeatism that overwhelmed . . . [them] . . . in their cruel and unequal struggle up through the years, making them virtually outcasts, at last, at the mercy of the white man."[15]

Private enterprise and Pres. Herbert Hoover's limited surplus food and clothing program of 1931 were only marginally successful. Moreover, almost all of the relief money distributed to destitute members of the tribe during the Hoover years came from the Cherokee's own local fund, which was comprised of revenues derived from a tribal tax on the sale of reservation timber and the rental of Indian lands to whites. This limited financial source was insufficient to aid all the Indians who needed help. The only other sources of aid were the American National Red Cross, which provided flour, and the federal government, which contributed surplus clothing. In a moving plea in 1933 for an additional appropriation of $500 with which to buy corn for the Cherokee, the superintendent of the Cherokee agency[16] declared that "the government has contributed nothing [i.e., no money] for their relief and they have never asked for such aid."[17]

Even had there been no economic difficulties, the Cherokee faced an impressive array of social problems. In 1935 a large number of them still had

[15] Foght to Youngblood, December 31, 1934, in RG 75, 61A931.
[16] The federal government appointed Indian agents for Cherokee residing east of the Mississippi River as early as 1792, but the Cherokee Agency was not permanently established until 1801. In 1839, however, after the majority of the tribe had been removed to Oklahoma, the Bureau of Indian Affairs discontinued its Eastern Cherokee Agency. Thereafter, the Cherokee who had fled to North Carolina had no regular agent assigned to them until 1882. By 1883 the title "Indian agent" had fallen into such nationwide disrepute that Congress transferred (27 Stat. 614, c. 209 [1893]) all the duties of the agent to the superintendent of schools on each reservation. Since that time, the chief federal representative on each reservation has been designated the superintendent regardless of whether or not there are any schools within the agency. After the reorganization, agency headquarters for the Qualla Boundary was moved from Bryson City to Cherokee, where it has remained ever since.
Agency superintendents were appointed by the president of the United States with the advice and consent of the Senate and were subject to civil service regulations. Their duties were wide-ranging and included supervising the purchase and sale of tribal land, acting as director of the reservation schools, promoting the economic advancement of the tribe, providing public health and sanitation facilities, procuring relief for indigent Indians, and administering the allotment of land among tribal members. Local government on the reservation was vested in a chief, a vice-chief (both elected by the tribe for four-year terms), and a tribal council comprised of two members from each township on the reservation (elected for two-year terms). Among other things, the council made decisions concerning the use of reservation land and the disbursement of tribal funds. Although the council made most of the decisions regarding tribal policy, some of its actions, particularly those dealing with tribal membership and land sales, were subject to the superintendent's approval. Moreover, as a leading employer on the reservation, the superintendent naturally exerted unofficial authority over the Indians. Nevertheless, the Cherokee enjoyed a large degree of autonomy, and there is little evidence that the agency suprintendent ever vetoed any of the council's major rulings during the 1930s.
Although Superintendents James Blythe (1889-1892) and H. W. Spray (1898-1903) were Indians, most superintendents were white. Not only was it difficult to find Cherokee with the necessary academic credentials and administrative experience for the job but also Indians who joined the civil service and were thus subject to transfer were likely to lose their political standing in the tribe. Collier was able to increase the number of Indians in the Bureau of Indian Affairs, but during the 1930s the position of superintendent of the Qualla Boundary was occupied by a Caucasian.
[17] Spalsbury to Collier, May 17, 1933, in RG 75, 61A931.

One of the most dynamic personalities of the first half of the twentieth century was John Collier (1884-1968). He served as executive secretary of the American Indian Defense Association from 1922 until his appointment by Pres. Franklin D. Roosevelt as commissioner of Indian Affairs in 1933. In 1945 Collier left the Bureau of Indian Affairs to "retire" but continued to teach, lecture, and write until his death. U.S. Office of War Information photograph supplied by the National Archives, Washington, D.C.

no formal education and were, for all practical purposes, illiterate. Although most of the Indians were law-abiding, some often engaged in "drunken carousals leading to shootings, knifings and worse" when under the influence of moonshine whiskey.[18] Common-law marriages, desertion, and illegitimacy were frequent occurrences (although the Indians had an extremely low rate of venereal disease—lower, in fact, than the neighboring whites). Because of inadequacies in housing, sanitation, and diet, sickness was common; and tuberculosis, to which Indians were particularly susceptible, was endemic.[19] Significantly, many poor mountain whites also suffered from most of these same difficulties.[20]

Although Franklin Roosevelt appears to have had a genuine interest in assisting the Indians,[21] the greater part of his administration's Indian program (the so-called Indian New Deal) was the work of John Collier. A sociologist and anthropologist, Collier devoted his life to the study and protection of American Indians. Born and reared in Atlanta, Georgia, Collier as a teenager (ca. 1902) developed a deep attachment for the North Carolina mountains when he went on frequent, extended camping trips in that region. There he first met Cherokee Indians and many years later recalled that, since that time, he had found his ". . . own thoughts and emotions bound in with theirs

---

18 Foght to Youngblood, December 31, 1934, in RG 75, 61A931.
19 Foght to Collier, October 19, 1935, in RG 75, 61A931.
20 Foght to Youngblood, December 31, 1934, in RG 75, 61A931.
21 Wise, Red Man in the New World Drama, 357.

and [had] visited many times in those mountain valleys. . . ."[22] Collier served as executive secretary of the American Indian Defense Association, an organization of social scientists, writers, and reformers involved in Indian affairs, from 1923 to 1933, when he was named commissioner of Indian affairs by Roosevelt.

During the 1920s Collier had been one of the most relentless critics of the Bureau of Indian Affairs. Notwithstanding his desire for long-range reform, Collier recognized the need for immediate relief for the impoverished Indians. Consequently, one of his first official acts as commissioner was the inauguration of an Indian Emergency Conservation Work Program (IECW), utilizing funds made available by the Civilian Conservation Corps. Collier hoped that the CCC program would serve the dual purposes of providing employment for destitute Indians and improving reservation lands through reforestation and erosion control. The Indian CCC was administered by the Department of the Interior, but the Indian projects were separate from and independent of white CCC camps. Collier insisted that projects on reservations should be "Indian-built, Indian-maintained, and Indian-used" to the maximum possible extent.[23]

The CCC was the most popular and successful phase of the Indian New Deal at the Qualla reservation in that it provided what the Cherokee needed most—money. Because of the unique situation of American Indians and their need to maintain their small agricultural holdings, each reservation conducting emergency conservation work was considered a CCC camp so that the Indians might continue to reside in their own homes. When the program was first introduced at Qualla, the response was so enthusiastic that over 500 Cherokee applied for 100 full-time vacancies. In order to secure an equitable distribution of the available funds, the agency superintendent enrolled the men in two shifts; this provided each man with two weeks of employment per month.[24] In addition to providing income and employment, the CCC projects brought to the Qualla Boundary such important physical improvements as roads, horse and truck trails, fire lanes, and a lookout tower for fire detection.[25] The Indian CCC remained operative until the first months of 1943.

Meanwhile, the Cherokee also benefited from other New Deal work-relief programs, including those of the Public Works Administration, the Civil Works Administration, the Works Progress Administration, and the National Youth Administration. These various agencies allocated appropriations to the Department of the Interior, which in turn assigned funds to the Eastern Cherokee through the Bureau of Indian Affairs. Like the Indian CCC money,

---

[22] John Collier, *From Every Zenith: A Memoir* (Denver: Sage Books, 1963), 54, hereinafter cited as Collier, *From Every Zenith*. Despite his hectic schedule, Collier visited the Qualla reservation in August and September, 1933. After retiring from government service he was professor of sociology and anthropology at the College of the City of New York from 1947 to 1954. He died in 1968.

[23] Collier, *From Every Zenith*, 186-187. Collier was also the author of several other books, including *The Indians of the Americas* (New York: W. W. Norton & Company, 1947), hereinafter cited as Collier, *Indians of the Americas*.

[24] Spalsbury to Collier, September 23, 1933, in RG 75, 61A931.

[25] Clyde M. Blair to Collier, "Annual Narrative Report, Education, 1939-1940," in RG 75, 61A931; CCC Project Reports, in RG 75, 61A931.

Jim Tail, full-blooded Cherokee, was born in 1844 and served in the Thomas Legion during the Civil War. He lived alone in the mountains and told a census taker that he had never been married and had no use for people who wore dresses. Photograph from the Federal Records Center, Atlanta, supplied by the author.

these funds were used for road construction, reforestation, and job training. Between 1933 and 1941 the North Carolina Cherokee received a total of approximately $595,000 from the New Deal emergency recovery agencies.[26]

The influx of money into the economy of the reservation also led to a decline in agriculture. Just as the logging industry had caused a deterioration in farming in the 1920s, so the public works projects of the New Deal introduced a short-term and artificial prosperity. So long as generous amounts of cash were available, many Cherokee tended to neglect their crops for relatively high-paying jobs. Similarly, Indian women were less inclined to produce handicraft work, another indigenous source of income.[27] These characteristics were especially distressing in that subsistence farming and, to a lesser degree, handicrafts and logging were the only sources of livelihood available to the Eastern Cherokee during the 1930s. Thus, the federal assistance, however welcome and necessary, weakened the economic base of the Cherokee without creating a viable substitute.

The main features of Collier's program were outlined in the Wheeler-Howard Bill. Although some of the provisions of this measure failed to emerge when it was finally approved by Congress as the Indian Reorganization Act (IRA) in 1934,[28] it contained most of the basic concepts which Collier sought to promulgate. One of the most novel features of the IRA was the stipulation that the provisions of the act would be applicable only to those tribes which approved it by majority vote in a secret ballot. The act also prohibited the further allotment to individual Indians of land owned by Indian tribes, appropriated funds for the purchase of additional Indian lands, encouraged the organization and incorporation of tribes to provide "self-government and self-management of economic resources," and established a credit fund for tribes

---

[26] Various monthly reports on the use of federal funds are found in the superintendent's correspondence, in RG 75, 61A931.
[27] Foght to Collier, October 19, 1935, in RG 75, 61A931.
[28] 48 Stat. 984, c. 576 (1934).

seeking to improve agricultural techniques and industrial potential. To assist enterprising Indian youths, the IRA also provided for education loans and granted preference to Indians for employment by the Bureau of Indian Affairs.[29] Thus, the Indian New Deal offered a comprehensive program designed to reverse a half century of misguided policy.

The Indian Reorganization Act enabled the Bureau of Indian Affairs to

Cherokee women grinding maize by hand, still a necessary household chore when this photograph was made. From the cover of *State*, November 2, 1935.

attempt to prepare Indians for economic and cultural advancement. Commissioner Collier hoped that by establishing "federal corporations chartered for economic enterprise," the Indians would be able to function more effectively in a modern economy.[30] Once a tribe voted to accept the IRA, it was required to draft and adopt a constitution which would incorporate tribal customs and the ideals of local self-government. With this modernized structure, Collier anticipated that the Indians could pool their resources and embark upon cooperative enterprises as a tribe.

On December 21, 1934, the Eastern Band of the Cherokee accepted the Indian Reorganization Act by the overwhelming vote of 700 to 101. It was

---

[29] U.S. Department of the Interior, *Annual Report, 1940*, 359, 394; Debo, *Indians of the U.S.*, 291. In an effort to break what he termed "the monopoly of the Indian Bureau," Collier sought to utilize the facilities of the Public Health Service and the Department of Agriculture to the greatest possible extent. He also sponsored the Johnson-O'Malley Act (48 Stat. 596, c. 147 [1934]) which promoted federal cooperation with state and local agencies in providing services for the Indians. The Indian Arts and Crafts Board, created by Congress (49 Stat. 891, c. 748 [1935]) on Collier's recommendation, sought to "teach the Indian modern distribution methods without commercializing the product of his skill." Originally intended as a reform, allotment was designed to divide reservations into small, individually owned plots of land. Because of the poverty of Indian lands, a complicated inheritance system, and an increase in Indian population on the reservations, allotment usually made it necessary for Indians to sell or lease their marginal lands to whites.

[30] Collier, *Indians of the Americas*, 266.

with obvious enthusiasm that agency superintendent Harold W. Foght reported to Collier that

> We are well satisfied with the way the Indians turned out and voted, particularly as the mountain roads were in bad condition after several days of rain and snow. . . . If I understand the wording of the Wheeler-Howard Act [IRA], we may proceed with the charter of incorporation . . . almost any time. Our people are in the mood to go through with this matter while they have it clearly in mind.[31]

Foght's optimism soon proved premature, for in the months and years ahead a small but determined group of "white" Cherokee waged a relentless fight against the new Indian policy. Indeed, during the 1930s this group was able to prevent any extensive implementation of the IRA.

By the 1930s the Cherokee Qualla Boundary, the main portion of the Cherokee reservation, consisted of approximately 45,000 acres in the foothills of the Great Smoky Mountains. Approximately 2,250 mixed- and full-blooded Cherokee lived on the reservation, while 970 mixed bloods resided on the marginal lands surrounding the government reserve. The latter were designated "white" Indians because of their close resemblances to the local white population. They were for practical purposes white—some even had red hair and blue eyes. Meanwhile, the mixed-blooded Indians who resided on the reservation tended to be less assimilated into white society in that their culture resembled more closely that of the full bloods than that of the "white" Indians on the borderlands. Sometimes the "white" Indians and the Cherokee who lived on the reservation clashed over tribal policies. For example, the reservation Indians attempted unsuccessfully to keep the "white" Indians off the official Cherokee rolls which had been compiled in accordance with the congressional act of 1924.[32] Being more familiar with the aggressive ways of competitive American society, however, the "white" Indians usually prevailed.

The "white" Indians who resisted the reforms of the Collier era were motivated by a wide assortment of ideals—personal self-interest, distrust of the federal government, extreme right-wing anticommunism, and the principle of private ownership. The leader of this faction, Vice-Chief Fred Blythe Bauer, was "a strong influence with the [tribal] Council due largely to the fact that he . . . [was] . . . emotional, dramatic, clever and capable of very persuasive speech."[33] Superintendent Foght described Bauer and his associate, Pearson

---

[31] Foght to Collier, December 21, 1934, in RG 75, 61A931.
[32] Foght to Collier, October 19, 1935, in RG 75, 61A931.
[33] Foght to Wm. Zimmerman (assistant commissioner of Indian Affairs), March 17, 1937, Foght to Collier, March 30, 1936, Blair to Collier, October 28, 1938, in RG 75, 61A931. Fred Blythe Bauer was the son of Adolphus Gustavus Bauer (ca. 1860-1898), a prominent Philadelphia architect who helped build the North Carolina Executive Mansion and other important public buildings throughout the state during the 1880s and 1890s, and Rachel Blythe Bauer, a full-blooded Cherokee Indian. After the death of his parents Bauer was reared on the Qualla Boundary by his mother's uncle James Blythe. A graduate of Pennsylvania's Carlisle Indian School and a veteran of World War I, Bauer returned to the reservation in 1933. As vice-chief of the Eastern Cherokee from 1935 to 1939, he was an outspoken critic of the Collier reforms. He was defeated in a 1939 election for vice-chief by his stepbrother Jarrett Blythe. Bauer died on May 30, 1971, in Brevard, North Carolina.

A controversial figure in the history of Qualla Boundary is Fred Blythe Bauer, son of architect A. G. Bauer and Rachel Blythe, a Cherokee. After the death of his mother in Raleigh in 1897 Fred B. Bauer was adopted by James Blythe and his wife Josephine, the daughter of Chief Jarrett Nimrod Smith. Photograph from *News and Observer* (Raleigh), December 1, 1935.

McCoy, as the "chronic trouble maker[s] of this reservation," who, together with "a number of other white Indians, and a few other misled Indians, have continued meetings, [and] through a system of insidious insinuations and false statements, have induced a group of parents to sign a petition asking for an investigation of the new educational set up."[34]

The Collier educational program, which sought to conserve Indian heritage, customs, and languages, was one of the most hotly debated issues on the Qualla Boundary. Superintendent Foght reported that the new school curriculum for the Cherokee was "planned to prepare the Cherokee Indian youth for happy, wholesome, and remunerative lives on the Cherokee Reservation [while] at the same time making it possible for those of real ability and desire to continue their education and to enter college and technical school on a par with white children."[35] To implement Collier's program, the Cherokee boarding school offered courses in agriculture, forestry, cooperative management, tourist camp maintenance, carving, weaving, basket making, and pottery making.[36]

The "white" Indians believed that the Cherokee's best hope for the future was in accelerating the pace of assimilation. For example, Bauer protested:

Suppose you, a white, born in a white community, see only white people, attend white schools, have only white associates. After you attain manhood you are suddenly dropped down in China, India, or Africa, with people of a different race, language, and social customs. Do you think you would be accepted without question into the social, economic, and political life of that community? And be happy there?[37]

---

[34] Foght to A. C. Monahan (director of education, Bureau of Indian Affairs), May 1, 1935, in RG 75, 61A931.

[35] Foght to Collier, October 19, 1935, in RG 75, 61A931.

[36] Foght to Collier, October 19, 1935, in RG 75, 61A931.

[37] U.S. Congress, House, Committee on Indian Affairs, *Investigate Indian Affairs: Hearings*

Bauer wanted the state of North Carolina to maintain an integrated public school system which would include both white and Indian children.

In their attempt to become part of the American socioeconomic system, the "white" Indians glorified private ownership of land and charged that the new school curriculum, which sought to perpetuate tribal ownership, destroyed "free speech, free press, free assembly, and religious liberty."[38] With the support of the American Indian Federation, a vociferous right-wing Indian organization, Bauer accused the Bureau of Indian Affairs of spreading communistic doctrines in the schools.[39] As evidence for his charge, Bauer pointed to several "communistic" practices:

(1) A compulsory mass bathing rule had been adopted for the day schools . . . ; (2) . . . flag raising and lowering ceremonies had been abandoned; . . . and the children did not sing the patriotic songs of America; (3) Sex was being subservicely [sic] taught to pupils . . . girls and boys ranging from 13 to 22 years of age; (4) teachers and employees had been instructed to teach socialism and communism.[40]

Such opposition was quite disconcerting to Superintendent Foght. Despite his training in rural education, Foght had little previous experience in dealing with Indians. He was a confirmed believer in the value of progressive education and was convinced that the Collier program would benefit the Cherokee.[41]

The agitation of Bauer and his followers, together with the unrelated aid of several teachers who opposed the new system, impeded the development of the Collier education plan among the Cherokee.[42] Although several minor changes were adopted, most of the major objectives of the Collier education program were not achieved during the 1930s. Owing to the policy of school segregation in North Carolina and the geographical inaccessibility of many areas of the reservation, it was impossible to discontinue the Cherokee boarding school. The introduction of Cherokee language and grammar had to be abandoned because few of the children were interested in learning to read and write in their native tongue.[43]

The "white" Indian opposition achieved its greatest success in its fight against the adoption of a constitution under the IRA. Thus, in March, 1936, Superintendent Foght informed Collier that "Messrs. Bauer and McCoy are leaders of the malcontent Indians here and have caused a great deal of trouble.

---

before a Subcommittee of the Committee on Indian Affairs on H. Res. 166, Seventy-eighth Congress, Second Session, 1944, 1102, hereinafter cited as Hearings on Investigate Indian Affairs.

[38] U.S. Congress, House, Committee on Indian Affairs, Wheeler-Howard Act—Exempt Certain Indians: Hearings before the Committee on Indian Affairs on S. 2103, Seventy-sixth Congress, Third Session, 1940, 405-406, hereinafter cited as Hearings on Wheeler-Howard Act.

[39] Sharlotte Neely Williams, "The Role of Formal Education among the Eastern Cherokee Indians, 1880-1971" (unpublished master's thesis, University of North Carolina at Chapel Hill, 1971), 41, hereinafter cited as Williams, "Formal Education among the Eastern Cherokee."

[40] Hearings on Wheeler-Howard Act, 41.

[41] Foght to Collier, May 13, 1937, in RG 75, 61A931.

[42] Foght to Collier, April 30, 1935, in RG 75, 61A931.

[43] Williams, "Formal Education among the Eastern Cherokee," 40-41.

VOLUME LIII. NUMBER 3. JULY. 1976

A photograph made during the New Deal era of a Cherokee, his wife and child at Qualla Boundary. From *State*, October 24, 1936, p. 7.

As a matter of fact, were it possible to eliminate these two and Mrs. Fred Bauer, we would have little difficulty . . . in adopting . . . the [IRA] Constitution, and By-laws. . . ."[44] Bauer believed that because the IRA encouraged common ownership and enterprise, it destroyed "initiative, interest, and progress . . ." and made "all phases of Indian activities . . . dependent upon a collectivist program."[45]

In 1935 the Bauer faction mustered enough support to defeat what it considered a "Bureau-prepared constitution."[46] During the campaign the reservation became tense, and Superintendent Foght complained that "the opposition . . . held many weird night meetings, and organized groups of election judges to displace judges legally appointed by the Tribal Council." In one voting precinct, "knives were drawn and the Superintendent's life was threatened."[47] Because of the constant agitation of the "white" Indians, the Cherokee never adopted a constitution or charter of incorporation and thus never fully accepted the IRA.[48]

During its battle against the policies of the Bureau of Indian Affairs, the Bauer faction received considerable support from the American Indian Federation (AIF). This pan-Indian organization, which originated in Oklahoma, favored the complete assimilation of American Indians. In one of its pamphlets the AIF warned that "to set the Indian apart in a racial group is an injustice to all citizens of all races and origins, [which] accomplishes no good purpose and tends to engender race hatred."[49] The federation advocated a program which proposed that each Indian in the United States be given $3,000 in return for renunciation of all claims on the federal government except treaty

---

[44] Foght to Collier, March 30, 1936, in RG 75, 61A931.
[45] *Hearings on Investigate Indian Affairs*, 1101.
[46] *Hearings on Wheeler-Howard Act*, 406.
[47] Foght to Collier, March 15, 1937, in RG 75, 61A931.
[48] Blair to Collier, February 16, 1939, in RG 75, 61A931.
[49] U.S. Congress, Senate, Committee on Indian Affairs, *Final Discharge—Certain Individual Indians: Hearings before the Committee on Indian Affairs on S. 2206*, Seventy-sixth Congress, First Session, 1939, 66, hereinafter cited as *Hearings on Final Discharge*.

rights.[50] Through its Washington lobbyist, Mrs. Alice Lee Jemison, a fiery right-wing activist, the AIF charged that the new policy of the Bureau of Indian Affairs was the result of "communism and distinctly Russian in variety . . ." and was "the program of the Christ-mocking, Communist-aiding, subversive, and seditious American Civil Liberties Union and its subsidiary, the Progressive Education Association."[51] Beginning in 1935, members of the AIF appeared before congressional committees and accused Collier of "communism, atheism, un-Americanism, sedition, maladministration and misuse of public funds. . . ."[52]

Mrs. Jemison, denounced as "a dangerous agitator" by Secretary of the Interior Harold Ickes,[53] claimed that she represented approximately 300 North Carolina Cherokee when she appeared before the Senate Committee on Indian Affairs in 1936, 1937, 1938, and 1939. Mrs. Jemison also appeared in 1939 before the House Committee on Indian Affairs at the request of Fred Bauer, who testified with several other members of the tribe. At the hearing Bauer and Mrs. Jemison demanded that the Eastern Cherokee be excluded from the Indian Reorganization Act[54] and that Superintendent Foght be removed from his post because he had threatened to dismiss from employment with the various work-relief agencies any Indian who opposed the New Deal education plan.[55]

Both Superintendent Foght and Clyde M. Blair, who succeeded Foght as superintendent and served in that office until 1945, vigorously denied the charges of the AIF. Foght admitted that in the excitement of the election he had hastily posted a notice which warned that anyone "Maliciously working against the best interests of the Government would not be put on the work rolls," but he added that the posters were removed and no Indians were ever denied work on this basis.[56] On February 12, 1940, the tribal council passed a

---

50 Hearings on Final Discharge, 465; Harold L. Ickes, The Secret Diary of Harold L. Ickes (New York: Simon and Schuster, 3 volumes, 1953-1954), II, 506-507, hereinafter cited as Ickes Diary.
51 Hearings on Wheeler-Howard Act, 80. Unfortunately, little is known of the career of Mrs. Jemison, except that she was a Seneca Indian and claimed that her father was a Cherokee. During the 1930s she was the Washington representative and lobbyist of the AIF. She apparently disappeared from public view after the outbreak of World War II. There is some evidence that Mrs. Jemison continued her right-wing activities after the war but was no longer active in Indian movements. See William Gellermann, Martin Dies (New York: John Day Company, 1944), 124; and O. John Rogge, The Official German Report: Nazi Penetration, 1924-1942: Pan Arabism, 1939-Today (New York: Thomas Yoseloff, 1961), 315.
52 Hearings on Wheeler-Howard Act, 78.
53 Ickes Diary, II, 507.
54 Hearings on Wheeler-Howard Act, 186.
55 Hearings on Wheeler-Howard Act, 429-435. With the coming of World War II, the AIF fell into disrepute because of its close ties with the German-American Bund and the bund's claim that American Indians were in fact a tribe of lost "Aryans." The AIF was approved by the right-wing extremist James True, an associate of William Dudley Pelley of Asheville, North Carolina. Pelley was the organizer of Asheville's Fellowship Press, which printed profascist propaganda and several pamphlets for Fred Bauer. See Hazel Hertzberg, The Search for an American Indian Identity: Modern Pan-Indian Movements (Syracuse, N.Y.: Syracuse University Press, 1971), 289; and John Roy Carlson [pseud. Arthur Derounian], Under Cover: My Four Years in the Nazi Underworld of America—The Amazing Revelation of How Axis Agents and Our Enemies Within are Now Plotting to Destroy the United States (New York: E. P. Dutton & Co., 1943), 145-146, 150-152, 218.
56 Foght to Collier, March 15, 1937, in RG 75, 61A931.

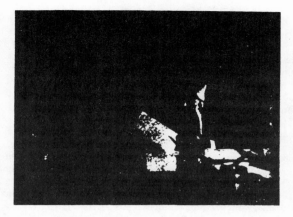

Chief Jarrett Blythe, left, and Superintendent C. M. Blair process the paperwork required to transfer $500 from the Cherokee communal fund to the Red Cross during World War II. Photograph from *State*, July 15, 1944, p. 5.

resolution which rejected Mrs. Jemison's claim that she represented the tribe.[57] In June the chief of the Eastern Cherokee, Jarrett Blythe, wrote to Collier informing him that the Cherokee desired to reconsider the adoption of the IRA Constitution.[58]

Although it is difficult to determine the validity of all the charges and countercharges in the debate over the IRA, it is obvious that most of the accusations of the Bauer faction were unfounded. The influence of the "white" Indians probably resulted from the fact that they were the most vocal element on the reservation. It is doubtful whether the great majority of the Cherokee had any real understanding of the goals and scope of the IRA. Consequently, the Bauer faction was able to prevent the tribe's approval of the IRA constitution and to hinder the Collier education policy. Although the IRA did provide education loans and jobs with the Bureau of Indian Affairs, it failed to make a radical change in the basic condition of the Cherokee Indians.

It is ironic that while the most effective New Deal programs for the Cherokee of North Carolina were the various work-relief projects—which unfortunately were a temporary expedient having no lasting effect upon the tribal economy—the program which in the long run proved most beneficial to the Cherokee was not initiated as part of the Indian New Deal. That program, which encouraged the Indians to invest tribal funds in the tourist industry, was a concept developed by Superintendent Foght. In 1935 Foght predicted that "new opportunities . . . are certain to come . . . with the great influx of tourists to the Great Smoky Mountain National Park with the

[57] Blair to Collier, February 17, 1940, in RG 75, 61A931.
[58] *Hearings on Wheeler-Howard Act*, 52. Blythe's letter notwithstanding, the Eastern Cherokee never did adopt an IRA constitution.

completion of the so-called Park to Park highway—throwing this portion of the Appalachians heretofore little known open to the nation."[59] Much to the chagrin of Foght and his successor C. M. Blair, the Bauer faction was able to delay the project for five years by influencing the tribal council to vote against a proposal which granted a right-of-way for the construction of a portion of the Blue Ridge Parkway through the reservation. Finally, in February, 1940, after Bauer had failed to win reelection as vice-chief, opposition was overcome, and the Cherokee council unanimously approved the right-of-way resolution.[60]

The Indian Reorganization Act made no profound changes in the social and economic condition of the Cherokee Indians. Except for minor changes in education policies, student loans, and the employment of more Indians at the local agency, the life patterns on the reservation remained basically unchanged during the New Deal era. The primary reason for the failure of the IRA at Qualla was the determined resistance of the "white" Indians, who viewed Collier's program as an invasion of their rights as Americans.

The obstacles encountered by the officials of the Bureau of Indian Affairs in attempting to implement the IRA in North Carolina demonstrate the extreme difficulty of formulating a federal policy for a group as heterogeneous as the American Indians. Great political, social, and economic differences existed not only between various tribes but also within each of them. Thus, at Qualla the IRA, which was directed toward assisting the conservative, tradition-oriented Cherokee, appeared to conflict with the interests of the "white" Indians, who generally constituted the wealthiest and most influential segment of the tribe. Because this latter group often farmed the best lands or operated local businesses, the "white" Indians advocated allotment, private ownership, and assimilation. In addition, both the "whites" and conservatives appear to have resented the paternalism of the Bureau of Indian Affairs.

Primarily because of tourism, the Eastern Cherokee are now well-known citizens of the southeastern United States, in contrast to the 1930s when the tribe inhabited the remote western North Carolina mountains and were largely ignored by most Americans. During the Great Depression, the Cherokee found their existence threatened by economic forces of which they had little understanding. It was fortunate that John Collier and Pres. Franklin Roosevelt did not forget the Cherokee of North Carolina.

[59] Foght to Collier, October 19, 1935, March 17, 1937, Blair to Collier, June 2, 1938, in RG 75, 61A931.

[60] *Hearings on Wheeler-Howard Act*, 39. Bauer considered the proposed highway construction a violation of Cherokee property rights. For a full discussion of Bauer's views, see Fred B. Bauer, *Land of the North Carolina Cherokees* (Brevard, North Carolina: Privately printed by the author, 1970), which the author dedicated to Alice Lee Jemison.

Anthropologists, Reformers, and the Indian New Deal

GRAHAM D. TAYLOR

For a generation of social scientists interested in the application of research findings to policy, Franklin Roosevelt's New Deal offered novel opportunities. A number of programs initiated by the federal government not only drew upon recent social and economic research but also brought into the government economists, sociologists, anthropologists, and psychologists. Earlier social scientists had contributed information and expert support for reform efforts, primarily at the local level. But "the New Deal made a permanent place for social scientists in government . . . as policy advisors and political appointees, roles traditionally assigned to lawyers and businessmen." [1]

This trend was particularly marked in the Bureau of Indian Affairs under Commissioner John Collier. Leader of an Indian reform movement in the decade before the New Deal, Collier brought to the Indian service a commitment to reverse the policies of the preceding fifty years, which had been shaped to assimilate Indians into white society. Collier proposed to revive traditional tribal institutions as part of his plan for social and economic development for Indians. This aim was central to the Indian

Reorganization Act of 1934, the keystone of the new policy. The Act proposed to give Indian tribes the political rights of American counties and municipalities and the power to form corporations for communal enterprises. [2]

Reviewing the course of Indian affairs under Collier, anthropologists Clyde Kluckhohn and Robert Hackenberg asserted that the Indian Reorganization Act was "a landmark not only for the American Indians but for social scientists in the United States because it brought to Indian affairs and to the United States government for the first time an explicit use of social science principles. . . . The Indian Reorganization Act was a deliberate attempt to induce certain kinds of changes in Indian society and to

[1] Gene M. Lyons, *The Uneasy Partnership: Social Science and the Federal Government in the Twentieth Century* (New York, 1969), p. 52. See also Richard S. Kirkendall, "Franklin D. Roosevelt and the Service Intellectual," *Mississippi Valley Historical Review* 49 (1962):459-463.

[2] Collier's concept of Indian policy and the role of anthropologists was succinctly outlined in John Collier's, "The Indian Administration as a Laboratory in Ethnic Affairs," *Social Research* 12 (1945):265-303. Important new work on the Indian New Deal has emerged in the last four years. Kenneth Philp and Lawrence C. Kelly are completing biographical studies of Collier; they presented papers on the Indian Reorganization Act at the 1973 convention of the Organization of American Historians in Chicago. See Kenneth Philp, "The American Indian New Deal, 1933-1945: An American Indian Renaissance"; and Lawrence C. Kelly, "The American Indian New Deal: Dream and Reality." See also Michael T. Smith, "The Wheeler-Howard Act of 1934: The Indian New Deal," *Journal of the West* 10 (1971):521-534; Donald L. Parman, "The Indian and the Civilian Conservation Corps," *Pacific Historical Review* 40 (1971):39-56; Peter M. Wright, "John Collier and the Oklahoma Indian Welfare

control other changes. In its inception the authors made conscious use of the knowledge of culture change then possessed by the social sciences."[3]

Anthropologists were brought into the bureau to assist in planning and executing the reorganization program. From 1935 to 1938 an applied anthropology staff worked with legal and economic advisers of the bureau, identifying tribal groups and helping to prepare tribal constitutions and charters. Subsequently, anthropologists were included in social surveys carried out by the Indian service and the Soil

John Collier, once a staunch critic of the Indian Bureau, presided over its affairs during the controversial New Deal era.

Conservation Service to develop long-range land use projects on various reservations. The

Act of 1936," *Chronicles of Oklahoma* 50 (1972):347-371; and G. D. Taylor, "The Tribal Alternative to Bureaucracy: The Indian's New Deal, 1933-1945," *Journal of the West* 13 (1974):128-142. Several of Philp's recent articles on the Indian reform movement, 1922-1932, are cited below.

[3] Clyde Kluckhohn and Robert Hackenberg, "Social Science Principles and the Indian Reorganization Act," in W. H. Kelley, ed., *Indian Affairs and the Indian Reorganization Act* (Tucson, 1954), p. 29.

educational unit of the bureau under Willard Beatty relied on anthropologists to prepare training programs to acquaint field agents with the variety and significance of Indian cultural groups.[4] In 1941 Collier arranged with the University of Chicago for joint financing of a major research project under Laura Thompson to determine the impact of his policies on various tribes. This project resulted in a series of monographs on cultural crisis and change among the Indians.[5]

Despite the intensive use of social science theory in the development of Collier's policies between 1933 and 1945, the anthropologists who participated were not entirely satisfied with the results. The reorientation of Indian policy away from an assimilationist stance to one respecting cultural differences was not completely successful; nor did the reforms in administration initiated in the New Deal period prove durable. By the early 1950s the Indian Bureau seemed to be sinking back into its former state of torpor. In Congress demands were growing for termination of federal responsibility for Indians, with the clear implication that Indians must accept the white man's way.

Kluckhohn and Hackenberg concluded that the limitations of Collier's policies could be attributed to lack of understanding of the intent of the reorganization program by the local field representatives of the bureau, reservation superintendents, and their agents. The reformers and anthropologists allied with Collier had paid "insufficient attention . . . to the habitual ways of thinking and reacting of the group out in the field. It was not that the Indian Service field representatives were irresponsible or insincere or unintelligent, by and large. It was

[4] See Edward A. Kennard and Gordon MacGregor, "Applied Anthropology in Government: United States," in A. L. Kroeber, ed., *Anthropology Today* (Chicago, 1953), pp. 832-835, for a summary of the tasks assigned to anthropologists during Collier's administration. For a more critical overview, see David L. Marden, "Anthropologists and Federal Indian Policy Prior to 1940," *Indian Historian* 5 (1972):19-26.

[5] A summary of the research with recommendations for changes in bureau administration is included in Laura Thompson, *Personality and Government: Findings and Recommendations of the Indian Administration Research* (Mexico, 1951). Among the important monographs completed during the project were: Laura Thompson and Alice Joseph, *The Hopi Way* (Chicago, 1944); Gordon MacGregor, *Warriors Without Weapons* (Chicago, 1946); Clyde Kluckhohn and Dorothea Leighton, *The Navaho* (Chicago, 1946); and Alice B. Joseph, Joseph B. Spicer, and Jane Chesky, *The Desert People* (Chicago, 1949).

simply that their own subculture screened both the instructions they got from Washington, and distorted their appraisal of the local situation." [6]

This hypothesis had been proposed earlier by H. Scudder Mekeel, director of the bureau's applied anthropology staff between 1935 and 1937. In an article published in 1944, Mekeel noted that many bureau field employees appointed before 1933 had been trained to carry out a program of forced, rapid assimilation, and even where they did not resist the new policies there had been a lag due to the difficulty of adjusting their views. Furthermore, few of them had any real knowledge of the Indian groups they dealt with, and their ignorance had been reinforced by the bureau practice of frequently rotating agents to different reservations. As field administrators, they were naturally resentful of outside advisers who, in effect, implied that they did not know their jobs. Consequently, there was continuous friction between the anthropologists and the local bureau people.[7]

Mekeel also implied that Collier had sacrificed the anthropologists to the demands of the old guard within the bureau by abolishing the applied anthropology staff in 1938. Collier denied this charge and many others that Mekeel made against his administration. He maintained that the decision to eliminate the staff of anthropologists was the result of heavy cuts in the bureau's budget after 1937, thus transferring responsibility for the cut to conservative congressmen hostile to Indian reform. Collier also came to the defense of his field agents, lauding their commitment to improving the health and social conditions of Indians. But he did not deny that there was serious friction between the anthropologists and other employees of the Indian service.[8]

This picture of conflict within the bureau between the old-line bureaucracy bound to the tradition of assimilation and the new reform leadership committed to cultural pluralism, allied with anthropologists who provided expert advice, appears satisfactory and logical. Certainly, the change in policy orientation was

complete enough that some degree of resistance or misunderstanding was to be expected.

The picture of internal cleavage resulting in frustration of reform is not complete, however, for it assumes a convergence of orientation and goals between anthropologists and reformers that was not the case. Moreover, it gives an inaccurate view of the general pattern of relationships between the bureau leadership under Collier and those working the field. As the dispute between Mekeel and Collier indicates, the reformers' ideas were not necessarily the same as those of their anthropologist ad-

Walter Woehlke, whom Collier brought with him to the bureau from the American Indian Defense Association, was the first coordinator of TC-BIA, the agency's planning group.

visers, and on many points the reform leaders and the bureau's old guard shared the goal of improving Indian life, even though they differed over the best means. Some of the bureau's anthropologists came to share the views of the administrators. Finally, the frustration of Indian reform did relate to internal problems of the bureau under Collier, but not in the way suggested by Kluckhohn, Hackenberg, and Mekeel.

[6] Kluckhohn and Hackenberg, "Social Science Principles," p. 31.

[7] H. S. Mekeel, "An Appraisal of the Indian Reorganization Act," *American Anthropologist* 46 (1944):211-212.

[8] Collier, "Collier Replies to Mekeel," *American Anthropologist* 46 (1944):422-426.

This essay will re-examine the relationships among the Collier reform leadership, the anthropologists involved in the bureau program, and the bureau field agents who applied the Indian Reorganization Act.

During the 1920s John Collier as head of the American Indian Defense Association emerged as the most militant advocate for reform of Indian policy. Beginning with a defense of the land claims of the Pueblo Indians in 1923, Collier and the A.I.D.A. relentlessly attacked the corruption, mismanagement, and dictatorial tendencies of the Indian service. Collier was equally critical of those who proposed more moderate or gradual reforms than his own, in particular the venerable Indian Rights Association, the traditional white spokesman for Indians. Even Charles Rhoads, who as head of the Indian Service from 1929 to 1932 tried to remove agents responsible for corruption and tyranny on the reservations and to improve health and educational standards of Indians, was criticized by Collier for failing to undertake the major changes required for lasting reform.[9]

Collier argued against the existing policy of assimilation because it was based on an ethnocentric concept of cultural evolution in which white society was viewed as constituting a superior form toward which the Indians should be guided. This rationale justified the extermination of traditional Indian customs and ceremonies; breaking up Indian families and the depletion of the Indians' land base, which had diminished from 139 million acres in 1887 to less than 48 million acres by 1931. Indians were ill-equipped to function in the emerging industrial society. Bereft of their traditional cultural institutions and values, they were poor, demoralized, and chronically susceptible to alcoholism and disease. Since the well-being of the individual Indian related directly to his cultural adjustment, any lasting change in Indian conditions required that the Indian cultural heritage must be revitalized, which meant allowing

[9] Randolph C. Downs, "A Crusade for Indian Reform, 1922-1934," *Mississippi Valley Historical Review* 32 (1945): 331-354. See also recent articles by Philp on the reform movement: "Albert B. Fall and the Protest from the Pueblos," *Arizona and the West* 12 (1970):237-254; "Herbert Hoover's New Era: A False Dawn for the American Indian, 1929-1932," *Rocky Mountain Social Science Journal* 9 (1972):53-60; and "John Collier and the Crusade to Protect Indian Religious Freedom," *Journal of Ethnic Studies* 1 (1973):22-38. Lawrence C. Kelly, *The Navajo Indians and Federal Indian Policy, 1900-1935* (Tucson, 1968), also has valuable information on the reform movement and Indian policy in the 1920s.

Indians more autonomy and reducing the paternalistic role of the bureau.[10]

Although Collier was familiar with, and presumably relied upon the research of contemporary anthropologists, particularly the students of Franz Boas, his own ideas about the sources of Indian problems and their solution derived from his background and education as a social worker in New York City and from his initial experiences with certain Indian tribes.

Before World War I Collier had been active in community organization among immigrant groups in New York where he came to share the the ideas of community pluralism developed by Mary Follett and E. C. Lindeman, among others. These thinkers advocated the organization of society into community groups representing different ethnic and regional cultural elements as an alternative to the emerging system of public policy made by economic interest groups representing large bureaucracies. In the context of these ideas, Indian tribes could indeed prove to be a "laboratory in ethnic affairs" whose experiments could be drawn upon for the elaboration of a program for renovating American society as a whole.[11]

Collier's notions about the cultural cohesion of Indian societies were shaped by his first encounters with the Pueblos in the early 1920s. These Indians had been relatively undisturbed by the policy of assimilation and the division of tribal lands into individual parcels, and they retained much of their economic and social cohesion. Furthermore, over ninety-five percent were fullbloods who had had little contact with white society. Although threatened and exploited by their white neighbors, these Indians retained a strong sense of cultural identity and social structure. Their situation, moreover, provided an instructive contrast with the tribes of the northern Great Plains who had been subjected to the full force of assimilation and allotment and who were totally demoralized. If the Indians of the southwestern United States could draw strength from their tribal traditions to resist white encroachments, presumably a reversal of bureau policies and a return to tribalism could stem the decline of their northern brothers.

[10] Collier, "The Indian Administration," pp. 267-270.

[11] Collier discussed the intellectual roots of his reform proposals and his ideas on social organization in *From Every Zenith: A Memoir* (Denver, 1963), pp. 93-100, 230-234, 308-309.

In summary, Collier's analysis of Indian cultural groups could be characterized as prescriptive rather than descriptive, instrumental in the reconstruction not only of Indian societies but in the reform of American society. This is not to say that Collier's interest in Indian cultures was not genuine; in a sense he had found his life's work when he witnessed Pueblo ceremonies on a journey to New Mexico in 1920.[12] But he perceived them in the context of his broader reform experiences and convictions. Furthermore, his observation of the living Indian cultures of the Southwest shaped his belief that the process of white acculturation not only should but could be reversed, and that the revival of traditional Indian cultural institutions was possible even among the disorganized Plains tribes. In these two aspects Collier's ideas on the subject differed from those of some of the leading scholars of North American Indian ethnography.

When he was appointed commissioner in 1933, Collier brought with him colleagues from the Indian Defense Association whom he installed in key positions in the bureau. Among these were Walter V. Woehlke, who headed the cooperative program for land use planning between the bureau and the Soil Conservation Service in 1937-1938; Allan G. Harper, who succeeded Woehlke in this position and was one of Collier's closest aides; F. H. Daiker, who headed the Tribal Organization Section; and Ward Shepard, a forestry specialist who held a number of positions in the commissioner's office between 1933 and 1945. In addition, Collier found sympathizers in other agencies of the Interior Department, notably the legal division under Felix Cohen, Nathan Margold, and Kenneth Meicklejohn, all of whom contributed to preparing and administering the Indian Reorganization Act.[13] Few of these men had any background in anthropology, and it is difficult to determine the extent to which they shared Collier's personal views on Indians. But they all believed strongly in the need to improve the material conditions of Indian life and to reverse the paternalistic policies of the Bureau.

Another factor that influenced Collier and his advisers was the sense of the impermanence of their tenure and the need to effect changes rapidly to lessen the chance of their being dismantled by future commissioners. That dilemma was sympathetically described by Oliver LaFarge:

It takes a good Commissioner of Indian Affairs about two years to learn his job. A good man . . . needs four years to get his program launched. Uncertainty of appointment clouds that first term, creating a sense of haste. The virtual certainty that eight years will be the limit is not as bad as the fear that the next Commissioner will belong to an administration with a totally different theory of government and will proceed to undo all that has been built up.[14]

The reformers certainly had no idea that they would be in control of Indian policy for more than ten years and could justifiably feel in the early years that a more gradual, systematically developed reform effort might well be stymied before reaching even initial goals.

These were the attitudes the reformers brought to the bureau and which figured prominently in the preparation of the Indian Reorganization bill in 1933. In November of that year, Collier sent out questionnaires to a number of anthropologists in the United States, requesting advice and information relating to formal patterns of tribal or community government, traditions of land and property rights, and similar information on various Indian groups with which they had contact.

Significantly, Collier chose not to rely exclusively on the aid of the Bureau of American Ethnology, a branch of the Smithsonian Institution that had been functioning since 1879. During the decade and a half before 1933, anthropologists had debated the use of culture as a unifying concept in their discipline and the validity of cultural pluralism as opposed to unilineal evolutionary schemes. The centers for support of cultural pluralism were in the universities, particularly in departments staffed by students of Franz Boas.[15] In drawing on this larger group of academics for advice, Collier could anticipate a sympathetic cross-section of responses to the reorganization program as a whole and perhaps some valuable information

---

[12] Ibid., pp. 125-127.
[13] Collier also benefited from support by prominent New Deal figures who had been involved in the Indian reform movement in the 1920s, most notably Harold Ickes and Adolph A. Berle, who were on the board of directors of the American Indian Defense Association. See Collier, *From Every Zenith,* pp. 132-133.

[14] Oliver LaFarge, *As Long As the Grass Shall Grow* (New York, 1940), p. 58.
[15] On divisions of opinion among anthropologists in the 1920s, I have relied on G. W. Stocking, Jr., *Race, Culture, and Evolution* (New York, 1968), especially pp. 273-307.

on the political situations among various Indian groups.

Collier's confidence was not entirely misplaced. Although one respondent asserted that "most anthropologists in this country have been comparatively uninterested so far in the practical problems of Indians,"[16] there were others who were highly favorable to the bill and who provided the specific details requested. Robert Lowie, for example, felt that the Crow Indians of Montana were well prepared to take over self-governing institutions and pointed to the fact that both the older full-bloods and younger boarding-school-educated Indians exhibited an interest in local politics and a willingness to cooperate that was unusual among Plains tribes.[17] A. L. Kroeber reinforced Collier's own impressions of the Pueblo villages, asserting that they "furnish perhaps the strongest case for collective administration, since these groups have succeeded to a large extent in maintaining their collective rights and therewith a tribal attitude."[18] H. Scudder Mekeel, a student of Clark Wissler, was particularly enthusiastic about the program and discussed at length the problems and potential for tribal organization of the Oglala Sioux at the Pine Ridge and Rosebud reservations in South Dakota. He noted especially the role that anthropologists could play in implementing new programs, ensuring that the organization of political and business groups such as cattle associations and agricultural cooperatives conformed to traditional cultural divisions among the Indians.[19]

Inevitably, the questionnaires also brought out differences of opinion among anthropologists on how to organize different tribes. Fred Eggan of the University of Chicago advocated a flexible approach that would provide for a substantial degree of federal tutelage for badly disorganized groups such as the Choctaws of Mississippi, but would allow greater autonomy and tribal self-government to other groups, for example, the Navaho and Hopi, who had preserved more of their tribal unity and traditions. Harold Colton of the Northern Arizona Museum, however, felt that "it will be a long time before members of these tribes [Navaho and Hopi] will be well enough trained to handle financial matters. . . . Complete home rule is something that can take place only in the dim future."[20]

There were some respondents who indicated that while the idea of Indian self-determination and an end to assimilation policies were laudable aims, they would not be particularly helpful to some Indian groups. Obviously Colton felt this to be the case for the Navaho and the Hopi. Ralph Linton, who had studied the Comanche, concluded that "they have no governing body and their whole pattern of life is such that I believe any attempt to establish one would be foredoomed to failure."[21] Linton also pointed to the preference on the part of the older Indians for the continuation of allotment. John Harrington of the Smithsonian Institution expanded Linton's pessimistic view to virtually all the Indian groups in the Southwest: "Outside the Pueblo areas, native government has all been battered down," and the activities of Catholic and Moravian missionaries had further divided and factionalized the tribal remnants.[22]

Of particular significance was the view of Franz Boas, who was not only the leading exponent of cultural anthropology in the United States and the mentor of the current generation of anthropologists but also an experienced ethnographer of North American Indian tribes. Boas's response may have been shaped in part by his opinion of Collier. Earlier he had written to Interior Secretary Harold Ickes opposing

[16] George Herzog to Collier, Feb. 27, 1934. Records relating to the Wheeler-Howard Bill, Records of the Bureau of Indian Affairs, Record Group 75, National Archives. Records relating to the Wheeler-Howard Bill, which became the Indian Reorganization Act of 1934, and the records relating to tribal organization are from the files of the Bureau of Indian Affairs (cited hereafter as Wheeler-Howard files or Tribal Organization files, RG 75, NA.)

[17] Robert Lowie to Collier, Mar. 5, 1934, Wheeler-Howard files, RG 75, NA. The Crow Indians in 1934 became the first tribe to elect their own superintendent, choosing Robert Yellowtail, a tribal leader with political connections to Sen. Burton K. Wheeler of Montana, cosponsor of the Indian reorganization bill.

[18] A. L. Kroeber to Collier, Jan. 15, 1934, Wheeler-Howard files, RG 75, NA. Kroeber was an anthropologist who had been actively involved in the reform movement before 1933. See Marden, "Anthropologists and Federal Indian Policy," p. 25.

[19] H. S. Mekeel to Collier, Apr. 7, 1934, Wheeler-Howard files, RG 75, NA.

[20] Fred Eggan to Collier, Jan. 11, 1934; Harold Colton to Collier, Apr. 17, 1934, Wheeler-Howard files, RG 75, NA.
[21] Ralph Linton to Collier, Feb. 15, 1934, Wheeler-Howard files, RG 75, NA.
[22] John Harrington, Smithsonian Institution, Wash., D.C., to Collier, Mar. 23, 1934, Wheeler-Howard files, RG 75, NA.

Collier's appointment on the grounds that he was unnecessarily opinionated and emotional about Indian reform.[23] In his comments on Collier's questionnaire, Boas echoed Linton's point that among Indians who were settled on allotments there was great reluctance "to merge it into the larger community," and that the allotment system had contributed largely to the breakdown of cultural ties among tribes of the northwestern coast and Plains regions with whom he was most familiar.[24] This response was carefully phrased to avoid making a direct judgment on the goals of Indian reorganization.

In summary, the initial responses of anthropologists to the proposals of the reformers revealed a variety of attitudes ranging from enthusiastic support to open skepticism; none were hostile but there was an undercurrent of doubt in many comments. Boas's opinion of Collier was not necessarily shared by his colleagues: Robert Zingg of the University of Chicago spoke of the high esteem that anthropologists held for both Ickes and Collier, particularly in comparison with their predecessors.[25] An appreciation of the good intentions of the reformers, however, did not imply uncritical acceptance of the reform proposals for all Indians.

Divisions of opinion also extended to the more practical question of the usefulness of anthropologists in implementing the reorganization program. Some of the younger anthropologists like Mekeel and Oliver LaFarge, who was then head of the National Association on Indian Affairs, believed that they could play a direct role in guiding the tribal organization process and helping it to conform to traditional Indian institutions. Boas, on the other hand, asserted "it is very difficult at the present time to find anyone who is well prepared for dealing with the practical problems of Indian life for the reason that no position of this kind was ever open to anyone who had studied anthropology." He recommended the use of anthro-

pologists in training schools for incoming bureau employees, a suggestion developed by Willard Beatty in the bureau's education division. More ambitiously, he urged the incorporation of anthropology into educational programs for Indian leaders and teachers that would focus on developing an understanding of Collier's social and economic programs.[26]

Other anthropologists favorable to Collier's proposals, like Kroeber and Lowie, submitted informative statements on tribal political situations in the obvious expectation that they would be useful in the reorganization program, but they had no suggestions for the systematic use of anthropologists in administration. Presumably there were many anthropologists who shared the view of Melville Herskovits, later vice-president of the American Association for the Advancement of Science, that social scientists involved in administrative tasks on behalf of the government ran the risk of becoming proponents of policies designed to serve political rather than genuinely scientific goals.[27]

The Indian Reorganization Act that emerged from Congress in June 1934 had been altered in significant ways from the bill originally drawn up by Collier and his fellow reformers in the bureau. A provision authorizing the new tribal organizations to consolidate individual allotments into tribal properties had been modified. Also, each tribe or reservation could decide by referendum whether or not it chose to come under the Act and undertake the creation of tribal governments and corporations. Those groups that rejected the Act would remain under the direct supervision of the bureau. Nevertheless, much of the basic structure of the Collier proposals remained. After deciding to come under the Act the Indian tribe or group could then draw up a constitution, which was subject to a referendum. Under a constitution, a tribal council or similar form of government could be established, and the tribe could incorporate itself for the purpose of setting up enterprises such as lumber mills, livestock associations, or farm cooperatives.[28]

[23] Franz Boas to Harold Ickes, secretary of the interior, Dec., 1932. Boas Papers, American Philosophical Society, Philadelphia. Pa. Marden, "Anthropologists and Federal Indian Policy," pp. 25-26, suggests that Boas's attitude toward Collier reflected his determination to remain aloof from contemporary issues and that this tendency was reinforced by his interest in primitive aspects of Indian life rather than in the problems of acculturation.

[24] Boas to Collier, May 9, 1934, Wheeler-Howard files, RG 75, NA.

[25] Robert Zingg to Collier, Apr. 16, 1934, Wheeler-Howard files, RG 75, NA.

[26] Boas to Collier, Dec. 7, 1933, Wheeler-Howard files, RG 75, NA.

[27] Melville Herskovits, "Applied Anthropology and the American Anthropologists," Science 83 (Mar. 6, 1936):215-222. The address on which this article is based was delivered a year earlier, before the Indian reorganization program was fully in operation.

[28] The final bill is printed in C. J. Kappler, ed., Indian

The most critical phase in the process involved preparing tribal constitutions, inasmuch as questions relating to representation of different groups and factions were raised. In a number of cases, Indian groups who had voted to come under the Act never got beyond this point because of irreconcilable differences among those who spoke different languages or between traditional religious and political factions and between older fullblood Indians and younger mixed-blood Indians. On these matters the assistance of anthropologists with specialized knowledge on tribal divisions was valuable.

Where possible, anthropologists were included on teams of lawyers sent to the reservations to advise and assist Indians in preparing constitutions and charters. Anthropologists were generally assigned to travel with a team covering an entire region rather than working intensively with a single tribe. This method was partly dictated by the scarcity of trained anthropologists willing and able to work full-time for the bureau. Collier arranged for the use of part-time consultants, where possible, drawing on graduate students who were doing field work and who were readily available. This rather unstructured organization was designated the Applied Anthropology Staff and was initially under the direction of W. Duncan Strong, himself a consultant anthropologist.[29]

As might be expected, most of the full-time anthropologists on the staff were young. Some presumably took positions with the government because of the Depression and the lack of jobs but others left academic positions to perform tasks to which they felt strongly committed. Among the best, and best-known of the anthropologists were Oliver LaFarge, the Indian reform lobbyist who worked primarily with the Hopi in the Southwest; Morris E. Opler who worked with the Apache, Kiowa, and Comanche; H.S. Mekeel who worked with the Dakota Sioux; Gordon MacGregor who worked among other Plains tribes; Oscar Lewis, John Harrington, and Ruth Underhill

who worked with the Navaho, Papago, and Pima in New Mexico and Arizona.

In 1936 when Mekeel succeeded Strong as chief, the work of the applied anthropology staff became more varied. Organizational work on tribal constitutions continued for several more years. New issues and problems arose among tribes already under constitutions when dissident groups sought to revise representational arrangements or when disputes occurred over the precedence of custom over legal procedures.

In January 1936, a new planning group was set up to coordinate the work of the bureau with the Soil Conservation Service on the reservations, called the Technical Cooperation-Bureau of Indian Affairs (TC-BIA). The objective of TC-BIA, according to Walter Woehlke, Collier's choice as the project coordinator, was "to outline the best possible use of the reservation's resources, a use which will bring the human carrying capacity on the reservation to its maximum, with complete conservation of the reservation's soil resources and with maintenance of an adequate standard of living."[30] Initial planning was carried out on an experimental basis on the Papago, Pima, and Hualapai reservations in New Mexico.

Mekeel, as head of applied anthropology activities, was placed in charge of the Socio-Economic Division of TC-BIA, which was to work in conjunction with agricultural economists, geologists, and other technical specialists from SCS carrying out intensive surveys of selected reservations. Mekeel described the function of his division: "to determine . . . the potentialities and limitations of the Indian population on each reservation in terms of its own economic system, its own standard of living as well as its economic drives"; and to ensure that resource use plans would strengthen traditional social and economic institutions and "foster the life-values of the people."[31] Elaborate procedures for the work were developed, including house-to-house surveys, a technique refined and extended by the Department of Agriculture for more wide-ranging rural economic projects. The survey also used conventional statistical studies of population,

Affairs: Laws and Treaties (Washington, D. C., 1941)5:380-387. On the congressional contest over the Wheeler-Howard bill, see Michael T. Smith, "The Wheeler-Howard Act of 1934: The Indian New Deal," *Journal of the West* 10 (1971):521-534; and John L. Freeman, Jr., "The New Deal for the Indians: A Study of Bureau-Committee Relations in American Government" (unpublished Ph.D. diss., Princeton Univ., 1952).

[29] Collier to Ickes, June 1, 1934. Collier Papers, Yale Univ., New Haven.

[30] Walter V. Woehlke, "SCS Project for Technical Assistance to the Office of Indian Affairs," Jan. 7, 1936. Records of Technical Assistance-Bureau of Indian Affairs project, Records of the Soil Conservation Service, Record Group 114, National Archives (cited hereafter as RG 114, NA).

[31] H. S. Mekeel, memo, Jan. 1936, RG 114, NA.

income, and other social characteristics.[32] Among the social scientists participating were Willard W. Hill, Frederica de Laguna, and Ruth Underhill, all of whom had done ethnographic studies of Indians.

The TC-BIA project marked a high point in the use of anthropologists by Collier. A year after the project was initiated, the applied anthropology staff was disbanded. Although the first TC-BIA surveys were completed and others initiated on thirty-five reservations in the Southwest and Plains regions, few of the planning proposals originated by the Socio-Economic Division went any further, and the work of TC-BIA as a whole was interrupted by the onset of World War II. Even before the war, serious difficulties had emerged in applying the planning group's recommendations. The underlying concept had been to develop economic projects on the reservations which would encourage Indians to participate because they would fit into the normal framework of tribal activities rather than being simply the imposition of an alien society. In practice, however, neither the bureau nor SCS were prepared to give priority to these proposals over more ambitious plans drawn up by the technical staffs.[33]

This situation fits the conventional view of relations within the bureau as portrayed by Mekeel, Kluckohn, and Hackenberg. Proposals by the reformers for tailoring new programs to traditional Indian practices, based on research performed by social scientists, were rejected or ignored by technical staff and field administrators who preferred to rely on more orthodox plans initiated and dominated by whites, while excluding Indians from any participation except as laborers. But differences in views and practices between the reformers and the anthropologists, differences that had been gradually crystallizing during the work on Indian reorganization, also emerged in the development of the TC-BIA.

Three months after the initial surveys began, Collier's office received complaints from field agencies about the anthropologists, and he asked Woehlke to investigate.[34] Woehlke's response was a bitter attack on the social scientists involved in the survey, whose work, he asserted, was based "on a pseudo-technique through which immunity or superiority is maintained at the expense of reality." The anthropologists were not making a systematic effort to gather information and as a group they appeared hostile both to Indians and to local bureau employees. Somewhat inconsistently he singled out Ruth Underhill for having "developed a proprietary interest in the Papagos and Pimas," presumably at the cost of objectivity.[35]

This incident indicates the low opinion of the social scientists held by Woehlke, one of the men closest to Collier in the Indian Service, a veteran of the reform movement with a definite interest in the success of the project and by no means an old guard administrator with an ax to grind. To some extent this unhappy encounter could be attributed to inexperience on the part of the anthropologists in this type of policy-directed research and with the methods of anthropologists. The rift created by the TC-BIA between reformers and anthropologists, however, was never completely healed. In a confidential letter written to Gordon MacGregor after the termination of the applied anthropology staff, Allan G. Harper, Woehlke's successor at TC-BIA, intimated that Mekeel and his colleagues "through the inept handling of a rare opportunity" had "discredited anthropology in the Indian Service."[36]

Collier's opinion was important in this critical area because his reformer aides reflected his own view of the role of social scientists in the reorganization program. Collier has sometimes been mistakenly identified as an anthropologist. He was not, but he did have a background in sociology, had taught applied social science at San Francisco State Teachers College in the 1920s and became a professor of sociology after retiring from the Indian service in 1945.[37]

[32] See Rensis Likert, "Democracy in Agriculture—Why and How," *Farmers in a Changing World, Yearbook of Agriculture* (Washington, 1940), pp. 994-1002, on the development of survey research in the federal government. The surveys predated Likert's Division of Program Surveys in the Department of Agriculture by two years.

[33] Alan G. Harper, coordinator, TC-BIA, to Woehlke, Apr. 25, 1938, Collier Papers; Harper, "Planning for the Economic Independence of Indians," paper delivered at the National Conference on Social Work, Buffalo, N.Y., June 22, 1939, Collier Papers.

[34] Collier to Woehlke, Apr. 18, 1936, Collier Papers.

[35] Woehlke to Collier, Apr. 22, 1936, Collier Papers.

[36] Harper to Gordon MacGregor, Apr. 19, 1938, RG 114, NA.

[37] Collier discussed his intellectual background in *From Every Zenith*, pp. 68-76. He is incorrectly described as an anthropologist in Robert Burnette and John Koster, *The Road to Wounded Knee* (New York, 1974), p. 115.

In the course of the tribal organization effort, Collier sought to clarify his own conception of the role of anthropologists, analyzing incoming reports on the basis of their methods and usefulness, and circulating his comments. The report of one hapless consultant anthropologist on the Blackfeet was used as an example of a poor methodology producing useless results:

In general the investigator seems to have considered that all facts which came to his attention were equally subject to being passed on by himself out of some kind of inner equipment, knowledge or wisdom. Factors economic, biological, cultural, governmental, moral—they are all on the same plane. The result is a general essay on the Blackfeet and their situation which is forcused on nothing in particular.[38]

He went on to express doubts whether "even a mature and thoroughly equipped anthropologist . . . could produce what we need, working alone. There is needed a focus of varied techniques upon specific problems within limited areas."[39]

Despite this pessimism, Collier reacted favorably to a report by Morris Opler on the San Carlos Apache: "Opler proceeds from a discussion of surviving culture patterns to a discussion of [tribal] organization and economic planning." The discussion of culture patterns is given clinical application to a specific case in which the emphasis by bureau officials on cattle breeding to the detriment of traditional small-scale communal farming was eradicating remaining tribal institutions among these Indians. The report was enhanced by the fact that "all of [its] factual statements are so definite that they can be corroborated or found faulty, and the report . . . requires administrative action if the facts and interpretations be found valid."[40]

There were several common threads running through the critical remarks on the work of anthropologists in the Indian program. First was the orientation toward problems and problem-solving as the determinant of research. Collier and his advisers were not interested in descriptive studies, even those with important implications for theoretical issues, unless they were addressed to immediate problems on which action could be taken. This

is a rather commonplace observation about the differences between pure and applied science and deserves further investigation.

The dominant approach to research in cultural anthropology in this era was that of Franz Boas who shunned generalization and emphasized a descriptive, eclectic study of cultural groups. Reacting against a generation of amateurish theorizing in anthropology, Boas trained his students in the inductive approach and never attempted to synthesize his own research results. Furthermore, insofar as there was a Boas theory it stressed the unity of culture and the dangers involved in extracting elements from this unified whole for the purpose of analysis leading to generalization.[41]

The impact of this approach on anthropological research techniques has been vividly described:

Boas' emphasis on systematic fieldwork led to the collection of whatever data became available. . . . This exhaustive collection which seems at the time to have little or no connection with any specific problem is peculiarly a feature of the natural history approach . . . . There is a fascination in following the details of a subject just for its intrinsic interest. . . . Masses of data may therefore be worked over with no clear knowledge of what is to be gained at the end.[42]

This description resembles closely the kind of research Collier criticized as being "focused on nothing in particular."

The point is important because Indian militants of the present, such as Vine DeLoria, Jr., echo the criticisms of the reformers of the Collier era that much of the work of anthropologists among Indians has been of little direct benefit to Indian policy and represents a waste of time and funds that would be better spent on the economic rehabilitation of Indians.[43] This charge, regardless of its accuracy, reveals the continuing gap between the social scientist and the policy-oriented reformer.

A second point of difference between anthropologists and reformers related to the goals of the Indian reorganization program. The Indian New Deal was erected on the premise

---

[38] Collier, "Comment on Blackfeet Report by Mr. [David] Rodnick," Oct. 6, 1936, Tribal Organization files, RG 75, NA.
[39] Ibid.
[40] Collier, "Comment on Report by M. D. Opler on Indian Organization and Related Problems at San Carlos," Oct. 7, 1936, San Carlos file, Tribal Organization files, RG 75, NA.

[41] Marvin Harris, The Rise of Anthropological Theory (New York, 1968), pp. 277-289.
[42] M. G. Smith, "Boas' 'Natural History' Approach to Field Method," in W. Goldschmidt, ed., The Anthropology of Franz Boas (Washington, 1959), p. 54.
[43] Vine V. DeLoria, Jr., Custer Died for Your Sins (New York, 1968), pp. 91-98. DeLoria included in his charge the works on MacGregor, Thompson, et al., that Collier had sponsored in 1941-45 to generate direct policy proposals from anthropological research.

that traditional Indian tribal groups were strong enough so that with encouragement from the Indian service they could take over the tasks of administration and economic organization. The mission of the anthropologist was to identify these traditional groups and to ensure that the bureau did not inadvertently undermine them as it undertook to improve the economic status of the Indian. But the premise that tribes did exist and could be revitalized went unquestioned. The anthropologist in the field who found that the particular situation did not fit the premise faced a dilemma since this task in the administrative system was defined by an assumption contrary to fact.

The clearest example of this dilemma involved Louis Balsam and the Minnesota Chippewa. Balsam was an anthropologist from Clark University in Massachusetts who had studied the Navaho in the Southwest. After working with the applied anthropology staff on tribal organization in several regions, Balsam was sent to Minnesota to investigate the problems encountered by the bureau in organizing the scattered Chippewa settlements. Balsam's conclusions were that the Chippewa in no way constituted a tribe, that most of the Indians were completely assimilated into neighboring white communities and that "many mixed bloods are Indians for revenue solely," that is, in order to qualify for tribal annuities and allotments. He recommended that the bureau undertake to help Indians needing jobs to relocate to Minneapolis-St. Paul and other urban centers and that the management of Indian Affairs for those who remained be transferred to the state government.[44]

Balsam's proposals were not accepted by Collier and he was transferred to the Colville reservation in Oregon where he subsequently performed well as agency superintendent. The problem of organizing the Minnesota Chippewa was not resolved and three years later Archie Phinney, an Indian who had studied with Franz Boas before entering the bureau,

reiterated Balsam's comments on the absence of tribal cohesion among the Chippewa, and further argued that the imposition of a basically artificial tribal government had done little to improve the condition of most of the Indians.[45]

H. S. Mekeel faced a similar problem with the Dakota Sioux. Initially he was enthusiastic about the development of tribal organizations based on traditional local kinship groups called "tiospaye." Mekeel reluctantly concluded, however, after several months of investigation in 1935, that on the Pine Ridge reservation, inhabited by descendants of Red Cloud's followers, any effort to establish tribal council electoral districts on the basis of the tiospaye would create too much friction among already divided Indians. There the process of land allotment had wrecked traditional tribal institutions to the extent that any effort to revitalize them would create as many problems as it solved.[46] The Sioux reservations were the scene of recurrent, virtually insoluble difficulties relating to tribal organization throughout the Collier era.

At the same time, in areas where Indian cultural groups remained strong, anthropologists were able to work effectively with other bureau officials and to contribute their knowledge directly to the development of reorganization policy. Among Indian groups in the Southwest such as the Papago, Hopi, Pueblo, and Navaho, effective cooperation between reformers and social scientists was particularly marked. The work of Oliver LaFarge on tribal organization with the Hopi in Arizona was one of the best examples of this kind of cooperation.

LaFarge was well known as a novelist and Indian reformer; in 1930 he won the Pulitzer Prize for *Laughing Boy*, a novel about Indians. He was elected president of the National Association on Indian Affairs, which in 1937 merged with Collier's Indian Defense Association to form the Association on American Indian Affairs. LaFarge was also a trained ethnologist who had studied Indian tribes of the American Southwest as well as the ancient Meso-Ameri-

---

[44] Louis Balsam to Collier, Feb. 11, 1939, Collier Papers. These proposals resemble the national program designed for Indians after 1952, which was applied most thoroughly to the Klamath Indians of Washington state and the Menominee Indians of Wisconsin, with devastating results for those better-organized tribes. Balsam's recommendations were not the best solution to the problem, but represented an effort to deal with a situation in which the underlying assumptions of the Indian reorganization program apparently did not apply.

[45] Archie Phinney to Collier, Aug. 30, 1942. Tribal Organization records, RG 75, NA. Phinney did not repeat Balsam's recommendations, but urged that greater attention be expended on local community organizations rather than on tribal councils.

[46] Mekeel to Collier, Oct. 31, 1935, Pine Ridge file, Tribal Organization files, RG 75, NA.

can cultures. In 1936 he accepted Collier's offer to come work with the bureau to establish a tribal constitution and council for the Hopi.[47]

As early as 1934, he had written to Collier concerning the special problems of organizing the Hopi under a tribal constitution: the tradition of independence, if not hostility, among Hopi villages, and the influence of religious ceremonies that limited the political power of leaders.[48] In preparing a tribal constitution LaFarge concentrated on the villages and had lengthy discussions with the Indians. The document that emerged in October 1936 emphasized the autonomy of local villages and the primacy of customary law administered by village councils in most tribal affairs. In the course of his work, LaFarge also prepared a descriptive guide to Hopi institutions and leaders to help bureau administrators in their work.[49]

LaFarge was not the only anthropologist who adapted well to administrative tasks. Others whose work among the southwestern tribes was regarded highly in the bureau were Morris Opler, Oscar Lewis, and Clyde Kluckhohn. After the applied anthropology staff was disbanded, individual anthropologists were integrated into the regular Indian service organization. Several were appointed reservation superintendents where their specialized knowledge and approach could be effectively employed. Among those who served in this capacity were Sophie Aberle, superintendent for the United Pueblos; Louis Balsam who as noted earlier went to Colville reservation after finishing his work with the Chippewa; Gordon MacGregor who worked with TC-BIA, then was superintendent at the Blackfeet reservation and also participated in the Chicago project, writing a monograph on the Pine Ridge Sioux. Still others, including John Harrington, Julian H. Steward, and Archie Phinney worked directly out of the commissioner's office, coordinating reorganization programs at the regional level and working on special projects,

such as the development of a written Navaho language.[50]

These were, however, individual cases of successful adaptation. They did not constitute a systematic use of social scientists in applying programs based wholly or primarily on theories of culture change developed by anthropologists. The notion of reviving Indian self-determination by building up tribal organizations was appealing to Collier with his experience in community work, because the Indian tribes appeared to be the natural communities in which Indians lived. As we have noted, tribal institutions had disappeared beyond retrieval in many instances and where traditional Indian groups still existed, such as among the Pueblo, Papago, and Hopi in the Southwest, the village was the center of Indian life. This was also true in Alaska, which received special legislative consideration for this reason.[51] Anthropologists were brought in to provide expert knowledge within the framework of this tribal concept, not to question the basic policy or to speculate on alternate ways of helping the Indians.

The reform administrators were also committed to rapid and radical improvement in the physical and economic conditions of Indian life, and to ending white domination in Indian civil and personal affairs. It was important to them that these changes should not unnecessarily damage traditional Indian cultures, but more important that something be done, some practical measures be taken to help Indians. Anthropologists such as LaFarge and MacGregor who shared this commitment and sense of urgency worked easily and effectively with the bureau both as anthropologists and administrators. Others whose commitments to professional and academic standards and to current social science methodology impinged on their work as applied anthropologists encountered hostility not only from local old guard bureau employees but also from the reformers. □

[47] D'Arcy McNickle, Indian Man: A Life of Oliver LaFarge (Bloomington, Ind., 1971), pp. 89-93, 107.

[48] LaFarge to Collier, Sept. 21, 1934, Collier Papers.

[49] McNickle, Indian Man, pp. 107-115, describes in detail LaFarge's activities in Hopi organization, based on LaFarge's papers and records of the Bureau of Indian Affairs. McNickle, an important figure in the tribal organization unit during this period, is favorable to LaFarge. Collier, in From Every Zenith, pp. 218-219, was more skeptical of lasting benefit from LaFarge's Hopi constitution and the work of anthropologists on the Indian reorganization program.

[50] Ibid., pp. 106-107.

[51] A. L. Kroeber, "The Nature of the Land-Holding Group," Ethnohistory 2 (1955):303-314, argued that the concept of "tribe" did not reflect the reality of most North American Indians. The tribe was primarily a structure created by whites to identify Indian groups and leaders so that their social systems would be comprehensible to the European mind. In practice, Kroeber maintained, most Indians functioned within smaller groups, such as villages and bands or as extended family organizations. This argument may be overstated but it has support from data on relatively acculturated Indian groups in the twentieth century.

The Elusive Ballot: The Black Struggle Against the Texas Democratic White Primary, 1932–1945

DARLENE CLARK HINE*

WHILE THE MAJORITY OF AMERICANS SOUGHT RELIEF FROM THE miseries of the Great Depression and riveted their hopes for a better future on President Franklin D. Roosevelt and the New Deal, black Texans viewed with increasing dismay the seemingly endless repertoire of disfranchisement schemes white Texas democrats devised to render them politically impotent. The Democratic white primary as used in Texas was one of the most blatantly discriminatory and, perhaps, most effective techniques employed to keep blacks from voting. In response to and in spite of a black frontal assault on the political system, the Texas white primary received the sanction of the United States Supreme Court, the United States Department of Justice, and the Division of Investigation (later known as the Federal Bureau of Investigation). On the state level, the attorney general of Texas defended and the Texas Supreme Court upheld the white primary against the frequent attacks of black lawyers, citizens, and the National Association for the Advancement of Colored People (NAACP). By employing a variety of techniques Texas white politicians on the state and county levels were able to nullify the Supreme Court decisions of 1927 and 1932 which had seemed to benefit the cause of the black voters.[1]

For black Texans the thirties represented no political New Deal. Efforts to gain access to the political system met with frustration and repeated failure. The political ostracism of blacks in Texas was, in a larger view, but one example of the general legal and social plight of black southerners.

After the Civil War and the adoption of the Fourteenth and Fifteenth Amendments, blacks armed with the ballot gained access to political positions and became actively involved in political affairs in Texas. In the 1870s and 1880s, as Reconstruction concluded, whites in

*Darlene Clark Hine is assistant professor of history at Purdue University. Research for this article was facilitated by a grant from Africana Studies and Research Center at Purdue.

[1]*Nixon* v. *Herndon*, 273 U.S. 536–541 (1927); *Nixon* v. *Condon*, 286 U.S. 73–106 (1932).

the black belt counties of East Texas organized clubs, unions, and associations for the expressed purpose of ousting blacks from local, county, and state politics. These groups, formed under the banner of the Democratic party, restricted membership to white citizens. They usually held primary elections to select Democratic candidates who then ran without opposition in the fall general elections. During the next quarter century, through fraud, intimidation, and murder, white democrats in counties such as Grimes, Wharton, Fort Bend, and Harrison achieved their objective, and the political complexion of those counties where blacks were in the numerical majority or, at least, represented sizeable proportions of the total population changed as blacks were eliminated from the political system. By the turn of the century, Texas was a one-party state with the Democratic party reigning supreme. The practice of holding primaries, begun on the local level, had become a statewide phenomenon, and nomination in the Democratic primary was tantamount to election. The general election was little more than a formal acknowledgment of the results of the primary. Therefore, to be excluded from participation in the primaries, where the important decisions were made, constituted disfranchisement.[2]

In an effort to make Texas politics as white as possible, a poll tax amendment was added to the state's constitution in 1902. This measure, however, did not completely eradicate the black vote. In 1903, at the urging of Travis County representative, Alexander W. Terrell, the state legislature adopted a mandatory primary statute. Terrell argued that the adoption of such a measure would ensure against selling of votes. In 1905 the legislature amended the statute to permit county Democratic Executive Committee chairmen to establish voting qualifications. Although the statutes did not mention blacks specifically, it was implicitly understood that blacks would be barred from voting in the party's primaries. Because white democrats never unanimously agreed upon the effective enforceability of this method of black disfranchisement many county executive committee chairmen were opposed to the

---

2.Alwyn Barr, *Reconstruction to Reform: Texas Politics, 1876–1906* (Austin, 1971), 17, 193–196; J. Morgan Kousser, *The Shaping of Southern Politics: Suffrage Restrictions and the Establishment of the One-Party South, 1880–1910* (New Haven, 1974), 196–200; Lawrence D. Rice, *The Negro in Texas, 1874–1900* (Baton Rouge, 1971), 114–119; Cortez Arthur Ewing, *Primary Elections in the South: A Study in Uni-party Politics* (Norman, 1953), 8–9; Paul Lewinson, *Race, Class and Party: A History of Negro Suffrage and White Politics in the South* (New York, 1932), 112–113; Lawrence C. Goodwyn, "Populist Dreams and Negro Rights: East Texas as a Case Study," *American Historical Review*, LXXVI (December, 1971), 1435–1456.

proscription, and white candidates continued to solicit the black vote. The uncertainty surrounding the issue created a climate in which various factions and personalities within the Democratic party intensified agitation for universal black disfranchisement and a law which would remove the question from the political arena altogether.[3]

As a result of pressure from local whites in Bexar County—particularly from the district attorney, D. A. McAskill (who proclaimed that the black vote had to be annihilated because of the degree to which it was manipulated by unscrupulous white and black politicians), with the combined support of prohibitionists and probably many Ku Klux Klan members—the Texas state legislature in 1923 enacted a law which declared that: "In no event shall a negro be eligible to participate in a Democratic party primary election held in the State of Texas, and should a negro vote in a Democratic primary election, such ballot shall be void and election officials shall not count the same." Lawrence A. Nixon, a black El Paso dentist, and L. W. Washington, the local El Paso branch president of the NAACP, contacted the national NAACP headquarters in New York and requested assistance to launch a campaign to have the law declared unconstitutional.[4]

Nixon, a fourteen year resident of El Paso, was born in Marshall, Texas, in 1884. He received his medical training at Meharry Medical College in Nashville, Tennessee, and established his dental practice in El Paso in 1910. Until the 1923 white primary statute, Nixon had regularly voted in Democratic primary and general elections. He agreed to serve as the plaintiff in legal action against the white primary. Washington quickly mobilized the members of the local El Paso NAACP branch to raise funds and financially support the suit. They retained white at-

[3]Charles Kincheloe Chamberlain, "Alexander Watkins Terrell, Citizen, Statesman" (Ph.D. dissertation; University of Texas, 1956), 462–468; Rice, *Negro in Texas*, 136; Paul E. Isaac, "Municipal Reform in Beaumont, Texas, 1902–1909," *Southwestern Historical Quarterly*, LXXVIII (April, 1975), 421–422; Conrey Bryson, *Dr. Lawrence A. Nixon and the White Primary* (El Paso, 1974), 12; Harold M. Tarver, "The Whiteman's Primary (An Open Letter to D. A. McAskill, 1922)." A printed copy of this letter from a black resident of San Antonio is in the Library, Barker Texas History Center, University of Texas, Austin. This letter is listed in the library card catalogue under "Tarver."

[4]*Texas Revised Civil Statutes*, Article 3107 (1925) (quotation); J. Alston Atkins, *The Texas Negro and His Political Rights: A History of the Fight of Negroes to Enter the Democratic Primaries of Texas* (Houston, 1932), 6–24; Lewis Gould, *Progressives and Prohibitionists: Texas Democrats in the Age of Wilson* (Austin, 1973), 48–49; Alwyn Barr, *Black Texans: A History of Negroes in Texas, 1528–1971* (Austin, 1973), 134–135; Lewinson, *Race, Class and Party*, 113; Charles C. Alexander, *The Crusade for Conformity: The Ku Klux Klan in Texas, 1920–1930*, Texas Gulf Coast Historical Association, Vol. VI, No. 1 ([Houston], 1962), v; Charles C. Alexander, *The Ku Klux Klan in the Southwest* (Lex-

torney, Fred C. Knollenberg to handle the case on the state level. Under the close supervision of NAACP Legal Committee chairman, Arthur B. Spingarn; the association's president, Moorfield Storey; and the organization's superb attorney, Louis Marshall; Knollenberg laid the groundwork for the first two white primary cases. The Supreme Court decisions in these two cases seemed to bode well for Texas blacks. In the first case, *Nixon v. Herndon* (1927), the United States Supreme Court in an unanimous decision delivered by Justice Oliver Wendell Holmes declared the Texas statute unconstitutional and a violation of the Fourteenth Amendment. The court found the state of Texas guilty of using its authority to deny blacks ". . . the equal protection of the laws."[5] In sum, the state of Texas could not enact a law barring blacks from participation in Democratic primary elections. However, the question of whether or not blacks could vote in primary elections in the absence of a state law remained unanswered.

Undaunted, the Texas state legislature repealed the offending statute and granted the executive committee of the Democratic party the power to prescribe membership qualifications and voting requirements for its primaries. The executive committee, as expected, declared that only whites could vote in the primaries.[6] The NAACP, again using Nixon as plaintiff, filed another suit to contest this latest action. In the second case, *Nixon v. Condon* (1932), Supreme Court Justice Benjamin Cardozo wrote the majority opinion in a five to four decision. The court held that the state of Texas had simply delegated its responsibility and authority to a quasi-public body and that the action taken by the executive committee was merely an extension of the power of the state. "Delegates to the State's power have discharged their official functions in such a way as to discriminate invidiously between white citizens and black" and in so doing had again abridged the Fourteenth Amendment. The court continued, "The Fourteenth Amendment, adopted as it was with special solicitude for the equal protection of members of

ington, Kentucky, 1966), 121; Kenneth T. Jackson, *The Ku Klux Klan in the City, 1915–1930* (New York, 1967), 71–73; Bryson, *Dr. Lawrence A. Nixon,* 12–13; Arnold S. Rice, *The Ku Klux Klan in American Politics* (Washington, D.C., 1962), 15; Tarver, "The White-man's Primary"; San Antonio *Express,* July 23, 1922, May 11, 1923.

[5] *Nixon v. Herndon,* 273 U.S. 536–541 (1927) (quotation); *Nixon v. Herndon,* 47, S.C. 446 (1927); Bryson, *Dr. Lawrence A. Nixon,* 34–51.

[6] *House Journal 40th Legislature, First Called Session* (Austin, 1925), 228, 268–271, 328–331; *General and Special Laws of the State of Texas, 40th Legislature, First Called Session* (Austin, 1927), 193; Bryson, *Dr. Lawrence A. Nixon,* 53–55; *Yale Law Review,* XLI (1932), 1212.

the Negro race, lays a duty upon the court to level by its judgment these barriers of color."[7]

The national officers of the NAACP and black Texans were ecstatic about the decision, but white attorney Nathan Margold, who had argued the NAACP case before the Supreme Court, expressed dissatisfaction and advised caution. Although the decision in the particular case had been favorable to the plaintiff, Cardozo had implied that a Texas Democratic Party Convention, as the truly representative body of the Democratic party in the state of Texas, could determine qualifications for voting, even though the executive committee could not. Margold's fears were justified. White Texas democrats quickly took advantage of the limitations of the decision and devised a new strategy to accomplish black disfranchisement, which would not bruise the constitutional sensibilities of the Supreme Court judges. The chairman of the Harris County Democratic Executive Committee and editor of the Houston *Chronicle,* W. O. Huggins, presented a disfranchisement plan on May 24, 1932, at the annual meeting of the state Democratic Convention. The Huggins Plan, as it was named, called for the repeal of the resolution of the state Democratic Executive Committee and the adoption by the state convention of a new restrictive measure. He convinced his fellow democrats that the Supreme Court would not rule that the state convention was an agency of the state of Texas and, therefore, any resolution adopted would not be viewed as originating in the mandate of the law. The convention, thus persuaded, adopted the resolution: "Be it resolved that all white citizens of the State of Texas who are qualified to vote under the constitution and laws of the state shall be eligible to membership in the Democratic party and as such to participate in its deliberations."[8]

Black leaders of the Harris County Democratic Club, attorneys James M. Nabrit and Carter W. Wesley (both graduates of Northwestern University Law School and relatively new residents of Houston), attempted to appear before the Resolution Committee before the convention adjourned.[9] They were repeatedly repulsed because—according to the

---

[7]*Nixon v. Condon*, 286 U.S. 73–106 (1932).

[8]Ibid.; Nathan Margold to Felix Frankfurter, May 5, 1932; Carter W. Wesley to Fred C. Knollenberg, May 30, 1932, NAACP Papers (Library of Congress, Washington, D.C.), Box D-63; W. R. Smith, District Attorney General for the Western District at San Antonio, Texas, to the United States Attorney General, % Joseph Keenan, September 18, 1934, Department of Justice Files (National Archives, Washington, D.C.), Folder 72-100-5; Bryson, *Dr. Lawrence A. Nixon*, 72; "Nixon v. Condon," *Yale Law Review*, IV, No. 8 (June, 1932).

[9]James M. Nabrit to D. C. H., April 6, 1974, interview.

claim of W. O. Huggins, chairman of the Resolution Committee—the vote had already been taken. Incensed over what they considered to be a flagrant disregard of the two Nixon decisions, black Texans filed numerous suits requesting injunctions against local democratic leaders and organizations in Bexar, Grayson, Tarrant, and Jefferson counties. Black lawyers spearheaded the legal attacks. R. D. Evans of Waco, W. J. Durham of Sherman, and Nabrit and Wesley of Houston quickly prepared individual cases to prohibit white democratic officials from interfering with black voting in the primaries. All of the cases met with defeat in the local courts.[10]

C. A. Booker of San Antonio employed white attorney Carl Wright Johnson to handle his suit. Booker sought an injunction to compel the county Democratic Executive Committee (specifically, John K. Weber, chairman, C. O. Wolfe, secretary, and Adolph Lassner, presiding officer of precinct number seventy-three) to permit him and other qualified black voters to exercise their franchise in the Democratic primaries. Judge T. M. Kennerly ruled against Booker but suggested that there was a possibility that the Democratic Convention's adoption of the resolution was illegal, for if the state could not enact such a restrictive law perhaps the same prohibition applied to the convention.[11]

Booker appealed the ruling and Johnson presented the case before the federal District Court in San Antonio. On July 22, 1932, the day before the first Democratic primary, the court granted Booker's request for an injunction. The District Court based its decision to a large degree on the second Nixon case. Booker was delighted with the ruling and the prospect of voting. His pleasure, however, lasted only hours. Bexar County white democrats quickly protested the decision and later in the same day, the Fourth Circuit Court of Appeals set aside the injunction. The Appeals Court held that a political party was a voluntary organization and possessed the power to determine its membership. Booker subsequently appealed to the Texas Supreme Court which dismissed the case and allowed the Appellate Court's decision to stand. Attorney Knollenberg wrote Walter White, executive secretary of the

---

10Wesley to Knollenberg, May 30, 1932, NAACP Papers, Box D-63; Robert Wendell Hainsworth, "The Negro and the Texas Primaries," *Journal of Negro History*, XVIII (October, 1933), 433–435; *White v. Harris County Democratic Executive Committee* 60F (2d) 973 (S.D. Texas, 1932); *Informer* (Houston), July 30, 1932.

11Knollenberg to Walter White, August 31, 1932, The Lawrence A. Nixon Papers, (Lyndon B. Johnson Library, Austin, Texas); O. Douglas Weeks, "The White Primary," *Mississippi Law Journal*, VIII (December, 1935), 135–153; Hainsworth, "The Negro and the Texas Primary," 434, 436–438; *Informer* (Houston), July 30, 1932.

NAACP, that the Supreme Court of Texas had "rendered a decision . . . which virtually denied the right to participate, on account of the fact that they [Booker and Johnson] had not included all of the persons who may have been responsible for passing the resolution that all white citizens are entitled to participate" in Democratic party primaries.[12] Knollenberg's exasperated comments were prompted by the Supreme Court's reliance upon the relatively weak judicial concept that a decree against one official could not be applied to other similar officials.

In the meantime, El Paso blacks desired to file a case but the NAACP advised them against doing so. The national officers closely observed the various proceedings but refrained from entering the fights against the convention's resolution until all the decisions were handed down in the local litigations. Legal Committee chairman Arthur Spingarn and Secretary White reviewed the pleadings and decisions and carefully devised a strategy which they hoped would avoid the mistakes and failures encountered in the other cases. With two victories to their credit the NAACP officials were torn between a desire to avoid tarnishing their record with a defeat and the importance of maintaining a leading role in the white primary fight. Coupled with these considerations, was the organization's lack of adequate financial resources.[13]

By late October, 1932, the NAACP was prepared, both from a legal and a financial point of view to venture forth once again into the legal fray. Spingarn, with assistance from attorney Margold, whom the NAACP had retained "to direct its proposed legal campaign under the Garland Fund Appropriations," and James Marshall, son of the late Louis Marshall, decided to sue the election officials who had denied Nixon the right to vote in the July and August primaries.[14] James Marshall outlined the three arguments which the association would utilize in the third case, *Nixon* v. *McCann*. First, the statutes of Texas originally set forth the qualifications of voters in primary elections and created and organized the structure of the state convention. Therefore, the state

---

[12]*County Democratic Executive Committee in and for Bexar County et al.* v. *Booker*, 53 S.W. (2d) 123 (Texas, 1932); *County Democratic Executive Committee in and for Bexar County et al.* v. *C. A. Booker*, 52 S.W. (2d) 908 (Texas, 1932); Knollenberg to White, August 31, 1932, Nixon Papers (quotation).

[13]Nixon to Robert Bagnall, August 3, 1932; White to Nixon, August 8, 1932, NAACP Papers, Box D-63.

[14]Margold to Knollenberg, October 21, 1930, Arthur B. Spingarn Papers, Library of Congress, Washington, D.C.), Box 5. Louis Marshall died in October, 1929. The Garland Fund, formally known as the American Fund for Public Service, had been established by Charles Garland.

committed an unconstitutional act when it permitted the state convention to modify the qualifications for participation in primaries in such
a way as to create a distinction between voters on the grounds of race
and color. Second, the state created a quasi-public body to perform a
quasi-governmental function and any discrimination by the state convention on the ground of race or color was prohibited by the Constitution. Regardless of whether there were state regulations as to participation in primary elections, any discriminatory resolution passed by this
quasi-governmental body (the Democratic State Convention) would be
unconstitutional. Finally, the judges of election, acting as election officials, were vested with their power by the state and they did not have
the right to deprive Nixon of his right to vote. When they denied Nixon
his ballot because of color, they violated the Fourteenth Amendment of
the Constitution.[15]

Fifteen months later, Federal District Court Judge Charles Boynton
held Justice Cardozo's decision in *Nixon* v. *Condon* binding and
declared that the resolution of the state Democratic convention unconsti-
tutionally deprived Nixon of his right to vote in the primaries. Boynton decided that the resolution passed by the convention did not exclude blacks from voting but merely established that white persons who
were qualified voters could participate in the primaries. Thus, the judge
continued, when the executive committee instructed the El Paso County
chairman to exclude blacks, it was an action of the executive committee
and not the convention. Ben Howell, attorney for the election officials
and the Democratic executive committee of El Paso did not appeal the
decision. Nixon was awarded five dollars for damages. This was the first
victory for the NAACP in a Texas white primary case in a court lower
than the United States Supreme Court.[16]

The decision in the *Nixon* v. *McCann* litigation was little more than
a pyrrhic victory. It had almost no effect on the political status of blacks
in Texas. Due to the lack of unanimity among white Texans some
blacks were allowed to vote in certain counties even before the *Nixon*
v. *Condon* decision and in spite of the Democratic party's resolution.[17]
But for the majority of black Texans, voting in Democratic primaries

---

[15]Marshall to Knollenberg, April 18, 1933, NAACP Papers, Box D-63.

[16]El Paso *Herald Post*, February 7, 1934; NAACP Press Release: "Third Texas Primary
Case Won in Federal Court," February 9, 1934, NAACP Papers, Box D-63.

[17]NAACP Press Release: "Outcome of Attempts of Negroes to Vote at Democratic Primaries in Texas on July 25, 1932," August 11, 1932, NAACP Papers, Box D-63; *Informer*
(Houston), July 30, 1932.

remained just a hope. The constant reminder of their political impotence goaded them into developing community-based political organizations through which they attempted to gain entry into the political process. Working from the outside was never satisfactory and blacks in Dallas, Houston, and San Antonio continued agitating for their political rights. Because Texas blacks refused to let the question of their voting in primary elections die, it became a perennial issue.[18] All white Democratic aspirants to political office confronted this issue and had to deal with it at one level or another during their election campaigns.

The gubernatorial election year of 1934 served as another setback for black Texans. Their defeats in the local courts in 1932 were compounded by political problems in 1934. There were seven contenders for the gubernatorial office in the 1934 primaries. One candidate, however, occupied a unique position insofar as the issue of black voting in the primaries was concerned. James V. Allred, born on March 29, 1899, at Bowie, Texas, had become the attorney general of the state in 1930. Allred had earned an impressive reputation as a trust-busting attorney general who was not afraid to challenge big business.[19] In 1934, having served two terms, Allred entered the governor's race and was promptly besieged with demands for some definitive statement of his position on black voting in that year's Democratic primaries.

Allred found himself confronted with a dilemma: should he or should he not use his official position for political advantage? As a gubernatorial candidate he was cognizant that many blacks supported one of his opponents, C. C. McDonald, and that any decision he rendered or statement he made regarding white primaries could affect the outcome of the election. His campaign advisers and organizers continually warned him that the black vote was going against him. The chairman of the Allred for Governor Club of Houston, Judge C. A. Teagle, for example, insinuated that one of his opponents was going to buy the black vote: "I know from experience what the negro vote means and that a little money will go a long way with them." Another principal Allred organizer, Jack Todd of Jefferson County, warned the attorney general of the adverse consequences of the black vote. The white pri-

18Melvin James Banks, "The Pursuit of Equality: The Movement for First Class Citizenship Among Negroes in Texas, 1920–1950," (Ph.D. dissertation; Syracuse University, 1962), 221–235; *Informer* (Houston), September 10, 1932.

19Knollenberg to James V. Allred, January 26, 1932, Nixon Papers; Walter B. Moore, *Governors of Texas* (Dallas, 1963), 31; Walter Prescott Webb, H. Bailey Carroll, and Eldon S. Branda (eds.), *The Handbook of Texas* (3 volumes; Austin, 1952, 1976), III, 21–22.

mary was a "hot issue" in Beaumont and some blacks had openly endorsed one of his opponents. Todd suggested that if Allred would wire him an endorsement of the white primary, it would "make lots of votes" in Beaumont.[20] In both of these counties blacks comprised a sizeable proportion of the total population.

Finally, as a result of the advice from his supporters and his belief that the opposition was using the black vote to his disadvantage, attorney general/gubernatorial candidate Allred issued an official declaration. In his "Opinion" Allred maintained that blacks were prohibited from the Democratic primaries under the resolution adopted in the Houston Convention of 1932: "In view of the resolution passed by the State Convention of the Democratic Party on May 24, 1932 you are respectfully advised that, in our opinion, negroes are not entitled to participate in the primary elections of the Democratic Party. . . ." Furthermore, he added, the legitimacy of the current resolution passed by the state Democratic Convention was based on the *Nixon* v. *Condon* decision. He found additional support for his "Opinion" in the ruling of the Texas Supreme Court in *County Democratic Executive Committee in and for Bexar County* v. *C. A. Booker*.[21]

The factionalism within the Texas Democratic party was apparent in the divided and heated reactions of county chairmen and the white press to Allred's "Opinion." Many Democratic county chairmen heartily approved Allred's decree, particularly those who were involved in local power struggles. In Jefferson County the county Democratic chairman, J. R. Edmunds, had unsuccessfully attempted to restrict Jefferson County balloting to white democrats. His actions had created divisions within the county's Democratic party leadership. Allred's ruling according to newspaper accounts, came just in time to unify Jefferson County's party organization. A few county chairmen and editors of major white dailies disagreed with Allred's "Opinion." Chairman Will A. Morriss, Jr., of the Bexar County Democratic executive committee decided that he would permit the approximately four to five thousand qualified black voters in Bexar County to vote. Morriss openly stated that the attorney general had acted without full knowledge and that he

---

20C. A. Teagle to Sidney Benhow, Assistant Attorney General, May 17, 1934 (first quotation); Jack Todd to Dick Watters, July 12, 1934, (second and third quotations), James V. Allred Papers (University of Houston, Houston, Texas), Containers 84–85.

21Allred to D. B. Wood, Williamson County Attorney, June 9, 1934, NAACP Papers, Box D-63.

would not adhere to the ruling.[22] The Dallas *Journal's* editor reportedly criticized the "Opinion" as "mighty poor law." The editor contended that it was "manifestly absurd" for the attorney general to assert, on the one hand, that the party was not the creature of the state and, on the other, that the attorney general, as the servant of the state, had the right to decide who was eligible to vote in the primary.[23] These responses indicated that the efforts to bar blacks were not unanimously supported by all white democrats in Texas.

Two black men from Jefferson County responded to this latest assault on their franchise rights. W. H. Bell and E. L. Jones, without NAACP assistance, filed a petition for a writ of mandamus against the governor of Texas, the attorney general, the state Democratic executive committee, the members of the Jefferson County Democratic executive committee, and the various election officers in Jefferson County. To guard against the court ruling against them on grounds of faulty pleadings and failure to name the right parties in the suit, Bell and Jones named approximately 200 individuals as defendants. The object of the suit was to invoke the jurisdiction of the court to require the election officials to permit them to vote in the Democratic primaries on July 28, 1934.

Eight days before the July primary the Texas Supreme Court denied Bell and Jones the mandamus. It held that since no other Democratic convention had revoked the resolution of 1932, it was still valid and was the policy of the Democratic party of the state. The court drew upon the decision in the case of *Bexar County et al.* v. *Booker* to support its ruling. In that case Special Associate Justice S. S. Searcy had proclaimed that "the Democratic Party of Texas [was] a voluntary political association," and that its convention possessed "the power to determine who shall be eligible for membership in the party, and, as such, eligible for participation in the primaries. A study of the election laws of Texas and their history can lead to no other conclusion." The Supreme Court of Texas concluded that, "The Attorney General of this state, in a recent able opinion, has likewise sustained the validity of the resolution passed by the Houston Convention. With the opinion of the Court of Civil Appeals at San Antonio and with that of the Attorney General we are in accord."[24]

22Bay City *Tribune*, July 14, 1934; Fort Worth *Star-Telegram*, July 8, 1934.

23The Dallas *Journal* as quoted in *Informer* (Houston), July 21, 1934.

24Tyler *Telegram*, July 21, 1934; *Bell et al.* v. *Hill, County Clerk, et al.*, 74 S.W. (2d).

An elated Allred immediately issued a statement asking every candidate for governor to request all election officials to follow the opinion of the court. In a speech before a cheering crowd of 700 in Longview, Texas, Allred pointed out that when he first released his "Opinion" the campaign manager of one of the candidates took issue with it and two of the "big city newspapers" attacked it. He added emphatically, "I now call upon the newspapers and all the candidates to follow the Supreme Court's opinion and keep the Democratic Party of Texas a white man's party."[25] His timely delivery of the "Opinion" proved to be the right political strategy. It won him the white vote and eliminated the black vote. The Texas Supreme Court's decision in *Bell* v. *Hill* unquestionably strengthened his candidacy.[26] (Predictably, Allred won the gubernatorial election.)

Ironically, Nixon and his business associate in El Paso were the only two blacks allowed to vote in the July and August primaries. White democrats chose not to risk involvement in another court action, so they provided Nixon with a ballot marked "colored," which Knollenberg thought a very "smart trick." The El Paso attorney theorized that this allowed election officials to ignore the ballot once cast and yet give the impression of compliance with the federal law as interpreted by the Supreme Court.[27]

Allred's "Opinion" and the *Bell* v. *Hill* decision seemingly closed another door on the possibility of blacks voting in Texas Democratic primaries. R. D. Evans of the National Bar Association, the formal organization of black lawyers, and Walter White of the NAACP were not at all satisfied with the turn of events in Texas. Leaders of both organizations, acting independently of one another, filed complaints with the United States Attorney General's Office and requested investigations of election practices in Texas. The National Bar Association's president, E. Washington Rhodes, expressed concern about the *Bell* v. *Hill* decision while White questioned the legality of Allred's "Opinion." Assistant Attorney General Joseph Keenan promised to give careful consideration to the matter to determine if any federal criminal laws had been violated. He also suggested that White contact Rhodes and assist

---

113–122 (Texas, 1934) (quotations). The case was argued before Texas Supreme Court, July 19, 1934.

25Tyler *Telegram*, July 21, 1934.

26John Speer to Allred, July 30, 1934, Allred Papers, Container 83.

27Nixon to White, September 8, 1934; Knollenberg to White, September 21, 1934 (quotation), NAACP Papers, Box D-63.

him in furnishing affidavits from black Texans who were denied ballots in the last primaries.[28]

From his office in Waco, Texas, attorney R. D. Evans alerted black lawyers across the state to the necessity of sending as many affidavits as possible to the attorney general's office. Scores of affidavits from the cities of Waco, Beaumont, and El Paso, and from Harris, Travis, Jefferson, and McLennan counties were forwarded to White to be sent to Keenan.[29] Rhodes and White met to work out other strategies to compliment the affidavits and to increase the pressure on the Department of Justice. To dramatize the role of the black attorneys in the struggle Rhodes proposed the appointment of a delegation of leading black lawyers who would go to Washington, D.C., to discuss the matter of the white primary directly with the attorney general. Evans enthusiastically supported Rhodes's idea of a delegation but White disagreed. White recommended that the National Bar Association and the NAACP jointly draft a memorandum brief for the attorney general setting forth not only the legal grounds on "which the Attorney General *may* act, but citing the grounds on which he *must* act if the law so indicated."[30]

Keenan forwarded the affidavits and related material to attorney generals S. D. Bennett of the Eastern District at Beaumont, Douglas W. McGregor of the Southern District at Houston, and W. R. Smith of the Western District at San Antonio. He ordered them to conduct a special investigation to review the allegations of voting discrimination and illegalities in violation of the United States Supreme Court decisions in the two Nixon cases. They were further asked to determine whether criminal prosecution of election officials was warranted under the Civil Rights Statute of Sections 19 and 20 of the Criminal Code.[31] Black lawyers in Texas exerted continuous pressure on the district attorney generals and carefully monitored the progress of the investigations.

28E. Washington Rhodes to Attorney General Homer S. Cummings, July 24, 1934; Joseph B. Keenan to Rhodes, July 26, 1934; White to Cummings, July 27, 1934; Keenan to White, July 28, 1934; White to Keenan, July 30, 1934; Department of Justice Files, Folder 72-100-5; White to Arthur Spingarn, Summary of all of the developments concerning the Justice Department and the NAACP, August 7, 1934, NAACP Papers, Box D-63.

29White to Keenan, August 3, 6, 1934, Department of Justice Files, Folder 72-100-5; White to Rhodes, August 9, 1934, NAACP Papers, Box D-63.

30Rhodes to White, August 1, 1934; R. D. Evans to Rhodes, August 15, 1934; White to Rhodes, August 9, 21 (quotation), 1934, NAACP Papers, Box D-63.

31Keenan to S. D. Bennett, U.S. Attorney, Beaumont, Texas, August 11, 1934; Keenan to Douglas W. McGregor, U.S. Attorney, Houston, Texas, August 11, 1934; Keenan to William R. Smith Jr., U.S. Attorney, San Antonio, Texas, August 18, 1934; Keenan to White, August 10, 1934; Bennett to Keenan, August 16, 1934; McGregor to Keenan, August 16, 1934; Smith to Keenan, August 21, 1934, Deparment of Justice Files, Folder 72-100-5.

Smith became defensive and refused to give out any voting information whereupon blacks suggested to the U.S. attorney general that Smith was remiss in conducting the investigations.[32]

The efforts of the NBA and the NAACP accomplished very little. The district attorney generals all agreed that prosecution of election officials who refused ballots to blacks was inadvisable. McGregor's staff concluded that "no grand jury in Texas would indict these officials, nor would a jury convict them." S. D. Bennett wrote, "I am of the opinion that criminal prosecution under the provisions of the statutes referred to could not be successfully maintained."[33]

Smith, perhaps because of the close attention blacks focused on him, filed a rather detailed report based upon James V. Allred's "Opinion" and the two cases adjudicated in Texas: *Bexar County* v. *Booker* and *Bell* v. *Hill*. Smith argued that the Texas Court of Civil Appeals in the case of *Bexar County* v. *Booker* had upheld the resolution adopted by the Democratic Party Convention on May 24, 1932. In that opinion the court had ruled that the Convention's resolution was in keeping with the expression of the *Nixon* v. *Condon* decision which had "strongly indicated that the Convention of the party itself could restrict its membership and determine the qualifications thereof in any way determined upon by the Convention." He concluded that the election officials who refused to allow blacks to cast their ballots were acting in good faith and without any criminal intent in following the decision of the court in the Booker case and in adhering to the "Opinion" of the attorney general of Texas. Furthermore, he added, the Supreme Court of Texas had sustained the Allred "Opinion" in the *Bell* v. *Hill* litigation.[34]

Shortly before these reports were filed, J. Edgar Hoover, director of the Justice Department's Division of Investigation assigned a special agent from the San Antonio Division Office to look into the issue of voting irregularities. The special agent in charge of the investigation arrived at the same conclusion as Smith. Agent Gus T. Jones informed Hoover that on the basis of preliminary study, no investigation was warranted because "the denial of the negro the right to vote was not

32White to Keenan, September 4, 1934; Keenan to Smith, September 6, 1934; Smith to Keenan, September 13, 1934, Department of Justice Files, Folder 72-100-5.

33Carlos G. Watson, Assistant to District Attorney General Douglas W. McGregor to the United States Attorney General, October 6, 1934 (first quotation); Bennett to the United States Attorney General, January 17, 1935 (second quotation), Department of Justice Files, Folder 72-100-5.

34Smith to the Attorney General, September 18, 1934, Department of Justice Files, Folder 72-100-5.

a matter of fact but a matter of law." That is, the Texas Supreme Court's decision in *Bell* v. *Hill* and the resolution of the Democratic Convention provided the legal justification for the disfranchisement of blacks.[35]

Keenan reviewed the reports and informed White that the Department of Justice would not institute criminal proceedings and that the case was closed. He summarized the findings and advised White that it would be difficult if not impossible to prove that the election officials had any criminal intent to break the law or that they had not acted in apparent good faith pursuant to a state statute and its interpretation by the Supreme Court of Texas. Keenan added that the *Nixon* v. *Condon* decision had not decided that white democrats violated the constitutional rights of blacks by excluding them from participation in the party's primaries. That, according to Keenan, would have to be decided in a new case by the United States Supreme Court. Until then, the present practice in Texas was constitutional.[36]

By the end of 1934 the NAACP, black lawyers, and local black leaders in Texas had almost reached a dead end. After a decade of obstinateness and legal maneuvering white Texas democrats who favored disfranchisement of blacks had seemingly achieved their objective. The Allred "Opinion," the *Bell* v. *Hill* decision, and the Justice Department's decision not to intercede left blacks virtually defenseless and voteless.

This disheartening situation steadily deteriorated in 1935. In 1934 the black law firm of Atkins, Nabrit and Wesley had filed a suit at the request of Houston barber and political activist, R. R. Grovey, against County Clerk Albert Townsend for denying Grovey an absentee ballot to vote in the Democratic primary of that year. The NAACP disapproved of the suit and the way it was presented and advised the Houston lawyers against pursuing the case. J. Alston Atkins, a Yale University Law School graduate, reasoned that because the county clerk was an elected official of the state of Texas and not an official of the Democratic party he could be charged with violation of the Fourteenth and Fifteenth Amendments for denying Grovey an absentee ballot. At-

---

[35]John Edgar Hoover, Director of the Division of Investigation to Keenan, October 17, 1934; Gus T. Jones, Special Agent in Charge of the San Antonio Division Office to Hoover, October 8, 1934 (quotation); McGregor to Jones, October 6, 1934; H. A. Fisher, Attorney, to Keenan, November 16, 1934, Department of Justice Files, Folder 72-100-5.

[36]Keenan to White, December 28, 1934, NAACP Papers, Box C-285; Keenan to Hoover, January 9, 1935, Department of Justice Files, Folder 72-100-5.

torney Atkins then, in a striking move, took the case before a justice of the peace court instead of filing it in Houston Federal Court. He asked for ten dollars damage to Grovey for his loss of the voting privilege. The justice of the peace court ruled against Grovey, whereupon the lawyers asked the United States Supreme Court for a writ of certiorari from the justice of the peace court. By this mechanism Atkins was able to bypass the Appeals Court.[37]

The United States Supreme Court agreed to review the transcript of the case on March 11, 1935, and delivered a devastating decision less than three weeks later on April Fools Day, 1935. Justice Owen J. Roberts wrote a unanimous opinion that was an outright rejection of the black Texan's appeal. The Supreme Court held that: "We find no ground for holding that the respondent has in obedience to the mandate of the law of Texas discriminated against the petitioner or denied him any right guaranteed by the Fourteenth and Fifteenth Amendments." The decision rested to a considerable extent on *Bell v. Hill*.[38]

The decision stunned the blacks in Texas and across the country. Under banner headlines Carter Wesley declared in the *Informer*: "In 1935 the Supreme Court of the United States in *Grovey* v. *Townsend* makes political slavery in Texas and the South constitutional, just as the Dred Scott decision made bodily slavery constitutional seventy-eight years ago." When the Associated Negro Press asked William J. Thompkins in the Recorder of Deeds Office in Washington, D.C., to comment on the decision, he stated: "I regard this decision as being infinitely worse than the Dred Scott decision. . . ." He continued, it "affects directly every colored person in the State of Texas and might eventually affect every adult man and woman in every state in the Union." NAACP executives were equally disturbed by the Grovey decision. Secretary Walter White noted in his autobiography, "It should not be difficult to imagine the gloom we all felt. Years of hard work and heavy expense appeared to have gone for naught."[39]

37James M. Nabrit to D. C. H., April 6, 1974, interview; Walter White, *A Man Called White: The Autobiography of Walter White* (Bloomington, Indiana, 1970), 88.

38Bryson, *Dr. Lawrence A. Nixon*, 74–75; Banks, "The Pursuit of Equality," 220–232; *Grovey v. Townsend*, 295 U.S. 45–55 (1935) (quotation); Walter Lindsey, "Black Houstonians Challenge the White Democratic Primary, 1921–1944" (M.A. thesis; University of Houston, 1969), 26–27.

39*Informer* (Houston), April 6, 1935 (first quotation); William J. Thompkins to Marvin Hunter McIntyre, Assistant Secretary to President Roosevelt, April 23, 1935 (second and third quotations) (Franklin Delano Roosevelt Library, Hyde Park, New York); White, *A Man Called White*, 88 (fourth quotation).

The *Grovey* decision should not be considered in isolation. The Supreme Court justices who rendered the *Grovey* decision handed down, on the same day, a landmark civil rights decision in a case originating out of the famous Scottsboro trials. Nine black youths were accused of raping two white girls in Alabama. After a hasty trial, amidst an atmosphere of intense racial hostility, the boys had been summarily convicted and sentenced to die. The communists became involved in the case after the initial trials and in two separate instances (1932 and 1935) appealed the convictions to the United States Supreme Court. In 1932 in *Powell* v. *Alabama* the Supreme Court overturned the convictions on the basis that the defendants "were not accorded the right to counsel in any substantial sense"; thus their constitutional rights to due process had been violated.[40] A retrial resulted in the same verdict and a return to the United States Supreme Court. Chief Justice Charles Evans Hughes on April 1, 1935, delivered the unanimous decision in *Norris* v. *Alabama* invalidating the convictions on the grounds that blacks were systematically excluded from jury service.[41]

The Norris decision gave blacks back their rights to serve on juries which would, perhaps, mitigate the excesses of southern justice meted out to blacks. In most southern states, however, jurors were selected from the pool of property-owning, poll tax-paying voters. Blacks who could not afford to vote did not serve on juries. The ineffectiveness of the *Norris* decision was further highlighted by the attitudes and actions of white lawyers who utilized their peremptory challenge to keep off blacks who were called for grand and petit juries.[42]

In another decision delivered the following month, the Supreme Court retreated from ruling upon other civil liberties, some as fundamental as the freedom of speech. On May 20, 1935, the Supreme Court in a six to three decision dismissed Angelo Herndon's appeal. Herndon, a young black communist, was convicted by the Georgia Supreme Court of attempting to incite a communist-led insurrection or conspiracy against the state of Georgia. Before the United States Supreme Court Herndon's defense attorneys presented an eloquent plea for the protection of free speech and other civil liberties and argued that Georgia's

---

[40]*Powell* v. *Alabama*, 287 U.S. 45–77 (1932).

[41]*Norris* v. *Alabama*, 294 U.S. 587–599 (1935); Dan T. Carter, *Scottsboro: A Tragedy of the American South* (Baton Rouge, 1969), 319–324.

[42]Henry J. Abraham, *Freedom and the Court: Civil Rights and Liberties* (2nd ed.; New York, 1972), 331–333; Ralph Bunche, *The Political Status of the Negro in the Age of FDR*, Dewey W. Grantham, editor, (Chicago, 1973), 297.

insurrection law violated the due process clause of the Fourteenth Amendment. The majority opinion, prepared by Justice George Sutherland, declared that Herndon had failed to raise the correct constitutional questions at the appropriate time and thus the court lacked jurisdiction. The dissenting opinion, written by Justice Benjamin Cardozo with Justices Louis Brandeis and Harlan Fiske Stone concurring, asserted that the court did have jurisdiction and was essentially side stepping the complicated constitutional issues posed.[43] Occurring as they did within a six week span, these three court cases reflect the United States Supreme Court's ambivalence in regards to the civil rights of blacks. The *Norris* decision was pro-civil rights although it had limited effect in practice. The *Grovey* decision was blatantly against civil rights and the *Herndon* decision evaded the issue.

Nine years elapsed before the NAACP and black Texans were again able to challenge the white primary before the United States Supreme Court. During the interim, significant domestic changes and international crises occurred. Only two of the nine justices who had ruled on *Grovey* remained on the Supreme Court: Owen Roberts and Harlan F. Stone. The seven justices appointed by Franklin D. Roosevelt were of decidedly more liberal views. The United States' entry into World War II and the rise of Nazism in Germany with its concomitant emphasis on theories of racial superiority had forced many Americans to question the continued denial of basic citizenship rights to blacks. The hypocrisy of fighting a war against Nazism and for the freedom of people external to America while denying the rights of first-class citizenship to the Negro population at home had become obvious. The situation was almost too much for most black Americans to bear. With renewed vigor blacks, during the late thirties and the war years, pushed forward and increased their demands to be treated as equals, particularly in the political arena.

As early as 1936 the NAACP Legal Committee, under the leadership of Thurgood Marshall began to lay the groundwork for a new white primary case. Acute shortage of funds prevented Marshall and the NAACP from developing a case before the 1938 elections. This did not deter leaders in the Houston branch, however. C. F. Richardson, editor of the Houston *Defender*, William Greene, William M. Drake, a prominent Houston physician, and Julius White, an active leader in the

---

[43]Charles Martin, *The Angelo Herndon Case and Southern Justice* (Baton Rouge, 1976), 108, 149–150; *Herndon v. Georgia*, 295 U.S. 446–455 (1935).

Harris County Negro Democratic Club, filed the case of *C. F. Richardson et al.* v. *Executive Committee of the Democratic Party for the City of Houston, Harris County*, asking for damages for deprivation of the right to vote and for an injunction to prevent further interference with black voters. The suit focused on whether blacks could be prohibited from voting in municipal primary elections.

Shortly after the hearings, Judge T. M. Kennerly denied the requests for a preliminary injunction and refused to consider any of the other contentions of the plaintiffs. Kennerly maintained that there was no substantial difference between this case and one that had been brought to the court in 1933, in *Drake* v. *Executive Committee of the Democratic Party for the City of Houston*. In both cases the plaintiffs had requested an injunction against the Democratic party of the city. The decision in the *Drake* case and the Texas Supreme Court's decision in *Bell*, according to Kennerly, had fully discussed and settled the laws involved in the whole primary issue. Moreover, he added, the United States Supreme Court had delivered the final word in *Grovey* v. *Townsend*.[44]

By 1941 the NAACP was ready to move. In January, 1941, NAACP attorneys filed suit in behalf of Sidney Hasgett, a black Houston, Texas, hod carrier, against election judges Theodore Werner and John H. Blackburn. They asked for five thousand dollars in damages for the refusal to permit Hasgett to vote in the Democratic run-off primary held on August 24, 1940. District Justice T. M. Kennerly set the trial date for April 14, 1941. After being postponed several times, the case was heard in court on April 25; on May 3 Judge Kennerly ruled against Hasgett.[45] While the *Hasgett* v. *Werner* litigations were underway, a case dealing with primary elections in Louisiana was making its way up to the United States Supreme Court. Black attorneys in Texas and the NAACP immediately focused their attention on the case of *United States* v. *Classic*.

Although the *Classic* case was not concerned with questions of race, it

[44]C. F. Richardson to Charles Houston. July 25, 1938, NAACP Papers, Box D-92; *Informer* (Houston), October 22, November 5, 1938; *C. F. Richardson et al.* v. *Executive Committee of the Democratic Party of the City of Houston* 20F (2d) (S.D. Texas, 1938); Memorandum and copy of Judge T. M. Kennerly's decision, Legal Files, November 2, 1938, NAACP Papers, Box D-92.

[45]Memorandum from Legal Department to members of the National Legal Committee, Re: Activities and Developments during January and February, 1941, Texas Primary Case, *Hasgett* v. *Werner*, NAACP Papers, Unprocessed Files; *Informer* (Houston), February 8, March 8, April 5, 19, 26, May 10, 1941.

was a harbinger of things to come. In the *Classic* case five white commissioners of election including Patrick B. Classic were charged with conducting a primary election under Louisiana law to nominate a candidate of the Democratic party for the United States House of Representatives in which they willfully altered and falsely counted and certified the ballots cast in the primary election. The United States Supreme Court was called upon to decide whether the right of qualified voters to vote in the Louisiana primary and to have their ballots counted was a right "secured by the Constitution."[46]

Chief Justice Stone delivered the five-to-three opinion. The court held that "the authority of Congress . . . includes the authority to regulate primary elections when . . . they are a step in the exercise by the people of their choice of representative in Congress." Thurgood Marshall termed the decision "striking and far reaching" and after brief consideration persuaded the NAACP and black Texans to drop their appeal of the *Hasgett* decision and begin a new case more in accordance with the *Classic* decision.[47]

On April 20, 1942 Marshall argued the new *Smith* v. *Allwright* case before the District Court. In his presentation he stressed that the Democratic party in Texas possessed few characteristics of a closed organization. He observed that it had no constitution, no by-laws, membership rolls, etc. Marshall further asserted that under the facts and laws, the case was almost identical to that of *United States* v. *Classic*. Neither the District Court nor the Circuit Court of Appeals agreed with Marshall's interpretations. He subsequently petitioned for a writ of certiorari in the United States Supreme Court.

In January, 1944, the Supreme Court heard final arguments in *Smith* v. *Allwright*. After deliberation, Justice Stanley Reed author of the eight-to-one decision declared the white primary unconstitutional. Neither the state nor the Democratic party possessed the power to deny blacks the right to vote in primary elections. The court acknowledged that the primaries were an integral part of the election process and effectively controlled the choice of the officials elected.[48]

---

[46]*United States* v. *Classic et al.*, 313 U.S. 299–341 (1941).

[47]Ibid. (first quotation); Richard Claude, *The Supreme Court and the Electoral Process* (Baltimore, 1970), 31–36; Thurgood Marshall to Belford V. Larson, December 19, 1941 (second quotation), NAACP Papers, Unprocessed Files; Judge William H. Hastie to D. C. H., November 27, 1973, interview.

[48]*Smith* v. *Allwright*, 321 U.S. 649–670 (1940); *United States* v. *Classic* 61 S.C. 1031, 85 L.Ed. 867 (1941); Robert E. Cushman, "The Texas 'White Primary' Case—*Smith* v. *All*-

White Texans did not immediately cave in to the *Smith* decision. They made yet another attempt to preserve, if not resurrect, the white primary. For sixty years white citizens in Fort Bend County had held preliminary elections under the auspices of the Jaybird Democratic Association. The Jaybirds conducted what amounted to privately financed "pre-primary" primaries to endorse candidates for the Democratic nomination. Of course these pre-primary primaries were open to whites only. In 1952 the United States Supreme Court agreed to hear arguments in *Terry et al.* v. *Adams et al.*, the last of the white primary cases. The Court ruled that the Jaybird Association was more than a private club and that exclusion of blacks violated the Fifteenth Amendment. Thus sounded the death knell of the Democratic white primary.[49]

It would be incorrect to assert that the 1930s witnessed a steady deterioration in the status of southern blacks. Their status was already fixed on the lowest rung of southern society. While many blacks had made significant strides since the Reconstruction era, during the 1930s the masses were still relegated to an inferior position within America. They remained economically destitute, largely uneducated, socially segregated, and politically powerless. The court cases and legal battles of the thirties reflect the extent of black debasement and concomitantly the lengths to which whites would go to preserve white supremacy. The struggles in the judicial arena then, merely lifted the veil and permitted the world to observe the underside of American justice.

Most accounts of the white primary struggle center around the final and determinitive cases heard and ruled upon by the Supreme Court in the 1940s. The impact of Supreme Court decisions was largely contingent upon the political predispositions and social attitudes of the black and white participants in the struggle. To ignore their roles and the events which transpired before a case reached the High Tribunal results in an incomplete understanding of the effects of judicial decisions, the development of political strategies and the operation of organizations such as the NAACP. The black quest for the elusive ballot reveals the many ways in which local politicians can negate laws and Supreme

---

wright," *Cornell Law Quarterly*, XXX (September, 1944), 66–76; Bryson, *Dr. Lawrence A. Nixon*, 78.

[49] *Terry et al.* v. *Adams et al.*, 345 U.S. 461 (1952); Nina Benware Margraves, "The Jaybird Democratic Association of Fort Bend County: A White Man's Union" (M.A. thesis; University of Houston, 1955), 45–61; Banks, "Pursuit of Equality," 328; Thurgood Marshall, "The Rise and Collapse of the 'White Democratic Primary'," *Journal of Negro Education*, XXVI (Summer, 1957), 249–254.

Court decisions. Against seemingly insurmountable white obstinance and repeated failures blacks persisted in the white supremacy struggle because somehow, the conviction that justice was ultimately color-blind could not be destroyed. More importantly, however, was the realization that to be barred from participation in the selection of public officials indicated more than anything else that blacks were only half free.

The New Deal and the Negro Community:
Toward a Broader Conceptualization

CHRISTOPHER G. WYE

WITH rare exceptions, research that evaluates the significance of the New Deal public housing and emergency work programs for Negroes has been conceptualized around certain well-defined questions. Most scholars who have approached the subject have focused their attention on the extent to which Negroes were included in these programs in an effort to assess the degree to which the New Deal was successful in alleviating the problems which Negroes faced as a result of the Depression, especially unemployment and the need for low cost housing. These studies have noted that, although Negroes received less assistance than their relatively greater needs warranted, they also received more than their proportionate share. Largely on this basis scholars concluded that the New Deal symbolized a salutary turning point in the attitude of the federal government toward Negroes.[1]

However, if research is conceptualized on a broader basis to include not only questions relating to the extent of Negro participation in the New Deal programs but also questions concerning the impact of these programs on the anatomy of the Negro community, notable qualifications are added to this conclusion and new insight is gained into the problems which the government faced at the local level. If the experience of Cleveland Negroes is representative, it is apparent that the New Deal's inclusion of Negroes in programs designed to relieve the special problems created by the Depression must be balanced against certain adverse side effects which these programs had on the social structure of

This essay received the Organization of American Historians' Pelzer Award for 1971. Christopher G. Wye is a graduate student in Kent State University. The author acknowledges the financial assistance of the Ford Foundation.

[1] Richard Sterner and others, *The Negro's Share: A Study of Income, Consumption, Housing and Public Assistance* (New York, 1943); Gunnar Myrdal and others, *An American Dilemma: The Negro Problem and Modern Democracy* (New York, 1944); Leslie H. Fishel, Jr., "The Negro in the New Deal Era," *Wisconsin Magazine of History*, XLVIII (Winter 1964-1965), 111-26; Raymond Wolters, *Negroes and the Great Depression: The Problem of Economic Recovery* (Westport, Conn., 1970); St. Clair Drake and Horace R. Cayton, *Black Metropolis: A Study of Negro Life in a Northern City* (New York, 1945); Robert C. Weaver, *The Negro Ghetto* (New York, 1948); Robert C. Weaver, *Negro Labor: A National Problem* (New York, 1946); Robert C. Weaver, "Negro Labor since 1929," *Journal of Negro History*, XXXV (Jan. 1950), 20-28. These sources occasionally note that the New Deal housing program encouraged segregation and that the emergency work program employed Negroes below their level of ability or training.

TABLE I

DISTRIBUTION OF NEGRO AND WHITE FAMILIES IN NEW DEAL
PUBLIC HOUSING PROJECTS IN CLEVELAND

	Outh-waite Homes	Outhwaite Extension	Carver Park	Cedar Central Homes	Wood-hill Homes	Lake Shore Village	Berea Homes
Negroes	574	1,217	1,226	9	0	1	72
Whites	14	4	21	645	568	800	1,644

Compiled from Cleveland *Call and Post*, Oct. 14, 1937, Aug. 31, 1940, March 8, 1941; and Robert C. Weaver, *The Negro Ghetto* (New York, 1948), 171-72, 197-98.

the black community, especially on patterns of residential and occupational distribution.

On the one hand, the housing projects provided many Negroes with inexpensive and well-maintained living accommodations and the public work programs furnished jobs for a large number of Negroes who would otherwise have been unemployed. On the other hand, the housing projects encouraged residential segregation, contributed to the disruption of the normal pattern of socioeconomic differentiation within ghetto neighborhoods, and played a crucial role in spreading slum conditions to new areas of the city, while the public work program appears to have depressed the Negro job structure to lower levels by employing Negroes in occupational categories below those which had been open to them in the private sector of the economy.

In Cleveland, there is evidence to substantiate the familiar conclusion that the New Deal low cost housing program provided Negroes with more than their share of new dwelling units. First through the Public Works Administration (PWA) and later through its successor, the United States Housing Authority (USHA), the federal government sponsored the construction in Cleveland of seven housing projects comprising 7,192 apartments. Three of these projects totaling 3,223 units were eventually occupied by Negroes. Since these 3,223 dwellings represented nearly 50 percent of the total number of units erected and since Negroes made up just under 10 percent of the city's population,[2] this meant that Negroes received approximately five times their share of public housing (see Table I).

At the same time, the experience of Cleveland Negroes also confirms the conclusion that the public housing provided for Negroes fell far short of meeting their need. The 3,223 slum clearance units made available to Negroes replaced only one third of the nearly 10,000 homes located within the ghetto

[2] Howard Whipple Green, *Census Facts and Trends by Tracts* (Cleveland, 1954), 5.

which the city's Real Property Inventory classified as "unfit for human habitation."[3] Nevertheless, the fact that the housing projects did not entirely solve the problem of substandard housing in the Negro community should not obscure the fact that they did provide a substantial number of modern and relatively inexpensive homes in an area which had become notorious for its poor condition.

Yet, while the housing projects rejuvenated certain slum sections, their distribution also encouraged residential segregation. Before the advent of the New Deal, more than 90 percent of Cleveland's 72,469 Negroes were concentrated in twenty-nine contiguous census tracts, comprising a compact ghetto on the city's east side.[4] Generally referred to as the Central Avenue district, the ghetto was bordered on the north by Euclid Avenue, an important shopping thoroughfare which marked the fringe of white settlements; on the east by the city's exclusive Shaker Heights suburb; on the south by the New York Central railroad tracks and the industrial zone beyond; and on the west by Cleveland's downtown shopping area. By constructing three projects—Outhwaite Homes, Outhwaite Extension, and Carver Park—in the very heart of the ghetto, designating them as "Negro projects," and then failing to ensure Negroes free access to "white projects" located outside the Central Avenue district, the federal government lent its considerable influence toward preserving the local pattern of segregated housing (see Map I).[5]

Moreover, several of the "white projects" actually had the effect of intensifying residential segregation. Cedar Central Homes, which was erected just inside the northwest border of the ghetto, and Woodhill Homes, which was constructed on the southeast boundary of the Negro district, were located in racially mixed neighborhoods. In both locations Negroes had constituted approximately 50 percent of the residents. However, when these projects were rented, only nine Negroes were admitted to the Cedar Central projects and none were accepted at the Woodhill complex.[6] Cartographic data indicating the final residence of each family who moved to make way for the construction of Cedar Central Homes makes it possible to establish with certainty that Negroes were pushed inward toward the center of the ghetto (see Map II). And, although similar data is lacking for the families who moved from the Woodhill Homes site, the absence of a significant increase in the number of Negroes in adjoining

[3] Howard Whipple Green, *Substandard Housing as Determined by the Low Income Housing Area Survey* (Cleveland, 1940), 5-6.

[4] Green, *Census Facts and Trends by Tracts*, 108-10.

[5] For reports of official references to the housing units as either "Negro projects" or "white projects," see Cleveland *Press*, Jan. 19, 21, 23, 1935; L. P. Mitchell to Harold L. Ickes [1935], National Association for the Advancement of Colored People Branch Files (NAACP Branch Files) (Library of Congress).

[6] Howard Whipple Green, "Cedar Central Apartments are 100 Per Cent Leased," *Sheet A Week*, Nov. 26, 1937; Cleveland *Plain Dealer*, Jan. 22, 1935; Cleveland *Call and Post*, April 25, Oct. 21, Nov. 23, 30, 1937, Dec. 7, 1940; Cleveland *Gazette*, Oct. 30, 1937.

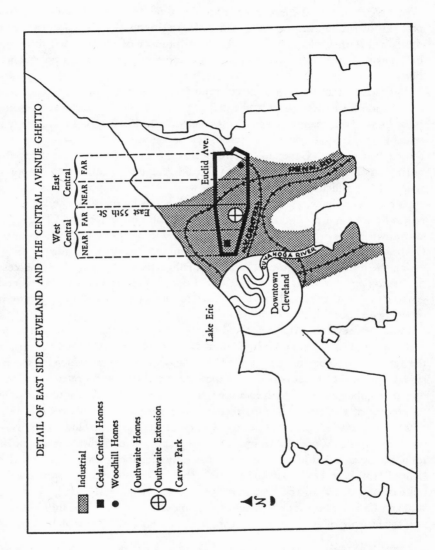

MAP I

DETAIL OF EAST SIDE CLEVELAND AND THE CENTRAL AVENUE GHETTO

Industrial

Cedar Central Homes

Woodhill Homes

Outhwaite Homes
Outhwaite Extension

Carver Park

West Central   East Central

NEAR | FAR | NEAR | FAR

NEAR | FAR

East 55th St.

Euclid Ave.

Lake Erie

Downtown Cleveland

CUYAHOGA RIVER

census tracts outside the Central Avenue district suggests that they too were forced deeper into the Negro section.[7] The influence of the two projects was reflected in the decline in the number of census tracts in which 90 percent of the Negro population lived from twenty-nine in 1930 to twenty-four in 1940.[8] Thus, as a result of the New Deal's housing program, ghetto borders were pushed inward, Negroes were even more heavily concentrated in the Central Avenue area, and segregation was increased.

Negroes were not silent. Protests made by the local National Association for the Advancement of Colored People (NAACP), the Urban League, and Negro politicians eventually resulted in a delegation that was sent to Washington to seek an end to the discrimination in the projects.[9] The director of PWA, Secretary of the Interior Harold L. Ickes, personally sought to assure the group that he was in sympathy with their cause. He pointed to his record as a former president of the Chicago NAACP and indicated that he was "in hearty accord that all groups must work together in the housing program." Moreover, at the conclusion of the meeting, Ickes made it clear that "PWA never had any intention of adopting a race segregation policy."[10] Yet, despite these assurances, Negroes never gained more than token representation in any of the projects located outside the Central Avenue ghetto (see Table I).

If PWA was in fact committed to opposing segregated housing, its practice of handling the actual construction and rental of the project units through local personnel sometimes worked at cross purposes to this policy. In Cleveland the man chosen to oversee PWA housing program, Warren C. Campbell, was a local businessman whose career in real estate offered very little to suggest that he was in sympathy with the principle of integrated housing.[11] As a past president of the Cleveland Real Estate Association, Campbell represented an organization which made it a policy not to rent or sell homes to Negroes in neighborhoods outside the ghetto.[12] Moreover, during World War II, the same organization was primarily responsible for the fact that needed defense housing units were not built for Negroes because it refused to approve the construction site selected by Washington officials.[13] At the same time, as a trustee of the

[7] Green, *Census Facts and Trends by Tracts*, 108-10.

[8] *Ibid.*

[9] Cleveland *Gazette*, Feb. 2, 1935; Cleveland *Call and Post*, Jan. 26, 1935; Cleveland *Eagle*, Jan. 17, 1936; Cleveland *Press*, Jan. 22, 1935; Cleveland *Plain Dealer*, Jan. 22, 1935. See also Mitchell to Walter White, Oct. 6, 1937, H. A. Gray to White, Sept. 28, 1937, C. K. Gillespie to White [1935], NAACP Branch Files.

[10] Cleveland *Gazette*, Feb. 2, 1935.

[11] *Ibid.*, July 25, 1936.

[12] Cleveland *Eagle*, April 3, 1936; Cleveland *NAACP Branch Quarterly*, NAACP Branch Files.

[13] The Federal Housing Administration was ready to construct war housing for Negroes in Cleveland. A local financial institution was ready to finance the projects if the Cleveland Real Estate Board would approve the construction site. The board, however, failed to approve the location and the local source of finance then

Apartment House Owners Association, Campbell represented an organization which had opposed the slum clearance projects and had proposed to solve the problem of congestion in the Central Avenue district by sending recently arrived southern Negro migrants back to the South.[14]

Although the evidence concerning both Campbell's attitudes and the influence which they had on the housing program in Cleveland is circumstantial, it was under his administration that a variety of techniques were employed with the apparent purpose of ensuring that Negroes and whites were separated.[15] One such strategy was to open two units simultaneously, permitting Negroes to enter only one. This practice had the advantage of making it appear as though Negroes were being equitably included in the public housing program. When Cleveland's first two projects, Cedar Central and Outhwaite Homes, were made available in 1937, a special dedication ceremony featuring prominent Negro leaders was held at the Outhwaite complex, and a Negro project manager was appointed who conducted a special campaign to sell the units to the Negro community; no such activities attended the opening of Cedar Central Homes.[16]

For Negroes who persisted in seeking apartments at Cedar Central, other methods were used. Those who made their race evident by applying in person encountered the suggestion that apartments could be obtained more quickly at Outhwaite.[17] Those who applied by mail were compelled to answer a question asking for their "race or nationality" and found that their applications were transferred to the Negro project.[18] Moreover, as it became evident that Negroes were not being accepted at certain projects, a psychology of avoidance seemed to develop within the Negro community. Many Negroes refused even to apply at projects located outside the ghetto, feeling that "What's the use when we know they don't let Negroes live there anyway."[19]

The housing projects not only encouraged residential segregation but also disrupted the normal pattern of socio-economic differentiation within the ghetto neighborhoods, a process which eventually led to the spread of slum conditions into new sections of the city. Prior to the construction of the units, Negroes were distributed according to a definite pattern of socio-economic gradation

withdrew its offer. As a result, no units were built in Cleveland for Negroes. For details of this episode, see Weaver, *Negro Ghetto*, 216.

[14] Cleveland *Gazette*, Sept. 24, 1932.

[15] In 1940 when the Cleveland Metropolitan Housing Authority took over the management of the housing projects from the United States Housing Authority, Warren C. Campbell was replaced by Marc J. Grossman, a civic leader well known for his interest in philanthropic movements. But, the policy of segregating Negroes and whites did not change under his administration before 1944.

[16] Cleveland *Call and Post*, July 12, 1937, Feb. 1, 1941.

[17] Cleveland *Gazette*, Oct. 16, 1937; Cleveland *Call and Post*, Nov. 30, 1940. See also Gillespie to Ickes, Sept. 23, 1937, Campbell to Gray, Oct. 4, 1937, Mitchell to White, Oct. 22, 1937, NAACP Branch Files.

[18] Cleveland *Gazette*, March 20, 1937; Cleveland *Call and Post*, Aug. 25, 1937.

[19] Cleveland *Call and Post*, Feb. 15, 1941.

MAP II

FAMILIES WHO MOVED FROM THE CEDAR CENTRAL
HOMES CONSTRUCTION SITE

One Family

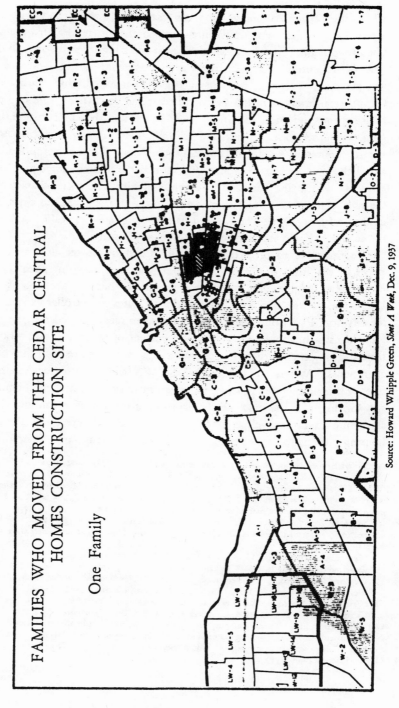

Source: Howard Whipple Green, *Sheet A Week*, Dec. 9, 1937

within the Central Avenue ghetto. East 55th Street, a main thoroughfare which bisected the Negro community on a north-south axis, represented the dividing line between a lower-status area on the west and a higher-status area on the east. The West Central Avenue district was predominantly a slum and vice area. It was here that Negroes were most heavily congested, that educational and occupational levels were lowest, that disease and death rates were highest, that housing and sanitation conditions were worst, and that prostitution, bootlegging, and other forms of vice and crime flourished.[20] In contrast, most of the Negro community's affluent families, those whose incomes permitted them to afford the more expensive homes and apartments located closer to Cleveland's suburbs, lived in the East Central Avenue district. The social characteristics of the two sections were aptly summarized in the phrases that the city's Negroes used to refer to them.[21] The western half of the ghetto was called "the jungle"; the eastern half was termed the "Blue Stocking District."[22]

The three Negro projects were built in a tight cluster close to East 55th Street in the heart of the West Central slum and were intended to provide inexpensive lodgings for low-income groups in that neighborhood (see Map I).[23] Yet, as a result of a ruling by the United States comptroller general that the returns from PWA units had to be sufficient to repay the federal government's total investment, only an estimated 10 percent of those Negroes who moved from the project construction sites were able to afford the rents in the completed apartments.[24] When USHA succeeded PWA and an attempt was made to remedy this problem by providing a government subsidy, the rental figures were still too high for the most bereft elements of the Negro community.[25] Negro and white leaders, as well as local housing officials, all agreed that the low cost housing projects had failed to reach the lowest income groups.[26] Instead, most of

[20] Robert Bernard Navin, *Analysis of a Slum Area* (Washington, 1934), 24-56; Howard Whipple Green, "Slums—A City's Most Expensive Luxury," *Sheet A Week*, Sept. 22, 1934; Gordon H. Simpson, "Economic Survey of Housing in Districts of the City of Cleveland Occupied Largely by Colored People" [mimeographed report of the Cleveland Chamber of Commerce, 1931], 20-50; "The Central Area Social Study" [mimeographed report of the Welfare Federation of Cleveland, 1944], 42-53, 124-46.

[21] Simpson, "Economic Survey of Housing," 51-135; "Central Area Social Study," 42-53, 124-46; Wellington G. Fordyce, "Immigrant Colonies in Cleveland," *The Ohio State Archaeological and Historical Quarterly*, XLV (Oct. 1936), 320-40.

[22] "Central Area Social Study," 124; Cleveland *Call and Post*, March 16, 1939.

[23] Cleveland *Gazette*, May 16, 1931; Cleveland *Call and Post*, Feb. 6, 1936.

[24] Cleveland *Gazette*, Feb. 1, 1936; Sterner, *Negro's Share*, 317; Cleveland *Call and Post*, Feb. 1, 1941.

[25] Cleveland *Gazette*, Nov. 23, 1935; Cleveland *Call and Post*, March 21, 1940; Howard Whipple Green, "The Families That Moved to Make Way for the Outhwaite Housing Project," *Sheet A Week*, June 11, 1936.

[26] Cleveland *Gazette*, May 28, 1938; Cleveland *Press*, Aug. 8, 1932. Grossman, who became head of the Cleveland Metropolitan Housing Authority on January 1, 1940, remarked in answer to a query from local Negro leaders: "The Housing projects built and to be built in the city of Cleveland do not and will not permit members of the lowest income group for whom they were first ... [intended] to become tenants ..." Cleveland *Gazette*, Nov. 25, 1939.

the new apartments went to middle-class Negroes whose incomes required them to seek more modest accommodations.[27]

It was the failure of the slum clearance projects to provide homes for the lower-class Negroes whom they displaced that provided the impetus for a shift in the pattern of socio-economic differentiation within the ghetto. Cartographic data available for the Outhwaite Homes complex disclose that most of the middle-class Negroes who were eventually housed in the new units came from the upper-status East Central district and that most of the lower-class Negroes who moved from the construction site were forced across East 55th Street into the same higher-status section (see Maps III and IV). This meant that the housing projects pulled middle-class Negroes from the upper-status East Central area into the lower-status West Central district, while they pushed lower-status Negroes from the lower-status West Central section into the upper-status East Central area. In effect, the construction of Outhwaite Homes led to a reversal of residential zones.

Other statistics add weight to this conclusion and suggest that the effects of Outhwaite Extension and Carver Park were similar. Data calculated for two socio-economic indices—education as measured by illiteracy rates and income as measured by median rental figures—reveal that before the projects were constructed there was a pattern of upward gradation from lower levels in the near West Central area through to higher levels in the far East Central area. However, in 1940 when all the three Negro units were completed, this pattern was no longer the same. Statistics for three socio-economic indices—education as measured by years of school completed, income as measured by median rental figures, and occupations as measured by percent of white collar workers—demonstrate that, while in all cases except occupations the near West Central area was still lower than the far East Central area, the two middle areas located on either side of East 55th Street were now reversed with the far West Central area higher than the near East Central area (see Table II).

The slum clearance housing projects, therefore, actually succeeded only in moving the slum area from one neighborhood to another. Both black and white observers agreed that the penetration of lower-class Negroes into the upper-status East Central section was attended by a marked deterioration in neighborhood conditions.[28] One and two family homes were converted into "kitchenette apartments," which usually consisted of one room with modest cooking facilities and which generally violated all of the city's building, safety, and sanitation codes.[29] In an area to which Negroes had once pointed with pride as "our

[27] Cleveland *Press*, Nov. 23, 1932, June 2, 1933.
[28] Cleveland *Gazette*, May 15, 1937; Cleveland *Press*, June 2, 1933.
[29] Cleveland *Call and Post*, Nov. 8, 1941; Cleveland *Press*, Aug. 22, 1935, Dec. 1, 2, 3, 4, 1941.

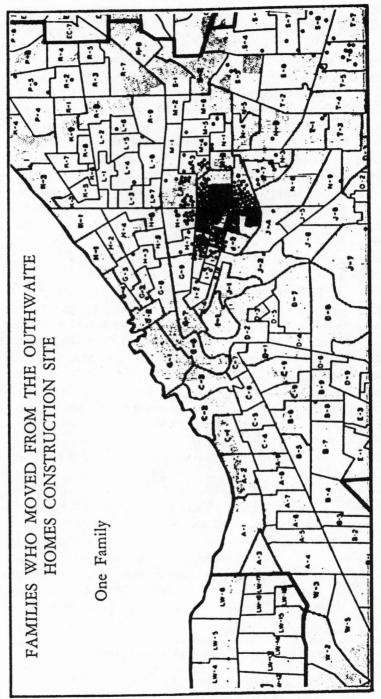

MAP III

FAMILIES WHO MOVED FROM THE OUTHWAITE
HOMES CONSTRUCTION SITE

One Family

Source: Howard Whipple Green, *Cleveland Real Property Inventory, 1936.*

showcase of progress ... [where] many of our outstanding businesses [as well as] several of our outstanding churches ... and fine homes add their dignity to the landscape ... " surveys conducted by social agencies and the white press now found "shacks that even in the most vivid imagination never again can be termed houses ... " with "holes in the walls and floors, paper falling off, lights out of order, plumbing faulty ... [and] rats 'so big they look like cats.' "[30] Negro leaders commented bitterly that for those Negroes who had been forced to move by the housing projects, the notice posted on the construction sites which read "Property of the ... United States Housing Authority" had become an "emblem of despair, desperation and disease."[31] Others went so far as to call USHA the "greatest menace to the Negro ... in Cleveland today."[32]

Moreover, as lower-class Negroes moved into the East Central section, the "sporting element" appeared with greater frequency east of East 55th Street. Prostitutes, both Negro and white, plied their trade as far east as East 80th Street in a district referred to as "Little Hollywood."[33] Speakeasies dispensing liquor obtained from Cleveland's Italian bootleggers, the Mayfield Road Gang, which was itself centered on the eastern fringe of the ghetto, became numerous along the Pennsylvania railroad tracks which cut across the area.[34] And, policy, a form of nickle-and-dime gambling, was ubiquitous.[35]

While the New Deal low cost housing projects had both positive and negative effects on ghetto residential patterns, the public work program had a similarly mixed impact on the structure of Negro employment. Because Negroes were concentrated in jobs that were particularly vulnerable to dislocation in a contracting economy—primarily in unskilled labor and domestic service—the Depression hit Negroes with unusual severity. Although they made up only 10 percent of the available workers, they constituted 27 percent of the unemployed.[36] Within the Central Avenue ghetto unemployment averaged 50 percent and in some sections was as high as 90 percent.[37] Moreover, the effects of the Depression on Negroes were not relieved to any appreciable extent by the

[30] Cleveland *Press*, March 12, 1934, Dec. 1, 2, 1941.

[31] Cleveland *Call and Post*, Feb. 1, 1941.

[32] *Ibid.*, Sept. 13, 1941.

[33] Gordon H. Simpson to White, June 24, 1932, NAACP Branch Files; Cleveland *Press*, Aug. 12, 1930; Cleveland *Call and Post*, Oct. 24, 1935.

[34] Cleveland *Press*, June 2, 1932.

[35] *Ibid.*, March 14, 1935; David H. Pierce to Roy Wilkins, July 9, 1932, NAACP Branch Files; Cleveland *Gazette*, June 1, 1935; Cleveland *Call and Post*, Oct. 24, 1935.

[36] *Fifteenth Census of the United States: 1930. Population: Occupations, by States: Reports by States, Giving Statistics for Cities of 25,000 or More* (Washington, 1933), 1269.

[37] Weaver, "Negro Labor since 1929," 22; "Press Release," Cleveland NAACP, April 15, 1942, NAACP Branch Files.

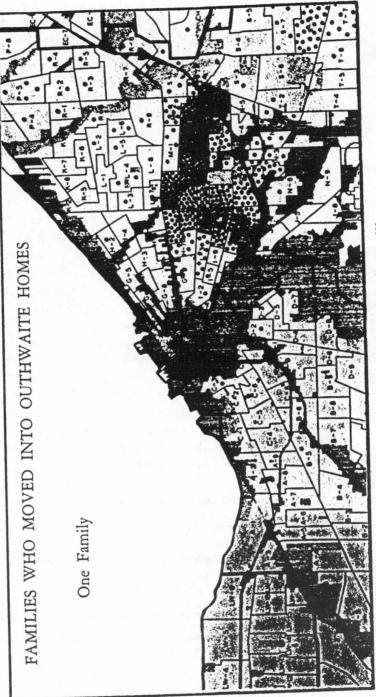

MAP IV

FAMILIES WHO MOVED INTO OUTHWAITE HOMES

One Family

Source: Howard Whipple Green, *Cleveland Real Property Inventory*, 1936.

TABLE II

SOCIO-ECONOMIC AREAS IN CENSUS TRACTS OVER 50 PERCENT
NEGRO WITHIN THE CENTRAL AVENUE GHETTO, 1930–1940

	1930			
	Near West Central Area	Far West Central Area	Near East Central Area	Far East Central Area
Education by percent illiterate	7.5	5.5	5.0	2.0
Income by rent per month	23.0	27.5	29.7	34.2
	1940			
Education by years completed	7.2	8.5	7.7	8.7
Income by rent per month	16.3	20.3	16.3	21.6
Occupation by percent white collar	32.2	28.0	20.5	24.6

Both illiteracy and rental data for 1930 were derived from census tract statistics presented in Howard Whipple Green, *Population by Census Tract*, Cleveland Health Council, 1931. There were no data for occupations for 1930.

Of the data for 1940, those for education were derived from figures in Howard Whipple Green, *Sheet A Week*, February 11, 1943; those for rentals from Howard Whipple Green, *Cleveland Real Property Inventory, 1941*; and those occupations from *16th Census of the United States: 1940. Population and Housing: Statistics for Census Tracts: Cleveland, Ohio and Adjacent Areas* (Washington, 1943).

To correlate the statistical areas indicated here with ghetto neighborhoods see Map I.

limited relief and emergency work projects sponsored by local agencies.[38] The seriousness of the Negroes' plight was summed up in reports made by the Negro community's two leading social welfare agencies. A survey conducted by the Phyllis Wheatley Association expressed the belief that "the race is standing on a precipice of economic disaster," while the Annual Report of the Cleveland Urban League for 1933 indicated that conditions among Negroes had "reached a state approaching chaos."[39]

[38] Lucia Johnson Bing, *Social Work in Greater Cleveland: How Public and Private Agencies Are Serving Human Needs* (Cleveland, 1938), 14-26; Joanna C. Colcord, *Cash Relief* (New York, 1936), 59-63.

[39] Cleveland *Call and Post*, Jan. 12, 1935; "Annual Report of the Negro Welfare Association, 1933,"

Although the New Deal public work programs did not entirely meet the needs of the Negro community, Negroes received more than their share of the jobs which were provided.[40] The result was a substantial reduction in the high unemployment rate within the ghetto. Negroes generally constituted more than 10 percent of all workers assigned to the Civilian Conservation Corps from Cuyahoga County.[41] Central High School, which was located within the ghetto and was attended almost entirely by Negroes, regularly received larger grants from the National Youth Administration than any other single school in the city.[42] PWA—the same agency which built the low cost housing units—operated under a percentage formula which assured Negroes at least the number of jobs equal to their proportion of the total labor force.[43] And in the Works Projects Administration (WPA) activities, which accounted for the largest share of emergency work in Cleveland, Negroes averaged approximately 30 percent of the work force.[44] Moreover, Negroes held nearly 40 percent, or about four times their proportionate share, of all the jobs that were created by emergency work programs.[45] By at least the mid-1930s, New Deal public work projects had succeeded in reducing unemployment among Negroes from about 50 percent to 30 percent and the federal government had become the largest single employer of Cleveland Negroes as well as the most important new influence on the Negro job structure.[46]

However, while the federal government's emergency work programs significantly reduced the high rate of unemployment within the Negro community, they also appear to have depressed the Negro job structure by engaging many workers in job categories below those which they had filled in the private sector of the economy before the Depression began. A comparison of the occupational distribution of Negro workers with that of whites indicates that on eve of the Depression Negroes were underrepresented by from 30 percent to 80 percent in occupations above the skilled level, while they were overrepresented by from 20

Cleveland Urban League Papers (Western Reserve Historical Society). The Negro Welfare Association was the Cleveland affiliate of the National Urban League.

[40] Interview with Russell W. Jelliffe, Oct. 20, 1969.

[41] "Minutes of the Board of Trustees of the Negro Welfare Association, June 1, 1936," Cleveland Urban League Papers; Cleveland Call and Post, July 14, 1936; C. V. Colwill to Clayborne George, June 11, 1933, NAACP Branch Files.

[42] Cleveland Call and Post, July 6, 1939.

[43] "Minutes of the Board of Trustees of the Negro Welfare Association, May 3, 1935," Cleveland Urban League Papers.

[44] Cleveland Press, April 18, 1941.

[45] Statistics derived from data in Sixteenth Census of the United States: 1940. Population. Vol. III, The Labor Force: Occupation, Industry, Employment, and Income. Part 4: Nebraska-Oregon (Washington, 1943), 639.

[46] Census of Partial Employment, Unemployment, and Occupations: 1937: States from North Carolina to Wyoming, Alaska, and Hawaii. Part 4: Nebraska-Oregon (Washington, 1938), 71-75. "Annual Report of the Negro Welfare Association, 1938," Cleveland Urban League Papers.

percent to 300 percent in occupations below this category. As a result, 79 percent of all Negro males and 93 percent of all Negro females were employed below the skilled level, primarily in Cleveland's iron and steel mills and as servants in white homes.[47]

Yet, there is evidence to suggest that Negroes may have sunk to lower occupational levels. On public work projects the experience of Cleveland Negroes with PWA illustrates this point. PWA was especially important to Negro skilled workers in the building trades since, during the Depression-engendered lull in private building, it held a virtual monopoly over the available jobs in the construction industry. But at best the policies of PWA could have accomplished no more than to maintain the occupational color line.[48] This was evident from the terms of an agreement worked out between the Cleveland Urban League and the Department of the Interior that provided only that "the percentage of Negroes in each skilled craft shall equal the ratio that the number of Negro skilled workers bore to the number of white workers in each skilled craft as shown by the census of 1930."[49] Even this minimum standard, however, was widely disregarded.[50] The Negro press reported that "only four to five lonely Negroes are polka dotted among the hundreds of skilled workers" and concluded that "the percentage agreement from Washington . . . is apparently not being followed."[51] A survey conducted by the Cleveland Urban League confirmed this conclusion when it found that only five Negro carpenters, two cement finishers, six bricklayers, and one engineer were employed on all of PWA projects.[52]

More detailed information regarding the concentration of Negroes in unskilled occupations on the New Deal projects is available for WPA. The

[47] These statistics were obtained by reclassifying all of the occupations of blacks and whites in the 1930 census according to the ranking system developed by Alba M. Edwards. This system involves a six category classification from unskilled labor at the bottom, through semiskilled, skilled, clerical, business, and finally to professional workers at the top. But for the purpose of brevity the procedure followed here has been to refer to all jobs in the skilled, clerical, business, and professional categories as simply skilled labor. The advantage of Edwards' system is that it permits an orderly ranking of jobs according to desirability and, therefore, provides a good basis for comparing the structure of Negro and white employment. The concept of a proportionate share, on which the figures concerning underrepresentation and overrepresentation are based, assumes that all other things being equal Negro workers might be expected to approximate the percentage which they represent of the total labor force in each occupational category. Drake and Cayton, *Black Metropolis*, 223-32; Alba M. Edwards, *A Social-Economic Grouping of the Gainful Workers of the United States: Gainful Workers of 1930 in social-economic groups, by color nativity, age, and sex, and by industry, with comparative statistics for 1920 and 1910* (Washington, 1938).
[48] Wolters, *Negroes and the Great Depression*, 203-12.
[49] "Minutes of the Board of Trustees of the Negro Welfare Association, May 3, 1935," Cleveland Urban League Papers.
[50] Interview with George W. Hanzly, Sept. 15, 1971.
[51] Cleveland *Eagle*, Nov. 22, 1935.
[52] "Minutes of the Organization of Building Trades Craftsmen [an organization sponsored by the Negro Welfare Association], Oct. 13, 1936," Cleveland Urban League Papers.

Cleveland Urban League in 1936 made a survey to determine what jobs Negroes held on eight sample public work projects, and the national *Census of Unemployment* in 1937 obtained information relative to the *former* occupations of Negroes temporarily employed on the government projects." A comparison of these data shows that, while the former occupations of Negroes on emergency work constituted a representative cross section of the total Negro labor force, the jobs which Negroes held on government projects were disproportionately unskilled labor. Among Negro males, 819, or 16.7 percent, of those on public work had been formerly employed in skilled jobs, yet of these, only thirty-four, or .6 percent, held similar jobs on the emergency work projects. Similarly, among Negro females, 213, or 20.4 percent, of those in the public work programs had been formerly occupied in skilled jobs, but of these only, five, or .3 percent, held comparable jobs on federal projects. Thus, in the private sector of the economy 79 percent of all Negro males and 93 percent of all Negro females were employed in unskilled labor, on eight WPA projects sampled by the Urban League these percentages increased to 99.4 percent for men and to 99.7 percent for women."

The tendency for Negroes to be employed at lower job levels on the New Deal projects than those which they had occupied in private industry was the result of several factors. Of primary importance was the occupational design of the relief effort. Despite the attempts of government administrators to provide employment for skilled, white collar, and professional workers, the greatest number of federally sponsored jobs were in manual labor. For this reason occupational depression on the work projects was a characteristic of the white as well as the Negro labor force. The problems of black workers, however, were intensified by an apparently widespread pattern of discrimination in job classification at the local level. A survey by the Negro press both summed up this pattern and revealed the resentment Negroes felt toward it:

Not a single Negro has a job on the state WPA staff. Not a single Negro ... has an executive position on the WPA county staff. Out of the hundreds of clerks employed by the WPA headquarters not one is a Negro. Of the hundreds of foremen on the scores of projects that are being operated by the WPA here there are only two Negroes. Practically all of the jobs the WPA has to offer above the role of menial labor are given to whites. We have good ground for the charge that there is widespread and deliberate discrimination against our people. There are practically no promotions of Negroes on projects. When Negro workers reach the point where they are eligible for promotion their jobs are abolished or some trumpted up charge against them brings their dismissal. When Negroes are fortunate enough to be placed on a project where the work is

" Cleveland *Eagle*, Jan. 3, 1936; *Census of Partial Employment*, 83.
" These data were obtained by using the Edwards classification.

pleasant they are mysteriously laid off. . . . All of our men are not ditchdiggers, neither are all of our women domestics. . . . The administration of WPA in Ohio and especially in Cuyahoga County has about reached the point of scandal."

Although a continuous stream of protest from Negro leaders prompted Washington administrators to action on several occasions, very little improvement was effected. A conference in 1935 of the Cleveland Urban League and WPA officials resulted in the employment of a "few Negro supervisors and foremen," mostly on Negro projects.* Negroes continued to complain, however, and three years later representatives of the national administration conducted an investigation of WPA operations in Cleveland which confirmed the existence of discrimination but which resulted only in a promise to employ Negroes in "several white collar jobs" and to appoint "at least three [Negroes] in a supervisory capacity."* A similar investigation made in 1939 ended with the dismissal of several local white executives on charges of discriminating against Negro skilled workers. But it appears that none of these actions achieved more than temporary improvement. A Negro leader observed, "When there is a rumor of an investigation they seem to find [skilled] Negroes from somewhere, but as soon as the heat is off the Negroes . . . on the projects begin to disappear. It is about as difficult for a skilled Negro operator to be assigned to a power machine as it is for him to find a job in private industry."*

The failure of the federal government to curb discrimination on the public work projects was due largely to its ineffectiveness in dealing with lower echelon personnel. Washington officials might attempt to eliminate the discrimination exhibited by administrators in executive positions at county headquarters, but only rarely did they make a determined effort to curtail the discriminatory practices of project leaders in the field, especially among foremen and supervisors. Yet it was the project leaders who controlled the allocation of jobs on the emergency work programs. Effectively, it was they who determined the final job classification for most workers; it was they who determined who was to be laid off when cutbacks were made; it was they who administered discipline (which could result in dismissal); and it was they who recommended promotions and demotions.

The variety of techniques employed by foremen and supervisors to restrict Negroes to unskilled occupations were frequently documented in the Negro press. Sometimes a project leader would refuse altogether to accept a skilled Negro. In one such instance, WPA county headquarters assigned two Negro

" Cleveland *Call and Post*, Feb. 24, 1938.
* "Minutes of the Board of Trustees of the Negro Welfare Association, Dec. 13, 1935," Cleveland Urban League Papers; *ibid.*, Jan. 10, 1936; Cleveland *Call and Post*, June 16, 1938.
" Cleveland *Call and Post*, June 2, 1938.
* *Ibid.*, Sept. 14, 1939.

typists to an indexing project, but the project supervisor wrote on the back of their assignment slips, "This project cannot use colored typists" and then sent them back to the county office.[59] More frequent was the practice of accepting a skilled Negro worker on a project and later demoting him to an unskilled job. This was the experience of a Negro electrician who was reclassified as a common laborer and put to work washing light bulbs.[60] Moreover, when Negro skilled workers who had been demoted to unskilled positions applied for reclassification their application forms were frequently lost between the office of the project foremen and the office of county headquarters.[61] And, Negroes who sought to register a complaint about their failure to be reclassified were threatened with dismissal, demotion, or a disciplinary reduction in pay.[62]

That lower echelon personnel in the field rather than executives at county headquarters were primarily responsible for the discrimination against Negro skilled workers on the public work projects was widely recognized by Negro leaders who considered them to be "czars" in the matter of job classification.[63] By the late 1930s comments of Negro leaders reflected a respect for the efforts of the county officials to secure a fair distribution of work for Negroes, while at the same time they displayed a certain resignation to the role of prejudiced foremen. In 1939 the Cleveland *Call and Post*, which had been one of the leaders in the campaign conducted by the Negro press to secure skilled jobs for Negroes, concluded that, "Despite the obvious efforts of departmental heads to do something about the violation of orders with reference to the classification ... of workers ... [their] efforts to secure a square deal for Negro skilled ... workers ... has continued to be obstructed by prejudiced foremen and office underlings."[64] A year later the same paper remarked that "while the central office WPA is innocent of responsibility for discrimination against Negro applicants, it is known that under officials at that office have turned their heads in the opposite direction while some underling supervisor or project foreman did the dirty work."[65]

These findings suggest that new perspectives on the relationship between Negroes and the New Deal are revealed if research is conceptualized on a basis broad enough to embrace both questions concerning the extent of Negro participation in government programs as well as questions relating to the impact of these programs on the social structure of the Negro community.

[59] *Ibid.*, June 23, July 7, 28, 1938, Feb. 1, 1940.
[60] *Ibid.*, June 16, 1938.
[61] *Ibid.*, July 14, 1938.
[62] *Ibid.*, July 28, 1938.
[63] *Ibid.*, April 27, 1939.
[64] *Ibid.*, July 14, 1938.
[65] *Ibid.*, Feb. 1, 1940.

Specifically, the Cleveland experience demonstrates that although the New Deal public housing and emergency work programs played an important part in alleviating the problems generated by the Depression, they also contributed to the preservation of perhaps the two salient components which combine to produce a caste-like Negro social structure—residential segregation and a distinctly racial occupational pattern.

BEYOND THE FAMILY ECONOMY: BLACK AND WHITE WORKING-CLASS WOMEN DURING THE GREAT DEPRESSION

LOIS RITA HELMBOLD

To cope with unemployment, poverty, and uncertainty during the Great Depression, working-class women devised many ingenious strategies. Flexibility and creativity defined their actions. Yet cooperation and increased female responsibilities did not always provide greater family cohesiveness or stave off the economic effects of the crisis; the Depression disrupted people's lives. The expectations and actualities of female self-sacrifice resulted in conflict between parents and daughters, between husbands and wives, among members of doubled-up households, and between "unattached" women and their children and siblings. Although families changed their form and structure and increased their responsibilities, they also fell apart from the strains of the Depression.

To understand the family tensions and conflicts that occurred during the Depression, it is necessary to look at women and families in a broad historical context. Yet much historical work on the family economy, recent scholarship on black families, and discussions of the Great Depression generally treat families within a framework of cooperation. Scholars in these three areas usually fail to account for widespread evidence of families' inabilities and/or unwillingness to meet the needs of their members. Does evidence from the Great Depression suggest that current interpretations are wrong or inadequate, or does the atypicality of the Depression place it in a category of its own? Two stories illustrate the issues.

A white working-class woman born in Chicago in 1902, Catherine T., like most urban adolescent girls of her race and

Feminist Studies 13, no. 3 (Fall 1987). © 1987 by Feminist Studies, Inc.

class, left school at age fourteen and began to work. For more than fifteen years she held steady jobs, sewing in garment and drapery factories and assembling parts in an electrical manufacturing company. After 1930, when she lost a job she had held for six years, she worked sporadically at a number of short-term and seasonal jobs, often employed on rush orders which lasted only a few weeks. Each summer she worked as a counter waitress at a concession stand in Riverside Park. During the first five years of the Depression, Catherine continued to support herself by taking any job she could find and by dipping into her savings when she was unemployed. Catherine's diligence, according to her interviewer from the Women's Bureau, could be read in her appearance. She described Catherine as "rather plain," "very neat," a "hardworking type," who "always had her nose to the grindstone."

As a single woman, Catherine maintained close ties with her family. She lived with and supported her invalid mother until her financial resources dwindled, then both of them moved in with one of Catherine's married sisters. Catherine paid room and board and her siblings took over their mother's expenses. When her mother's health worsened dramatically in December 1935, Catherine left the labor force and nursed her mother full-time for the remaining months of her life. After her mother's death the following spring, Catherine received $390 from her insurance policy. In earlier years, Catherine had borrowed money to keep up the policy payments and her mother had made her the sole beneficiary. Her sister, however, demanded $150 for the assistance she claimed she had provided Catherine, a paying boarder, and so Catherine moved out of the house.

Catherine attempted to find full-time work again, but harsh working conditions, an inadequate diet, worry, and the strain of her mother's illness had taken their toll. Seriously ill and completely run down, she could not stand the stress and noise of a sewing factory or her thirteen-hour days and seven-day weeks at Riverside Park. For the next year and a half she lived on the insurance money, earnings from occasional brief jobs, small bits of assistance from friends, and by gathering rags and papers to sell to junk dealers. When her interviewer "commented that it was hard to visualize a woman like herself rummaging about in alleys, Catherine said, 'If you're hungry you'll do anything.'" In September 1936, still ill and having exhausted all her resources, Catherine applied to the Chicago Relief Authority. The CRA stipulated that an "unattached" woman could qualify for relief payments only if she were unemployed, unemployable, and unable to secure support from her family. Catherine had been a dutiful daughter, but her siblings, still jealous of her inheritance, resented her and cut her off. Virtue, in other words, went unrewarded.[1]

Dutiful daughters were not the only women shaken by familial dissension. Mothers of adult children could not necessarily rely on their offspring in hard times either. Another Chicago resident, Mary P., a fifty-three-year-old widow, and a black Pentecostal preacher, had supported herself and her family for forty years by doing domestic work. When she lost the last of her day work in 1932, Mary attempted to get help from her sons. The youngest, unmarried and living in Chattanooga, never contributed to her support. Another son, William, she described as a "good boy" and his wife as "a lovely girl. I love her like my own." William and his wife usually gave Mary twenty-five or fifty cents each payday over the next several years. Mary had never lived with them, however, which she explained by the fact that they had no furniture and had always roomed in other people's homes.

In 1932 Mary moved in with Ossie, her third son, and his wife, Maud, a "good girl." Her affection for her daughter-in-law, however, could not sustain the relationship. Mary and Ossie did not get along and after three months she left his home in despair and applied for relief. Five years later Mary told an interviewer that she had received scarcely any help from Ossie since then. Maud had died and Ossie had moved in with another woman and her three children. Although Ossie's failure to marry his new partner may have contributed to his religious mother's displeasure with him, even a marriage of which she had approved had not sustained the mother/son relationship. Mary said emphatically to her interviewer, "He's no good, that boy, I'd sooner see him dead. He curses me out."[2]

Between 1932 and 1937, Mary, who suffered from a variety of ailments, got by on a combination of work relief jobs and direct relief payments. One son never helped her, a second contributed regularly but minimally, and a third son had earned his mother's wrath and disapproval. Raising children did not necessarily entitle a mother to support, help, or even respect from them.

The experiences of Catherine and Mary challenge current

scholarship about familial cooperation. After summarizing recent scholarship and debates about white working-class families, Afro-American families, and women during the Depression, I want to illustrate gaps in each analysis. I will then describe the disharmonies and destruction that characterized many families during the 1930s and suggest alternative explanations that do account for Depression experiences.

Social historians have created one model of the (white) family economy to analyze the connections between women's productive work, domestic activity, and reproduction. Louise A. Tilly and Joan W. Scott, in *Women, Work, and Family,* an influential work in the field, place the family at the center of their attempt to understand women's work, because the family is "the unit of decision-making for the activities of its members," and its decisions "implicitly assign economic value to all household tasks."[3] Whether women contributed unwaged but necessary labor or earned wages, whether they lived in preindustrial or industrial societies, women's economic significance was central to their families' survival. Thus, this model counters the myths that women do not work and that the "private" family is separate from the "public" economy.

Those scholars who use this model assume a harmony of interests among family members, who choose "overall strategies to maximize the economic goals of the family group."[4] But this view, as many feminists have pointed out, often disregards the exercise of power within families and thus ignores or bypasses the feminist theory of the early 1970s that characterized the family as an oppressive institution structured by the dominance of men over women and old over young.[5] As Rayna Rapp, Ellen Ross, and Renate Bridenthal have warned, the family should not be regarded as a "natural" institution with a unity of interests. Similarly, Heidi I. Hartmann reminds us that "mutual dependence by no means precludes the possibility of coercion."[6]

Yet historians such as Miriam Cohen, Sarah Eisenstein, Tamara K. Hareven, and Leslie Woodcock Tentler, like Scott and Tilly, discuss dependence and mutuality but ignore or minimize coercion, conflicts, and differences of interest.[7] Judith E. Smith's recent study of Italian and Jewish immigrant families in Providence,

Rhode Island – although acknowledging challenges to familial and patriarchal authority by the young adult children of immigrants in the prosperous 1920s – also focuses on mutual dependence.[8] The problem with this work is that it fails to specify the power and authority exercised in family decision making. Cohen, for example, in her essays on Italian immigrants, claims that "the girls were pulled out of school because families needed their labor," and "Italian families were faced with a strong financial motive for sending women to work."[9] Who was pulling and sending? Fathers? Mothers? Did parents jointly make and enforce these decisions? Did daughters dutifully comply or did they ever resist? What did the resistance accomplish and what price did it exact from the rebels? Working-class female writers of the early twentieth century, such as Anzia Yezierska, Agnes Smedley, and Emma Goldman, have portrayed rampant conflict within families. But surely we cannot conclude that only socialists and anarchists ever fought with their families, ever turned aside from tugs on their heart strings and appeals to their guilt.

The family economy model has created two archetypes – the dutiful daughter and the malleable matron. Paying insufficient attention to the entire life cycle and ignoring women who do not fit into either of these categories, historians have excluded many women. Older single women, who may not continue to live with their families; women whose marriages end in divorce, desertion, or separation (with or without children to support); widows, more likely to be older – with problems comparable to women with broken marriages, although lacking the stigma of failure – and lesbians, all fail to appear in the paradigm. Far more than one-quarter of adult women, I would argue, are likely to spend some part of their lives in one of these categories. A model, then, that fails to account for at least one-quarter of the adult female population at a given time certainly cannot be used uncritically.[10]

But although historians of the family economy account for the lives of millions of women on two continents across several centuries, and often write as though their model were universally applicable, they have applied their model only to white women. The history of Afro-American women does share certain characteristics with that of white women, but there are also important dissimilarities – due, most importantly, to the experiences of slavery, racism, and African and Afro-American cultural practices and values. Writers of black history, unlike historians of white women, have not needed to demonstrate the economic centrality of black women. Slave owners appropriated female and male productive labor, and women's reproductive labor was similarly a source of profit to the masters.[11] In the years of freedom, black married women have consistently worked outside their homes at rates far surpassing the labor force participation of white married women; only within the past decade has white women's labor force participation grown close to that of black women.[12] So instead of concentrating on the importance of women's work to the family, recent scholars of the black family have focused their work on countering the claim that black families—particularly poor and working-class black families—are pathological when they are not similar to white nuclear families.[13] Recent scholarship has analyzed the extensive kinship networks that provided security, stability, and the wherewithal to provide daily sustenance and to raise children. Although the nuclear family form characterized the majority of black families from Reconstruction onwards, black people also survived by relying on larger kin communities.[14]

Yet the revisionist focus on black kin cooperation creates some of the same problems as the white family economy model. To be sure, there are differences in the scholarly approaches. Historians have noted that the power relationship between black women and men is not parallel to that between white women and men.[15] Moreover, scholars of black families have broadened their focus to consanguine families, including relations among siblings, aunts, uncles, nieces, nephews, cousins, and nonfamily kin-like relations.[16] The advantage of this approach is that an analysis of kinship and cooperation based on consanguine families does not exclude from consideration women who are neither wives nor daughters, nor does it credit marital and parental relations with the sole power to explain family decisions. In other words, black family history, because of its focus on kinship, accounts for the lives of more black women than does the model of the white cooperative family economy. But both white family history and the history of the black family share a common theme of cooperation, even though they developed from separate historical and scholarly roots. And neither adequately describes Depression America, when many urban black and white working-class families proved incapable of meeting the needs of their members.[17]

What explains the conflicts between parents and daughters, the broken marriages, the dispersal of families, and the failure of kin to aid one another when hard times hit? Was the shock of the Depression so severe that it destroyed cooperative mechanisms?

Examining the impact of the Depression on daily life, contemporary scholars have focused on the themes of family stability or destruction and on the increase in married women's employment despite depressed economic conditions.[18] Social scientists of the 1930s concluded that the relative strength of a family determined whether it could survive hard times. "Weak" families, characterized by problems prior to the crisis, more frequently fell apart under the additional strain, and "strong" families more often pulled together and survived. This facile social Darwinian judgment fails to examine the family as an institution.[19]

But this view still affects recent work on women in the Depression. The increase in married women's employment, for example, a subject of controversy during the 1930s, has become an expression of "family values" in historical interpretations. Both Lois Scharf and Winifred Wandersee cite the rising patterns of consumption in the 1920s which enlarged the definition of necessity as the impulse sending white married women into the labor force. Although white married women seemingly discarded their traditional roles, the public need not have worried. Rather than being a sign of women's dissatisfaction, their employment symbolized commitment to their husbands, children, and homes.[20] Married white women of the 1930s were not significantly different from the group described by Leslie Tentler who, earlier in the century, worked to fulfill "wifely and motherly obligations."[21] Julia Kirk Blackwelder, author of the only comparative history of women of the Depression era, finds evidence of emotional stress in divorce, abandonment, mental illness, and suicide, but she concludes that most families remained intact. Comparing black, Mexican, native-born white, and immigrant white women in San Antonio, Texas, Blackwelder sees black families as most likely to be broken by separation or abandonment and black women as more likely to work outside their homes. She explains these differences by cultural factors—for example, expectations of male authority and female deference account for the lower incidence of labor force participation among Mexican women. Her conclusions in general substantiate the judgments of earlier family historians who look at common survival goals.[22]

In my own comparative work, however, I have found that differences between urban black and white women during the Depression were most pronounced in their experience of paid work, but that the experience of family life was comparatively similar. White women – particularly white married women in their twenties and thirties – increased their share of the female labor force, but black women's share declined. Married women's proportion of total female employment grew 28 percent from 1929 to 1940, and the share of women in the twenty-five to forty-four-age group increased 13.8 percent. Nationally, black women's proportion of the labor force declined 22.6 percent in eleven years; in the four cities I studied, black women's rate of decline varied from 42.3 percent at its highest to 32.3 percent at its lowest.[23] White women replaced black women by moving down the occupational ladder of desirability. For black women already on the bottom rung, there was no lower step, and they were effectively pushed out of the labor force. Yet the existing literature does not provide an adequate explanation for the comparative similarity regarding family situations.

Using interviews which the Women's Bureau of the Department of Labor conducted during the 1930s, I have constructed a sample of 1,340 women from Chicago, Cleveland, Philadelphia, and South Bend, Indiana – black and white; immigrant and native-born; young, middle-aged, and old; and of all family and marital statuses. Employed, unemployed, job applicants, relief applicants, relief recipients, or outside the labor force, these women span the demographic and employment spectrum of urban working-class women during the 1930s. Some had never worked before the Depression, others had been steadily employed for years, and still others had a sporadic history of employment, usually remaining out of the labor force while raising children. My criterion for inclusion in the sample was that a woman held a service or clerical job at some point during the late 1920s or the 1930s.[24]

Thus, the women in these samples are a cross-section of urban working-class women in the Northeast and Midwest during the

Depression. White women of all family and marital statuses are included. Because most of the black women in the samples had been previously married, young, single black women and married black women are underrepresented.[25] Black women accounted for no more than 11 percent of the adult female population in any of these cities in 1930; (the majority of North American black people still lived in the South during the Depression).[34] The black women in the samples were either Northern-born, or more frequently, recent immigrants from the South. The white immigrants came from virtually all the countries of Europe and from Canada. No Asian women appear in my samples (only a tiny number of Asians lived in these cities in the 1930s).[26] Although Chicago claimed a Mexican population of almost 20,000 in 1930, no Mexican woman showed up in either Chicago sample. Deportation removed many Mexicans from the area during the Depression, but it is unclear why none of those who remained appeared in either of my samples. The Chicago sample groups consisted of relief applicants and relief recipients. Discrimination against Mexicans may have made them ineligible or unwilling to apply for relief; Mexican women may have wanted to avoid public attention for fear of being deported.[27]

What are the biases of these sources? The Women's Bureau conducted studies in order to answer questions about women's employment, unemployment, and remedies for unemployment. Although the interviewers elicited some information about marital and family relationships, this was not their focus. The fact, then, that so much evidence of familial distress did surface in the interviews is a clear sign of how much this issue was on women's minds. The samples from Chicago and Philadelphia consisted of "unattached" women who were unemployed and unable to obtain financial help from their families; thus, lack of family support was, for some of them, a motivating factor in filing their applications for relief jobs or relief. Some had no family nearby; others had experienced marital or family breakups as a result of the Depression. These surveys might therefore contain more evidence of family dissension than a random sample of the adult female population. Yet the other two samples—one a house-to-house survey in working-class neighborhoods in South Bend, Indiana, and the other a study of women applying to an employment agency run by the Cleveland YWCA—also provide many examples of familial dissension and disruption.[28]

These sources are unique. Most histories of working-class women rely on government studies and statistics, observations by middle-class reformers and journalists, or a small number of auto-biographical accounts and oral histories. The differences in my conclusions derive in part from my using interview sources in which large numbers of working-class women documented their daily life experiences.

During the Depression, women played out the theme of family cooperation in numerous ways as they attempted to stave off the effects of joblessness, poverty, and uncertainty. Housework increased dramatically. When cash income declined, housewives replaced purchasing with subsistence production. Whether they planted gardens, canned food, remade old clothing, made do with less heat, or moved into poorer housing which required extra effort to keep clean and comfortable, women worked harder. Their families apparently expected them to do so. Virtually all of the sample of South Bend working-class families utilized such strategies in the early Depression years. These families were less likely to rely on financial strategies such as using up their savings, taking out loans, going into debt for unpaid bills, or cashing in insurance policies.[29] Rather, they depended on additional work from women as their first line of defense.

At the same time, unemployment and economic insecurity deepened tensions and aggravated problems, creating more emotional work for women. A working-class wife, for example, might find her home occupied by her unemployed husband and sons while the utilities had been shut off for nonpayment and the kitchen stove provided the only heat for the entire house. In such situations, trying to do her housework, at the same time mediating the tensions of enforced, constant crowding was no easy task. Younger women had to throw out their expectations about life proceeding in an orderly fashion; they sacrificed education, independence, marriage, and children in order to help their families. The birth rate, for example, plummeted from an average of 98 per 1,000 women of childbearing age in 1925 to 1929, to 76 in 1933 and again in 1936.[30] To soothe frightened men unaccustomed to unemployment, coordinate the activities of increased numbers of people living in a small number of rooms, and cope with changes in their own lives—all required women's stamina and ingenuity.

Family economies also depended on women's wages more heavily during the Depression, a result, in part, of the comparative protection afforded to women by the sex-segregated labor force.[31] By 1930 the female-intensive clerical and service sectors of the economy accounted for more than one-half of the female nonagricultural labor force and employed the majority of urban working-class women, both black and white.[32] Because layoffs began in production jobs, women in clerical and service occupations continued to work when male production workers lost their jobs or worked intermittently. When the men on the assembly line at Studebaker, for example, worked one partial shift every few weeks or did not work at all, their daughters, sisters, wives, mothers, and girl friends continued to work as clerical, janitorial, and food service employees in the corporate headquarters.

Young, single urban women—working-class daughters—almost without exception, worked for wages. In the four cities I studied, 85 percent of single women between the ages of twenty and forty-four were employed in 1929.[33] The presumption of their families was that "when the children are grown, they can make a piece of bread for themselves," as one Russian immigrant described her father's attitude. Most lived with their parents and contributed all or most of their wages to their familes.[34] The assumption of daughters' allegiance to and financial support of their parents and siblings intensified under the weight of the Depression, when the male wage earners in these families were more likely than not to be unemployed. The portion of family income provided by daughters or sisters increased dramatically. By the fall of 1932, for example, twice as many households in the South Bend sample had full-time female workers compared with those with full-time male workers.[35] Women alone supported one-third of these 183 households and another one-third received one-quarter or more of their incomes from female members. Although the interviews did not detail wages prior to the Depression, there were male wage earners in 157 or 85.7 percent of the households in 1929 compared with male financial contributors in only 111 or 60.7 percent of the households in the fall of 1932. "Normally" 228 men and 259 women were employed in these households. By the fall of 1932, only 124 men were working, either part-time or full-time, a drop to 54.4

percent of the previous group. Among women, 164 worked, 63.3 percent of the previous number. Women's financial contributions to family survival were critical.

In interview after interview, young single daughters living with parents described themselves as the sole or primary source of familial support during the Depression. Although women volunteered this important information, the nature of the interviews made it less likely that they would express their emotional response to this burden.[36] The important financial contributions of daughters raised their status in some families; in others, the expectation that daughters' wages would go to their parents caused resentment among the daughters. Helen M., the daughter of Polish immigrants living in Cleveland, began to work at age fourteen, doing housework after school and on Saturdays. She quit this job at age fifteen to take "regular" work, and by sixteen, in the spring of 1933, she had left school to work full-time. Helen supported a sick mother, a father who had been out of work for two years, and four younger siblings. Earning five dollars a week for sixteen-hour days at housework, she reported, "I'm just about keeping the family."[37] Many young daughters reported, sometimes proudly, sometimes resentfully, that they were contributing "every cent" they earned to their families.

Familial obligation also required other kinds of self-sacrifice from young women. Many daughters, like Helen, cut short their educations, often at the behest of their parents. Although the proportion of young people graduating from high school increased during the Depression, some young women who wanted an education could not obtain it. The young women leaving high school in the early thirties who appear in my samples were more than balanced, numerically, by their younger sisters remaining in school later in the decade as government programs employed some of their fathers and as younger women found it more and more difficult to secure work.[38] A seventeen-year-old American-born daughter of Slovak parents described herself and her sister in 1935. "There are hundreds of girls just like herself and me. Neither of us could finish our high school education, we had to go to work. My mother works a little, my father very little, yet he must have his tobacco and beer."[39] For this young woman, who signed her letter to Frances Perkins "One of the Hundreds," her resentment of her father was unmistakable.

235

For other young women, the dream of a college education had to be put aside. Ruth K., the eighteen-year-old daughter of Bohemian immigrants, had to turn down a college scholarship. Her father, a fur finisher, had little work, and her brother could not find a job when he graduated from high school in 1933. Ruth, however, had two jobs; she held a full-time position as a secretary and medical assistant to a physician and worked at a part-time clerical job three evenings a week. Her earnings, $55 a month from her full-time job and perhaps another $10 from the part-time job, provided almost the entire income for a family of six. Although Ruth could not "take advantage of" the scholarship she had won, she persevered and took a chemistry class in night school. Her comments do not make clear whether her parents insisted she go to work or whether her own feelings of responsibility framed her choice, but it is obvious that the Depression altered her plans dramatically.[40]

Although parents could decide that their daughters had to leave school, this strategy did not necessarily yield the desired results. Josephine and Constanti B., Polish immigrants, employed as operatives at two different South Bend factories, had not worked full-time since 1929. Raising four children and trying to make mortgage payments on their home, Josephine reported that she had taken her daughter Irene out of high school in 1932 because she "needed her wages." Irene worked as a domestic, "off and on," but the following fall, chafing under parental authority, Irene married and left home.[41]

Irene's case was not typical, however, because, during the Depression, marriage rates dropped dramatically. By 1932, only three-quarters as many people were marrying as had during the late 1920s.[42] Consequently, more young women lived with their families longer into adulthood, and their responsibility for providing some, and frequently all, of the family income grew accordingly. This situation exacted a high emotional price. Daughters who lived with parents were not always happy about their circumstances, but loyalty, parental authority, or a lack of alternatives compelled them to remain.

Other women chose to live on their own. Although they had many reasons for leaving home, they faced a common problem when the loss of work forced them to reconsider their futures. Some women "adrift" entertained thoughts of returning home to their parents, but not all parents would take them back.[43] Grace S.

and Margaret T., both young white women living in Cleveland, one a native-born clerical worker and the other a Canadian immigrant household worker, reported that after their mothers died, their fathers had remarried, and their stepmothers had made it clear that they were not welcome at home.[44] Neither stepparents nor parents were always willing to support unemployed young adults.

On the other hand, some independent daughters resisted returning to parental supervision. Helen B., a twenty-five-year-old single white woman, lived with a friend and was employed as a clerical worker in Philadelphia. When she was laid off in 1931, another friend whom she knew through a basketball club helped her to get a job at a department store. This job ended after a year. Helen searched for work for two months and, finally, nine weeks behind in her rent, applied to the Bureau of Unemployment Relief in the spring of 1933. This young woman, whose social and work relationships revolved around her peers, responded to her interviewer's suggestion that she move back home by insisting that "difficulties" made it impossible to do so.[45]

There are similar stories about young black women. After a year teaching school in rural Missouri, Mandolyn B. moved to Chicago in 1928 at age twenty-three. She had not been able to find work commensurate with her normal school education and had, instead, supported herself as a beautician for seven and a half years. In 1937, unemployment and lack of resources pushed her to apply for relief. She would not consider returning to Missouri, she told her interviewer, because she had "felt hindered a great deal socially in a small town."[46]

Older women also expressed loyalty to their families in their actions, but disappointment, anger, and bitterness over marriages and families was, if anything, more direct. Married women's participation in the wage labor force grew during the Depression, in spite of the considerable opposition to their working. Nationally, only 11.7 percent of all married women were employed in 1930, but the proportion varied dramatically by race and according to opportunities available in the particular city. One-third of black married women worked for wages, more than three times the employment rate of either native-born or immigrant white married women.[47] Despite a decade of Depression, however, by 1940 married women as a group had increased their proportional share

237

of the labor force by almost one-third. Because black women lost jobs disproportionately during the 1930s, the increase of white married women's labor force participation was even greater.[48]

The growth of employment among married white women, despite public opinion and even legislative action seeking to restrict it, reflected more than increased consumer pressures, particularly in working-class homes.[49] Married working-class women entered the labor force because their husbands and sons were unemployed and underemployed and their families needed the income. Edna H. decided to look for a job in 1931 although she had not been employed in more than twenty years since she had married. She worked sporadically at the South Bend Bait Company. Her daughter Ruth, a clerical worker, alternately worked a month and took half a month layoff. Edna's husband, Leland, a printer, had suffered an industrial accident; although he expected to receive some compensation, the amount would be quite small because he had been working only three days every other week. A younger child had not yet entered the labor force, and a grandmother planned to move to South Bend to live with them because she had lost everything in a bank failure. Edna explained, "We were having such a hard time getting along on the little the others could make, I thought I'd try to help some too." Yet women did not always assume this burden cheerfully. Emma D., an assembler at Studebaker, worked because her husband's employment was so irregular. A forty-three-year-old immigrant, she had only one child still at home, a son in high school, but she regarded housework as her responsibility and breadwinning as her husband's. Emma said that she "wished he could work more so I could stay home and tend my business."[50]

The additional burden of a woman's paid job strained some marital relations, and among married women of both races the breakup of marriages was a widespread phenomenon. Separations and desertions multiplied. Divorces declined in the early 1930s because of the expense, but by 1936 the divorce rate had surpassed its previous high in the late 1920s and continued to grow.[51] Lack of money and the husband's unemployment often precipitated the splitup. After nineteen years of marriage, Gertrude W.'s husband had deserted his fifty-year-old white wife in 1936. With tears in her eyes, she told her interviewer that her husband had "forced" her to work to supplement his wages, and when he refused to work to "preserve his own health," she had worked too hard and could "hardly drag along." Gertrude W. attributed the breakup of their marriage to the fact that he "drank and told lies."[52] Elizabeth H., a black woman of forty-nine who lived in Chicago, described her husband as a "good provider" until he lost his job in 1931. They subsequently lost their home, and Elizabeth said he "got the big head" after these crises and "dropped" her.[53] A wife's unemployment could also precipitate a break. An interviewer described Mary B., a black woman, as "quite depressed and entirely through with men." Mary had married at fifteen and had supported her husband through most of their marriage. When her health broke down after years of hard physical labor, her husband was "cruel" and "mistreated" her and finally went off with another woman in 1935, when Mary was forty-six. "She has trouble avoiding tears when speaking of her husband's abuse of her when she became too ill to work, after supporting him for so many years," wrote her interviewer. Mary stated that she had "looked through her life and decided that she was too easy, that she was a fool." When questioned about whether she would marry in the future, Mary responded, there's "no next time for me—never no more for me."[54] We might expect the bonds of marriage to hold people more tightly in hard times, because poverty made them more dependent on one another. For many people the family economy did serve this purpose, but for a growing number of women and men, the Depression fostered family disintegration instead.

Although acrimonious breakups wreaked havoc on many women's lives, other family economies split apart by mutual agreement, albeit reluctantly, when husbands and wives decided to go their separate ways because it was not possible for them to survive financially while living together. Husbands often left wives and children to search for work, some returning to the old country, others traveling to other areas of the United States. Rose W.'s husband, for example, left South Bend because no work was available there and found a job in Kiwana, a small Indiana town, where he earned only his own keep. He was unable to contribute anything to his wife and child, so Rose and their infant moved in with her mother.[55]

Rose's move represents a common working-class method for coping with the Depression—the addition of more people to a household. In South Bend, between 1930 and 1932 alone, more than one-third of the households had doubled up at some point.[56] Most frequently, a married daughter and her husband and children moved into her parents' household; less frequently, a married son's family moved in with his parents or other relatives joined the home. These doubled-up households expanded the family economy by providing more potential wage earners as well as providers of unpaid services, such as grandmothers who cared for their grandchildren while the mothers worked. Yet doubled-up households did not necessarily function harmoniously. Mary T. and her three children lived with her in-laws for two years while her husband was undergoing treatment in a tuberculosis sanitarium. She explained that they left because the children were "too lively" for their grandmother and made her "nervous."[57] Similarly, in black households, various combinations of relatives and lodgers lived together in an attempt to survive the Depression – Richard Wright, his mother, brother, and aunt, for example, lived together in Chicago in the 1930s.[58]

Other families fell apart because there were not enough resources to enable them to stay together. Beatrice T., once a well-paid clerical worker earning $150 a month, reduced to physically onerous, around-the-clock housework for $8 a week in 1933, mirrored in her job experiences her family's financial plight. Her Irish immigrant parents had lost their home and furniture in the spring of 1933. The entire family had scattered across Cleveland to the homes of various relatives. Beatrice's declining income must have contributed to the disaster. Retta K., widowed at the beginning of the Depression, worked as an attendant at Warrensville Institution and later as a housekeeper/manager at a fraternity house; both jobs provided her with lodging. She also worked as a saleswoman and a domestic and rented a place with her high school-age son during those periods. When she was unemployed, she lived with a married daughter on a farm in rural Ohio. After their home broke up, a single daughter, Doris K., a twenty-five-year-old clerical worker, had stayed with a married sister and subsequently lived with a friend of her sister. Doris reported, optimistically that "when the Depression is over we'll all get back together again." In 1933 she had no way of knowing that the Depression would drag on for another eight years.[59]

These stories of daughters and wives illustrate experiences that theories of family cooperation do not take into account. The histories of Catherine T. and Mary P. which opened this article exemplify women who existed outside nuclear families. In 1940, only three-quarters of the female population lived as wives or daughters; the other one-quarter were female heads of household, grandmothers, granddaughters, other adult relatives, lodgers, or live-in servants.[60] Although social scientists of the 1930s termed "unattached" women "nonfamily" women, many of them, in fact, did have families – siblings and children – who were unable or unwilling to provide for them.

The "nonfamily" women often supported their families by contributing part of their paychecks and by assuming additional responsibillities in times of crisis. Once their services were no longer necessary, their families might desert them. Mary H., a white woman born in Chicago in 1889, was nine years old when her father died. At fourteen she left school to help her mother with the laundry she took in to support the three children. Mary did not marry but continued to live at home and to help support her family. In 1928, laid off from her job at a wire company, she decided to stay at home with her invalid mother, whose ill health probably could be attributed to years of hard physical labor as a laundress. During the next six years, Mary cared for her mother, and her two younger brothers supported them. Both brothers married during the Depression; their underemployment and responsibilities for their new families ended their financial contributions to Mary and their mother, who consequently went on relief. After her mother's death in 1934, Mary could not find steady work, partly because of her own poor health; three years later her situation had not changed. Her brothers' allegiances lay with their own conjugal families.[61] Although women were expected to contribute to the families in which they lived, "unattached" women – divorced, deserted, separated, widowed or single – had no one from whom they could claim support. Responsibility and sacrifice were expected and taken for granted, but reciprocal support was not necessarily forthcoming.

Stories like these were not limited to adult siblings or adult children. Esther O., a young married immigrant from the Netherlands, lived with her mother, step-father, husband, and siblings in Cleveland. She voluntarily quit her job in 1929 to care for her sick mother. When her husband lost his job and was unable to contribute to the household, he moved back to his own family's home in Marion, Ohio. By 1933 Esther's mother's health had improved so that she no longer required constant help, and Esther's step-father decreed that she had to "get out." Esther had voluntarily left her job and then separated from her husband to help her family; subsequently, the family rejected her.[62]

Thus, adult siblings, parents, and adult children, the kin most likely to provide aid in time of trouble, frequently failed to support needy women. They used women's energies when they needed them but disdained returning the favor at a later time when the women themselves were needy. Both black and white women, often in their fifties, sixties, or older, applied for relief because they could not find work and could not obtain aid from children or siblings. In 1937 there were 12,000 "unattached" women receiving relief in Chicago alone.[63] Among those in my sample of this group who had once been married, approximately two-fifths had ended their marriages during the Depression. Rose W. "seemed to think that her children should have supported her when she was old," but Rose's children had "kicked out" the sixty-two-year-old Hungarian immigrant.[66] Many older women tried to live with their children, but if they could not get along with them or with their sons- and daughters-in-law, they were forced to move out. Maud J., a white widow of fifty-one, cashed in her insurance policies for living expenses after losing her job. When her daughter learned that she could no longer inherit anything, she refused to take her destitute mother into her home.[67] Stella P., a black woman of sixty-two, refused to live with her daughter because she disapproved of her living with her boyfriend.[64]

Although families relied on women's care and in some cases on their financial contributions, the "nonfamily" women learned that their families were not their most reliable sources of aid. Among the three samples of women applying for or receiving relief as "unattached" persons (who comprise 59 percent of my total sample group), the women reported receiving material aid from their friends much more frequently than from their families. In the sample of single women relief cases in Chicago in 1937, almost three-fifths had received help from friends prior to applying for relief; in contrast, less than one-fifth had gotten any support from their families.[65]

Why were there so many conflicts in families during the Depression? Why did the family economy fail to meet its obligations to its members? What accounts for similarities in the experiences of black and white working-class women? The impact of the Depression, particularly on people who were either economically marginal or dependent, was cataclysmic. This was a long-term crisis. Throughout the thirties, the official unemployment rate never dropped lower than 14.3 percent; estimates of unemployment among nonfarm employees never fell lower than 21.3 percent. Despite the economic gearup for war, the nonfarm unemployment rate still remained 21.3 percent in 1940.

Black women's deprivation was far more severe than that of white women, particularly with regard to jobs. There was the racial and sexual stratification of the labor force already in place, which relegated black women to a few of the worst jobs at the bottom of the occupational ladder. The Depression added endemic unemployment, employers' preferences for white women, and white women's willingness to accept jobs they previously had disdained. The result was a dismal employment situation.

Black women who lived in cities like Chicago, where black communities were relatively new, were probably least likely to have nearby kinship circles on which to rely. Recent migrants left most of their kin behind in the South. Some younger black women did rely on their mothers, sisters, relatives, and friends to raise their children, sending the children South while they remained in the North where wages were higher. Women also turned to friends for help, shaping relationships of cooperation and concern from among available human resources.

Blackwelder's observation that we know little about the internal workings of families deserves emphasis. Analyses of the family economy stress the economic nature of cooperation. Historians have not understood or examined the disruption to family economies because of the compartmentalization of our research. Study of the family economy usually relies on sources quite different from studies of familial discord. Pursuing the records of divorce courts or of social service agencies yields materials for students of family strife but offers little information about economic arrangements; the reverse is equally true.

Although black women's labor force experiences were especially difficult, other aspects of the histories of black and white women were similar during the Depression. The effect of these years on family relations in the urban North and Midwest cut across the races. Families simply could not bear all the strains of the Depression, and they frequently came unglued. Cooperation is the quality that makes families work. It is also the quality whose strength is tested in hard times. Families demanded much from women members, both married and unmarried alike; all too often they gave little in return.

NOTES

The author would like to express her thanks for comments on earlier versions of this article to Miriam Cohen, Joanne Meyerowitz, Mary Ryan, and anonymous reviewers from *Feminist Studies*.

1. Catherine T., 378, I 42, Northern, box 346: Survey Material, Bulletin 158. All interviews are contained within the records of the Women's Bureau, Record Group 86, National Archives, Washington, D.C. The Women's Bureau assigned each interview record a number. In some studies, the Women's Bureau used a single number to record each woman, but in the 1937 Chicago study, each woman was given two different case numbers, and her relief district was also noted. I have not used the last names of the women in order to protect their privacy. When the Women's Bureau conducted the studies with organizations of more well-to-do women, such as the American Association of University Women, it discarded interview records in order to protect the women's privacy. Working-class women deserve the same respect.

2. Mary P., 098, C 24, Canal, box 345: Survey Material, Bulletin 158.

3. Louise A. Tilly and Joan W. Scott, *Women, Work, and Family* (New York: Holt, Rinehart & Winston, 1978), 6.

4. Louise A. Tilly and Miriam Cohen, "Does the Family Have a History? A Review of Theory and Practice in Family History," *Social Science History* 6 (Spring 1982): 151.

5. See, for example, Linda Gordon, "Functions of the Family," in *Voices from Women's Liberation*, ed. Leslie B. Tanner (New York: New American Library, 1970), 181-88; Shulamith Firestone, *The Dialectic of Sex: The Case for Feminist Revolution* (New York: Bantam Books, 1970); Juliet Mitchell, *Woman's Estate* (New York: Random House, 1971).

6. Rayna Rapp, Ellen Ross, and Renate Bridenthal, "Examining Family History," *Feminist Studies* 5 (Spring 1979): 174-200; Heidi I. Hartmann, "The Family As the Locus of Gender, Class, and Political Struggle: The Example of Housework," *Signs* 6 (Spring 1981): 376.

7. Miriam Cohen, "Changing Education Strategies among Immigrant Generations: New York Italians in Comparative Perspective," *Journal of Social History* 15 (Spring 1982): 447; Miriam Cohen, "Italian-American Women in New York City, 1900-1950: Work and School," in *Class, Sex, and the Woman Worker*, ed. Milton Cantor and Bruce Laurie (Westport, Conn.: Greenwood Press, 1977), 122; Sarah Eisenstein, *Give Us Bread but Give Us Roses: Working Women's Consciousness in the United States, 1890 to the First World War* (London: Routledge & Kegan Paul, 1983); Tamara K. Hareven, *Family Time and Industrial Time: The Relationship between the Family and Work in a New England In-*

dustrial Community (Cambridge: Cambridge University Press, 1982); Leslie Woodcock
Tentler, *Wage-Earning Women: Industrial Work and Family Life in the United States,
1900-1930* (New York: Oxford University Press, 1979).

8. Judith E. Smith, *Family Connections: A History of Italian and Jewish Immigrant Lives in
Providence, Rhode Island, 1900-1940* (Albany: State University of New York Press, 1985).

9. Cohen, "Changing Education Strategies among Immigrant Generations," 447, and
"Italian-American Women in New York City," 122.

10. U.S. Bureau of the Census, *Sixteenth Census of the United States, 1940, Population*,
vol. 4, *Characteristics by Age*, pt. 1: *U.S. Summary* (Washington, D.C.: GPO, 1943), 26.
The Fifteenth Census (1930) offers no comparable information about a person's relationship to the head of the household in which she/he lives. Far more than one-quarter
of adult women are likely to spend some part of their lives in one of these categories. I
do not intend to imply that women who are neither wives nor daughters are never
discussed in this literature, but they are certainly not its focus. Although I am critical of
the family economy analysis, I believe it answers more historical questions than either
the demographic or sentiments interpretations of family history. See Tilly and Cohen
for a useful summary of interpretations of family history.

11. Angela Y. Davis, "Reflections on the Black Woman's Role in the Community of
Slaves," *Black Scholar* 3 (December 1971): 2-16, and *Women, Race, and Class* (New York:
Random House, 1981), 5-12.

12. U.S. Department of Labor, Women's Bureau, *Time of Change: 1983 Handbook on
Women Workers*, Bulletin 218 (Washington, D.C.: GPO, 1983), 44.

13. The classics of the family disorganization school are E. Franklin Frazier, *The Negro
Family in the United States*, revised and abridged edition (Chicago: University of Chicago
Press, 1966); Daniel P. Moynihan, *The Negro Family: The Case for National Action*,
Department of Labor, Office of Policy Planning and Research (Washington, D.C.: GPO,
1965); reprinted in *The Moynihan Report and the Politics of Controversy*, ed. Lee Rain-
water and William L. Yancey (Cambridge: MIT Press, 1967), 41-124.

14. Carol Stack, *All Our Kin: Strategies for Survival in a Black Community* (New York:
Harper & Row, 1974); James Borchert, *Alley Life in Washington: Family, Community, and
Folklife in the City, 1850-1970* (Urbana: University of Illinois Press, 1980); Shepard Krech
III, "Black Family Organization in the Nineteenth Century: An Ethnological Per-
spective," *Journal of Interdisciplinary History* 12 (Winter 1982): 429-52; Herbert G. Gut-
man, *The Black Family in Slavery and Freedom, 1750-1925* (New York: Pantheon, 1976);
Harriet Pipes McAdoo, "Black Mothers and the Extended Family Support Network," in
The Black Women, ed. LaFrances Rodgers-Rose (Beverly Hills: Sage Publications, 1980);
Jualynne Dodson, "Conceptualizations of Black Families," in *Black Families*, ed. Harriette Pipes McAdoo (Beverly Hills: Sage Publications, 1981); Harriette Pipes McAdoo
and Rosalyn Terborg-Penn, "Historical Trends and Perspectives of Afro-American
Families," *Trends in History* 3 (Spring/Summer 1985): 97-111.

15. Andrew Billingsley, *Black Families in White America* (Englewood Cliffs, N.J.:
Prentice-Hall, 1968); Gutman; Elizabeth H. Pleck, "A Mother's Wages: Income-Earning
among Married Italian and Black Women, 1896-1911," in *The American Family in Social-
Historical Perspective*, 2d. ed., edited by Michael Gordon (New York: St. Martin's Press,
1978), 510; Davis, *Women, Race, and Class*, 5-12.

16. Niara Sudarkasa, "Interpreting the African Heritage in Afro-American Family
Organization," in *Black Families*, 37-53.

17. Measuring family disintegration over the course of the decade is difficult. The census, however, confirms the interview evidence. Comparing the proportion of families
headed by women in each of the four cities at the beginning and end of the decade, I
found that female-headed households increased at a rate between 20.9 percent in
Cleveland to 25.9 percent in South Bend (see Table 1).

Table 1. – Increase of Female-Headed Households

City	Households Headed by Women, 1930 (%)	Households Headed by Women, 1940 (%)	Rate of Change
Chicago	13.6	17.1	25.7
Cleveland	13.4	16.2	20.9
Philadelphia	15.9	19.5	22.6
South Bend	10.8	13.6	25.9

Source: Figures calculated from U.S. Bureau of the Census, *Fifteenth Census of the United States, 1930, Population*, vol. 6, *Families by States*, 68, (Washington, D.C.: GPO, 1933), *Sixteenth Census of the United States, 1940, Population*, vol. 4, *Characteristics by Age*, pt. 1, 169; pt. 2, pp. 624, 695; pt. 4, pp. 27, 227.

18. Susan Ware, *Holding Their Own: American Women in the 1930s* (Boston: Twayne Publishers, 1982), 13-17; Robert S. McElvaine, *The Great Depression: America, 1929-1941* (New York: Times Books, 1984), 175-81; Lois Scharf, *To Work and to Wed: Female Employment, Feminism, and the Great Depression* (Westport, Conn.: Greenwood Press, 1980), 158; Ruth Milkman, "Women's Work and the Economic Crisis: Some Lessons from the Great Depression," *Review of Radical Political Economics*, 8 (Spring 1976): 83; Winifred Wandersee, *Women's Work and Family Values, 1920-1940* (Cambridge: Harvard University Press, 1981), 112.

19. E. Wright Bakke, *Citizens without Work: A Study of the Effects of Unemployment upon the Worker's Social Relations and Practices* (New Haven: Yale University Press, 1940); Robert Cooley Angell, *The Family Encounters the Depression* (New York: Charles Scribner's Sons, 1936); Ruth Shonle Cavan and Katherine Howland Ranck, *The Family and the Depression: A Study of One Hundred Chicago Families* (Chicago: University of Chicago Press, 1938); Mirra Komarovsky, *The Unemployed Man and His Family: The Effect of Unemployment Upon the Status of the Man in Fifty-Nine Families* (New York: Dryden Press, 1940).

20. Scharf; Wandersee.

21. Tentler, 147.

22. Julia Kirk Blackwelder, *Women of the Depression: Caste and Culture in San Antonio, 1929-1939* (College Station: Texas A & M University Press, 1984), 25-42.

23. Lois Rita Helmbold, "Downward Occupational Mobility during the Great Depression: Urban Black and White Working-Class Women," *Labor History*, forthcoming, 1988.

24. See the following U.S. Department of Labor, Women's Bureau publications: *Wage-Earning Women and the Industrial Conditions of 1930: A Survey of South Bend*, Bulletin 92 (Washington, D.C.: GPO, 1932); *The Effects of the Depression on Wage Earners' Families: A Second Survey of South Bend*, Bulletin 108 (Washington, D.C.: GPO, 1936); *Women Unemployed Seeking Relief in 1933*, Bulletin 139 (Washington, D.C.: GPO, 1936); and *Unattached Women on Relief in Chicago, 1937*, Bulletin 158 (Washington, D.C.: GPO, 1938).

In South Bend, Indiana, the Women's Bureau conducted a house-to-house survey of employed women in working-class neighborhoods in 1930, followed by a repeat study of the same households two years later. Data were obtained from all household members, including women outside the labor force. The group was overwhelmingly white, as was South Bend in the 1930s. Only 2 of the 183 households were black. One-fifth of the 274 women workers were immigrants, mostly Polish and Hungarian, and many more were daughters of immigrants. One-half were single (mostly young daughters), more than one-third were married, and the remainder were formerly married. Because the interviews examined the entire household, women in occupations besides clerical and service work, primarily factory operatives, were included and serve as a useful comparison for conditions in different sectors of the labor force. Although employment had been a criterion for inclusion in the first study, by 1932 the employment status of these women spanned the range of possibilities.

The Cleveland study was a record of applicants for work at the Friendly Service Bureau of the Cleveland YWCA. Because the YWCA did not offer services to black or Jewish women, the sample was completely white and Christian. More than one-quarter were immigrants and many more were daughters of immigrants. Like the YWCA's clientele, the group was predominantly young and single, but approximately three-tenths were over thirty and one-quarter were married or formerly married. Although the women were seeking jobs, some were already employed and others became employed in jobs offered to them by the placement service. My sample contained 294 women.

Unemployed, "unattached" women who applied to several pre-New Deal agencies for make work, relief, or other assistance in 1932 and 1933 were studied in Chicago and Philadelphia. The two groups were quite similar; about one-half were over forty-five and one-half were younger; two-thirds had been married previously. About four-tenths were black, one-tenth were immigrants, and one-half were native-born white women. All had been employed, although sometimes only briefly. Unemployment and/or the end of their marriages through death or separation had left these women without support and led them to apply for help. Although these samples contain some young women, they are most representative of middle-aged and older women living outside families. Presumably, the women lived alone, but in fact many shared living quarters with friends.

The School of Social Service Administration of the University of Chicago, the Chicago Relief Administration, and the Women's Bureau investigated and interviewed a representative group of the 12,000 women receiving relief payments as single-person cases in Chicago in January 1937. In my sample of 219, half were black, one-third were native-born whites, and the rest were immigrants. This group was the oldest of the five samples; one-half were fifty or older. Only one-fifth had never married.

25. Young, single black women and married black women do appear in the samples, but not in proportion to their share of the population. The two samples that contained the bulk of young, single white women and married white women, South Bend and Cleveland, contain few black women. I was unable to locate another source that provided a comparable group of black women.

26. U.S. Bureau of the Census, *Fifteenth Census of the United States, 1930, Population,* vol. 2, *General Report, Statistics by Subjects* (Washington, D.C.: GPO, 1933), 118, 120, 127, 129.

27. Abraham Hoffman, *Unwanted Mexican Americans in the Great Depression: Repatriation Pressures, 1929-1939* (Tucson: University of Arizona Press, 1974), 119-20. Blackwelder (p. 112) found that San Antonio relief administrators discriminated against both black and Mexican applicants.

28. Furthermore, the interviewers and the interviewees were separated by class and sometimes by race. An encouraging and sympathetic interviewer might gain more detailed information about her subject's life and emotions. Yet the interviewers made many negative judgments, revealing racist and classist attitudes in their notes. The original purposes of the studies did not concern familial relations, the interviewer/interviewee dynamic in many cases militated against personal information being revealed, and yet we have widespread evidence of familial distress and destruction.

29. Of the households studied, 77.3 percent used three or more strategies that demand-

ed additional labor from women. Only 37.6 percent of the households relied on as many as three financial strategies.

30. Figures were calculated from U.S. Bureau of the Census, *Historical Statistics of the United States, Colonial Times to 1970*, Bicentennial Edition, pt. 1 (Washington, D.C.: GPO, 1975), 49.

31. There are no reliable national unemployment data enumerated by sex. Having examined various regional data and estimates of national data, Milkman (pp. 75-81) has concluded: "the available data clearly indicate that, insofar as their paid labor force participation was concerned, women were less affected than men by the contraction."

32. Figures were calculated from U.S. Bureau of the Census, *Fifteenth Census, 1930, Population*, vol. 5, *Occupations, General Report*, (Washington, D.C.: GPO, 1933), 74.

33. Figures were calculated from U.S. Bureau of the Census, *Fifteenth Census, 1930 Population*, vol. 2, 954, 955, 965, 1005; vol. 4, *Occupations, by States*, (Washington, D.C.: GPO, 1933), pp. 454, 510, 1301, 1425; vol. 5, p. 274. The census constructed age groups of fifteen to nineteen, twenty to twenty-four, and twenty-five to forty-four. I would have preferred to examine the experience of women aged eighteen to thirty-five, but that was not possible. Single black women between the ages of twenty and twenty-four were slightly less likely to work for wages than white women in three of the four cities. In Philadelphia, the city characterized by the longest-standing black community, young black women's labor force participation rates were the same as those of young white women. Nationally, the average was lower; urban residence caused all young single women to be more likely to be employed.

34. Pauline H., 261, box 306: Survey Materials, Bulletin 139.

35. Of the households studied, 40.4 percent reported having full-time female workers, compared with only 20.2 percent having full-time male workers.

36. In Cleveland, brief interviews were conducted at the YWCA Friendly Service Bureau and were oriented primarily to the job-finding functions of the bureau. In South Bend, the interviews lasted longer and covered more areas of daily life, but they were conducted in the homes of the women. Other family members were often present, possibly inhibiting the women interviewed.

37. Helen M., 435, box 306.

38. Overall, school attendance of sixteen-year-old and seventeen-year-old women and men increased greatly between 1930 and 1940. Slightly more than one-half of sixteen-year-old and seventeen-year-old women attended school in South Bend and Cleveland in 1930; by 1940 over three-quarters of the age group was in school. The men in these cities followed the same pattern but were a few percentage points more likely to be in school in both years. See U.S. Bureau of the Census, *Sixteenth Census of the United States, 1940, Population*, vol. 2, *Characteristics of Population*, (Washington, D.C.: GPO, 1943), pt. 2, p. 822; pt. 5, p. 711. Women between fourteen and nineteen lost 43.6 percent of their share of the female labor force between 1929 and 1940. See Helmbold.

39. One of the Hundreds to Frances Perkins, 28 July 1935, Cleveland, Ohio, box 926: Correspondence–Household (Domestic) File, File: Household Employees, 1934-35, Records of the Women's Bureau, Record Group 86, National Archives.

40. Ruth K., 351, box 306.

41. Josephine B., Irene B., 0850, box 253: Household Schedules, Matched with 1930 Schedules, Bulletin 108. "Matched with 1930 Schedules" refers to interview schedules from South Bend in 1932 which were matched up with interview schedules for the same people from 1930. (There were two separate studies of South Bend, 1930 and 1932.) This contrasts with some archival boxes that contain only the 1930 schedules, for people the interviewers could not locate in 1932.

42. Samuel A. Stouffer and Lyle M. Spencer, "Marriage and Divorce in Recent Years," *Annals of the American Academy of Political and Social Science* 18 (November 1936): 58.

U.S. Bureau of the Census, *Historical Statistics* of the U.S., pt. 1, p. 64. No breakdowns by class or race are available.

43. See Joanne J. Meyerowitz, *Women Adrift: Wage-Earning Women Apart from Family in Chicago, 1880-1830,* (Chicago: University of Chicago Press, forthcoming, 1988). Social workers and social scientists of the period used the term "adrift" to describe any woman not moored to a family or at least to a husband. They also used the terms "unattached" and "nonfamily" for the same purpose.

44. Grace S., 617, box 305; Margaret T., 663, box 305.

45. Helen B., 0201, box 589: Survey Materials, Bulletin 139.

46. Mandolyn B., 296, J 11, Oakwood, box 344: Survey Materials, Bulletin 158.

47. U.S Bureau of the Census, *Fifteenth Census, 1930, Population,* vol. 5, p. 329. Of black married women, 33.2 percent worked for wages, compared with 9.8 percent of native-born white and 8.5 percent of immigrant white married women. This national pattern held true in the four cities I studied.

48. In 1940, 14.3 percent of married women were employed, an increase of 22.2 percent and an increase of 28 percent of their share of the female labor force. The Sixteenth Census did not compare women's employment status with both their race and their marital status at the same time, to make possible comparisons with 1929 by specific groups. Black women's labor force participation declined from 43.3 percent to 33.5 percent between 1929 and 1940. *Fifteenth Census, 1930, Population,* vol. 5, p. 274; *Sixteenth Census, 1940, Population,* vol. 2, pt. 1, pp. 44, 47; vol. 3, pt. 1, p. 18. See Helmbold.

49. For the consumer theory, see Scharf, 147-53; and Wandersee, 1-54. Their conclusions may be accurate for middle-class homes. Wandersee avoids dealing with the class nature of this issue by using the term "middle income." Her definition of middle income was $1,000 or more a year. See Winifred D. Wandersee Bolin, "The Economics of Middle-Income Family Life: Working Women during the Great Depression," *Journal of American History* 65 (June 1978): 63. Only 30 percent of the working-class households in the South Bend sample would have qualified for this middle-income range, based on a one-month's report of income during the fall of 1932.

50. Edna H., 0538, box 255 and Emma D., 0665, box 256: Household Schedules, Matched with 1930 Schedules, Bulletin 108.

51. Although there are no official data for an unofficial end to marriages, contemporary reporters offered this observation. See *Historical Statistics of the United States,* pt. 1, p. 64. No data are available by class or race.

52. Gertrude W., 474, K 26, Union Park, box 346.

53. Elizabeth H., 056, B 20, Bridgeport, box 347: Survey Materials, Bulletin 158.

54. Mary B., 430, J 45, Oakwood, box 344.

55. Rose W., 0284, box 263: Household Schedules, Matched with 1930 Schedules, Bulletin 108.

56. Thirty-five percent lived doubled up.

57. Mary T., 0243, box 260: Household Schedules, Matched with 1930 Schedules, Bulletin 108.

58. Richard Wright, *American Hunger,* (New York: Harper & Row, 1977). The Chicago and Philadelphia samples containing black women have anecdotal evidence about doubling up, but these studies provide no systemic detail comparable to that presented in the South Bend sample.

59. Beatrice T., 661, box 305.

60. Retta K., 311, Doris K., 309, box 306. Figures calculated from U.S. Bureau of the Census, *Sixteenth Census, 1940, Population,* vol. 4, p. 169.

61. Mary H., 262, G 16, Lawndale, box 346.

62. Esther O., 483, box 306.

63. Women's Bureau, *Unattached Women on Relief, 1937.*

64. Rose W., 216, F 7, Irving Park, box 344. Maud J., 365, box 304. Stella P., 514, L 11, Washington Park, box 345.

65. In this sample of single women, 58.9 percent had received help from friends, but only 18.7 percent had received any aid from their families. A significant proportion of these women had become "unattached" during the Depression, either through the death of their spouses or through the dissolution of their marriages.

66. *Historical Statistics of the United States*, pt. 1, p. 126; *Sixteenth Census, 1940, Population*, vol. 3, *Labor Force*, pt. 1, *U.S. Summary*, p. 18.

RACE, SEX, AND CLASS: BLACK FEMALE TOBACCO WORKERS IN DURHAM, NORTH CAROLINA, 1920-1940, AND THE DEVELOPMENT OF FEMALE CONSCIOUSNESS

BEVERLY W. JONES

This article examines how race, sex, and class affected the lives and consciousness of black female tobacco workers in Durham, North Carolina, and how they conceptualized work and its meaning in their lives. The research was based on fifteen interviews. The interviewees fall into three broad age categories: five were born before 1908, seven between 1908 and 1916, and three between 1916 and 1930. All were born in the rural South. The majority migrated to Durham in the 1920s, subsequently entering the labor force.

Historically, black labor of both females and males has been critical to the tobacco manufacturing industry. As cigarette manufacture became mechanized, blacks were hired as stemmers, sorters, hangers, and pullers. These "dirty" jobs were seen as an extension of field labor and therefore as "Negro work" for which whites would not compete.[1] The rapidly expanding number of tobacco factories employed the thousands of black females and males migrating from the rural South. The pull of better paying jobs and the push of falling farm prices, perennial pests, and hazardous weather induced a substantial number of black sharecroppers, renters, and landowners to seek refuge in Durham.

Charlie Necoda Mack, the father of three future female tobacco workers, remembered the difficulties of making an adequate living out of farming in Manning, South Carolina. "I was a big cotton farmer; I made nine bales of cotton one year. Next year I made, I think, one or two, and the next year I didn't make none. I left in July, I had to leave. I borrowed money to get up here—

Feminist Studies 10, no. 3 (Fall 1984). © by Feminist Studies, Inc.

Durham. I had six children and I know no jobs available. Well, then I came up here in July in 1922 and got a job at the factory. And by Christmas I had all my children with clothes and everything." Unlike the Mack family who were pushed out of South Carolina, others were pulled into the city. Dora Miller, after marrying in 1925, left Apex, North Carolina, because she heard of the "better paying jobs in Durham." Mary Dove, at age ten and accompanied by her family, left Roxboro, North Carolina, because a "Duke agent told us that a job in the factory at Liggett Myers was waiting for my daddy." Rosetta Branch, age eighteen and single, left Wilmington, North Carolina, because her mother had died, and "there were no other kinfolks."[2]

Thus, Durham's gainfully employed black population swelled from 6,869 in 1910 to 12,402 in 1930. (The city's total black population in 1930 was 23,481.) According to the census, the number of black female tobacco workers in 1930 was 1,979 out of a total black female population of 12,388. (See table 1.)

TABLE 1   Tobacco Industry Employment by Race and Gender

Durham County: 1930

White		Negro	
Male	Female	Male	Female
2,511	2,932	1,336	1,979

North Carolina: 1940

White		Negro	
Male	Female	Male	Female
6,517	3,175	5,899	5,898

Source: U.S. Bureau of the Census, *Population: 1930* (Washington, D.C.: GPO), vol. 3, pt. 2, pp. 355, 378; *Labor Force: 1940* (Washington, D.C.: GPO, 1940), vol. 3, pt. 4, p. 566.

Durham and Winston Salem tobacco factories employed more black females than other cities: one-half of the number of women employed in tobacco factories in 1930 in these cities were black compared with the 19.7 in Petersburg and Richmond in Virginia.[3]

Upon disembarking the central train station, the newly arrived southern migrants were immediately faced with race restrictions. Rigidly segregated communities were the dominant feature of

Durham's black life. Many of the migrants settled in the dilap-
idated housing in the larger communities of East End and Hayti, a
bustling commercial district of black businesses, and in the
smaller areas of Buggy Bottom and Hickstown. Almost all black
workers rented either from the company and white landlords or
from black real estate agents. The comments of Annie Barbee, the
daughter of Necoda Mack, reflect her first impressions of
Durham.

We were renting in the Southern part of Durham—the Negro section—on
Popular Street, second house from the corner, across the railroad tracks. The
house was small, two rooms, but somehow we managed. The street was not
paved and when it rained it got muddy and in the fall, the wind blew all the dust
into your eyes and face. There were no private family bathrooms. But it was an
exciting life. See, in the country things were so dull—no movie houses. . . . Up
here people were always fighting and going on all the time.[4]

Despite the exploitive living conditions described by Barbee, urban employment did have some liberating consequences for rural
daughters.

Race restricted the black population to segregated neighborhoods and also determined the kinds of jobs black females could
get. Black female tobacco workers also faced discrimination as
poor people and as females. Although class and sex restraints
punctuated the lives of white female tobacco workers, their impact was reinforced by management policies. Although white
females' wages were a fraction of white males' and inadequate to
support a family, black females' wages were even lower. According to some black female tobacco workers, the wage inequity
led many white women to consider black women inferior. This in
turn led to an atmosphere of mistrust between black and white
females. Management strengthened racial and class inequities in
hiring practices, working conditions, and spatial organization of
the factory, and therefore impeded the formation of gender
bonds among working-class women.

Black females were usually hired as if they were on an auction
block. "Foremen lined us up against the walls," one worker
stated, "and chose the sturdy robust ones." Mary Dove recalled
that she had "to hold up one leg at a time and then bend each
backwards and forwards."[5] Once hired, black and white women
were separated on different floors at the American Tobacco Company and in entirely different buildings at the Liggett Myers
Tobacco Company. In the 1920s and 1930s, according to a report
by the Women's Bureau (the federal agency created in 1920), and

confirmed by my interviews, 98 percent of these black females were confined to the prefabrication department where they performed the "dirty" jobs—sorting, cleaning, and stemming tobacco.[6] White females had the "cleaner" jobs in the manufacturing and packing department as they caught, inspected, and packed the tobacco. However, both jobs were defined by the sex division of labor—jobs to be performed by women. Black men moved between the areas pushing 500-lb hogsheads of tobacco while white men worked as inspectors, safeguarding the sanctity of class and sex segregation.[7]

Reflecting on these blatant differences in the working conditions, some fifty years later, many black women expressed anger at their injustice. Annie Barbee recalled: "You're over here doing all the nasty dirty work. And over there on the cigarette side white women over there wore white uniforms. . . . You're over here handling all the old sweaty tobacco. There is a large difference. It ain't right!" Rosetta Branch spoke of her experience with anger. "They did not treat us Black folks right. They worked us like dogs. Put us in separate buildings. . . thinking maybe we were going to hurt those white women. Dirty work, dirty work we had to do. Them white women think they something working doing the lighter jobs."[8] These comments reflect both the effectiveness of management policies to aggravate racial and sexual differences in order to preclude any possible bonds of gender, but also illustrate the unhealthy working conditions to which black women were exposed.

In fact, the interviews indicate that the health of some black women suffered in the factories. Pansy Cheatham, another daughter of Necoda Mack, maintained that the Georgia leaf-tobacco "was so dusty that I had to go to the tub every night after work. There was only one window and it got so hot that some women just fainted. The heat and smell was quite potent." Mary Dove recounted one of her fainting spells. "You know on the floor there was a salt dispenser, because it would get so hot. I did not feel so well when I came to work but I had to work. After about two hours standing on my feet, I got so dizzy—I fell out. My clothes was soaking wet from my head to my feet. When I woke up I was in the dispensary."[9]

Blanche Scott and another worker were forced to quit for health reasons. Scott, who began working for Liggett Myers in 1919, quit four years later. "When I left the factory, it became difficult for me to breathe. The dust and fumes of the burly tobacco made me cough. The burly tobacco from Georgia had chicken feathers and even manure in it. Sometimes I would put an orange in my mouth to keep from throwing up. I knew some women who died of TB." The other worker had miscarried twice. Pregnant again, she decided not to return to the American Tobacco Company. "I felt that all that standing while I stemmed tobacco," she stated, "was the reason I lost my two children." Some women found momentary relief from the dust by retreating outside the confines of the factory complex to breathe the fresh air while sitting under trees or on the sidewalk during lunch.[10]

These comments on the poor, unhealthy, working conditions were verified by research on Durham's death records between 1911 and 1930. In many instances, the records were imprecise and failed to provide information about race and occupation. Of the 105 certificates that identified black women as tobacco workers, who died between 1911 and 1920, 48 (about 46 percent) died of tuberculosis, sometimes listed as phthisis and consumption. Of the 134 recorded deaths of black female tobacco workers between 1920 and 1930, 86 (64.5 percent) died of tuberculosis. Because tuberculosis is a bacteria that can be transmitted by a tubercular person through the cough, it is likely that poorly ventilated rooms and incessant coughing by workers, possibly by a carrier, made some workers susceptible to the disease, although deplorable living conditions of workers cannot be dismissed as a contributing factor.[11]

As studies have found in other cities, black females in Durham were more likely to work than white females.[12] Black females also earned lower wages than white females. In the early 1900s, wages for black tobacco workers, both female and male, ranked the lowest in the nation. In 1930, 45.5 percent of native-born white women in Durham were gainfully employed—27.7 percent in tobacco. While 44 percent of black women were working, 36.2 percent were employed in tobacco. From 1920 to 1930, Durham's white female tobacco workers averaged about 29 cents per hour, while black female hand stemmers earned about 11.9 cents an hour. However, black men, as well as black women who stemmed tobacco by machine, averaged about 27 cents an hour, still less than white women.[13]

Wage differential continued and worsened throughout the 1930s. By the eve of the New Deal, a Women's Bureau survey reported figures for North Carolina which revealed an even higher wage discrepancy. White women working in the making

and packing departments reported a median weekly wage of
$15.35. Wages ranged from $14.10 earned as catchers to $20.50
on older packing machines. On the newest packing machines, the
median wage was $18.15. Black women, working in the leaf de-
partment, reported a median weekly wage of $7.95. Hand stem-
mers earned a median wage of $6.50.[14]

The low wage was itself demeaning to black female workers.
But the inadequate wages also forced many into the labor force at
an early age. Black women thus worked for a longer part of their
lives, and henceforth were more vulnerable to diseases and other
health problems. Blanche Scott, for example, began working at
the age of twelve. "Since my mother stayed so sick, I had to go to
work. I worked at Liggett Myers after school got out. I attended
West End School. I'd normally get out at 1:30 and worked from
two o'clock to 6 p.m. I was just twelve years old. In the summer,
they're let children come and work all day until four o'clock."
Pansy Cheatham began working at age thirteen. "My father talked
to the foreman," she stated, "I worked because my sisters Mae
and Annie worked; I stemmed tobacco by hand. But Papa did collect the money and use it for food and clothing." Cheatham's
statement would indicate that the gender hierarchy of the black
family resided in the father who controlled the daughter's
wages.[15]

Many women saw their employment as a means of "helping
out the family." Better stated in the words of Margaret Turner,
"that's what a family is all about, when we—the children—can
help out our parents."[16] Out of the fifteen interviewees, the ten
women who entered the work force at an early age all conceptualized the central meaning of their work in relation to their
families.

By the late 1920s and early 1930s, the enforcement of the Child
Labor Law of 1917 arrested the practice of employing children
under the age of sixteen. "They began to ask for your birth cer-
tificate," one worker stated. A study done by Hugh Penn Brinton,
substantiated the decrease of child labor employment in
Durham's factories. Brinton found that from 1919 to 1930 the
percentage of black laboring-class households sending children
into the labor force had decreased from 35 to 14 percent.[17]

However, the legislation against child labor did not force the
wages up for black tobacco workers, and the constant low earning power of both female and male breadwinners continued to affect the lives of black female workers psychologically. Many

women submitted to the demands of the foreman and other company officials. Viewed as short-term cheap labor, some females submitted to physical and verbal harassment, because in many instances defiance would have certainly resulted in the loss of jobs. Dora Miller asserted that "since the foreman knew you needed the job, you obeyed all of his demands without question. He called you dirty names and used foul language but you took it." Mary Dove recalled what it was like to work under one "of the toughest bosses." "Our foreman was a one-eyed fella named George Hill. He was tight! He was out of South Carolina, and he was tight. I mean tight! He'd get on top of them machines—they had a machine that altered the tobacco—he'd get on top of that machine and watch you, see if you was working all right and holler down and curse. Holler down and say, "GD. . . get to work! GD. . . go to work there you ain't doin' nothin." Janie Mae Lyons remembered one who walked in on her while she "was in the sitting position on the stool" and told her "that if you ain't finished then you can pack up and leave. I was so embarrassed and that's what I did."[18]

Lyons's departure from the factory represented a form of militancy—a definitive stance against further harassment. Other women resisted verbally. Annie Barbee publicly castigated "women who allowed the foreman to fumble their behind" and further stated that if "one did that to me he would be six feet under." She indicated no one ever did. One worker resisted "by playing the fool." "The foreman thought I was crazy and left me alone."[19]

Constantly resisting physical and verbal abuse and trying to maintain their jobs, the workers were further threatened by increased mechanization. "I don't think it is right," one woman stated, "to put them machines to take away from us poor people." "Because of the strain we work under," another maintained, "they don't care nothing for us." One woman recalled crying at the machines because she could not quit in the face of high unemployment. "With them machines you have to thread the tobacco in. Them machines run so fast that after you put in one leaf you got to be ready to thread the other. If you can't keep pace the foreman will fire you right on the spot. Sometimes I get so nervous but I keep on goin'."[20]

The increased mechanization of the tobacco factories resulting in physical hardships of female workers can to some degree be attributed to Franklin D. Roosevelt's National Industrial Recovery

Acts of 1933 and 1934. On the one hand, President Roosevelt's New Deal measure fostered economic stability for many black families by establishing standard minimum wages and maximum hours. On the other hand, this standardization exacerbated the job insecurity of black workers by indirectly catalyzing many companies to maximize profits by replacing hand labor with technology. During the latter part of the 1930s, Liggett Myers closed its green leaf department that had employed the majority of black women.[21]

The long-term insecurities of their jobs led black female stemmers to organize Local 194. The limited success of the union was reflected in the decline of its membership of two thousand in January 1935 to less than two hundred by May 1935. Black female union members found little support from either Local 208, black controlled, or Local 176, white controlled. In the eyes of the male unionists, the temporary nature of women's jobs excluded them from any serious consideration by the locals.[22] Conscious of their auxiliary position and the lack of support from male-led unions, black females chose not to support the April 16, 1939, strike at Liggett Myers. Reporting for work on that day, they were turned away as management had no other recourse but to close the factory. Dora Miller recalled that the black stemmery workers "were never involved in the strike because demands for wage increases did not include us."[23] On April 26, 1939, the company capitulated. The contract indeed reaffirmed Miller's assessment because the stemmery workers were not mentioned.[24]

The factory policies of hiring, wages, working conditions, and spatial segregation, inherently reinforced by racism, the "cult of true white womanhood," and the inadvertent effect of New Deal governmental measures, all came together to touch the lives of black women tobacco workers, with sex, race, and class exploitation. These practices further dissipated any possible gender bonds between black women and white women workers. As a race, black female tobacco workers were confined to unhealthy segregated areas either in separate buildings or on separate floors. As a working class, they were paid inadequate wages. As a sex, they were relegated to the worst, lowest paid, black women's jobs.

Black females conceptualized work as a means of "helping out the family." Denied self-respect and dignity in the factory, black female tobacco workers felt a need to validate themselves in other spheres. Victimized by their working conditions, female tobacco workers looked to the home as a preferred if not powerful arena. The home became the inner world that countered the factory control over their physical well-being. The duality of their lives—workers of production and nurturers of the family—could be assessed as a form of double jeopardy. But it was their role as nurturers, despite the hardship of work, that provided them with a sense of purpose and "joy." As Pansy Cheatham described her daily routine, "I get up at 5:30 a.m. I feed, clothe, and kiss my children. They stay with my sister while I work. At 7 a.m. I am on the job. A half-hour for lunch at about twelve noon. At 4 p.m. I quit work. At home about 4:30 then I cook, sometimes mend and wash clothes before I retire. About 11:30 I go to bed with joy in my heart for my children are safe and I love them so."[25]

Black females who worked together in the tobacco factories also had the positive experience of creating networks of solidarity. Viewing their plight as one, black females referred to one another as "sisters." This sisterhood was displayed in the collection of money during sickness and death and celebration of birthdays. The networks established in the factory overlapped into the community and church. Many of these workers belonged to the same churches—Mount Vernon, Mt. Gilead, and White Rock Baptist Church—and functioned as leaders of the usher boards, missionary circles, and Sunday School programs. These bonds were enhanced in the community by the development of clubs. These church groups and female's clubs overlapped the factory support networks and functioned in similar ways.

Finally, the resistance to the physical and verbal abuse that was a constant in the work lives of black women fostered among some a sense of autonomy, strength, and self-respect. Annie Barbee was one of those women. The assertiveness, dignity, and strength she developed through work became an intricate part of her private life. At age forty and pregnant, she decided to obtain private medical assistance despite her husband's resistance. "When you know things ain't right God gave you a head and some sense. That's my body. I knew I wasn't going to Duke Clinic. And I was working and making my own money, I went where I wanted to go. You see, being married don't mean that your husband controls your life. That was my life and I was carrying his child, it's true, but I was going to look after myself."[26]

Although the work experience of black women tobacco workers was one of racial, sex, and class oppression, the early advent into the labor force, the resistance to exploitation, and the longevity of work created a consciousness that fostered a sense of strength and dignity among some women in this working class. Management tactics of wage inequity, hiring practices, and racial-sexual division of labor pitted black women against white women economically as workers, and made the formation of gender bonds across race lines all but impossible. Yet among black women, the linkages of sisterhood engendered a consciousness of female strength, if not feminism.

NOTES

I am deeply grateful to North Carolina Central University for a Faculty Research Grant and for the excellent editorial comments of the *Feminist Studies* editors.

1. For discussion of the historical involvement of black labor in tobacco manufacturing, see Joseph C. Robert, *The Tobacco Kingdom* (North Carolina: Duke University Press, 1938).
2. Charlie Necoda Mack, interview with author, 22 May 1979, on file in the Southern Oral History Program, University of North Carolina, Chapel Hill, hereafter cited as SOHP/UNC. Dora Miller, interview with author, 6 June 1979, SOHP/UNC; Mary Dove, interview with author, 7 July 1979, SOHP/UNC; Rosetta Branch, interview with author, 15 Aug. 1981.
3. The 1940 labor force figures do not include information for Durham County. U.S. Bureau of the Census, *Population: 1930* (Washington, D.C.: GPO, 1930), 3:341. In 1900, the major tobacco industries in the South were the American Tobacco Company and Liggett Myers in Durham; R.J. Reynolds in Winston Salem; and P. Lorillard in Richmond, Virginia.
4. Annie Barbee, interview, 28 May 1979, SOHP/UNC.
5. Interview, 30 May 1981; Mary Dove, interview.
6. Women's Bureau, *The Effects of Changing Conditions in the Cigar and Cigarette Industries,* Bulletin no. 110 (Washington, D.C.: GPO, 1932), 774-75. The Women's Bureau was established by Congress in 1920 under the aegis of the United States Department of Labor. Its purpose was to gather information and to provide advice to working women.
7. Mary Dove, interview; interviews, 15 and 28 Aug. 1981.
8. Annie Barbee and Rosetta Branch, interviews.
9. Pansy Cheatham, interview with author, 9 July 1979, SOHP/UNC; Mary Dove, interview.
10. Blanche Scott, interview with author, 11 July 1979, SOHP/UNC; interviews, 8, 15 June, 1981; Mary Dove, Annie Barbee interviews.
11. Death Certificates, 1911-1930, Durham County Health Department, Vital Records, Durham, North Carolina. I was also interested in the correlation of working conditions and female-related maladies such as stillbirths, miscarriages, and uterine disorders. Further perusal of death certificates of stillbirths were less valuable for there were no indications of mothers' occupations. Even hospital statistics lacked occupational data. This area of inquiry as it relates to the health of black female workers and working conditions needs further research. Further questions that will have to be explored include: Was there a higher percentage of female tobacco workers dying of

tuberculosis than non-female tobacco workers? How long were stricken female workers employed in the factory? How much weight must be given to the working environment over that of home environs? Despite the lack of solid data on these questions, the interviews and death records clearly indicate that racial division of labor negatively impacted upon the health of many black female tobacco workers.

12. Elizabeth H. Pleck, "A Mother's Wage: Income Earning among Married Italian and Black Women, 1896-1911," in *The American Family in Social-Historical Perspective*, 2d ed, ed. Michael Gordon (New York: St. Martin's Press, 1978), 490-510; "Culture, Class, and Family Life among Low-Income Urban Negroes," in *Employment, Race, and Poverty*, ed. Arthur M. Ross and Herbert Hill (New York: Harcourt, Brace and World, 1967), 149-72; "The Kindred of Veola Jackson: Residence and Family Organization of an Urban Black American Family," in *Afro-American Anthropology: Contemporary Perspective*, ed. Norman E. Whitten, Jr., and John F. Szwed (New York: Free Press, 1970), chapt. 16.

13. U.S. Bureau of the Census, *Population: 1930*, vols. 3 and 4; U.S. Department of Labor, Women's Bureau, *Hours and Earning in Tobacco Stemmeries*, Bulletin no. 127 (Washington, D.C.: GPO, 1934).

14. Women's Bureau, *Effects of Changing Conditions*, 172-75.

15. Blanche Scott and Pansy Cheatham, interviews.

16. Margaret Turner, interview with author, 25 Sept. 1979, SOHP/UNC.

17. Interview, 8 June 1981; Hugh Penn Brinton, "The Negro in Durham: A Study in Adjustment to Town Life" (Ph.D. diss., University of North Carolina, Chapel Hill, 1930).

18. Dora Miller, and Mary Dove, interviews; Janie Mae Lyons, interview with author, 4 Aug. 1981.

19. Annie Barbee, interview; interview, 10 July 1981.

20. Interviews, 4 and 15 June 1981.

21. For the best discussions of the National Industrial Recovery Acts' impact on blacks, see Raymond Wolters, *Negroes and the Great Depression: The Problem of Economic Recovery*, ed. Stanley E. Kutler (Westport, Conn.: Greenwood Publishing Co., 1970); and Bernard Sternsher, ed., *The Negro in the Depression and War: Prelude to Revolution, 1930-45* (Chicago, Ill.: Quadrangle Books, 1969). Also see Dolores Janiewski, "From Field to Factory: Race, Class, and Sex and the Woman Worker in Durham, 1880-1940" (Ph.D. diss., Duke University, Durham, North Carolina, 1979).

22. *Durham* (N.C.) *Morning Herald*, 17, 18 Apr. 1939, p. 1; Janiewski.

23. Dora Miller, interview.

24. For terms of contract, see *Durham* (N.C.) *Morning Herald* and *Durham* (N.C.) *Sun*, 27 Apr. 1939, pp. 1, 2; Janiewski.

25. Pansy Cheatham, interview.

26. Annie Barbee, interview.

CHALLENGING "WOMAN'S PLACE": FEMINISM, THE LEFT, AND INDUSTRIAL UNIONISM IN THE 1930S

SHARON HARTMAN STROM

An important work which helped us see the history of women's work in a new way is Alice Kessler-Harris's 1975 article, "'Where Are the Organized Women Workers?'" Attacking the traditional question asked by organizers and historians, "Why don't women organize?" Kessler-Harris argued that the sexual segregation of women's jobs, their life cycles of work and marriage, and the overwhelming sexism of male unionists made the organization of any women workers remarkable. She suggested that a focus on women workers who had organized would be a more positive and instructive category in the new women's history.[1]

Historians have begun to look for more organized women workers, and, not surprisingly, have found them, particularly in the industrial sector.[2] The fact remains, however, that women have organized less frequently than men; by the mid 1970s 12 percent of working women were unionized while 29 percent of working men were. Some observers of women's work still see the relatively low level of organized female workers as evidence that women are inherently less organizable than men. Although acknowledging that women have had more difficulties to overcome in organizing, these observers still believe there is a psychological component in women's attitudes toward union organization that makes them less assertive, less willing to take risks, more willing to be victims of employer exploitation. For instance, in a recent book on women wage earners from 1900 to 1930 Leslie Tentler argues that women were more passive than men at work. Women saw themselves as powerless in the world outside the home, and they relinquished any notions of rebelling against male coworkers or bosses in order to inherit their tradi-

Feminist Studies 9, no. 2 (Summer 1983). © by Feminist Studies, Inc.

tional authority at home as wives and mothers.[3] On being presented with evidence of clerical organizing in the 1930s, one male sociologist who commented on a paper I gave at a convention several years ago was still not convinced. "Large numbers of male workers," he argued, "rose up and demanded industrial unions in the thirties. For whatever reason, large numbers of women didn't." Although the romantic content of this view is obvious, it is not enough, evidently, to show that women workers may have organized. We need to go beyond the question, "Where are the organized women workers?" and explain why women workers haven't been able to organize as effectively as men. In other words, what historical conditions needed to be present for women to perceive that protests against employers and sexist unions were worth risking their jobs? Why haven't such protests led to the forming of viable trade unions? What will make it possible for women to organize *en masse* in the primarily female occupations? When can women organize?

In this article I will explore depression-era organizing with these questions in mind. In so doing I will avoid attributing psychological motives to women workers. Instead I will try to show that economic, ideological, and political variables can explain why some women workers succeeded in organizing, but did not organize in as large numbers as men. The most important of these variables were women's occupational positions in the American economy, the discriminatory policies of the New Deal, prevailing cultural and ideological views of women's roles in the work force, the failure of industrial unionism to reach most women workers, the lack of community and family support networks for striking women workers, and the absence of a feminist critique within the progressive labor movement, especially the Communist party. I will argue that although women did engage in job actions and spontaneous labor protests in the thirties they were at an intrinsic disadvantage in getting the kind of wholehearted support men received. That support could not have been provided without a feminist ideology to justify changing the status of working women. As Ruth Milkman has argued, "minimally any successful struggle to organize women had first to challenge the ideology of 'women's place'—a problem that did not arise in organizing men."[4]

Unemployment, underemployment, and drastically reduced wages became a national experience during the 1930s. Under the banner of Franklin D. Roosevelt's New Deal, the federal government responded on a number of levels to ease the suffering of working people. Women did not receive equal assistance. The 1933 National Industrial Recovery Act (NIRA) minimum wage codes sanctioned lower pay rates for women workers than for men in the same occupations, and they excluded domestic and agricultural jobs—both major occupations for women, especially poor and minority women. Salaried workers and clerical workers in the insurance industry were also excluded. There was widespread evasion of maximum hour codes for clerical workers as employers changed titles, assigned salaries, increased duties, and then forced secretaries to work overtime with no extra pay. Women workers paid the same Social Security taxes as men, but received fewer benefits upon retirement. The domestic work, agricultural, and government sectors were not covered by Social Security; all three were employers of large numbers of women. The NIRA work relief section ignored women altogether, and the Civilian Conservation Corps camps were originally for men only. When camps for females were set up women received one-half of what men were paid. The Works Projects Administration (WPA) provided more jobs, but only one member of a family could earn relief, and that member had to be the main wage earner. Aid to Dependent Children (ADC) was widely seen in local communities as a way to get women off the WPA rolls and therefore out of the work force, although ADC payments were lower than WPA work rates. When the NIRA was found to be unconstitutional and was replaced by the Fair Labor Standards Act of 1938, clerks, seasonal employees, and domestic workers found themselves with no protection against substandard wages.[5]

National legislation lashed out at married women workers. Section 213 of the Economy Act of 1932 allowed the firing of one spouse if both husband and wife worked for the government, and of the fifteen hundred married persons fired within the next year, nearly all were women. A crop of proposed state laws tried to follow suit. Frances Perkins, secretary of labor and the first woman to hold a cabinet position, had, as state industrial commissioner of New York, called on women who did not need jobs to stay at home and deplored women who worked for "pin-money."[6]

Federal and state governments were in some ways merely expressing sentiments held by the public at large. Many people believed that working married women were partly responsible for unemployment, and there was widespread sentiment for the firing of married teachers and government workers. The president of the California Institute of Technology proposed that 75 percent of all jobs be reserved for men, and George Gallup, who repeatedly polled Americans on their attitudes toward working wives, claimed that he had never seen poll respondents "so solidly united in opposition" to an economic issue.[7]

Section 213 and other discriminatory policies against married women played a direct role in forcing women out of better jobs in the 1930s. Local and state employees had increased by 400 percent between 1900 and 1930, civilian employees of the federal government had tripled, and school workers had grown by two and one-half times. Women received many of these new jobs, and one-fifth of the women were married. The Women's Bureau found that Section 213 was usually applied to married typists and stenographers and rarely to married charwomen or elevator operators. These policies were repeated in private industry. In 1931, New England Telephone and Telegraph fired all its married women workers. Most large companies, and almost all banks and insurance firms, simply refused to hire married women as clericals. Numerous commentators observed that many workers lied about their married status in order to get or keep jobs. When Social Security cards were issued for the first time in 1937, regional offices were besieged by calls from women who feared their marriages would be revealed to their employers.[8]

Married women were not excluded from the labor force during the depression. In fact, the number of married women at work increased because families were forced to earn a living in any way they could. Overall, women's status in the job market declined in the thirties; men made gains in proportion to women in teaching, library work, social work, and nursing. Meanwhile, many women had to enter the lower-paid female occupations like domestic service, part-time work, canning, and farm labor. These were also job categories either not covered or only partially covered by Social Security, collective-bargaining legislation, NIRA, and the Fair Labor Standards Act. They were also the only job categories available to most black and minority women.[9]

The ramifications of attacks on married women workers were of grave import for all women workers, married or not. Because most women eventually married, the working woman was by default considered to be a young adult, or "working girl." She was not a permanent member of the work world, and therefore should not have the same say in government and union policy as the "working man." Every married working woman was an anomaly, present in the work force either through temporary financial necessity or personal selfishness. The implication for women was that work outside the home was a stage, not a right, and that the mature woman belonged at home.

Movies hammered home the same message. As Molly Haskell has observed, although many movies of the thirties portrayed an adventurous young working woman who could hold her own in a man's world, she usually capitulated to marriage and home by the film's end.[10] In any event, she worked because she had to; she was either a Jean Arthur, on her own and earning a living, as in *Mr. Smith Goes to Washington,* or a Barbara Stanwyck, supporting her brother and a widowed mother, as in *Meet John Doe.* Or if she didn't really need to work, she was a Katharine Hepburn, a silly, unfeeling snob who finally learned that suicide might be the consequence of taking a deserving young woman's job, as in *Stage Door.*

Thus, the makers of popular culture, government legislators, the general public, and private industry, while somewhat sympathetic to the plight of the working man, were ambivalent about the working woman. She was evidently a necessary evil but should remain confined to the lower-paying feminized occupations, which did not, for the most part, deserve the same benefits as male jobs. She faced a complicated range of problems in the work force, only one of which was union organization.

Women workers responded to Section 7 (a) of the NIRA in 1933. They were often given organizing help from Communist activists, many of them women, in the Trade Union Unity League (TUUL) and the Unemployed Councils. In Detroit, 6,000 workers, 2,000 of them women, went on strike at the Briggs Mack Avenue plant and won substantial wage gains for women. In Philadelphia, female and male workers at the Philadelphia Storage Battery Company (Philco) won an agreement which gave a 10 percent wage increase to men and a 15 percent increase to women aimed at narrowing the disparity between female and male wages. In May of 1933, 4,500 workers, mostly women, struck nonunion Philadelphia dress plants. A revitalized International Ladies Garment Workers' Union (ILGWU) was able to launch a general strike of dressmakers, mostly female, in New York, New Jersey, and Connecticut and won an agreement in four days. Similar strikes were conducted by the Amalgamated Clothing Workers in Pennsylvania, New York, and Connecticut. In St. Louis 1,400 women, mostly black, went on strike to protest a piece-rate reduction in the city's pecan-shelling factories. The strikers, who had gone out in 1927 as well, had the support of the TUUL and the Unemployed Councils. Husbands and children of the strikers joined them on the picket line, and sympathetic unionists and businesses in the black community provided food for meals. After the employers brought in scabs and strikebreakers, the local Jewish community and the American Civil Liberties Union provoked sympathy for the strikers in the press, and the mayor of the city helped to mediate negotiations.[11]

In 1934, textile workers went out on strike from Maine to Mississippi, and women, who made up 40 percent of all textile workers, were instrumental in the protracted and bloody strike which ensued. They fought state militias, participated in huge demonstrations, sat down on railroad tracks, and led "flying squadrons" from plant to plant to recruit new strikers and intimidate scabs. Thirty thousand women and men hotel workers struck fifty hotels in New York early in 1934 to gain union recognition. In December 1936, 4,000 female and male workers struck five of Philadelphia's six leading department stores. Warehouse workers, truckers, sales clerks, packers, porters, and waitresses were joined on the third day of the strike by seventy-five bookkeepers and office workers. Although the strike was hushed up in the newspapers and numerous arrests were made, workers achieved union recognition and a forty-eight-hour week.[12]

The entire labor movement entered a dynamic new phase in 1936 and 1937 when workers in basic production waged sit-down strikes. In both Akron, Ohio, and Flint, Michigan, despite the fact that they made up substantial numbers of workers in both the rubber and automobile industries, women workers—many of them young and single—were sent home by strike leaders and not allowed to sit-down. Women were discouraged from sitting in with men in factory strikes, for mixed groups of women and men might give employers a chance to charge sexual promiscuity or to provoke "unfit mother" cases in the courts.[13] Both men and married women, given the traditional allocation of childcare responsibilities in the thirties, probably feared that children would be neglected if mothers were not at home to care for them.

Sit-downs were perceived as men's affairs in the Congress of Industrial Organizations (CIO). One union official defined a sit-down in 1937 as "a cessation of work with the men remaining at work." But women workers throughout the country were quick to perceive that sit-downs might be of use to them. Jeremy Brecher found that both Chicago and Detroit experienced waves of sit-down strikes in stores and smaller factories following the great General Motors Strike in the spring of 1937. There were eighty-seven sit-downs involving 3,000 workers in Detroit alone, many of them in the auto parts and manufacturing firms which employed large numbers of women. Two hundred women, not allowed to participate in the Flint sit-down strike which led to a United Automobile Workers (UAW) contract with General Motors, sat down in a sewing room in the Fischer Body Plant No. 1 and were joined in sympathy an hour later by 280 additional women sewers. When sixty men in the shipping department also sat down, the entire plant was forced to close.[14] Clerks sat down in Detroit, Chicago, and New York department stores and five-and-tens, and women workers barricaded themselves in three tobacco plants in Detroit for several weeks. When 150 police attacked sit-downers at one of them, "hysterical cries echoed through the building as, by ones, and twos, the eighty-six women strikers, ranging from defiant girls to bewildered workers with gray hair, were herded into patrol wagons and sped away, while shattering glass and the yells of the street throng added to the din."[15] The UAW protested against such forced evictions, threatened to call 180,000 auto workers out on strike, and even raised the specter of a citywide general strike. The police stopped their raids. In Chicago there were sixty sit-downs in a two-week period in March of 1937, including 9,000 female and male Loop workers, ranging from peanut baggers to stenographers. Brecher reports that "1,800 workers, including 300 office workers, sat down at the Chicago Mail Order Company and won a ten percent pay increase; 450 employees at three deMet's tea rooms sat down as 'the girls laughed and talked at the tables they had served' until they went home that night with a twenty-five percent pay increase. . . ."[16]

We should also remember that women participated in strikes and job actions not only as workers, but also as wives or relatives of workers, mainly in women's auxiliaries. Male unionists at the time were more likely to respond to women who participated in women's auxiliaries than to women workers. The image of the woman standing behind her man and his job became a sentimental theme in union rhetoric, while the working woman was conspicuously absent. Women's auxiliaries often picketed and even fought the police, and they also provided meals for the duration of strikes, clearly an important key to their success.[17] There were obviously no "men's auxiliaries" to provide meals and childcare for striking women, although we need to know more about the ad hoc arrangements created by the friends, relatives, and communities of striking women. Working women and wives and relatives of working men all belonged to the auxiliaries; women workers who were sent out of plants in the Akron and Flint sit-downs of 1934 and 1937 participated by joining the UAW and United Rubber Workers (URW) auxiliaries.[18]

The auxiliaries did not lead to permanent union organizations which might have begun to articulate women workers' grievances. Although most male sit-downers were happy to have the support of women's emergency brigades during strikes, they expected that women would return to traditional roles once the emergencies were over. Some women resented this idea and saw the auxiliaries as a forum for discussion of women's concerns. Sometimes they were encouraged by Communist party (CP) organizers to address such issues as birth control, childcare, and who should do the housework, but the mere fact of organizing together as women was evidently a problematic idea for all concerned.

In some cases the women through their activities won the respect of their striking husbands, and were given representation on strike committees. In other situations, the militancy of the CP-led auxiliaries enraged the male union leadership, who wanted women to stay home. Women in auxiliaries, as in the CP's women's units, developed some cooperative methods of child care, and occasionally forced their husbands to assume some of these responsibilities. These organizations did not equal liberation, of course, as tasks such as preparing food for the strikers still remained for the women. The CP often failed to push the auxiliaries and unions to go beyond sex-stereotyped roles.[19]

Yet some working-class women clearly articulated the larger issues their organizing as women had raised; one participant in the Flint Emergency Brigade said, "Just being a woman isn't enough anymore. I want to be a human being with the right to think for myself."[20] Beatrice Marcus reported in a December 1934 issue of the CP's *Working Woman* that women from coal miner families in Hillsboro, Illinois, had organized to demand adequate relief. They "held meetings, travelled through the countryside, raised money, and, in defiance of the male leadership of the Progressive Miners' Association, led demonstrations. As one march began on City Hall, the male demonstrators 'made vain efforts to

keep their wives from the front ranks.'''[21] One of the most salient
features of the thirties is the failure of any organized groups to
develop this working-class womens' new consciousness and
militance into a feminist position.

Middle-class feminist organizations were on the defensive in
the thirties. In fact, because they had not recruited many younger
women to join their ranks, older feminists found themselves increasingly talking to each other. Many of the goals they had been
working toward since 1920 seemed to be under attack, particularly the right to combine marriage and work. In an attempt to gain
some protection for the jobs of married women, feminists tended
to emphasize that women workers did not usually compete with
men and that most of them needed their wages to support
families. Although useful in the short run, these arguments tended
to reinforce popular notions of the thirties that women should
work only when they had to and only when they did not take
men's jobs.[22] Feminists in the thirties were also unable to establish
any sustained point of view in the industrial union movement;
they either ended up criticizing the role of Communists and other
leftists, or they joined popular front alliances in which leftist
women—most of whom were suspicious of traditional
feminism—dominated. Although they had never been very successful in attracting working-class women to their groups, the
failure of feminists to remain visible in the thirties meant that
working-class women had no public sanction for articulating
feminist ideas.

Feminist ideology might have survived if women on the Left
had been interested in it. But although they often acted like
feminists and addressed women's issues in their organizing efforts, most leftist women refused to associate themselves with the
legacy of the movement for women's rights. While Trotskyists,
Lovestoneites, Socialists, and A.J. Muste's Independent Labor party all made significant contributions to labor organizing in the
thirties, Communist party members were clearly the most effective segment of the Left, and one of the most important in
organizing women.

Communist party dogma officially viewed feminism as a
bourgeois reform movement; women's problems would automatically be corrected with the arrival of true communism. Yet this
view, as Robert Schaffer has recently argued, barely kept the lid
on a smoldering debate within the party and in its publications on
the "woman question." Party writers did discuss birth control,

unequal pay, maternity insurance, and the role of men in housework. It was always clear, however, that industries dominated by male workers would be the target of vanguard organizing. Official writings also did not "admit to any conceivable antagonism between working-class men and women," and any struggle against male supremacy within the party had to be balanced against the party's desire to have its members live like ordinary workers and therefore accept ordinary workers' behavior—including the subordination of women to men.[23] These party lines, however, must be counterpointed by the actual experience of Communist women in the 1930s. There is no doubt that the experience of party membership, of organizing women's auxiliaries, consumer boycotts, and picket lines gave many a female Communist the organizing experience and self-respect she needed to become an independent woman. We must remember, however, that sometimes standing up for women, working with women, or becoming independent of men was not the same as possessing a feminist consciousness. One office worker organizer who was also in the CP in the thirties summed this up precisely: "My interest in the women's movement as such was quite peripheral if it was even conscious. It's not that I wasn't aware that women had problems, but I have always believed that . . . the basic problems of women will not be solved until we have socialism."[24] The consequence of this view was that women were always subject to having their grievances—whatever they were—superseded by the overall struggle of the working class, a struggle in which men and their families—not men and women—were participants.

The labor struggles of the Great Depression took on a new dimension after 1937 as the CIO rapidly expanded. The effects of increasing bureaucratization on women's organizing efforts were somewhat contradictory. Certainly the financial resources, institutional support, and power to impose a closed shop of the CIO made it possible to bring unionism to women who would otherwise have missed it. Any unionized shop was likely to raise women's wages significantly.[25] But there is also evidence to suggest that the early militancy of strikes and the wide-ranging scope of issues they raised in the early thirties began to disappear by 1937, as collective bargaining replaced confrontation and focused on the narrow range of issues laid out by contract negotiations.[26]

Frances Fox Piven and Richard A. Cloward have argued in their *Poor People's Movements* that legitimized workers' organizations like the CIO had a vested interest in discontinuing "unauthorized" job actions on the shop floor once they had large enough constituencies and had won agreements with employers. Communist organizers, now in their popular front phase, went along. The CP editor of the Flint *Auto Worker,* Henry Kraus, announced that the UAW's goal was "not to foster strikes and labor trouble. The union can only grow on the basis of established procedure and collective bargaining."[27] In a primer on how to organize an industrial union Clinton S. Golden and Harold J. Ruttenberg argued that "the written collective-bargaining contract is the means through which workers secure . . . a voice. This is one path to industrial peace that cannot be by-passed, either by managment or union officials. . . . Once wage earners successfully establish organization and collective bargaining at their point of actual employment, their relationship with management undergoes a transition from one of conflict in varying degrees to that of cooperation in some degree."[28] Both the General Motors (GM) and the U.S. Steel contracts signed by CIO unions in 1937 prohibited local strikes.[29] Unions called for grievances to be handled by shop stewards and union committees. In many unions women were denied access to this hierarchy, although they were a significant influence in locals of the United Electrical Workers (UE).[30]

These new developments probably prevented women from capitalizing on effective use of job actions to rectify their grievances. Complaints they had aplenty; Ruth Meyerowitz found that although the automobile industry was the biggest employer of women workers in Flint, it confined them to "women's jobs" like upholstery sewing and tedious assembly line work like spark plug manufacturing. Before the Flint strike they earned an average of ten to thirteen cents an hour while men made four or five times as much.[31] Although women in union plants did make gains in wages, the UAW abandoned a universal minimum wage in its contract with GM, which stipulated that wages could be determined by local plants in conjunction with local conditions. This was no different from the NIRA codes, which had allowed employers to maintain geographical, racial, and sexual differentials in wages. CIO unions continued the American Federation of Labor (AFL) tradition of setting lower wages for women's jobs than for men's jobs in their contracts.[32]

Although the CIO was more receptive to women workers than the AFL had been, women usually joined when they were present in industries with large numbers of men, as in, for example, the garment and electrical industries, or when they organized themselves. This was particularly true of minority women. When 400 black women stemmers in Richmond, Virginia, tobacco factories walked out in a spontaneous strike in 1937, they were told by the AFL that black workers couldn't be organized. The Southern Negro Youth Congress and the National Negro Congress, not the CIO, helped them form the Tobacco Stemmers and Laborers' Union. The ILGWU, which had a better record on helping southern workers than some other CIO unions, sent 500 women pickets to a Richmond tobacco strike in 1938, and the newly formed locals were passed on to the CIO in 1939. A similar strike by Mexican-American pecan shellers in San Antonio, Texas, in 1938 helped to establish the United Cannery, Agricultural, Packing and Allied Workers of America, a leftist union which was expelled from the CIO in 1950.[33] When women did organize, men saw little wrong with unequal pay; one male picket line protesting "girl's wages" dressed in drag and carried picket signs reading "Restore Our Manhood" to make its point.[34] When women did come into mixed CIO locals or tried to assume leadership roles they were often accused of being loose women and were asked to conduct union business in spaces like saloons, pool halls and union halls, where they were bound to feel uncomfortable.[35]

Only a "negligible proportion" of the 519 delegates to the first CIO convention were women (most of them from office worker unions); and by 1946 only 20 of the 600 delegates to the national convention were female. Only one woman, Eleanor Nelson of the United Federal Workers (UFW) was ever a president of any of the unions chartered by the CIO in the thirties. None of the 1938 constitutional convention's resolutions mentioned working women. The only specific reference to women thanked members of the women's auxiliaries, "the mothers, wives, sisters and daughters of industrial workers," thus ignoring entirely the contribution made by women workers to the auxiliaries. The *CIO News* either buried articles on women's strikes or failed to report them at all, and pictures of women workers in cheesecake poses were far more common than pictures of women on picket lines. Beauty contests for CIO women abounded in every affiliate, and mothers, wives, and girlfriends of unionists who "stood by their men" received the most praise. Wisconsin CIO members in 1938 thought "a good union girl" should only work to support herself or her family, be intelligent, a good housekeeper, and shorter than her boyfriend. She should use makeup moderately and keep her stocking seams straight. She should go out on the picket line "with her man," because having "girls come on the line . . . puts more pep in the gas." Although she should listen "with interest when a man wants to talk about his union," she mustn't ever "try to get bossy."[36]

Secretaries for labor unions complained that their employers did not pay them the minimum salary advocated by the CIO office workers' union, the United Office and Professional Workers of America (UOPWA). Joining the union itself was evidently seen as a threat to male unionists; a former secretary for the National Maritime Union (NMU) in Boston thought union men were "outraged, really in their hearts . . . when the secretaries of labor unions joined the UOPWA and dared to organize against them! There they were, the great champions of labor, (and) those ungrateful women sitting in those offices dared to organize a union to fight them. Disrupting the labor movement!" This same secretary, however, had taken the floor to explain police brutality to an enormous crowd in the Everett (Massachusetts) town hall after a bloody tear gas assault on an NMU picket line in 1937; the men were all too nervous to speak in public. Male unionists clearly had trouble maintaining the contradiction of the ornamental "union girl" that their ideology upheld with the militant union woman who they frequently encountered. One UFW member told a meeting of unionists that he wanted "to say a word in praise of this little girl of ours, Eleanor Nelson, who . . . has the tenacity of a bulldog and has been out there facing the guns for our union!"[37]

The narrow application of industrial unionism by the CIO to workers in basic production and manufacturing hurt women workers as well. Less than 22 percent of all working women worked in manufacturing by 1940, and more than 60 percent worked in other occupations, so the failure to reach out to service, domestic, sales, and clerical workers by the CIO played a crucial role in excluding women. Whether this failure was based on disinterest in nonindustrial occupations or on disinterest in women is not very important because it amounted to the same thing.[38]

Although it was not so obvious in the thirties, it is very clear now that the decision to ignore clerical workers was especially portentous. The census of 1940 indicated that more than 21 percent of all women workers were in clerical work, and the size of the occupation increased by nearly 85 percent from 1940 to 1944.[39] To ignore clerical workers was, then, to ignore a significant portion of women workers. Inevitably, however, clericals also caught the union spirit. Leftist clericals and office workers, both female and male, had begun by the mid thirties to agitate within long-dormant AFL locals for industrial unionism. In 1937 the CIO agreed to charter three office worker unions: the UFW, the State, County and Municipal Workers of America and the UOPWA. These unions grew substantially during the 1930s and 1940s, but were all purged by the CIO in 1950 and rapidly disappeared. Only the UOPWA could really follow the male industrial union model, because national state and local government employees were usually prohibited by law from going on strike.

The CIO never poured any effort into organizing assistance for the UOPWA and in fact repeatedly restricted its influence. Conceding to the protests of male industrial unions like the UAW and the URW, the CIO prohibited the UOPWA from organizing clerical workers in industries already represented by CIO nationals. Or, if such clericals did organize, their membership and dues would be handed, upon request, to the industrial union in question. The UOPWA was thus left with clericals in banks, insurance offices, small offices, social work agencies, paper work factories like the direct mail industry, and department stores. None of these workplaces had ever been strongholds of unionism, and especially not of industrial unionism.[40]

Office workers in the steel, mining, auto, rubber, and electrical industries were left to the whims of industry or of male unionists, none of whom made any significant attempt to organize clericals. In fact, many manufacturing unions tried to exclude office workers from their locals, a significant action because office workers made up 14.2 percent of all workers in manufacturing by 1938. The 1941 UAW contract with Ford Motors, for instance, specifically excluded most white collar workers. Sometimes industrial unions made gains explicitly at the expense of white collar workers. A UE contract with General Electric in 1937 cut salaries for office workers. In the late thirties, rubber workers in Jeanette, Pennsylvania, and Akron, Ohio, agreed to contracts which raised factory wages significantly, but cut or froze those of office workers.[41]

Not all office workers or blue collar workers wanted to be grouped with each other, and the National Labor Relations Board (NLRB) usually ruled that office workers should not be members of the same locals. One of the consequences of this bifurcation of the work force was that blue collar wages increased at a faster pace than white collar wages, with clerical workers increasingly earning lower wages than organized workers in manufacturing. Some office employees formed independent unions, but we don't know whether women clerical workers were in favor of this arrangement or not, or if they were even involved in the decisions to organize these. Certainly these independent unions were dominated by men, who had the better-paying and more responsible office jobs. The Federation of Westinghouse Independent Salaried Unions even tried to exclude married women from the Westinghouse offices.[42]

Although the CIO was indifferent at best and hostile at worst to the organizing of clericals, the office worker unions embodied important contradictions which helped prevent the widespread organizing of clericals. Young Communist women were particularly likely to be in a position to organize in the offices. The social character of the Communist party had changed dramatically since World War I, with many of the second-generation children of working-class parents receiving high school and even college educations by the 1930s. Many young leftist women with degrees in teaching could not find jobs and were forced to work as secretaries. By 1938 the CP estimated that 22 percent of its new recruits were technically "middle class." Young Communist women were working in business offices, social agencies, publishing houses, government offices, and trade union offices. As Communists they were expected to participate directly in the building of militant unions. They had received speaking, organizing, and protest experience in the CP, a vitally important ingredient for women workers, who often had trouble getting this experience elsewhere. They became the main leaders and organizers of the fledgling office worker unions which emerged in 1936 and 1937, an activity encouraged by the CP during the popular front.[43] Leftists helped break new ground in the organization of clericals in the thirties, but their antifeminist position and their class analysis of clericals hindered their effectiveness.

What class did clerical workers belong to in the thirties? Certainly many secretaries, especially older ones, came from the middle class, and some were college-educated women who had been pushed into lower-status jobs by the effects of the Depression. However, the new compulsory school laws and fewer industrial jobs for teenagers during the Depression meant that countless young working-class women were taking a "business curriculum" in high school and becoming clericals. Business had partly responded to hard times by reducing wages for office workers, instituting speedup, and increasing mechanization. This process involved a more clear-cut sexual division of labor with male office workers doing the managing and earning the best salaries and women performing the more tedious "assembly line" functions and earning the lowest wages. Most hard data on office workers indicated that female secretaries, typists, filing clerks, and other clericals were rapidly descending into the working class.[44] Nonetheless, most leftist observers continued to lump all female and male office workers together as though their interests and values were the same.

Two social scientists frequently quoted by leftists, Hans Speir, who wrote about German white collar workers, and the American economist Lewis Corey, both emphasized the increasing "proletarianization" of office work. Corey argued that most white collar workers were not "middle class in their relations to production and income: *they are economically and functionally a part of the working class: a 'new' proletariat.*" Speir acknowledged that "it is the man who typically has the principal authority, the girl who is typically the subordinate . . . . The majority of the subordinate employees in the large offices perform duties which are specialized and schematized down to the minutest detail." As his lengthy analysis continued, however, Speir left behind his reference to women as subordinates, giving the reader the impression that all this had little to do with sexual roles:

In the case of the salaried workers who serve as subordinates in one of the many modern office machines, . . . the difference in the nature of the duties between such workers and the manual workers is completely wiped out . . . . Especially revealing with regard to the sinking of the social level of the white collar workers is, finally, the change in the social antecedents. The growing tendency to employ salaried workers of "proletarian origin" indicates that the number of untrained and poorly paid positions is increasing faster than the number of middle and principal positions. In other words, the salaried employees as a whole are being subjected to a process of decreasing social esteem.[45]

Speir's confusion rested on two traditional assumptions about clerical workers which most other analysts were unwilling to abandon: that the "social prestige" of office workers always made them identify with the middle class, and that female and male office workers' interests were necessarily inseparable. No one in the Left in the thirties was able to fully articulate the sexual division of office work or to grasp that women might prefer to be or even should be organized *as women* in an industrial clerical workers' movement. Organizers were also unable to discard the notion that because they were theoretically—if not actually—"middle class," office workers were a kind of parentheses to the main thrust of the industrial labor movement.[46]

In fact, the motives for organizing office workers sometimes bordered on the cynical. Communists routinely asserted in the thirties that fascism in Germany and Italy had relied on the support of the *petite bourgeoisie,* including white collar workers, for its political success. Fearful of the same social phenomenon in the United States, leftist theorists and organizers argued that the American middle class—especially the white collar sector—should be organized primarily to prevent it from supporting right-wing political causes and to facilitate the spread of unions in the industrial sector. According to Len DeCaux, editor of the *CIO News,* "if democracy and liberalism are to prevail over the menacing forces of fascism, unionization of white collar, office and professional workers is one of the most effective means of spreading labor sympathy and understanding among the middle classes."[47] This line of reasoning often obscured the actual grievances of working-class clericals and made them mere supporters of the struggle to help industrial workers. As one organizer told her UOPWA local: "It's important to you that all labor should be organized, stand together for legislation, better hours and wages, the right to organize, strike and picket. . . . Office workers if organized can help labor improve conditions and laws. . . . If manual workers in a shop strike, it would help them if the office workers were with them; the shop could be shut up tight. . . . Sometimes bosses take votes on who is for a strike or for a union, and count all the office workers against, even if they don't vote at all."[48]

Despite all these obstacles, thousands of female clerical workers joined the UOPWA in the thirties and hundreds went out on strike.[49] Some of these strikes were successful; others were not. A few examples should illustrate that female office workers could be militant, determined, and effective unionists and should also indicate the problems they might encounter.

In early 1936 machinists at the Margon Corporation, a small manufacturing firm in New York City, went on strike. The entire office staff of seven workers, all of them women and members of the leftist Bookkeepers, Stenographers, and Accountants Union

(BSAU), precursor of the UOPWA, refused to cross the machinists picket line. The strike was quickly won, and the factory workers went back to work with "increased wages, union recognition, and improved working conditions." On January 18, Sunny Grill, who had worked for Margon for six years, was fired and given her severance check. Officially told there was a slowdown in business, she was "privately told that she could no longer be 'trusted.'" Three days later union shop steward Claire Mitchell "interviewed the employers and told them that Miss Grill's discharge made them all feel insecure and that for the sake of efficiency and harmony in the office she should be reinstated, and if it were actually necessary to have any layoff, it be done on the basis of seniority." Mitchell was fired, and the remaining women were asked to sign pledges that "under no circumstances, especially in the case of a strike of the factory workers, would they go on strike or refuse to walk through the inside workers' picket lines." When they refused to sign, the women were fired, and the BSAU called a strike. Pickets were set up in front of Margon and the employers' homes. The company hired scabs and professional strikebreakers, and the police were called in to protect the scabs. Fifty-eight arrests were made in front of the Margon office in the next eight days, and eighteen members of BSAU were arrested in front of one of the owner's homes in Brooklyn. One picketer was beaten by a hired thug. Arrests finally halted after the intercession of Mayor La Guardia and the police commissioner. Two hundred factory workers, minus supervisors and skilled workers, did not honor the office workers' picket line until March 2, and by then the position of the owners was frozen. The strike continued into April, when the Margon owners moved their factory to Bayonne, New Jersey, where they had received "assurances that they would not be annoyed with labor disputes."[50]

Margon was the kind of small firm UOPWA often organized, and the 1936 strike typified some of the special dilemmas of organizing clericals. First, the clerical staff was far outnumbered by the industrial workers. That industrial workers, usually male, would honor clerical picket lines was not a foregone conclusion. One also senses here that employers were more threatened by the betrayal of their office staffs than they were by the militancy of factory workers; they were willing to move the factory rather than "tolerate the idea of their office girls belonging to a union and being as loyal to their fellow workers as they had been" to their bosses.[51] As for the factory workers, the message was crystal clear; saving jobs and union membership might necessitate throwing clerical workers overboard.

The advantages of penetrating a "clerical worker factory" were obvious in the wave of credit clearinghouse strikes in the Northeast in 1937-38. The 225 employees of the New York Credit Clearing House, the largest credit information bureau in the country, won union recognition and negotiated a contract under the leadership of office chair Lena de Pasquale. Salaries were as low as $11.88 a week, and employees were expected to work as much as two extra days a week without pay. An arbitrator set new minimum pay rates at $14 a week, but a strike ensued in 1940 over continued union recognition and new wage scales. Workers devised a new strike tactic—telephone picketing. New York Credit Clearing House had seventy-seven trunk lines, and unionists and their friends and relatives kept two thousand calls an hour coming in to jam the phones and stop business.[52] When the union's no-strike pledge prevented a strike in early 1942, UOPWA officials took workers' demands for a new contract to the U.S. Conciliation Service:

> The day before the UOPWA called upon the conciliation service, CCH workers tried their own hand at winning a settlement without a strike.
> With the boss directly behind her, little Lena de Pasquale, office chairman and leader of the 1940 strike, blew a signaling whistle. From every corner other whistles resounded. All employees left their desks and walked quietly over to one section of the office.
> A boss asked the cause. Lena bluntly told him it was a protest against the firm's stalling tactics. . . .
> Another boss told the workers "Whoever wants to go back to work, go right ahead." No one budged.[53]

Taking on a huge corporation, however, was far more difficult. At the New York office of L. Sonneborn Sons, Inc., an oil and paint company with widespread operations throughout the Northeast, Beatrice Limpson and six of her officemates organized and won a NLRB election for Local No. 16 in 1941. A strike in February ensued when contract negotiations broke down, and sympathetic picket lines were thrown up by UOPWA locals around Sonneborn operations all over the country. Longshoremen, seamen, teamsters, and painters all refused to cross picket lines, and names of scabs were advertised daily on picket signs. In an interesting reversal of family sympathies, Joseph Sonneborn, nephew of the company president, walked the picket line, while

Jack Gompers, nephew of AFL founder Samuel Gompers, went to work at Sonneborn as a scab. Picket captain Ruth Nettborn, "who once vowed she would never be seen on a picket line," was arrested while picketing Gompers's home. One observer reported that despite arrests, the strikers were "gay and lively," with one clerical worker teaching sister picketers the rumba to the music of a donated phonograph.[54]

UOPWA organizers realized early on they would have to reach Sonneborn's customers to make the strike effective. Accounts had to be visited, and if persuasion failed they were to be picketed or boycotted. The company's executives were hit with a barrage of telephone calls from strikers and their families; the "swanky Savoy Plaza," residence of the company president, was the target of a demonstration. Although Sonneborn eventually agreed to some of the union's demands, it refused to reinstate strikers, and rumor had it that new defense orders were making the company stronger than ever. Office workers at Sonneborn went back to work without a contract.[55]

The UOPWA had a better record than most CIO unions in organizing women workers, but it also reflected prevailing sexual attitudes of the period, despite its leftist leadership. The president of the national was always a man, and national organizers of the UOPWA frequently aired patronizing views of clerical workers in articles like the condescending weekly column signed by "Susie the Secretary." Susie said in 1937 that she didn't know if there were "any other girls in my department who have sense enough to stick together. They seem to be just out for themselves and not to care about how anyone else gets along. I used to be pretty dumb too, thinking that unions were just for common laborers and mechanics, so perhaps I can show them that organization is the thing."[56]

The UOPWA consistently allowed professional and higher-paid office workers, most of whom were men, to write contracts which excluded clerical workers or bargained away their contract rights. And in 1939 the union decided to launch a major campaign to organize insurance agents, almost all of whom were men. Although the insurance agents had suffered reduced salaries and worsened working conditions as a result of the Depression, they were not really devoted to industrial unionism, and routinely excluded clericals from their contracts and their locals. Clericals had to join separate locals of the UOPWA. The national accepted this sexism as the price it had to pay for attracting insurance agents to the union, but it meant that dues collected from clerical workers were sent to male locals with no intention of ever serving them.

The UOPWA had successfuly organized insurance agents at most of the major insurance corporations by the middle of World War II. In its desire to make these inroads, however, it essentially abandoned any attempt to include clerical workers in the insurance industry. Eventually the insurance workers bolted from the CIO and created independent craft unions or joined the AFL.

Not surprisingly, these unions specifically excluded clericals. In 1952 striking AFL insurance agents set up a picket line outside a Prudential office building in Newark, New Jersey, hoping to convince clericals not to go to work; the clericals crossed the line. This episode was recorded as another example of how women workers, especially clerical workers, will not honor picket lines, but the story, as we have seen, was far more complicated.[57]

The arrival of the CIO in the 1930s must be viewed as a mixed blessing for women workers. Although many made gains in wages and working conditions, countless others were never offered industrial unions. The CIO acquiesced in the sexual division of labor and even actively sought to maintain it. And, whenever women were organized into unions without some sense of themselves as women, they tended to abrogate their rights. They usually became an adjunct to male unionism, paying in dues and receiving little else but a union card in return.

Women workers needed to challenge women's place to organize effectively in the thirties. They were not only establishing unions, but also the right to work, to have feminized occupations accorded equal treatment under federal statute, to earn comparable pay, and to win the support and cooperation of working-class men. In other words, women faced a complicated mesh of ideological, social, and economic obstacles in organizing that were peculiar to them. Where was this challenge to come from? To argue that working-class women could somehow have mounted a viable feminist movement on their own is to engage in the worst sort of wishful thinking. To perceive as an individual woman that one's exploitation as a wife, a mother, a daughter, an employee, and a unionist were all connected was one thing; to struggle collectively on occasion against one or more of these conditions was another; to band together in the face of women's economic dependence on men and attack them all at once was impossible. There were no existent forms of protest or organization along these lines, no popular symbols to evoke, no terms with which to identify the process of liberation, no audiences who would have taken such rhetoric seriously. Unions should have been the forum where the connections between women's problems as workers and as women were made; where the beginnings of a feminist consciousness should have emerged.

Leftist activists from both the working and middle classes were most likely to perceive these connections and to be able to act on them at the same time. Already in an antiestablishment posture, they might be able to see similarities between forms of patriarchy and forms of capitalism. As members of political groups or parties they would have alternative means of personal support other than traditional patriarchal families.[58] Socialist feminists had developed such connections earlier in the century. Women in the Socialist party articulated a far-reaching platform of goals for working women, including suffrage, birth control, and pay for housework. Anarchist Emma Goldman and socialist theorist Charlotte Perkins Gilman had attacked marriage as a capitalist institution ensuring male property rights. Their point of view was missing from leftist ideology in the thirties. The Communist party viewed women's issues as important but inferior to the issues of race and industrial unionism. When all three of these issues combined, as in the pecan sheller's strike in St. Louis in 1933, the Communists did some of their best work. But in organizng women they were prone to use them for the greater good of the party, not for engaging in an ongoing struggle to eliminate sexism. Yet Communist women were probably more engaged with women workers than were any other groups in American politics during the Depression. They helped women to articulate their own issues in a movement which would otherwise probably have ignored women as much as possible.

Whatever the failings of both feminists and leftists in the thirties, they did try to organize women workers and pioneered in the organization of clerical workers. Hundreds of clerical workers responded by joining CIO office worker unions, and their numbers grew larger during World War II. The contributions of leftist and feminist women during the thirties and during the war stand out in high relief when we look at women in unions in the fifties, a time when feminism was at its lowest point since the early nineteenth century. The Left was driven from the industrial union movement, and all three industrial unions for office workers were expelled from the CIO.

When can women organize? Women workers—whether they

are domestics, nurses, clericals, hairdressers, or seamstresses—
must be given the impression by someone—male unionists,
middle-class feminists, or leftist activists—that unions are appropriate for women, that unions are receptive to the elimination
of sexism, and that taking the risks of losing jobs by striking will
be worth the effort. The recent public attention paid to such
sobering examples as Crystal Lee Jordan, on whom the film
character Norma Rae was based, and the Willmar Eight may provoke more fear than courage, and it is easy to see why; women
fighting for unions seem to get themselves fired.

It may also be true that years of experience with unresponsive
male-dominated unions may account for the deep and abiding
antiunion sentiment which many organizers find in women
workers. Women may very well prefer dealing with one form of
patriarchy—in the workplace—to adding another layer of patriarchy—the union—to their lives.

Women workers no longer have the vitality of a growing industrial union movement from which to draw inspiration. They
do have a more consciously feminist atmosphere. There is considerable disagreement, however, over how strongly unions
should be tied to the women's movement. Working Women has
recently forged an alliance with Service Employees International
Union to organize clerical workers for the AFL-CIO, and it will
continue to maintain an independent existence as an organization
representing women's interests. Yet workers as a group remain
ambivalent about their feminism and its role in union organizing.
Although they want to draw on some of the issues related to
equal pay and equal representation raised by the feminist movement they are also reluctant to identify themselves as "women's
libbers."[59] Recent strikes have shown that union women can use
some aspects of feminist ideology to bolster their own self-esteem
and create a rationale for the redressing of their grievances.
"Feminist baiting," however, is also a tactic available to the opposition, and it will probably be increasingly used in the next
decade.[60] Feminists who are also socialists will probably be particular targets of the corporations, hospitals, banks, and insurance
companies, just as Communist women and men were particular
targets in the McCarthy era. A unionist movement for women in
this country will be successful to the extent that it acknowledges
its past in radical industrial unionism and its future in militant
feminism.

NOTES

I would like to thank Susan Porter Benson, Kate Dunnigan, Ruth Milkman, and Bruce Laurie for reading an earlier draft of this paper and providing helpful suggestions.

1. Alice Kessler-Harris, "'Where Are the Organized Women Workers?'" *Feminist Studies* 3 (Fall 1975): 92-110.

2. Some recent sources include Rosalyn Baxandall, Linda Gordon, and Susan Reverby, eds. *America's Working Women: A Documentary History—1600 To the Present* (New York: Random House, 1976); Ellen Cantarow with Susan Gushee O'Malley and Sharon Hartman Strom, *Moving the Mountain: Women Working for Social Change* (Old Westbury, N.Y.: Feminist Press, 1980); Phillip S. Foner, *Women and the American Labor Movement,* 2 vols. (New York and London: Free Press, 1979-80); James J. Keneally, *Women and American Trade Unions* (St. Aibans, Vt., and Montreal: Eden Press, 1978); Alice Kessler-Harris, *Out to Work: A History of Wage-Earning Women in the United States* (New York: Oxford University Press, 1982), Alice Lynd and Staughton Lynd, eds., *Rank and File: Personal Histories of Working-Class Organizers* (Boston: Beacon Press, 1973); Meredith Tax, *The Rising of the Women: Feminist Solidarity and Class Conflict, 1880-1917* (New York and London: Monthly Review Press, 1980); Barbara M. Wertheimer, *We Were There: The Story of Working Women in America* (New York: Pantheon, 1977).

3. Leslie Tentler, *Wage-Earning Women: Industrial Work and Family Life in the United States, 1900-1930* (New York: Oxford University Press, 1979).

4. Ruth Milkman, "Organizing the Sexual Division of Labor: Historical Perspectives on 'Women's Work' and the American Labor Movement," *Socialist Review* 10 (January-February 1980): 119.

5. Foner 2: 279-81; and Lois Scharf, *To Work and To Wed: Female Employment, Feminism, and the Great Depression* (Westport, Conn., and London: Greenwood Press, 1980), 110-33. Scharf provides the most thoroughgoing analysis to date of the New Deal's impact on women.

6. Scharf, 45-50; Foner 2: 278.

7. Foner 2: 257; Scharf, 50.

8. Scharf, 45, 104, 106-7; Grace Coyle, "Women in the Clerical Occupations," *Annals of the American Academy of Political and Social Science* 143 (May 1929): 183-84; U.S. Department of Labor, Women's Bureau, *The Employment of Women in Offices,* by Ethel Erickson, Bulletin no. 120 (Washington, D.C. 1934), 12-13.

9. For an overall analysis of the impact of the Depression on women's work see Ruth Milkman, "Women's Work and the Economic Crisis: Some Lessons from the Great Depression," *Review of Radical Political Economics* 8 (Spring 1976): 73-97; Scharf, 86-109.

10. Molly Haskell, *From Reverence to Rape: The Treatment of Women in the Movies* (New York: Holt, Rinehart & Winston, 1974), 141-52.

11. Keneally, 155; Foner, 2: 270, 272-73, 281-82, 285, 314-18.

12. Foner 2: 286-88; Keneally, 155-56; Irving Bernstein, *The Turbulent Years: A History of the American Labor Movement, 1933-1941* (Boston: Houghton Mifflin, 1970), 122-23; "Store Clerks Win Philadelphia Strike," *Ledger* 2 (December 1936): 1.

13. Sidney Fine, *Sit-down: The General Motors Strike of 1936-1937* (Ann Arbor: University of Michigan Press, 1969), 156; Robert Schaffer, "Women and the Communist Party, USA, 1930-1940," *Socialist Review* 45 (May-June 1979): 99.

14. Jeremy Brecher, *Strike!* (San Francisco: World Publishing, 1972), 203, 207-9; Foner 2: 311-12.

15. Foner 2: 312-13.

16. Brecher, 208-9.

17. For discussions of women's auxiliaries see Baxandall, Gordon, and Reverby, 264-65; Fine, 200-1, 279-80; Foner 2: 290-92, 302-12. One of the most important sources on the auxiliaries is the 1977 film, *With Babies and Banners: The Story of the Women's Emergency Brigade,* directed by Lorraine Gray, produced by Anne Bohlen, Lyn Goldfarb, and Lorraine Gray and distributed by New Day Films, P.O. Box 315, Franklin Lakes, N.J. 07417.

18. *With Babies and Banners;* Foner 2: 303-4. Ruth Meyerowitz found that working women were instrumental participants in the brigade ("Organizing the UAW: Wives, Workers, and Leaders, 1933-1974," Ph.D. diss. in progress).

19. Schaffer, 99-100. I have been influenced in this article by the views of Heidi Hartmann, who argues that working-class men actively tried to maintain traditional patriarchal controls over guilds and unions during the historical evolution of modern capitalism. They also convinced many capitalist employers to maintain the sexual division of labor, even when it was in the interest of capitalists to create a totally exchangeable labor market. See her "Capitalism, Patriarchy, and Job Segregation By Sex," in *Capitalist Patriarchy and the Case for Socialist Feminism,* ed. Zillah R. Eisenstein, (New York and London: Monthly Review Press, 1979), 206-47. Ruth Milkman argues persuasively that Hartmann ignores the extent to which working-class *families* (my emphasis), not just working men, used traditional patriarchal ideology to protect capitalist relations from totally encompassing the home and its members. Moreover, union men sometimes support equal rights and wages for women; the question is when and why. See Milkman, "Organizing the Sexual Division of Labor," 95-150, and her article "Redefining 'Women's Work': The Sexual Division of Labor in the Auto Industry During World War II," *Feminist Studies* 8 (Summer 1982): 337-72. Hartmann and Milkman both agree that working-class men have a vested interest in maintaining women's dependence on men in order to secure female childcare and housework services.

20. Fine, 201.

21. Beatrice Marcus, quoted by Shaffer, 89.

22. Scharf, 43-65.

23. Shaffer, 86-87.

24. Anne Prosten, interview with author, 5 February 1977, Brookline, Massachusetts. Vivian Gornick's recent book based on interviews with members of the CP, despite its judgmental style, does hint at the wide variety of sexual relationships within the party. The CP membership evidently encouraged some women to establish fuller and more assertive lives, but doomed others to horrible marriages in which they sacrificed themselves to the dual tyranny of their husbands and party discipline. One senses, however, that the activism of women in the party kept the "woman question" alive on a personal basis, whatever the official view. This ongoing struggle may explain the attraction of the current women's movement for many Old Left women. See Gornick's *The Romance of American Communism* (New York: Basic Books, 1977).

25. See Milkman, "Redefining 'Women's Work,'" 357, for an important discussion of this idea and its likely effect on women's militancy.

26. For a more detailed explanation of this argument see David A. Brody, *Workers in Industrial America: Essays on the Twentieth-Century Struggle* (New York: Oxford University Press, 1980), 127-35.

27. Henry Kraus, quoted in Frances Fox Piven and Richard A. Cloward, *Poor People's*

Movements: Why They Succeed, How They Fail (New York: Pantheon, 1977), 156. The authors do not consider sex as a variable in their analysis.

28. Clinton S. Golden and Harold J. Ruttenberg, *The Dynamics of Industrial Democracy* (New York and London: Harper & Brothers, 1942), 82, 310.

29. See Foner 2: 316-17 for a brief discussion of women in the UE; Piven and Cloward, 156.

30. Ruth Milkman, "The Reproduction of Job Segregation by Sex: A Study of the Changing Sexual Position of Labor in the Auto and Electrical Manufacturing Industries in the 1940's" (Ph.D. diss., University of California, Berkeley, 1981). Milkman argues persuasively that the greater numbers of women working in industry during World War II allowed them to exert more influence in the CIO and to raise women's issues more frequently.

31. Ruth Meyerowitz generously shared this information with me.

32. Fine, 324; Foner 2: 332; U.S. Department of Labor, Women's Bureau, *Women in the Economy of the United States of America* by Elizabeth Pidgeon, Bulletin no. 155 (Washington, D.C., 1937), 76-78.

33. Foner 2: 322, 324.

34. *CIO News* 2 (11 Sept. 1939): 7.

35. Genora Johnson Dollinger makes this point in *With Babies and Banners*. Also see the interview with Stella Nowicki in Lynd and Lynd, 83-84.

36. U.S. Department of Labor, Women's Bureau, *The Woman Wage Earner: Her Situation Today* by Elizabeth D. Benham, Bulletin no. 172 (Washington, D.C., 1939), 44; *Office and Professional News* 13 (December 1946): 4; Foner 2: 327, 329; "Stenos Strut," *CIO News* 2 (20 Feb. 1939): 3; and "Sweetheart of the CIO," *CIO News* 1 (6 Aug. 1938): 7.

37. Anne Prosten interview; "Regions Give 'All-Out' Aid to Organizing Drives," *Federal Record* 4 (3 Apr. 1941): 1.

38. Valerie Kincade Oppenheimer, *The Female Labor Force in the United States: Demographic and Economic Factors Governing its Growth and Changing Composition* (Westport, Conn.: Greenwood Press, 1976), 149.

39. Milkman, "Women's Work and the Economic Crisis," 530.

40. For a brief history of these unions see Sharon Hartman Strom, "Clerical Workers in the CIO, 1937-1950" (paper presented at the Society for the Study of Social Problems, San Francisco, 3 Sept. 1978); and Jurgen Kocka, *White Collar Workers in America, 1890-1940: A Socio-Political History in International Perspective* (London and Beverly Hills: Sage Publications, 1980), 218-37.

41. Kocka, 20, 218-19, 226; Carl Dean Snyder, *White-Collar Workers and the UAW* (Urbana: University of Illinois Press, 1973); "Wage Cuts in Steel Offices Hit by Union," *Ledger* 4 (February 1938): 1, 8; "Union Grows in Rubber Company," *Office and Professional News* 6 (March-April 1940): 1; "Organizing the Unorganized White Collar Workers," *Career* 2 (15 Oct. 1949): 4.

42. Kocka, 224-25, 227, 230-31.

43. Nathan Glazer, *The Social Basis of American Communism* (New York: Harcourt, Brace & World, 1961), 116-17, 130. When Jessica Mitford worked in Washington for the Office of Price Administration during World War II, she assumed that joining the UFW would put her in touch with the CP *(A Fine Old Conflict* [New York: Knopf, 1977], 49). Len DeCaux, editor of the *CIO News,* said that the "new-type" leaders of white collar unions "differed little from the blue collars. Some college was common for all . . . many . . . were trained in the Communist movement as I knew it—a movement, that is, of militant unemployed; of Union pioneers before New Deal permitted or

CIO paid salaries; of rebels against corrupt inaction or reaction in AFL unions." See his *Labor Radical: From the Wobblies to CIO, A Personal History* (Boston: Beacon Press, 1970), 288-89.

44. For some sources that discuss the mechanization of clerical work, see Harvey Braverman, *Labor and Monopoly Capital: The Degradation of Work in the Twentieth Century* (New York and London: Monthly Review Press, 1974), 293-358; Coyle, "Women in the Clerical Occupations"; Erickson; C. Wright Mills, *White Collar: The American Middle Classes* (New York: Galaxy Paperback, 1956), 189-212; Orlie Pell, *The Office Worker—Labor's Side of the Ledger,* pamphlet published by the League for Industrial Democracy (New York, January 1937); and Strom, "Clerical Workers in the CIO."

45. Lewis Corey, *The Crisis of the Middle Class* (New York: Covici, Freide, 1935), 259; and Hans Speir, "The Salaried Employee in Modern Society," *Social Research* 1 (February 1934): 116-18. Also see J. Raymond Walsh, *C.I.O. Industrial Unionism in Action* (New York: W.W. Norton & Co., 1937), 148-155.

46. For instance, Joseph Starobin recalled that at a June 1945 meeting of the CP that a "Lew,"—certainly Lewis Merrill, president of the UOPWA—argued in favor of openly admitting membership in the party. However, as a representative of white collar workers party leaders felt his union was not among "the most crucial elements in the working class." See Starobin's *American Communism in Crisis, 1943-1957* (New York: Harvard University Press, 1972), 96-97.

47. Len DeCaux, "Unionizing the White Collared," *CIO News* 1 (21 May 1938): 4.

48. "Typewritten notes for speeches," circa 1936-40, Florence Luscomb Papers, Schlesinger Library, Cambridge, Massachusetts.

49. The UOPWA claimed 22,000 members and forty locals in 1937 out of an estimated white collar work force of four or five million. See "Merrill Article Shows White Collar Progress," *Ledger* 3 (November 1937): 5. By 1943 the UOPWA had 43,000 members and 118 locals. See Florence Peterson, *Handbook of Labor Unions* (Washington, D.C.: American Council on Public Affairs, 1934), 259.

50. Murray Nathan, "The Margon Strike," *Ledger* 2 (March 1936): 5-6; "Unity Pledged at Joint Rally," *Ledger* 2 (March 1936): 9; Murray Nathan, "The Margon Strike Continues," *Ledger* 3 (April 1936): 9.

51. Nathan, "Margon Strike."

52. "Union Recognized in Credit Firm. . . .," *Ledger* 3 (September 1937): 1; "Local 16 Pickets CCH by Telephone," *Office and Professional News* 6 (February 1940): 1, 3.

53. "Government Mediation Averts Credit House Strike," *Office and Professional News* 8 (11 Feb. 1942): 1.

54. "Local 16 Wins NLRB Poll in Oil Office by Two to One," *Office and Professional News* 7 (January 1941): 1; "Sonneborn Strikers Win Coast to Coast Support," and "Strikers Burned Up—Put Heat on Oil Company" 7 (February 1941): 1, 2, both in *Office and Professional News.*

55. "Strike Spirit Rises as Sonneborn Accounts Fall" (March 1941): 8; "Sonneborn Begins Talk in Strikes' 9th Week" (April 1941): 12; and "Local 16 Maps Changes in Sonneborn Strike" (May 1941): 8, all in *Office and Professional News.*

56. "Susie Steno Discovers the Union," *Ledger* 3 (June 1937): 6.

57. Harvey J. Clermont, *Organizing the Insurance Worker: A History of Labor Unions of Insurance Employees* (Washington, D.C.: Catholic University Press, 1966), 176; and Strom, "Clerical Workers in the CIO."

58. Ronald Schatz found that the women organizers of union locals at electrical plants in the thirties were even more likely than men to be children of radicals, socialists, or

union activists, although none had belonged to a union before joining the UE. They were also more likely than other female workers to come from female-headed households. See his "Union Pioneers: The Founders of Local Unions at General Electric and Westinghouse, 1933-37," *Journal of American History* 66 (December 1979): 586-602.

59. "Women's Group Set to Organize Office Workers," *New York Times,* 4 Mar. 1981: A12; "Women Clerical Workers and Trade Unionism," Interview with Karen Nussbaum, *Socialist Review* 10 (January-February 1980): 151-59.

60. See for instance, Gail Gregory Sansbury, "'Now, What's the Matter With You Girls?' Clerical Workers Organize," *Radical America* 14 (November-December 1980): 67-75; and the 1980 film *Willmar 8,* directed by Lee Grant, produced by Mary Beth Yarrow and Julie Thompson, and distributed by California Newsreel, 630 Natoma St., San Francisco, Calif. 94103.

THE DIALECTICS OF WAGE WORK:
JAPANESE-AMERICAN WOMEN
AND DOMESTIC SERVICE, 1905-1940

EVELYN NAKANO GLENN

INTRODUCTION

The work of women has been a much neglected topic in the economic and social history of Japanese Americans. Yet, from the moment they arrived, Japanese-American women labored alongside the men to secure their own and their families' livelihood.[1] Although much of their work took the form of unpaid labor on family farms and businesses, many women turned to wage work to supplement family income. Up until World War II, the most common form of nonagricultural employment for the immigrant women (*issei*) and their American-born daughters (*nisei*) was domestic service.

As was true for immigrant women from other rural societies, domestic work served as a port of entry into the urban labor force.[2] The demand for domestic help among urban middle-class families ensured a constant pool of jobs, but the occupation's low status and unfavorable working conditions made it unattractive to those who could secure other kinds of jobs. Thus, the field was left open to the newcomer and the minority woman.[3]

For European immigrants, domestic service was a temporary way station. By the second generation, they had moved into the expanding, white collar clerical and sales occupations.[4] The Japanese, however, like blacks and other minorities, were barred from most industrial and office settings.[5] Thus, Japanese women remained heavily concentrated in domestic work even into the second generation. Only after World War II did institutional racism diminish sufficiently to enable the *nisei* and their children to move into other occupations. Involvement in domestic service was thus an important shared experience for Japanese women in the prewar years, serving as one basis for ethnic and gender solidarity.[6]

This paper examines that experience, using the case of *issei*

Feminist Studies 6, no. 3 (Fall 1980). ©1980 by Evelyn Nakano Glenn.

women in the San Francisco Bay Area in the period from 1905 to
1940. The account is based primarily on interviews with domestic
workers and community informants.[7] The first three sections
describe the historical context in which *issei* women's specialization in domestic work evolved: the development of Bay Area
Japanese communities, the arrival of *issei* women, and the labor
market structure they confronted. The next five sections give a
detailed account of domestic workers' experiences: the circumstances leading to involvement in domestic work, the entry and
socialization process, the conditions of work, relations with employers, and the interaction between the women's wage work and
their unpaid work in the family.

What is highlighted in this account is the contradiction between
the multiple forms of oppression to which the women were subjected and the resilience that they developed.[8] *Issei* domestic
workers were subjugated by institutional racism, by conditions
of work in domestic employment, and by the structure of *issei*
family life; yet, they were not passive victims, but active participants shaping their own lives. Faced with oppression, *issei* women
strived, often in covert and indirect ways, to gain control over their
work and other aspects of their lives. Out of this effort, I argue,
grew a sense of autonomy and self-reliance that enabled them to
transcend the limitations of their circumstances and gain a measure
of satisfaction from essentially menial work.

HISTORY OF BAY AREA JAPANESE COMMUNITIES

We begin by examining the historical context in which Japanese
women's involvement in domestic work developed. The pre-World
War II history of Japanese communities in the San Francisco Bay
Area can be divided into three periods: frontier, settlement, and
stabilization, each demarcated by specific historical events that
shaped the immigrants' lives.[9]

The "frontier" period, roughly 1890 to 1910, was when the
first wave of immigrants arrived. The *issei* were remarkably homo-
geneous, and most of the immigrants were young single males from
rural villages in southern Japan, with an average of eight years of
education.[10] They came as sojourners, expecting to work a few
years to amass sufficient capital to establish themselves in Japan.
They started out as unskilled wage laborers in agriculture, rail-
roading, mining, and lumbering, or in domestic service.[11] Later,
as they accumulated capital and know-how, many launched small
enterprises, usually laundries or stores. In place of their old kin
ties, the *issei* men formed mutual aid associations with those from

291

the same prefecture (*kenjinkai*) and organized rotating credit associations (*tanomoshi*) to raise capital.[12]

Up until 1907, San Francisco, as a port city, was one of three main centers of Japanese population.[13] The Japanese congregated in a section of the Western Addition, a district of low-rent rundown housing that became known as Little Osaka. From San Francisco, the *issei* spread to other cities in the East Bay. By 1910, the Japan populations of the four main cities were: San Francisco, 4,518; Oakland, 1,520; Berkeley, 710; and Alameda, 499.[14]

Growing anti-Japanese agitation led to a series of legal measures designed to reduce immigration and to discourage permanent settlement. The 1907 "Gentlemen's Agreement" between Japan and the United States closed entry to laborers. Between 1910 and 1929, more men returned to Japan than entered.[15] However, those who remained began to think in terms of a longer stay. The "Gentlemen's Agreement" contained a loophole: it permitted the entry of wives and relatives. The *issei* began returning to Japan to marry and bring back wives or began sending for picture brides.

The arrival of *issei* women marks the beginning of the "settlement" period. Between 1909 and 1923, over 33,000 *issei* wives immigrated.[16] During this period of family and community building, the sex ratio became less-skewed, and the population came to include children as well as adults. Extensive infrastructures developed with the establishment of ethnic churches, newspapers, language schools, and business and service establishments.[17] Ethnic enclaves formed in San Francisco's Western Addition, on the borders of Chinatown in downtown Oakland, and around City Hall in Alameda. Except for jobs, the *issei* could fulfill most of their social and material wants within the ethnic community. According to one observer, "very few Japanese ventured beyond those comfortable environs."[18]

Meanwhile, partly in response to more permanent settlement, anti-Japanese sentiment grew. An Alien Land Law was passed in California in 1913, prohibiting the *issei*, who were ineligible for citizenship, from owning land or leasing it for more than three years. Finally, the Immigration Act of 1924 cut off all further immigration from Asia.[19]

The end of immigration marks the start of the "stabilization" period, 1924 to 1940. Henceforth, the growth of population depended entirely on births. There was little room for expansion of ethnic enterprises serving a largely Japanese clientele. Thus, the *issei* found their opportunities shrinking and began to pin their hopes for the future on their children, who by virtue of American citizenship had rights denied their parents.[20]

The restriction on immigration also created distinct generational cohorts. The majority of *issei* were born between 1870 and 1900, and their children, the *nisei*, were born mainly between 1910 and 1940. By the mid-1930s, the *issei* were primarily middle-aged, while the eldest *nisei* were just reaching maturity and entering the labor force. Despite American citizenship and education, the *nisei* confronted the same racist restrictions as their parents; they were still barred from union jobs and employment in white-run offices and stores. It is unclear what course ethnic assimilation would have taken over the next decade under normal circumstances, for the Japanese community was shattered almost overnight by the commencement of World War II. The Japanese were evacuated and incarcerated in concentration camps. Those who returned to the Bay Area after the war settled in scattered areas, rather than concentrating in the old enclaves, so the old physical communities were never fully reconstituted.

ISSEI WOMEN

Most of the *issei* women who arrived in the United States between 1907 and 1924 were from the same southern rural backgrounds as the male immigrants. They had levels of education comparable to the men: the fifteen *issei* domestics in the study averaged six years of education, with two having no schooling and two having completed ten years, the equivalent of high school. The typical *issei* woman was in her early twenties and was married to a man ten years her senior who had lived for some years in the United States, working as a wage laborer or small entrepreneur.[21]

Following Japanese custom, the marriages were arranged by the families of the bride and groom through a go-between (*baishakunin*). Many *issei* men managed to save or borrow money to return to Japan to meet their prospective brides and to get married. Many others, for financial or other reasons, could not return. In such cases, the match was arranged by the go-between through an exchange of photographs, hence the term "picture marriage." The union was legalized by registering it in the husband's home prefecture.

For the most part, the women felt they had little say in the selection of a husband; daughters were expected to go along with their parents' judgment. Yet, the extent to which women felt forced or manipulated by their parents and by circumstances varied.[22]

At one extreme is Mrs. Takagi, 23, who recalls that her father tricked her into going to stay with her adopted grandfather on the pretext that she would receive training to become a midwife:

Otherwise, I wouldn't have gone, you see. I knew my mother needed help. . . . I stayed one week and helped my uncle [a doctor]. I was thinking I would stay to help him. Pretty soon, they took me to see this man. I'd never seen or heard of him. He was my second cousin. You don't know the Japanese system: they just pick out your husband and tell you what to do. So, I just did it, that's all. . . . I never gave my parents a fight.

Another *issei*, Mrs. Nishimura, falls somewhere in the middle of the continuum. She was only fifteen when she was persuaded by her father to marry Mr. Nishimura:

In the Japanese style, we used a go-between and the husband would come to Japan to pick up his bride. My father was rather new in his thinking, so he told me that rather than stay in Japan to attend school, I should come to the U.S. My mother told me even then that I was too young. But, it's something that had to be done so. . . . I was rather big for my age, and . . . but I cried at the time, and I'll always remember that. My parents felt a little guilty about it, almost as if they had forced me to come, and apparently they kept asking about me, about how I was doing, until they died.

At the other extreme, we have Mrs. Shinoda who claims she dreamed of going to the United States even as a child:

I told my father that I wouldn't get married, unless I could come to the United States. [Did your parents oppose you?] Yes, they were all against me. [How did you know you wanted to come to the United States?] I don't know. When I was small, in elementary school, we had to write an essay on "What I Wish For." I wrote in that essay that I'd like to go to America. My friends read it and told what I had written. That's funny, huh?

Mrs. Shinoda was stubborn enough to hold out until her father gave in. She didn't marry until she was twenty-eight, but she got her way.

In leaving their families and going to the United States, the *issei* women were following usual Japanese practice. Custom dictated that a woman leave her parents' household or village to live in her husband's home. The *issei* were simply traveling a much greater geographic and cultural distance.[24] Despite the pain of separation and fear of the unknown, the majority of the women said they left Japan with positive expectations. Just as the men came to the United States to better their lot, *issei* women came with their own hopes: to further their education, to help their families economically, to seek a happier homelife, and to experience new adventures.

The boat trip to the United States, usually from Yokohama to Seattle or San Francisco, normally took over a month. The women report feelings of homesickness and physical illness, although they also recall fondly the friendships they developed with other women during the voyage. Upon arrival, the women confronted many new and strange experiences. The first shock for the picture brides was meeting their new spouses. Mrs. Yoshida, who traveled with a number of other picture brides, recalls the responses of some of her companions upon catching glimpses of their husbands:

A lot of people that I came together with said, "I'm going back on this very boat." I told them, "You can't do that; you should go ashore once. If you really don't like him, and you feel like going back, then you have to have a meeting and then go back. . . ." Many times, the picture was taken twenty years earlier and they had changed. Many of the husbands had gone to the country to work as farmers, so they had aged and became quite wrinkled. And very young girls came expecting more and it was natural.

As for herself, Mrs. Yoshida says she was disappointed that her husband (sixteen years her senior) looked much older than a neighbor at home the same age. However, many people from her village in Hiroshima had traveled to Hawaii and to the mainland United States, and she wanted to go too: "I didn't care what the man looked like."

The second shock was having to discard the comfort of kimonos and slippers for constricting dresses and shoes. The women were generally taken straight off after clearing immigration to be completely outfitted. Mrs. Nomura, who arrived in Seattle in 1919, said:

At that time, ships were coming into Seattle every week from Japan, carrying one or two hundred Japanese brides. So, there was a store set up especially for these new arrivals. There was a hotel run by a Japanese and also Japanese food available. The Japanese wouldn't go to the stores run by Whites, so there there were stores run by Japanese to deal with Japanese customers. We did all of our shopping there. The lady there would show us how to use a corset— since we had never used one in Japan. And how to wear stockings and shoes.

Mrs. Okamura, who came in 1917, laughs when she remembers her first dress:

It felt very tight. I couldn't even move my arms. That was the first time I had ever worn Western clothes, so I thought they were supposed to be like that. . . . Later, Mrs. S. taught me to sew my own clothes. She had a pattern that we all used to make the same dress in different materials. So I found out that first dress was too small.

As Mrs. Okamura's account indicates, earlier immigrants taught new arrivals "the ropes," and living quarters were usually secured within the ghetto. Many couples rented rooms in a house and shared kitchen and bathroom facilities with several other Japanese

families. Thus, help and comfort were close at hand. Mrs. Hori-
uchi says the best time in her life was when she was a new bride,
just after arriving in the United States. All her husband's friends
dropped in to welcome her and bring gifts. Sometimes, husbands
who had worked as "Schoolboys" or domestics, taught their wives
how to shop, cook, and clean. Community agencies such as the
YWCA, and the public schools, sponsored housekeeping and
English courses for newcomers. Most of the women in the study
took some of these classes, but claimed that they were unable to
continue their studies once children arrived. Partly for this reason,
most never fully mastered English, Another reason was that the
women rarely ventured outside the confines of their ethnic community, except to do domestic work for wages. The ethnic community provided for most of their needs and insulated them from
the hostility of the larger society.

The *issei* women arrived at a time of accelerating anti-Japanese
agitation. Their arrival was itself a focus of attack because it signaled an intention on the part of the *issei* to settle on a long-term
basis. Anti-Japanese propaganda depicted the practice of picture
marriages as immoral and a ruse to contravene the Gentlemen's
Agreement. As a result of mounting pressure, the Japanese government stopped issuing passports to picture brides in 1921.[25]

Mrs. Takagi was outspoken about the racism of the period,
saying:

I think all the [Japanese] people at that age had a real hard time. [They had
to work hard, you mean?] Not only that, they were all thinking we were
slaves, you know, sleeping in the stable upstairs. And even when we'd get
on a streetcar, they'd say, "Jap, get away." Even me, they always threw stuff
from up above. [They did? What do you mean?] I don't know why they
did that. I was so scared. . . . One man, he was going on a bicycle and someone threw cement. That night he lost an eye. But they never sued, they
never reported it because they didn't speak English. . . . I don't know what
other people think, but we didn't have very much fun. We didn't have very
many jobs. A lot of people graduated from college and still no job, before
the war.

The *issei* downplay personal difficulties they encountered as a
result of racism. Although they were able to avoid hostile encounters by remaining within their own world, nevertheless, it is
clear that their lives were affected in a variety of ways, especially
economically. Furthermore, discrimination reinforced the *issei*'s
sojourner orientation. Mrs. Adachi notes that because of discrimination, her husband always opposed putting down permanent
roots, and they always rented apartments, rather than buying a

house, even after they could afford to do so. Her husband also became increasingly nationalistic, keenly following the political and
military developments in Japan.

ECONOMIC ACTIVITIES OF ISSEI WOMEN

Issei women had little time to brood about their situations.
Whether rural or urban, they found they were expected to be full
economic contributors almost immediately upon arrival. Like
other working-class women of that era, they were manufacturing
many basic household necessities, such as foodstuffs and clothing,
as well as performing the maintenance and childcare tasks.[26] In
addition, according to an early observer of the *issei*:

The great majority of wives of farmers, barbers and small shopkeepers take
a more or less regular place in the fields or shops of their husbands, while a
smaller number accept places in domestic service, or in laundries or other
places of employment. Thus, a larger percentage of those admitted find a
place in the "labor supply."[27]

According to U.S. Census figures, 20.8 percent of all Japanese
women over age fifteen were gainfully employed in 1920. This
proportion is similar to the proportion of women employed in the
overall population (23.3 percent). However, because virtually all
Japanese women over fifteen were married, the *issei* rate of employment was remarkably high. In the population at large, only 9.0
percent of all married women were in the labor force.[28] Also, because Japanese men were concentrated in agriculture and small
businesses, which relied on wives' unpaid help, the extent of *issei*
women's gainful activity is probably underestimated.

It is difficult to specify the occupational distribution of *issei*
women, for the women frequently divided their time between
housework, unpaid work in family farms and businesses, and
paid employment. In these cases, the main occupation cannot
be pinpointed. However, there are data that indicate the range
of their activities. Edward K. Strong surveyed 1,716 *issei* women
in a 1933 study of Japanese-American occupations. He classified
998 (58 percent) as housewives, 438 (26 percent) as part-time
assistants to their husbands, 53 (3 percent) as full-time assistants,
and 227 (13 percent) as engaged in independent occupations. He
noted, however:

Undoubtedly, the last two figures are too low and the first figures too high.
Accuracy in this connection was very difficult to secure because many of
these women speak very little English and are unaccustomed to talk to
strangers, and in some cases the Japanese men prevented or interfered in
the interviewing of their wives.[29]

297

TABLE 1

OCCUPATIONS OF EMPLOYED JAPANESE WOMEN IN THE UNITED STATES, 1900-1940[a]

	1900		1920		1930		1940[b]	
	Number	Percent	Number	Percent	Number	Percent	Number	Percent
Total females 10 years of age or older	985		25,432		36,693			
Total females in gainful occupations	266	100.0	5,289	99.9[c]	6,741	100.0	6,693	100.0
Occupations								
Agricultural, including farm and nursery labor	13	4.9	1,797	34.0	2,041	30.3	2,525	37.7
Servants, including cooks, chambermaids, some waitresses and other servants	151	56.8	1,409	26.6	1,195	17.7	690	10.3
Other personal services, including barbers, waitresses, lodging house keepers, laundry operatives, etc.	57	21.4	951	18.0	1,463	21.7	1,579[d]	23.6
Trade, including saleswomen, clerks, etc.	9	3.4	369	7.0	946	14.0	683[e]	10.2
Dressmaking, seamstresses, tailors	23	8.6	124	2.3	121	1.8	NAp[f]	[f]NAp
Other manufacturing, mechanical pursuits	8	3.0	378	7.1	348	5.2	801[g]	12.0
Professional services (teachers, nurses)	5	1.9	145	2.7	329	4.9	214	3.2
Clerical occupations	NAp.	NAp.	75	1.4	271	4.0	NAp[h]	NAp
Other	NAp.	NAp.	41	.8	27	0.4	201	3.0

SOURCES: For 1900: U.S. Department of Commerce, Bureau of the Census Special Reports, *Occupations of the Twelfth Census* (Washington, D.C.: U.S. Government Printing Office, 1904), table 35: Distribution, by Specified Occupations, of Males and of Females in the Chinese, Japanese, and Indian Population Gainfully Employed; 1900.

For 1920: U.S. Department of Commerce, Bureau of the Census, *Fourteenth Census of the United States Taken in the Year 1920*, vol. 4, *Population, Occupations* (Washington, D.C.: Government Printing Office, 1923), table 5: Total Persons of 10 Years of Age and Over Engaged in Each Specified Occupation: Classified by Sex, Color, or Race, Nativity, and Parentage) for the United States: 1920.

For 1930: U.S. Department of Commerce, Bureau of the Census, *Fifteenth Census of the United States*, vol. 5, *Population*, General Report on Occupation, (Washington, D.C.: Government Printing Office, 1933), table 6: Chinese and Japanese Gainful Workers 10 Years Old and Over by Occupation and Sex, for the United States and Selected States; 1930.

For 1940: U.S. Department of Commerce, Bureau of the Census, *Sixteenth Census of the Population, 1940. Population Characteristics of the Non-White Population by Race*. (Washington, D.C.: Government Printing Office, 1943), table 6: Non-White Employed Persons 14 Years Old and Over, By Major Occupation Group, Race, and Sex, for the United States, by Regions, Urban and Rural; 1940.

[a]Data for 1910 are omitted because occupational figures for Japanese and Chinese were combined in the census report.

[b]Only foreign-born (*issei*) women are included in the figures for 1940. The 1940 census for the first time separated out native and foreign born. The figures for 1930 contain some native born (*nisei*), but they probably constitute only a small proportion of the total. Because of immigration patterns, most *nisei* were born after 1910.

[c]Due to rounding.

[d]Consists of two categories, "proprietors, managers, and officials, farm" and "Service workers, exc. domestic."

[e]The category is named "clerical, sales and kindred workers" in the 1940 census.

[f]This category is no longer separately reported, presumably; these occupations are included under manufacturing.

[g]This category is named "operatives and kindred workers" in the 1940 census.

[h]Included in trade category, see also [e].

There are similar limitations in the U.S. Census data.[30] The figures in table 1, which show the occupational distributions for 1900, 1920, 1930 and 1940.[31] should be seen as a rough estimate of the proportion of women engaged in various fields. As table 1 shows, agricultural work, including work in plant nurseries (which was an early Japanese speciality), was the largest field of employment.[32] The figures also show that domestic service was by far the most common form of nonagricultural employment. In 1900, over one-half of all women were so employed; however, the numbers are so small as to make the data inconclusive. By 1920, domestic service accounted for 40.3 percent of all women engaged in nonagricultural occupations. Overall, there seems to have been a trend away from concentration in domestic work between 1920 and 1940.[33]

During this period, there was increased employment in personal service (which in the Bay Area was primarily laundry work) and in retail trade. The growth of employment in service and trade reflects the move of Japanese men away from wage labor into small enterprises, which employed women as paid and unpaid sales, service, and clerical workers. A small but steady percentage of women found work in manufacturing, primarily in food processing and garment manufacturing. With the establishment of ethnic community institutions, there was a small demand for professionals, such as teachers in Japanese language schools.

The occupations in which Japanese women specialized shared several characteristics. The work could be fit in around family responsibilities (for example, children could be taken to work, or the hours were flexible); they were an extension of women's work in the home (such as food preparation, laundry, and sewing); they were in low-technology, labor-intensive fields in which low wages and long hours reduced competition from white women; they took place in family-owned or ethnic enterprises in which language or racial discrimination did not constitute barriers to employment. Domestic service included the first three characteristics and was, therefore, consistent with the general run of occupations open to Japanese women. Because of the common characteristics of the occupations, one would expect the jobs to be highly substitutable. The job histories of the women support this expectation, for the women in the study moved easily between these occupations, although never outside them. The eleven women with experience in nondomestic employment had worked in one or more of the following fields: farming, hand laundry at home, embroidery at home, midwifery, and assisting in family-owned cleaning store, hotel, or nursery work. Domestic service, thus, can be seen as belonging to a set of occupations that constitute a distinct and narrow labor market for Japanese women.

Evidence from the 1940 census indicates that the labor market in the Bay Area was particularly restricted. A comparison of the proportion of *issei* women engaged in domestic work in four cities with substantial Japanese populations shows that domestic work was a speciality among *issei* women only in the Bay Area. Over one-fourth (26.8 percent) of all employed *issei* women in Oakland and over one-half (50.4 percent) in San Francisco were found in domestic work. By contrast, only 6.4 percent of *issei* women in Los Angeles and 3.3 percent in Seattle were so employed. A comparison of the occupational distributions for women in Seattle and San Francisco, cities with comparable Japanese populations, is instructive. Nearly two-thirds of Seattle women were employed as proprietors, service, and clerical workers (table 2). These figures reflect the opportunities for small entrepreneurs in Seattle, where the *issei* ran hotels, restaurants, and shops catering to transient male laborers in lumbering and canning. Such opportunities were more limited in the Bay Area, leaving domestic work as the main employment for women and gardening as the main occupation for men.

TABLE 2

MAIN OCCUPATIONS OF ISSEI WOMEN
IN SAN FRANCISCO AND SEATTLE, 1940

	Seattle		San Francisco	
	Number	Percent	Number	Percent
Total employed	611	100.0	367	100.0
Proprietors	11	18.2	41	11.2
Clerical	112	18.3	21	5.7
Operatives	143	23.4	58	15.8
Domestic	20	3.3	185	50.4
Service	167	27.3	28	7.6

Source: U.S. Department of Commerce, Bureau of the Census. *Sixteenth Census of the Population: 1940. Population Characteristics of the Non-white Population by Race* (Washington, D.C.: Goverment Printing Office, 1943), table 38: Japanese Employed Persons 14 Years Old and Over, by Major Occupation, Group, City and Sex for Selected States, Urban and Rural, and for Selected Cities.

ISSEI WOMEN'S ENTRY INTO DOMESTIC WORK

Having now described the historical and economic context of *issei* women's wage labor in the Bay Area, I now turn to an analy-

sis of the circumstances that came together in the lives of *issei*
women to lead them into domestic service.

Unlike other immigrant groups that specialized in domestic
service, these women did not have a prior tradition of service in
their homelands. Generally, only indigent and unattached women
became servants in Japan. Most of the immigrants who came to
California were better off economically than the average rural
peasant. They had sufficient resources to pay their fares and as
much cash on hand as immigrants from Northern Europe.[34] Thus,
becoming a domestic worker meant a drop in status, as well as a
break with tradition. Given the lack of previous experience in
wage labor generally, and a cultural prejudice against domestic
service, the explanation for *issei* women's involvement in domestic
work must lie in the situations they confronted in the United
States.

One unusual historical circumstance was that the path into
domestic work was paved by *issei* men starting in the early days
of immigration. Many had gained their first footholds in the
United States as "Japanese Schoolboys." This designation was
reportedly coined in the 1880s by a Mrs. Reid, who enrolled a
few Japanese students in her boarding school in Belmont, California. These students earned their tuition and board by doing
chores and kitchen work.[35] The term came to refer to any Japanese apprentice servant, whether or not he had any involvement
in formal schooling. The job itself was the education: it provided
the new immigrant with an opportunity to learn English and become familiar with American customs. In return for his services,
the Schoolboy received token wages of about $1.50 a week in
1900 ($2.00 a week by 1909), in addition to room and board,
compared with the $15.00 to $40.00 a month earned by trained
servants. It has been estimated that at the height of male immigration (1904 to 1907), over 4,000 Japanese were employed as
Schoolboys in San Francisco.[36]

Still other immigrants earned their first wages in the United
States as Dayworkers; they hired out to do yard chores and housecleaning on a daily or hourly basis. Groups of men from the same
prefecture sometimes took lodgings together and advertised their
services. Newcomers were invited to join the household and were
quickly initiated into the work. H. A. Millis found 163 Japanese
Daywork firms listed in the 1913 San Francisco City Directory.[37]
In addition, *issei* who had their own businesses sometimes acted
as agents for dayworkers. Ads for a Japanese nursery included
notices such as the following, which appeared in the *Alameda
Daily Argue* in 1900: "Japanese Help. Also, first class Japanese

help for cooking, general housework, or gardening, by day, week
or month, furnished on short notice."

Both forms of domestic service were temporary stopgaps.
Schoolboy jobs and daywork were frequent first occupations
for new arrivals; after a short time, the *issei* moved on to agricultural or city trades.[38]   In the Bay Area, many dayworkers graduated into a specialized branch of domestic service—gardening.
The Japanese gardener became a status symbol, but the indoor
male domestic had largely disappeared by 1930. The early association of men with domestic service, however, established the
stereotype of the Japanese domestic—a stereotype inherited by
the *issei* women when they arrived. The situations wanted columns in Bay Area newspapers, which prior to 1908 had been
dominated by ads for Japanese Schoolboys now began to include
ads for women, such as "Japanese girl wants situation to assist
in general housework and taking care of baby. Address, Japanese
Girl, 1973 P . . . . . Street."

The path into domestic service was, thus, clearly marked. The
issue remains, what were the personal circumstances that launched
many *issei* women on the journey?

The case of Mrs. Yoshida is a good place to begin. Ninety-one-
years old at the time of the interview, she arrived in 1909 as a
picture bride. Her husband, sixteen years her senior, had lived in
the United States for almost twenty years and had managed to
acquire a laundry in Alameda, which the couple ran together.
Because they had one of the few telephones in the Japanese community, they began acting as agents for dayworkers. Employers
called to request help for cleaning, or other jobs, and the Yoshidas referred the requests to the *issei* men who dropped by. By
1912, Mrs. Yoshida had two small children, and she felt that they
needed extra income. She explains:

I started to work because everyone went on vacation and the summer was
very hard for us. The cleaning business declined during the summer. . . . I
bought a second-hand bicycle from a friend who had used it for five years.
I paid $3 for it. So, at night I went to the beach and practiced on that bicycle.
At night nobody was at the beach, so even if I fell down, I didn't feel embarrassed. And then I went to work. I worked half a day and was paid $1. . . .
We didn't know the first thing about housework, but the ladies of the house
didn't mind. They taught us how at the beginning: "This is a broom; this is
a dustpan." And we worked hard for them. We always thought America was
a wonderful country. At the time, we were thinking of working three years
in America and then going back to Japan to help our parents lead a comfortable life. . . . But, we had babies almost every year, and so we had to give up
that idea. [She had 10 children between 1910 and 1923.]

303

Although the specific details are unique, Mrs. Yoshida's account reveals several common elements which came together in the lives of *issei* women who entered domestic work. First, the Yoshidas' intention of accumulating a nest egg and returning to Japan was shared by other immigrants during this period. The women in the study all claimed that they expected to return to Japan eventually. Many were sending remittances to support parents or other relatives in Japan. Because the sacrifice was seen as short term, the immigrants were willing to work long hours and in menial jobs. In this context, wage work could be viewed as a temporary expedient which, therefore, did not reflect on the family's social standing.

A second common element was the economic squeeze experienced by many *issei* families, especially after children arrived. Some families managed to accumulate enough capital to return to Japan.[39] Those who were less well off postponed their return and continued to struggle for day-to-day survival. The majority of women in the study were married to gardeners, whose earnings fluctuated. As Mrs. Yoshida's case illustrates, even those who owned small businesses found their marginal enterprises did not generate sufficient income to support a family. Some women were in even more dire straits: a husband who was ill, who refused to turn over his earnings, or who died and left children to support. Three women, facing this situation, took or sent their children to Japan to be cared for by relatives, so they could work full-time.

Mrs. Shinoda was part of this group. Her husband, a college graduate, was killed in an accident in 1928. She was thirty-nine and had two young sons:

I started work after my husband died. I went to Japan to take my children to my mother. Then, I came back alone and started to work. . . . My sons were ten and eight . . . and I worked in a family. At that time, I stayed in the home of a professor at the University of California as a live-in maid . . . I got the job through another Japanese person. She was going back to Japan, so I took her place. [What kind of things did you do?] Cleaned house, and cooking, and serving food. [Did you know how to cook and things like that?] No, I didn't, at first. The lady told me.

Given the factors pushing the *issei* to seek wage work, what factors drew them particularly into domestic work? The basic limiting factor was the labor market situation described earlier. Race segregation, family responsibilities, and the lack of English and job skills severely limited job options. Given limited choices, domestic work offered some desirable features. Its main attraction was flexibility; those with heavy family responsibilities could work part-time, yet during times of financial pressure, they could work extra days or hours, as needed. A further pull was the demand for domestic labor. Dayworkers were sought by the growing number of middle-class urban families who could not afford regular servants. The demand was great enough so that, as Mrs. Yoshida and Mrs. Shinoda noted, employers were willing to take on someone with no experience and provide on-the-job training.

ENTRY AND SOCIALIZATION PROCESS

The know-how for obtaining and working in domestic jobs was widespread in the community as a result of the early experience of *issei* men in Schoolboy jobs and in daywork. The women sometimes resorted to advertisements, but primarily they found employment through informal job networks. They heard about jobs through friends or acquaintances working as gardeners or domestics, and sometimes they inherited a position from another *issei* who was taking another job or returning to Japan. As the Japanese gained a reputation in domestic work, employers began to make requests through Japanese churches, businesses, and social organizations. Once one job was secured, other jobs were easily obtained through employer referrals.

Among the women in the study, two patterns of entry emerged. One pattern was to begin as an apprentice just as the Japanese Schoolboys had done; in fact, some women used the term Schoolgirl to refer to these positions. A Schoolgirl job was typically entered soon after the woman's arrival and before she had children; she was more or less thrust into the position without a specific intention of beginning a career of domestic service. The job was arranged by a husband, relative, or friend. Wages were nominal, and in return, the employer provided training in housekeeping and cooking. Many of the *issei* women actually attended classes part-time to learn English. The job was, thus, intended as part of the socialization of the newcomer. However, in many cases, it portended the beginning of a career in domestic service.

The experience of Mrs. Takagi, who arrived as a nineteen-year-old in 1920, illustrates the entry into domestic service by way of a Schoolgirl job. Mrs. Takagi's husband's parents had immigrated with him, and the couple lived with them in Oakland:

I was here 28 days, and my mother-in-law took me to the first job on the 29th day. So I didn't even know "yes or no." I was so scared to go out then. [She took the trolley.] I got off at ——Street. I just did it the same way, counting "one, two, three stops." If I lost my way home, I couldn't ask anybody.... I couldn't hardly sleep at night.... The first time I went, she [employer] taught me all the things I said. . . . they had a coal stove, a big one. Burned coal just like a Japanese hibachi. It has a pipe inside and heats the water from down below. I had to bring the coal up, all the time I went up and down. Then I had to wash diapers. Me, I grew up on a farm, so I never had to do that. When I came to America, I didn't know anything. So I just had to cry. She said, "What happened to your eyes?" Then she gave me $5.00 and gave me a note and said to take it home. . . . My mother [in-law] and father [in-law] said, "Oh, that's big money." They thought it was supposed to be $5.00 a month.

Mrs. Takagi was fortunate in having an employer who treated her as an apprentice and who encouraged her to attend English classes: "She put a hat on me, put a book in my hand, and gave me carfare. She said, 'Go to school.'" After six months, Mrs. Takagi went on to a general housekeeping job with a banker, and then with a widow, before finally settling into daywork.

The second pattern was to enter into daywork on a part-time basis after the arrival of children, when family expenses began to outrun income. Mrs. Yoshida, who was discussed earlier, followed this path. In these cases, the women entered into domestic work deliberately. They initiated the job search themselves, after deciding that they needed to work to make ends meet. The example of other *issei* women working as domestics provided both the impetus and the means to secure employment. Mrs. Yoshida's account indicates that her husband attempted to discourage her employment; yet, she persisted in her resolve. The conflicting wishes of husband and wife are even more apparent in the case of Mrs. Adachi. She began daywork in her mid-thirties after several years of taking in laundry:

When the kids got to be in junior high school, Mrs. S. said, "Why don't you go out to work?" Other people with small children did go out to work but Mr. Adachi was sickly when he was young, so he didn't want the children left alone. He said, "What if the children got hurt. You couldn't get their lives back. The children are worth more than a few dollars. Just as long as we have enough to eat, that's enough." So, I went out secretly to work in one place. And that one became two and that became three. By three, I stopped [adding more jobs] because by that time, my husband found out, and, of course, there was still work at home, because I was still taking in home laundry.

Mrs. Adachi's decision to secretly defy her husband is interesting and illustrates the contradictory nature of *issei* women's involvement in domestic labor. On the one hand, circumstances beyond their control appear to have ruled these women's lives. They were forced to seek employment because of economic deprivation, husbands' inability to provide adequate support, and the needs of parents and other relatives in Japan. They had to travel in unfamiliar neighborhoods and enter strange households without any experience or knowledge of English. Some confessed that they felt fearful and helpless in the beginning. Yet, on the other hand, some women actively sought out employment, even in the face of opposition from husbands. And, among those who took School-girl jobs more or less passively, many continued in domestic work even without great financial pressure. These latter instances suggest that employment, even in a menial capacity, provided some resources the women desired, but lacked when they worked exclusively within the family.

The most obvious resource provided by wage work was an independent source of income. Although the women put most of their wages into a common family pool, their contribution was more evident when it was in the form of money, than when it was in the form of unpaid labor. Moreover, because of informal pay arrangements and flexible work hours, the women could hide the amount of their earnings. (Some women reported keeping their own bank accounts.) They could use some of their earnings to purchase things for their children or themselves without having to ask their husbands. It is also important to note that some women were largely self-supporting and/or were supporting others. This was a source of considerable pride and an option that married women did not have in traditional Japanese society. This was pointed out by Mrs. Takagi. After describing "killing myself" working forty to sixty hours a week as a domestic to support herself and her children and helping her mother and her brothers, who were able to attend high school because of her, she concluded: "I'm glad to be able to do that. I'm so lucky to be in the United States. In Japan, I wouldn't have had the chance as a woman."

Going out to work also took women outside the confines of the family, away from the direct control of their husbands. They could form outside relationships with employers, and at the very least, these relationship expanded the *issei* women's store of knowledge and experience. Some employers provided material and emotional support. Mrs. Takagi's employer visited her in the hospital when she was sick and gave her the money to return to Japan to retrieve her son. She also credits this employer with helping her weather many personal crises. For women who were cut off from kin, the ties with employers could be a valuable resource. If we recall Strong's remark that *issei* men prevented interviewers from talking to their wives, we can see the significance of outside alliances to internal family power relationships. Thus, it is not surprising that some *issei* men opposed their wives' employment, even when the extra wages were needed, and that some *issei* women persisted in working, despite their husband's opposition and in the absence of overwhelming financial need. Domestic service offered a compromise resolution. It permitted women to work and form relationships outside the family, yet, it kept them within a female sphere in which they were supervised by other women.

CONDITIONS OF WORK

Domestic service encompasses a variety of specific situations. The jobs that the *issei* women entered were of three types: live-in service, full-time nonresidential jobs, and daywork.

For most of its history, domestic service was a live-in occupation, and up until World War I, this was the most common pattern in the United States. This merging of residence and workplace stood as a marked exception to the increasing separation of production from the household and the accompanying segregation of of work and nonwork life brought about by industrialization. For the live-in domestic, there was no clear delineation between work and nonwork time. Work hours were open-ended, with the domestic "on call" most of her waking hours, and with little time to devote to family and outside social relationships. As other forms of wage work which gave workers greater autonomy expanded, the confinement and isolation of domestic service grew more onerous. Observers noted that women preferred factory or shop employment even though wages and physical amenities were frequently inferior.[40] Two *issei* in the study had worked as live-in servants; a widow who needed a home as well as a job, and a woman who arrived as an adolescent with her parents and worked as a live-in Schoolgirl before marriage.[41]

Their situations were unusual for *issei* women. Unlike European immigrant domestics, who were primarily young and single, almost all *issei* domestics were married and had children. Their circumstances were similar to those of black women in the South, and like them, the *issei* turned to nonresidential work. Until the 1930s, full-time positions with one employer were fairly common. Some *issei* women worked as general household help for middle-class families, performing a wide range of tasks from laundry to cooking to cleaning. Other *issei* worked as "second girls" in multiservant households, where they carried out a variety of tasks under the direction of a paid housekeeper.

The nonresidential jobs gave workers stable employment, set hours, and a chance for a private life. However, for the worker to provide all-around services, she had to put in an extended day, which typically began with breakfast cleanup and ended only after supper cleanup. The day was broken up by an afternoon break of one to three hours, during which the women returned home to prepare meals or do chores. Mrs. Kayahara described her workday, which began at 6:30 in the morning when she left home to catch a trolley. She arrived at work before 8:00. Then: "Wash the breakfast dishes, clean the rooms, make lunch and clean up. Go home. Back at 5:00 to help with cooking dinner and then do the dishes. Come, go, and back again. It was very hard. I had to take the trolley four times."

Partly because of the extended hours in full-time domestic jobs and partly because of the greater availability of day jobs, all the women in the study eventually turned to daywork. They worked in several different households for a day or half-day each week and were paid on an hourly or daily basis. The workday ended before dinner, and schedules could be fitted around family responsibilities. Many women worked part-time, but some women pieced together a forty- or forty-eight-hour week out of a combination of full and half-day jobs.

The duties of the dayworker generally consisted of housecleaning and laundry. Sometimes the worker did both, but many employers hired different workers for the two sets of tasks. Laundry was viewed as less skilled and more menial, and was often assigned to minority women, such as the Japanese.[42] Both cleaning and laundry were physically demanding, because of low-level household technology. Ruth Cowan suggests that the availability of household help slowed the adoption of labor-saving appliances by middle-class housewives.[43] Moreover, employers felt that hand labor created superior results. Workers were expected to scrub floors on hands and knees and to apply a lot of elbow grease to waxing and polishing. Some sense of the work is conveyed by Mrs. Tanabe's description of her routine, when she began work in 1921.[44]

When we first started, people wanted you to boil the white clothes. They had a gas burner in the laundry room. I guess you don't see those things any more—an oval shaped boiler. When you did daywork, you did the washing first. And, if you were there 8 hours, you dried and then brought them in and ironed them. In between, you cleaned the house from top to bottom. But, when you go to two places, one in the morning and one in the afternoon, you do the ironing and a little housework.

The *issei* express contradictory attitudes toward the demands of the work. On the one hand, they acknowledge that the work was menial, that it consisted largely of unskilled physical labor.

As one put it, "You use your body, not your mind." The women also say that the reason they were satisfied with the work is that they lacked qualifications; for example, "I'm just a country person." Yet, one is also aware that the women are telling stories of their own prowess when they describe the arduousness of the work. What emerges out of their descriptions is a sense of pride in their physical strength and endurance, a determination to accomplish whatever was asked, and a devotion to doing a good job. Mrs. Yoshida explains that she never found housework difficult; even today she can work for hours in her garden without being aware of it, because

From the time I was a little girl, I was used to working hard. I was born a farmer and did farm work all along. Farm work is very hard. My body was trained so nothing was hard for me. If you take work at a hakujin [caucasian] place, you have to work hard. There was a place where the lady asked me to wash the ceilings. So I took a table and stood up on it. It was strenuous, but I washed the whole ceiling. So the lady said: "That was hard work, but next time it won't be so hard." She gave me vegetables, fruits and extra money and I went home.

This kind of pride in physical strength is talked about in relation to men in manual occupations, but is rarely seen as relevant to women. Similarly, an orientation toward completing a task is seen as more evident among skilled craftsworkers than among those engaged in devalued work. Yet, we find evidence of both among this group of older women engaged in what has been called "the lowest rung of legitimate employment."[45]

The evolution from live-in service to nonresidential jobs to daywork can be viewed as a modernizing trend that has brought domestic work closer to industrialized wage work. First, work and nonwork life became clearly separated. Second, the basis for employment became more clearly contractual; that is, the worker sold a given amount of labor time for an agreed-upon wage. Yet, as long as the work took place in the household, it remained fundamentally preindustrial. While industrial workers produced surplus value that was taken as profit by the employer, the domestic workers produced only simple use value.[46] In a society based on a market economy, work that produces no exchange value is devalued.[47] Whereas the work process in socially organized production is subjected to division of labor, task specialization, and standardization of output, domestic labor remained diffuse and nonspecialized. The work consisted essentially of whatever tasks were assigned by the employer. While industrial workers were integrated into a socially organized system of production, the domestic worker

remained atomized. Each domestic performed her tasks in isolation, and her work was unrelated to the activities of other workers.

Because of its atomization, domestic work remained invisible
and was not subject to regulation. Domestic workers were excluded from protections won by industrial workers in the 1930s, such
as social security and minimum wages.[48] Although sporadic attempts to organize domestics were made in large cities, such efforts
rarely succeeded in reaching more than a small minority. The *issei*
in the study appear never to have been included in organizing efforts. Thus, there was no collectivity representing their interests,
and, of course, the *issei* received none of the benefits accorded
more privileged workers, such as sick days or paid vacations. In
fact, when the employer went out of town, the worker was put
on unpaid leave. The *issei* claimed, in any case, that they never
took vacations before World War II.

It also follows that wages depended on idiosyncratic factors.
Informants and subjects reported that the rate for dayworkers
around 1915 ranged from $0.15 to $0.25 an hour. The top rate
rose to around $0.50 an hour by the late 1930s. Full-time domes-
tics earned from $20.00 to $45.00 a month in 1915, while School-
girls earned from $2.00 to $5.00 a week. I was unable to find
wage data on other semiskilled occupations in the Bay Area, but
other studies have found that domestic wages during this period
compared favorably with those of factory, sales, or other low-level
female occupations.[49]

Some of the variation in wages can be attributed to market factors. Wealthier households were expected to pay more. The rate
in some communities was higher than in others, probably due to
the balance of labor supply and demand. Alameda had a higher
proportion of Japanese seeking domestic work and had among the
lowest wages. Still, what is striking is the seeming arbitrariness of
wages. Some workers were willing to work for less than the average
rate, and some employers were willing to pay more than they had
to to get a worker.

It may be useful to examine the process by which wages were
set in individual cases. Generally, the employer made an offer, and
the worker either accepted it or looked for another job at a higher
wage. Although the shortage of workers may have maintained a
minimum level for wages, the effect was not uniform. What employers offered depended a great deal on personalistic factors.
Sometimes, the worker benefited, if the employer especially
wanted to keep her for personal reasons. At other times, employers used their knowledge of the workers' personal situation
to push wages down. Both these elements are evident in Mrs.

Takagi's story. Her employers liked her and paid her more than
the average rate. However, during the depression, employers cut
back on help, and Mrs. Takagi couldn't find enough work to fill
the week. One employer knew about her situation and offered
her an extra day's work if she would take a cut in pay.

She said to me, "I tried another girl, because you get the highest wages. I
tried a cheaper one, but she wasn't good. She never put the clothes away
and never finished the ironing. . . . What do you think—take $4.50 and
I'll keep you? I'll give you 2 days a week." I wanted the money—I was
trying to save money to get my son [from Japan]. So I said, "fine." She
said, "I'll never tell anybody." Here, a month later, she told every friend. . . .
Everybody said, "You're working for so and so for $3.50 and here you're
getting $4.00." See, that's the way all the jobs were. A lot of people worked
for $2.50, so I was just crying.

Mrs. Takagi weathered this crisis and did not have to take cuts
from the others, but she felt humiliated at being found out.

EMPLOYER-EMPLOYEE RELATIONS

As this incident illustrates, the relationship between employer
and employee was, perhaps, the most distinctly preindustrial, as
well as the most problematic, aspect of domestic service. The relationship has been described as feudal[50] or premodern.[51] According
to Lewis Coser, the traditional servant role was

rooted in a premodern type of relationship in which particularism prevails
over universalism and ascription over achievement. . . . While post-medieval
man is typically enmeshed in a web of group affiliations and hence subject
to pushes and pulls of many claims to his commitment, the traditional servant
. . . is supposed to be entirely committed and loyal to a particular employer.
. . . Moreover, while in other occupational roles, the incumbent's duties are
largely independent of personal relationships with this or that client or employer, particularistic elements loom very large in the master-servant relationship.[52]

Although the totalism of the traditional master-servant relationship was much reduced under conditions of daywork, relations
between white employers and *issei* domestics retained two essential
and interrelated characteristics of the earlier period, personalism
and asymmetry.

Personalism pervaded all aspects of the employer-employee
relationship. Employers were concerned with the worker's total
person—her moral character and personality—not just her work
skills. The *issei* domestics in the study in turn judged their em-

ployers on moral and characterological grounds; for example, whether they were good Christians and clean and neat in their habits. The importance of the personal can also be seen in the *issei*'s preference for personal referrals for job placement. Compatibility and mutual trust were important because employer and employee were thrown together in a situation with little mutual privacy. The worker had access to the most intimate regions of the household where she might become privy to family secrets. The worker in turn was open to constant scrutiny by her employer.

A sense of mutual obligation, a carry-over of feudal values, also colored the tie between employer and employee. The domestic was expected to demonstrate loyalty, and the employer was expected to concern herself with the worker's welfare. This mutuality was viewed as a positive feature by some of the *issei*. Mrs. Shinoda recalls her first employer's concern fondly: "That lady was really nice. She would turn on the light and the heat in my room and stay up waiting for me to return. Usually, she would go to sleep early, but even if I returned late at night, she would wait up for me with the room heated up."

For some women, the tie with the employer became an extension of familial relationships. Mrs. Takagi described her second employer, Mrs. Cox, in these terms: "She was a Christian. Anytime I came down with a sickness, she said, 'Call a doctor.' If I go to the hospital, she came every day. She was almost a second mother. If I didn't have her help, I would have been badly off. I went to Japan and she gave me help with that."

Despite the intimacy, there remained a not quite surmountable barrier of status, which was reinforced by cultural and racial differences. Thus, the familial attitude of the employer usually took the form of benevolent maternalism. Even Mrs. Takagi, who formed close and long-lasting ties with her employers, recognized the employer's need to perform acts of *noblesse oblige*. She said she had learned to accept gifts, including old clothes and furnishings, even when she didn't want them. Otherwise, the employer was apt to feel the worker was "too proud," and would withhold further gifts and bonuses.

Thus, the second main feature of the relationship was its asymmetry. The traditional mistress-servant relationship exhibited in pure form the relation of superior to inferior. This aspect, though modified with the advent of daywork, continued to stigmatize the domestic as a menial and "unfree" worker. In extreme cases, the domestic was treated as a "nonperson." Mrs. Takagi recalls being offered a lunch consisting of asparagus stalks whose tips had been eaten off by the employer's son. This kind of treatment

313

was probably rare, at least according to the women in the study. However, less indirect expressions of asymmetry were common. For example, in an asymmetric relationship, the lower status person has to be attuned to the feelings and moods of the higher status person. Mrs. Nakashima provided an insight into this aspect when she described her approach to domestic work:

At first, since I hadn't had much chance to enter caucasian homes, I was a little frightened. But, after I got used to it, it became very easy. And I concluded, after working for a while, that the most important thing in this type of job is to think of and be able to predict the feelings of the lady in the house. She would teach me how to do certain things in the beginning, but after a month or two, I gradually came to learn that person's likes, tastes and ideas. So I try to fulfill her wishes—this is only my way of doing it, of course, and so, for example, I'll change the water in the vase when it's dirty or rearrange wilting flowers while I'm cleaning house. In that way, I can become more intimate with the lady of the house in a natural way and the job itself becomes more interesting . . . sometimes, I plant flowers in the garden without being asked . . . so, then I'll start to feel affection even for that garden.

Although her employers may have appreciated Mrs. Nakashima's aesthetic sensibilities, it is doubtful they were as aware of and responsive to her thoughts and feelings as she was of theirs.

The personalism and asymmetry in the employer-employee relation were complementary. The supposed inferiority and differentness of the domestic made it easy for the employer to be generous and to confide in her. The domestic was not in a position to harm her or make excessive demands, and secrets were safe with someone from a different social world. An informant suggested that the language barrier, though it hampered communication, may have contributed to the smoothness of relationships. The *issei* could not "hear" insulting or denigrating comments. One worker confirmed this by saying she had never minded being a domestic, but added that had she understood English, she might have gotten into quarrels with her employers.

Ultimately, however, the personalism and asymmetry created contradictions in the employer-employee relationship. As Coser put it: "The dialectic of conflict between inferior and superior within the household could never be fully resolved, and hence the fear of betrayal always lurked behind even the most amicable relationship between master and servant."[53] The fear is evident in *issei* women's complaints about employers who distrusted them. Mrs. Takagi once found money left under the corner of a rug. She carefully replaced the rug without touching the money or saying anything about it; she had been warned by her father-in-law that employers sometimes tested the domestic's honesty by leaving valuables about. Mrs. Nakashima indignantly reported an incident in which she was suspected of dishonesty:

There was a place I was working temporarily. They asked me whether I had seen a ring. I didn't know what kind of ring they meant, so I just told them no. I hadn't seen any ring while I was vacuuming. They sounded a little skeptical, saying it's strange I hadn't seen it. I felt insulted then, as though they were accusing me of something.

The conflict took its most concrete form in a power struggle between employer and employee over control of the work process. On one side, the employer attempted to exercise as much control as possible. Mrs. Noda echoes the sentiments of many of the *issei*, when she said that her greatest dislike was an employer who was *yakamashi* (noisy, critical): "Indeed, where they don't say too many things, the work is better. If they ask, 'Have you done this? Have you done that? Do you understand?' There is that sort of place. Most people don't say such things because they know [better]."

Some employers seemed to assume the worker would loaf or cut corners if she were not watched. Mrs. Nakashima said she quit one job because her employer spied on her. She said most of her employers left the house while she worked; if they returned, they announced themselves loudly. In this case: "The Mrs. would come in very quietly without warning, so it made me feel as if she were spying on me to make sure I wasn't doing anything wrong. I disliked that a great deal."

Another area of conflict was over the amount and pace of the work. Employers sometimes engaged in the household equivalent of work "speedup." If the worker accomplished the agreed-upon tasks within a designated period, the employer added more tasks. To finish everything, the worker was forced to "do everything fast." Employers were thus able to exploit the *issei* worker's conscientiousness.

The *issei* had only limited resources to resist employer's attempts to control their work and the conditions of employment. Yet, within their capabilities, they strove to wrest some degree of control over their work and their lives. The choice to shift to daywork can be seen as one means to gain greater autonomy.[54] By working for several families, the domestics became less dependent on one employer. Work hours could be adjusted to fit in with the workers' other interests and responsibilities. As Mrs. Tanabe said about her change from full-time work with one employer to daywork, "You're freer to yourself."

Within the structure of daywork, the *issei* maneuvered the situation to increase control over the work process. One way was to minimize contact with employers. Mrs. Adachi deliberately chose employers who went out during the day:

I liked it best when nobody was there. The places I worked, they went out. The children were in school, and I was all by myself, so I could to what I wanted. If the woman was at home, she generally went out shopping. I liked it when they didn't complain or ask you to do this or that. The places I worked, I was on my own. It was just like being in my own home, and I could do what I wanted.

Her sentiments were seconded by Mrs. Noda: "I don't like it when people stay home. I like nobody home. It's more easy to work— everything is smooth."

Mrs. Adachi retained her autonomy by adopting a utilitarian orientation toward her employers. She "picked up and dropped" jobs on the basis of convenience, rather than becoming attached to particular employers:

Sometimes I gave the job to someone else and looked for something else. I changed from this job to that job. If I had to walk too far to the bus, or the people were too messy. I kept the job until I found a better one, and then I changed. [How did you find the other job?] When they're playing cards, they talked about the help. If someone knew who is a good worker, they would give the other ladies my name, and they would call me. Then I'd go and see. If I like it better than the other places, I'd quit the other and move to the new one.

Some women maintained control over the work by defining and enforcing their own standards; they insisted on working on the basis of tasks, rather than time. The job was done when the tasks were accomplished to their own satisfaction. If they worked extra time, they did not want to be paid; if they accomplished it in less time, they reserved the right to leave.

The last recourse in the face of a recalcitrant or unreasonable employer was to quit. This was a difficult step for the *issei*. They felt it was a loss of face to complain about mistreatment, and furthermore, they felt employers should know how to act properly without being told. Thus, when they quit, they did so in a way that was designed to maintain both the employer's and their own dignity. If an employer asked why they were leaving, the *issei* usually made up an excuse that avoided any criticism of the employer. Mrs. Adachi was typical when she said, "I wouldn't say I didn't like it, so I would say I was tired or sick." Yet, their own pride was also important. Mrs. Yoshida reported this incident when she quit: "There was one place that no matter how much you do, that person would let you do more. So I thought I would quit. That day I did a lot of work—more than usual—and finished up everything she gave me." By meeting the challenge, no matter how unreasonable, Mrs. Yoshida was able to leave with her self-respect intact.

WORK AND FAMILY LIFE

Issei women's experiences in domestic employment cannot be understood without also considering the relationship between wage work and family roles. Some of the connections between work and family life have been alluded to in earlier sections, but I would like now to examine the dialectics of this relationship more systematically.

To do so, we must refer back to the family system of the society from which the immigrants came. In late nineteenth- and early twentieth-century southern, rural Japan, the basic social and economic unit was the *ie* (household), which typically included husband, wife, unmarried children, and in the case of an eldest son, the husband's parents. The *ie* served as the basic unit of production and as a corporate economic body. Ownership and authority were vested in the male head of household. Members were graded by gender, age, and insider-outsider.[55]

Most households were engaged in small-scale farming and petty manufacturing and trade, the economy of which relied on the unpaid labor of all members, including women and children.[56] Most of what was produced was directly consumed, and any income generated was corporate, rather than individual. There was no separation of work and family life because production, consumption, maintenance, and childcare were carried on more or less simultaneously. Women's work was thus incorporated into the overall work of the household and did not differ organizationally from men's work. There was, of course, a clear division of labor by sex. Women were assigned most domestic chores, as well as certain female-typed agricultural and manufacturing tasks; men supervised the household work and represented the family in relation to the larger community.

When they came to the United States, the *issei* were entering an industrialized economy in which wage labor was becoming the predominant mode. The majority of *issei* families found "pre-industrial" niches in farming and small business enterprises. In these families, the traditional system of household labor, as well as the old role relationships, were transplanted, more or less intact.[57] Many *issei* families, however—especially those in Bay Area cities—adapted to the urban economy by turning to multiple wage earning. Husband and wife and older children were individually employed, mostly in marginal, low-paying jobs. Each worker's earnings were small, but the pooled income was sufficient to support a household and to generate some surplus for savings, remittances, and consumer goods.

This strategy was in many ways consistent with the values of the *ie* system. Because multiple wages were needed, the economic interdependence of family members was preserved. Moreover, the employment of women was consistent with the assumption that women were full economic contributors. In other ways, however, the strategy was inconsistent with the traditional *ie* structure. Wage work represented a form of economic organization in which the individual, rather than the family, was the unit of production, and in which work and family life were separated, rather than integrated. Women working outside the home violated the principle that men had exclusive rights to, and control over, their wives' labor.

Perhaps because of this duality, *issei* men were divided in their attitudes toward their wives' participation in the labor force. As noted earlier, some men opposed their wives' employment on the grounds that their services were needed at home. In contrast, other men expected their wives to pull their full weight by being employed, regardless of the women's own inclinations. Thus, while Mrs. Adachi said she was defying her husband's wishes by going out to work, Mrs. Uematsu indicated that she felt compelled to seek wage work:

My husband didn't bring in enough money, so I went out to work. I didn't even think twice about it. If I didn't take a job, people would have started to call me "Madam" [i.e., accusing her of thinking she was too much of a lady to work] . . . . It was like a race; we all had to work as hard as possible.

The duality is further mirrored in the contradictory impacts of wage work on women's position in the family. On the one hand, to the extent that the traditional division of labor and the structure of male privilege persisted, wage work added to the burdens and difficulties experienced by women. On the other hand, to the extent that wage work reduced women's economic dependence and male control over their labor, it helped the women transcend the limitations of traditional role relationships. Evidence of both tendencies emerge from the women's accounts; the increased burdens are greater and more obvious.

Among the women in the study, the major share of housework

and childcare remained with them even if they were employed. All but two women claimed their husbands did no work "inside" the house. Mrs. Nishimura explained:

No, my husband was like a child. He couldn't even make tea. He couldn't do anything by himself. He was really Japan-style. Sometimes, I had too much to do, so although I would always iron his shirts, I might ask him to wait a while on the underwear, but he'd say no. He'd wait there until I would iron them. People used to say he was spoiled. He was completely a Japanese man. Some people divorce their husbands for not helping around the house, but that never entered my mind. I thought it was natural for a Japanese.

Although Mr. Nishimura might be viewed as extreme, even by other *issei*, there was unanimous agreement among the women that Japanese men expected to be waited upon by their wives.

The result was that the women experienced considerable overload. The men worked long hours, often at physically exhausting jobs, but the women's days were longer. Their days began earlier than other members of the household with the preparation of a morning meal and ended later with the preparation and cleanup of the evening meal; in between, they had to fit in laundry and cleaning. Some women were endowed with natural vitality. They could maintain an immaculate household and do extras, such as making clothes for children. Mrs. Nishimura described her schedule during the years she was doing seasonal garment work:

Since I had so many children, I asked my mother-in-law to take care of the children. I would get up at 5 o'clock and do the laundry. In those days— we'd do it by hand—hang up the laundry, then go to Oakland. I would come home and since my husband didn't have much work then, he'd get drunk and bring the children home. I would cook and eat, and then go to sleep. They all asked me how long I slept at night. But, since I was in my twenties, it didn't affect me too much.

Others, like Mrs. Uematsu, were exhausted at the end of the day and had to let things slide. She exclaimed: "My house was a mess. I went to work in the morning and when I came back from work, I'd cook a little and then go to sleep and that's about all."

As Mrs. Nishimura's account indicates, an additional problem was created by wage work that did not exist under the family work system—the need for separate childcare. Employers sometimes allowed domestics to bring a young child to work, but as more children arrived, other arrangements had to be made. Friends, neighbors, older children, and husbands were recruited to baby-sit. Women with older children often set their work hours to correspond to school schedules. When no other means were available, and employment was a necessity, the *issei* sometimes resorted to sending their children to Japan to be raised by relatives, as three of the women in the study did. They planned to return to Japan and rejoin their children. In all three cases, the women stayed in the United States, and the children returned as adolescents or adults.[58]

Despite the prevalence of male privilege, role relationships sometimes underwent change in response to new circumstances. The most common adjustment was for husbands to take on some child-care responsibilities. Even Mr. Nishimura, the "completely Japanese man," took on transporting and minding children when he was out of work. One woman, Mrs. Nomura, claimed that her husband did quite a lot around the house, including drying dishes. She explained:

He was considerably Americanized. He was young when he came over and he was a Schoolboy, so he was used to the American way of doing things. Even when we quarreled, he wouldn't hit me, saying it's bad in this country for a man to hit a woman, unlike Japan. In Japan, the man would be head of the family without any question. "Japan is a man's country; America is a woman's country," he often used to say.

Some respondents and informants reported cases of role reversal between husband and wife (although not among the women in the study). Role reversals occurred most often when the husband was considerably older than the wife. Because many *issei* men married late in life to much younger women, they were in their fifties by the time their children reached school age. As laborers, their employment prospects were poor, while their wives could easily find domestic jobs. Mrs. Tanabe, a *nisei* raised in Alameda, recalls that her husband was "retired" while she was still a young girl:

The Hiroshima men in Alameda were the laziest men. Their wives did all the work. My dad raised me while my mother went out and did domestic work. He did the cooking and kept house and did the shopping and took me when I went to work. So, he didn't do much really. But, in Alameda, they're known for being the lazy ones—most Hiroshima men are—so no one's rich.

One reason for this pattern may be that domesticity was considered appropriate for older men. Mrs. Yamashita, another *nisei*, reported that her father, a widower, acted as a housekeeper and baby-sitter while she and her husband both went out to work.

In addition to the division of labor by sex, the traditional Japanese family was characterized by what Elizabeth Bott[59] has called segregated conjugal role relationships; that is, husband and wife had a considerable number of separate interests and activities.

This pattern seems to have been maintained by the *issei* to a marked degree.[60] Leisure time was rarely spent in joint activities. Women's orbit was restricted to the home and the domestic world of women; men engaged in a wider range of formal church and community activities. Informal socializing, including drinking and gambling were common male activities. The men's drinking seems to have been a source of conflict in many families. Two women's lives were tragically affected by their husband's drinking. Mrs. Takagi's husband got into frequent accidents, and spent much of his earnings on alcohol. Mrs. Shinoda's husband was killed in a judo mishap that occurred while he was intoxicated. Perhaps, a more typical story is Mrs. Kayahara's, who described her husband in these terms:

Not so much nice, but not so bad. [Was he old-fashioned?] Just like a japan boy! So, I did everything—cook, wash, keep house. My husband drank. He drank so much, his stomach went bad. Once we were married, he would have five or six drinks every day—sake. All his life, he did that. But, he did work hard.

The extent of drinking among *issei* men can be gauged by the fact that women whose husbands did not drink thought it worthy of comment. Mrs. Nomura feels her life was much easier than other women's because her husband was straitlaced:

Yes, I've been lucky. I worked, of course, and encountered social problems [discrimination], but . . . I didn't suffer at all with regard to my husband. He didn't smoke, drink or gamble. . . . Very serious Christian with no faults. Everyone else was drinking and gambling. Park Street was full of liquor stores, and so they'd all go there; but my husband led such a clean life, so I was lucky.

Overwork and poverty exacerbated conflicts generated by gender division in the family: the discrepancy in power and privilege, the unequal division of household labor, and the separation of female and male emotional spheres. Far from being passive, the women actively fought with their husbands. Mrs. Nakashima had to send her three children back to Japan and work in a laundry to support herself because her husband was sickly. She reports: "My life in the U.S. was very hard in the beginning because my husband was ill so much and we had such totally different personalities. We were both selfish so we had many problems. But, after I started going to church, I became more gentle. So we had fewer quarrels. I think that is a gift from God." Mrs. Nishimura also reported that she and her husband quarreled a great deal. She explained: "Well, he was rather short-tempered . . . there were times when I thought he was stubborn, but we were far apart in age, so I would attribute

our differences to that. Being apart in age does create quite a lot
of differences. . . . But, I bore it all." Thus, while the *issei* women
express the traditional Japanese attitude that women must bear up
under hardship, it is evident that they did not always do so quietly!

Given these additional strains imposed by employment, what
did the women gain in the family through domestic employment?
There was, of course, the tangible benefit of income, part of which
could be retained for individual saving or spending. A less tangible,
but perhaps more significant, gain was increased control over their
economic circumstances. In Japan, women were ultimately at the
mercy of their husband's ability or willingness to provide support.
Mrs. Takagi's mother suffered extreme poverty as a result of her
father's irresponsibility and drinking. He ran up debts that led to
the loss of their farm in Japan. Her own husband proved to be
similarly unreliable. However, Mrs. Takagi felt less victimized than
her mother because she could work to support herself and her children. As she put it, "I killed myself, but did it all, myself." The
sense of self-sufficiency is clearly important to the women, for
they maintain an independence, even in later life, from their children. About one-half the women worked into their seventies and
even eighties, and all the women worked into their sixties.

In addition to working for their own independence, the *issei*
worked for their children. They gained a sense of purpose by
seeing their work as contributing to their children's future. Although most women agreed that the present was the best (that
is, easiest) period of their lives, many looked back nostalgically
to these days when their children were growing up. Mrs. Nishimura spoke for this group when she said: "This is my best time,
but my happiest time was then, when my children were small.
I was poor and busy then, but that might have been the best time.
It was good to think about my children—how they'd go through
high school and college and afterwards."

It is difficult to document the extent of special consideration
or deference the women received as a result of their sacrifices.
However, the long-term respect they earned is strikingly evident.
The daughters and sons of these women were uniform in their
expressions of respect toward their mothers. They were eager
to do whatever possible to make life comfortable for them. A
few spoke ruefully about their mothers' "stubbornness" or "independence," which prevented them from doing more.

The very difficulty of the *issei*'s circumstances and their ability
to "bear it all" gave them added respect. Looking back, the wom-
en expressed amazement at their own capacities: Mrs. Nishimura
concluded it was because she was young; while Mrs. Yoshida cited

her early conditioning in farm work. The hard work of the *issei* women has become legendary within the Japanese. community. Several *nisei* domestics claimed that even now they are unable to match the endurance of *issei* women in their seventies.

The good opinion of others was important in the close-knit· Japanese community. The comradery and common frame of reference eased some of the hardships and counteracted the isolating conditions of their work. Sharing their experiences with others in the same situation, they found sympathy and understanding. Mrs. Kayahara recalled:

In Alameda, the Japanese were living in five or six houses near the City Hall— all of them from Fukuoka were living together. That was so enjoyable. Myself, I never thought to be ashamed of doing domestic work. We had to do any sort of work that was available. Also our friends were doing the same sort of work, and we used to talk about it. . . . Sometimes, things that were worrying us, we'd talk about it. That helped us. If you don't talk to anyone, your heart gets heavy. So we told each other things right away.

CONCLUSIONS

This paper has analyzed the contradictions in *issei* women's involvement in domestic work in the pre-World War II period. The approach taken here has highlighted several aspects of these contradictions.

First, it draws attention to conflict as an underlying dynamic in women's relationship to paid and unpaid work. The attention to conflict makes it possible to see *issei* women as actors striving to gain control and self-respect, rather than as passive targets of oppression. The contest was obviously uneven: *issei* women had few resources for direct resistance, and they lacked collective strength in the form of worker organization or female kin networks. Thus, there is no evidence that they directly confronted their employers or their husbands, that they were militant, or engaged in collective action. If these are the criteria, it is easy to overlook the woman's resistance to control by employers and husbands. The strategies the *issei* adopted reflected their relative lack of power; they engaged in indirect forms of resistance, such as evasion. The *issei* maximized autonomy in employment by choosing work situations in which employers were absent or inactive. In the family, they went out to work secretly or withheld part of their wages as a means of gaining control over disposable income. Another strategy women used in both employment and family life was to define their own standards and goals. The *issei* had internalized criteria for what constituted a good day's work;

some women defined their jobs in terms of tasks accomplished, rather than hours, for example. They also set their own priorities in relation to housekeeping, education for their children, and the family's standard of living. There is evidence that the women gained satisfaction from meeting their own standards, irrespective of the employers' or their husbands' evaluations.

Second, as the previous discussion indicates, the analysis highlights the interconnectedness of different aspects of the women's experiences, particularly between paid and unpaid work. In both employment and family life, women were in a subordinate position in which their role was defined as service to another. The content of activities in both spheres was also similar, and the structures of employment and family life were, therefore, mutually reinforcing. The parallel structures in turn contributed to a similarity in the strategies used to cope with subordination. The reliance on indirect strategies in conflicts with employers, for example, can be related in part to *issei* women's experience of subordination in the household and the community and their inability to directly confront their husbands' authority. In contrast, black women domestics resisted or defied their employers more openly and were also less subordinate in the family.[61]

Coping stragegies are usually conceptualized as situationally specific; that is, as growing out of and being confined to a particular setting.[62] In this case, at least, the strategies appear to form a coherent whole. This is to be expected in part because of structural parallels in women's positions in work, family, and community life and in part because of internalized cultural attitudes, such as the value of hard work, which carried across situations. Perhaps, more important, the process of striving in one area developed orientations that carried over into other arenas. Thus, the theme of self-sufficiency pervaded all aspects of the women's life and has persisted over time.

Finally, the analysis points to the contradictory implications of employment for *issei* women's status. The issue has often been framed in either/or terms. Some theorists, including some Marxists, have viewed employment as a liberating force, arguing that women would gain status in society by becoming producers in the market economy, rather than remaining nonproductive household workers. By contributing to family income and by gaining a role outside the family, women would increase their power in the family. More recently, analysts have argued that employment, far from contributing to equality, actually reinforces women's oppression. They point out that women are relegated to low-status, routine, and low-paying jobs; that women remain responsible for unpaid domestic work and are, thereby, saddled with a double burden; that in both realms, women are subjugated by male authority.[63]   Although the present account shares this recent perspective and documents the multiple forms of oppression faced by *issei* domestic workers, the focus on contradictions makes it possible to see oppressive and liberating consequences as interrelated. *Issei* women were constrained by the larger economic and political system that forced them to seek employment, but limited them to the most marginal jobs. The conditions of domestic work subjected them to further oppression. But, out of these conditions, *issei* women gained advantages that enabled them to achieve certain goals (such as helping their families in Japan and providing extras for their children), to become less dependent on the ability or willingness of husbands to provide support, and to form ties outside the immediate family group. And, despite the menial nature of employment, the *issei* achieved a sense of their own strength, and in some cases, superiority to employer and husband within their own area of competence.

NOTES

The research for this paper was supported in part by a faculty grant from the Graduate School, Boston University. The author is grateful to Jean Twomey for assistance in organizing the data; Haru Nakano for help in arranging interviews; Peter Langer for detailed suggestions during writing; Murray Melbin for clarifying issues in an earlier version, and Edna Bonacich and Lucie Cheng Hirata for encouraging me to explore the topic. Special thanks are also owed to the Women and Work Group, Chris Bose, Carol Brown, Peggy Crull, Roz Feldberg, Myra Ferree, Heidi Hartmann, Alice Kessler-Harris, Dorothy Remy, Natalie Sokoloff and Carole Turbin. Our meetings were supported by a grant from the Problems of the Discipline Programs, American Sociological Association; and our discussions helped crystallize some key conceptual issues.

[1] H. A. Millis, *The Japanese Problem in the United States* (New York: The Macmillan Co., 1915); and Edward K. Strong, *Japanese in California* (Stanford, Calif.: Stanford University Press, 1933).

[2] David Chaplin, "Domestic Service and Industrialization," *Comparative Studies in Sociology* 1 (1978): 98-127; and U.S. Department of Labor, Women's Bureau, *Women's Occupations Through Seven Decades*, by Janet M. Hooks, Bulletin no. 218 (Washington, D.C., 1947).

[3] Lewis Coser, "Domestic Servants: The Obsolescence of a Social Role," *Social Forces* 52 (1973): 31-40.

[4] George J. Stigler, *Domestic Servants in the United States, 1900-1940* (New York: National Bureau of Economic Research, 1946).

[5] C.f. Gerda Lerner, *Black Women In White America: A Documentary History* (New York: Vintage Books, 1973).

[6] William L. Yancey, Eugene P. Ericksen, and Richard N. Julian, "Emergent Ethnicity: A Review and Reformulation," *American Sociological Review* 41 (June 1976): 391-403.

[7]The material for this paper is drawn from several sources. Information on the economic context and historical background was obtained from census material, a few early surveys, and secondary accounts. Newspaper files and documents furnished by community members provided valuable details; these sources included the files of the *Alameda Daily Argus* from the 1880s to 1920; surviving copies of the *Nichi-Bei Times* annual directories, 1910, 1914 and 1941; and privately printed church histories, *Eighty-fifth Anniversary of Protestant Work Among Japanese in North America* (1975) and *Buddhist Churches of America* (1976), which included the chronologies of individual churches and temples in the Bay Area. Overall, however, documentary evidence was scanty. Japanese community directories, organizational records, and newspaper files were lost during World War II, or they were destroyed by their owners prior to evacuation because they feared the material would be used as evidence of subversive activities.

The heart of the data for this paper was derived from in-depth interviews of fifteen *issei* women who worked as domestics, and for comparison, twelve *nisei* (American-born) and seven *kibei* (American-born, Japan-educated) domestics. These interviews were supplemented by informant interviews of thirty older *issei* and *nisei* who had lived in the prewar communities of San Francisco, Oakland, Alameda, Berkeley, and San Leandro. Interviews were semistructured; particular topics were systematically covered, but new ideas were explored if subject's remarks provided new insights. Topics covered included individual work histories, work attitudes, work experiences, and non-work areas such as health, ethnic identity, and social and family life. Initial interviews took from one to two and one-half hours with a follow-up of twenty minutes to one hour. With a few exceptions, interviews were taped, translated (if necessary), and transcribed verbatim. Only a small part of the information is reported in the present paper.

The analysis of the interview data was primarily qualitative. The aim was to identify patterns in the women's experiences and to generate hypotheses, rather than to test prior ones, see Barney G. Glaser and Anselm L. Strauss, *The Discovery of Gounrded Theory* (Chicago: Aldine Publishing Company, 1967).

[8]Cf. Bonnie Dill, "The Dialectics of Black Womanhood," *Signs* 4 (Spring 1979): 543-55, for a similar argument regarding black women.

[9]Frank Miyamoto, "Social Solidarity Among the Japanese in Seattle," *University of Washington Publications in the Social Sciences* 11 (1939): 57-130, first designated these three time periods in his study of the prewar Seattle, Washington, Japanese community. I have adopted his chronology, substituting the term "stabilization period" to designate the third period, which Miyamoto called the "second generation period." For a discussion of the social characteristics of frontier situations, for example, the preponderance of males, see Murray Melbin, "Night as Frontier," *American Sociological Review* 43 (1978): 3-22.

[10]Edward K. Strong, *The Second-Generation Japanese Problem* (Stanford, Calif.: Stanford University Press, 1934).

[11]See Yamato Ichihashi, *Japanese Immigration* (San Francisco: The Marshall Press, 1915) and his more detailed *Japanese in the United States* (Stanford, Calif.: Stanford University Press, 1932); also Roger Daniels, *The Politics of Prejudice* (New York: Atheneum, 1973).

[12]For an account of the immigrant associations, see Ivan H. Light, *Ethnic Enterprise in America* (Berkeley and Los Angeles: University of California Press, 1972).

[13]The other areas of concentration were around Sacramento and the upper San Joaquin Valley (Daniels, *Politics of Prejudice*).

[14]Strong, *Second-Generation Japanese Problem.*

[15]Ichihashi, *Japanese in the United States.*

[16]Census figures for 1900 show only 985 Japanese women over age fifteen. By 1910, the number had jumped to 9,087. Sydney Gulik compiled data showing that 45,706 Japanese females were admitted to the continental United States between 1909 and

1923, of whom 33,628 were listed as wives (reprinted in Ichihashi, *Japanese in the United States*, as appendix C).

[17] *1914 Yearbook of the Nichi-Bei Times* is a directory of residents, associations, and businesses in the Bay Area. Most Christian churches were founded in the 1890s with the aid of white Protestant churches. The Buddhist churches, which were ethnically supported, were founded and developed between 1900 and 1915. Oakland, 1901, was the earliest, followed by Berkeley, 1908, and Alameda, 1912. Japanese language schools were usually attached to the churches (see *Buddhist Churches of America,* and *Eighty-fifth Anniversary of Protestant Work*).

[18] Harry H. L. Kitano, "Housing of Japanese Americans in the San Francisco Bay Area," in *Studies in Housing and Minority Groups*, ed. Nathan Glazer and D. McEntire (Berkeley and Los Angeles: University of California Press, 1960), pp. 178-97.

[19] Daniels, *Politics of Prejudice.*

[20] Miyamoto, "Social Solidarity."

[21] Strong, *Japanese in California.*

[22] Although the women spoke of the decision as their parents', it appears to be the father as head of the household who had the power. See beginning of section on the Japanese family. The full range of attitudes among the women did not necessarily fall in one dimension; however, roughly scaling the women's attitudes from "most reluctant" to "most eager," the following attitudes can be identified: (1) felt tricked, went reluctantly, (2) persuaded, inveigled by promises for the future by parents, (3) "carefree," thought it would be a new experience, (4) felt that this mate or going to the United States was better than another alternative, (5) aspired to come to the United States; parents concurred, and (6) aspired to come to the United States; had to overcome parents' opposition.

[23] This and all other names in the text are pseudonyms. Other identifying details have been disguised to ensure anonymity.

[24] During this period, many Japanese women had to marry men who were emigrating for demographic reasons. This was a time of Japanese expansionism. Young men were colonizing Manchuria and Korea, as well as seeking their fortunes in Hawaii and the mainland United States. Among the various destinations, the United States was viewed as offering the easiest situation for women. Mrs. Nomura reported:

I was among the lucky ones, coming to the U.S. as I did. I almost wound up in Manchuria, you know. In Japan, the woman doesn't go out hunting for a husband. We used a go-between. The marriage arrangement offer from Mr. Nomura came a week before the one from the person going to Manchuria. So my father rejected the latter offer.

[25] Ichihashi, *Japanese in the United States.*

[26] Robert W. Smuts, *Women and Work in America* (New York: Columbia University Press, 1959).

[27] Millis, *Japanese Problem, p. 27.*

[28] U.S. Department of Commerce, Bureau of Census, *Fourteenth Census of the United States Taken in the Year 1920*, vol. 4, *Population, Occupations* (Washington, D.C.: Government Printing Office, 1923), and U.S. Department of Commerce, Bureau of the Census, *Women in Gainful Occupations, 1870 to 1920*, by Joseph A. Hill, Census Monographs 9 (Washington, D.C.: U.S. Government Printing Office, 1929).

[29] Strong, *Japanese in California*, p. 109.

[30] Unless special instructions were given to enumerators (as occurred in 1910) to count the unpaid work of women and children, such labor was likely to be overlooked. (See Hill, *Women in Gainful Occupations.*) Because the Japanese faced legal harassment, they were suspicious of outsiders and feared giving our personal information. Finally, the women's inability to communicate in English undoubtedly hampered accuracy in

reporting. Despite these shortcomings, the census remains the best source of detailed occupational information.

[31] Unfortunately, data for a key census, 1910, are missing because compilers aggregated occupational data for Chinese and Japanese, and so no separate figures exist for Japanese alone. Extrapolating from population and employment trends for the Japanese and Chinese, I would estimate that about 30 percent of all gainfully employed and about 45 percent of all non-agriculturally employed *issei* women were employed in domestic service in 1910. Because the Chinese female labor force grew very little between the 1900 and 1920 censuses, the distributions for the Japanese for 1910 can be estimated in the following way. We assume that the 1910 figures for the Chinese were the same as they were in 1900 and then subtract the 1900 Chinese figures from each 1910 combined total. The remainder in each case should be a rough approximation of the 1910 Japanese total. Using this method, I estimate that gainfully employed Japanese women numbered 1,800, of whom about 540, or 30 percent, were employed as "servants."

[32] This figure is lower than would be expected from geographic distributions. During the period between 1900 and 1930, slightly more than one-half of the Japanese (56 percent) lived in rural areas, according to a survey conducted by the Japanese consulate (Strong, *Japanese in California*). There appears to have been an undercount of unpaid agricultural labor among women.

[33] If data for *issei* and *nisei* are combined, however, the percentage in domestic work actually goes up slightly in 1940. This is because the *nisei* were even more heavily concentrated in domestic work than the *issei.*

[34] Ichihashi, *Japanese in the United States.*

[35] Ibid.

[36] Daniels, *Politics of Prejudice.*

[37] Millis, *Japanese Problem.*

[38] Strong, *Japanese in California.*

[39] An old-time resident of Alameda recalled that the early stores and businesses were owned by a succession of different families. The owners sold their businesses to other families and returned to Japan.

[40] Lucy M. Salmon, *Domestic Service* (New York: Macmillan Co., 1897); and Amy Watson, "Domestic Service," in *Encyclopedia of the Social Sciences* 5 (New York: Macmillan Co., 1937), pp. 198-206.

[41] Some other women later worked as live-in help right after World War II in order to have a place to live after returning from internment camp.

[42] C.f. Lerner, *Black Women in White America*; and David M. Katzman, *Seven Days a Week: Women and Domestic Service in Industrializing America* (New York: Oxford University Press, 1978).

[43] Ruth S. Cowan, "The Industrial Revolution in the Home: Household Technology and Social Change in the Twentieth Century," *Technology and Culture* 17 (January 1976): 1-23.

[44] Mrs. Tanabe is counted as one of the *nisei*, even though she is technically an *issei*, having arrived in Hawaii as an infant and later coming to California when she was five. She is one of the oldest nisei, however, having been born in 1898, and her work experience overlaps with those of the *issei.*

[45] Theodore Caplow, *The Sociology of Work* (New York: McGraw-Hill, 1954), p. 233.

[46] Perhaps, the point is made clearer by Braverman's remark that although the work of a cleaner employed by a firm that sells cleaning services generates profit and thereby increases the employer's capital, the work of the private domestic actually reduces the wealth of the employer, Harry Braverman, *Labor and Monopoly Capital* (New York and London: Monthly Review Press, 1974).

[47] Margaret Benston, "The Political Economy of Women's Liberation," in *From Femin-*

ism to Liberation, ed. Edith H. Altbach (Cambridge, Mass. and London: Shenkman Publishing Company, 1971), pp. 199-210.

[48] Social security coverage was extended to domestics in the 1950s, and federal minimum wage laws in the 1970s. See U.S. Department of Labor, Women's Bureau, *Handbook of Women Workers* (Washington, D.C.: Government Printing Office, 1975); and David M. Katzman, "Domestic Service: Woman's Work," in *Women Working*, ed. Ann H. Stromberg and Shirley Harkess (Palo Alto, Calif.: Mayfield Publishing Company, 1978), pp. 377-91).

[49] For example, studies by Katzman, *Seven Days a Week*, and Stigler, *Domestic Servants in the United States.*

[50] Jane Addams, "A Belated Industry," *American Journal of Sociology* 1 (March 1896): 536-50.

[51] Coser, "Domestic Servants."

[52] Ibid., p. 32.

[53] Ibid., p. 36.

[54] Katzman, *Seven Days a Week*, points out that employers preferred live-in help and deplored the trend toward living out, because they preferred the control they could exert over the time and behavior of the domestic who lived in.

[55] Chie Nakane, *Kinship and Economic Organization in Rural Japan*, London School of Economics Monographs on Social Anthropology, no. 32 (London: The Athlone Press, 1967).

[56] Sylvia J. Yanagisako, "Two Processes of Change in Japanese-American Kinship," *Journal of Anthropological Research* 31 (1975): 196-224.

[57] Ibid.

[58] These *kibei* children (American born, Japanese educated) frequently encountered the same difficulties as their parents. Language and cultural barriers handicapped them in the labor market. Mrs. Nishimura's three older children raised in Japan, for example, ended up in farming and domestic work, and the three younger children became white collar workers.

[59] Elizabeth Bott, *Family and Social Network: Roles, Norms and External Relationships in Ordinary Urban Families* (London: Tavistock Publications, 1957).

[60] This is in contrast to the Azorean immigrant families described by Louise Lamphere, Filomena Silva, and John Sousa, in "Kin Networks and Family Strategies: Working-Class Families in New England," (unpublished paper). These families also adjusted to the urban economy through mlutiple wage earning. Traditional division of household labor by gender was maintained, but social activities were joint, and centered around the extended family.

[61] See Dill, "Dialectics of Black Womanhood"; and Lerner, *Black Women in White America.*

[62] For example, Erving Goffman, in *Asylums* (Garden City, New York: Anchor Books, 1961) identifies several situationally specific strategies that patients develop for coping with conditions in total institutions.

[63] Heidi Hartmann, "Capitalism, Patriarchy, and Job Segregation by Sex," *Signs* 1 (Spring 1976): 137-69; and Natalie Sokoloff, "A Theoretical Analysis of Women in the Labor Market," paper presented at the meetings of the Society for the Study of Social Problems, San Francisco, 1978.

Women and the
New Deal

Susan Ware

The reunion in Washington of old New Dealers was breaking up.
They had come together, most of them now in their seventies and
eighties, to recall their glory days in Washington in the 1930s. Many
had provided poignant and humorous reminiscences of their dealings with President Franklin Delano Roosevelt, but consumer activist Caroline Ware realized that no one had paid tribute to
Eleanor Roosevelt for her special contributions to the New Deal.
Ware rushed to the microphone as people were beginning to leave
and shouted, "We can't go home without mentioning Eleanor."
Having said her piece, she then sat down.

This anecdote clearly is applicable to the task at hand: when
evaluating the New Deal, we "can't go home" without mentioning
women. While conventional accounts rarely cite women's activities
in the period, women were a vital part of the New Deal. In fact, the
New Deal provided opportunities for women in politics and government that make the 1930s one of the most creative and exciting
periods for women in twentieth century political history.

The topic of women in the New Deal has not been totally ignored by historians, but it rarely has been a central concern..
Eleanor Roosevelt and Lorena Hickok highlighted women's
political and governmental roles in their book, *Ladies of Courage*
(1952), as did William Chafe (1972) and Lois Banner (1974) in their
surveys of women's public roles. There are biographies of Eleanor
Roosevelt by Tamara Hareven and Joseph Lash, among others.
Lash's books, *Eleanor and Franklin* (1971) and *Eleanor: The Years
Alone* (1972), aroused much popular and scholarly interest. George
Martin's biography (1976) of Frances Perkins was one of the few
books to analyze an individual woman's impact on the emergence of

113

the New Deal. For the most part, however, standard works on the New Deal completely ignored the contributions of women. In both surveys and monographic studies, women have been practically invisible.

Several factors contributed to this neglect of women in the New Deal literature. Until recently, women were rarely considered topics worthy of attention from serious scholars. Unless a historian was specifically looking for women's contributions, it was far too easy to overlook evidence of women's active roles. In part, this was because women who served in the New Deal did not see feminism as their first priority: they were working to solve the crisis of the Depression. These women often did not hold the most visible top post in an agency or department. Many of these women shunned publicity in order to work quietly (and effectively) behind the scenes. These women felt just as much a part of the New Deal as did their male coworkers, but they rarely received commensurate credit. It was only with the revival of feminism in the 1960s that some of these women looked back on their own experiences in the 1930s from a different perspective.

The contributions of women to the New Deal had also been neglected until recently by scholars interested in the history of American women. Since the study of women's history drew heavily on the methodology of the new social history, attention to political elites (male or female) was a low priority. Another factor that limited attention was the prevailing view that the 1930s was a disastrous decade for women: in the midst of the economic crisis of the Great Depression, women's status declined as they struggled simply to make ends meet. Now this neglect is being supplanted by a burgeoning interest in twentieth-century women's history, especially the postsuffrage period between 1920 and the revival of feminism in the 1960s. This, in turn, has renewed interest in the 1930s, represented by recent work on women in that decade by Lois Scharf, Winifred Wandersee, Susan Becker, Alice Kessler-Harris, and others.

Historians have yet to arrive at a consensus on general trends for American women in the 1930s. Generalizing about women in the New Deal is only slightly more manageable. The most fruitful way to assess the dual questions of women's impact on the New Deal and the New Deal's impact on women is to begin with the realization that the category of "women" is too broad. A three-tiered approach to analyzing women in the New Deal provides a more workable framework. This scheme differentiates among elite women in top policy-making positions, a second level of women holding appoint-· ments in New Deal agencies and the federal bureaucracy, and a third level of ordinary women affected by the New Deal relief and welfare programs. Progress varied at each level, and an evaluation of women and the New Deal depends very much on which women are under scrutiny. For some, the record of the New Deal is superlative; for others, only mixed. On the whole, however, the story is a remarkable one.

THE WOMEN'S NETWORK

The level where the most progress undoubtedly occurred was for elite women in the politics and government of the New Deal. This historical moment for women to play vital roles in the planning and administration of New Deal programs resulted from several factors. The chief factor was the Depression itself—a crisis of such over-whelming proportions that it forced the American governmental system to strike out in new directions, which eventually led to the creation of the modern welfare state. Women flourished in this expe-rimental climate. As the majority of social workers, women were often the only ones with the necessary expertise to put large-scale relief and welfare programs into operation. In this case, broad trends of women's entry into professions such as social work intersected with the crisis demands of the Depression, and women moved forward.

Progress for women in the New Deal was also related to the historical circumstances that brought Franklin Roosevelt to the presidency in 1933. Along with Franklin came Eleanor, making the 1932 election one of the greatest two-for-one deals in American political history. Eleanor Roosevelt believed in women's capabilities, and she supported women's causes. She was especially useful to other women administrators in Washington by providing White House access to women who had a program or idea that they wanted brought to the attention of the President. More than once, if a program was stalled, Eleanor Roosevelt offered to hold a con-ference at the White House, and the resulting publicity soon broke the bureaucratic logjam. Eleanor Roosevelt could also command public attention in her own right through press conferences and her newspaper columns. Women were just one of the several constituencies that Eleanor Roosevelt served, but she served women well. It is practically impossible to imagine so much progress for women in the New Deal without Eleanor Roosevelt in the White House.

While Eleanor Roosevelt was the angel of women in the New Deal, Franklin Roosevelt deserves some credit as well. Without at least his tacit support for increased initiatives for women, even Eleanor would have been powerless. Franklin Roosevelt was a superb politician, and he realized that women could be an asset to the Democrats as they made themselves the dominant political party in the middle third of the twentieth century. He supported the efforts of women's Democratic leader, Molly Dewson, to increase women's access to patronage and to larger substantive and symbolic roles in the Democratic National Committee. In addition, Franklin Roosevelt felt comfortable in entrusting major responsibility to talented professional women like Frances Perkins and Molly Dewson, many of whom he had met through Eleanor. Yet Roosevelt was only willing to go so far: no woman, not even Eleanor, was ever part of his inner circle of advisers. On the whole, however, Franklin Roosevelt was open-minded about women's contributions, a trait not always found in male politicians. Given the experimental climate of the New Deal, his willingness to give women a chance was all that was needed for the flowering of women's talents.

The New Deal's record on opening opportunities for women to serve in major policy-making positions was not matched until the 1960s. The New Deal saw many "firsts" for women: first Cabinet member (Frances Perkins), first woman ambassador (Ruth Bryan Owen), first Assistant Treasurer of the United States (Marion Glass Banister), first Director of the Mint (Nellie Tayloe Ross), and first woman judge on the United States Circuit Court of Appeals (Florence Allen).

Women also held important positions in the new relief agencies, notably Ellen Sullivan Woodward who headed Women's and Professional Projects for the WPA, Hallie Flanagan, head of the Federal Theatre Project, and Hilda Worthington Smith, director of Workers Education for the WPA. In addition, Frances Perkins at the Labor Department gathered a talented group of women administrators, notably Clara Beyer at the Division of Labor Standards, Grace Abbott and Katherine Lenroot at the Children's Bureau, and Mary

Anderson at the Women's Bureau. Josephine Roche was nearby as Assistant Secretary of the Treasury, another first for women. Women active in the consumer and labor field in the National Recovery Administration included Mary Harriman Rumsey, Sue Shelton White, Emily Newell Blair, and Rose Schneiderman; Jane Hoey, Molly Dewson, and Ellen Woodward worked on Social Security. Finally, women found roles in the Democratic party hierarchy: besides Molly Dewson, who served as Director of the Women's Division, Carolyn Wolfe, Dorothy McAllister, Emma Guffey Miller, and Congresswomen Mary T. Norton and Caroline O'Day all played active roles in New Deal Democratic politics.

The women who served in the New Deal were a talented and dedicated group who brought years of experience in politics and social welfare administration to Washington in the 1930s. Strong similarities drew these women together in Washington. They were concentrated in certain areas of the bureaucracy, notably the newer relief agencies and the Labor Department, as well as the Women's Division of the Democratic party. Many of these women had been friends and professional colleagues since the Progressive period; at the least, most had known each other since the 1920s. They shared common ideas about extending the role of the federal government in modern America and about expanding roles for women in public life. From this shared ideology, they developed a network of professional cooperation and personal friendship, which was perhaps the most outstanding characteristic of women's participation in the New Deal.

The women's network comprised almost all the women who held prominent positions in the politics and government of the New Deal. Three women stand out for their contributions. As First Lady, Eleanor Roosevelt represented the most visible public center of this New Deal network. She also served as the network's emotional center, providing a model of public-spirited womanhood that was greatly admired and respected by women in Washington and throughout the nation. A close second to Eleanor Roosevelt in influence was Molly Dewson, who, as director of the Women's Division, was primarily responsible for badgering the men to give women jobs in the early New Deal. More than anyone else, Molly Dewson was the architect of the women's network: her almost daily contact with its members gave focus and shape to its influence. The other member of this triumvirate was Frances Perkins. Perkins has often been described as hostile to women's issues, but in fact she used her position

as Secretary of Labor to surround herself with like-minded professional women who worked for the social welfare goals so dear to
women in public life in the postsuffrage years. Like Dewson and
Roosevelt, Frances Perkins served as an inspiration to women in
Washington and in the country as a whole.

One of the few prominent women in the New Deal who was not
part of this network is almost the exception that proves the rule.
Mary McLeod Bethune, head of the Office of Minority Affairs for
the National Youth Administration from 1936 to 1944, held a job as
important as many network members, yet she was rarely mentioned
as a prominent "woman" in the New Deal. Instead she was seen, and
saw herself, as representing the interests of blacks. She served as the
unofficial leader of the Black Cabinet, which raised issues of concern to black Americans in ways very similar to the women's network on social reform and feminist issues. Bethune was concerned
about the special problems of black women, but for her, race took
priority over sex.

Mary McLeod Bethune, Frances Perkins, Molly Dewson, and
other women all benefited from the experimental climate of the early New Deal that made this progress for women possible. For the historical record, it is important to identify these women in positions of
power and influence, but in the end, what difference did it make
that so many women were prominent in the New Deal? In fact, it
made quite a lot of difference. Women affected the course of the
New Deal, both as individuals assisting in the planning and administration of New Deal programs, and as members of a network where
cooperation on common goals enhanced their influence. The wom-
en's network had its greatest impact on two areas of the New Deal:
Democratic party politics, and the developing social welfare policies
of the modern welfare states.

In political circles, women found larger roles in the newly revitalized Democratic party. Molly Dewson was the chief mover here,
building the Women's Division into a force of some 60,000 grass-
roots workers who publicized the accomplishments of the Roosevelt administration through the Reporter Plan. These Democratic
women really put the New Deal across in communities throughout
the United States. In the 1936 election, for example, Rainbow
Fliers — written by the Women's Division — made up 90 percent of
the Democratic National Committee's campaign material.

In the field of Democratic politics, Molly Dewson deserves

equal time with other well-known politicians such as James Farley, Stephen Early, or Louis Howe. Yet Molly Dewson cared little about the personalities of politics—she was interested in education and ideas. The social and economic changes of the New Deal supplied the perfect tool for educating women to the need for strong federal action in the areas about which women felt most strongly, especially economic security and social justice. The issue-oriented approach to politics, which Dewson mastered, has characterized women's political participation ever since. These enlarged political roles allowed Dewson to fulfill her second goal: to encourage women to take a more active part in Democratic party affairs. Dewson won increased support for women's activities from the financially strapped Democratic National Committee, and increased women's representation at national conventions and on key party committees. She did not reach her goal of equal numbers of women and men on all party committees, but she did make progress toward that objective.

Women had an even more wide-ranging impact on the social welfare policies of the New Deal. Historians may soon say that women founded the modern welfare state. In 1933, Frances Perkins had presented Franklin Roosevelt with a list of six reforms in the field of social welfare for his endorsement; by 1940, all but health insurance had been enacted. Women in the National Recovery Administration (NRA) drafted provisions setting maximum hours and minimum wages for workers covered by the NRA codes. Women also found scope in the consumer affairs division where they were among those raising protests against the business-oriented thrust of the NRA codes. Frances Perkins and her circle in the Labor Department supplied crucial expertise in the drafting of the 1935 Social Security Act, one of the New Deal's more lasting accomplishments. In addition, provisions for Aid to Dependent Children grew directly out of the collaboration between Grace Abbott and Frances Perkins. And, women in the network helped pass the 1938 Fair Labor Standards Act, which made permanent many of the reforms first enacted under the NRA codes. This 1938 law was the last liberal reform measure won by the Roosevelt administration in the face of opposition from an increasingly conservative Congress.

Women administrators and planners also oversaw the treatment of ordinary women in the relief agencies. When women's relief was lagging in the early days of the New Deal, Eleanor Roosevelt got the ball rolling with a White House Conference on the Emergency

Needs of Unemployed Women. Administrators in the Federal Emergency Relief Administration (FERA) and the Works Progress Administration (WPA) such as Ellen S. Woodward and Hilda Worthington Smith set up separate programs for women and won fairer treatment for women in existing programs. While progress was not uniformly positive, without the efforts of such administrators the needs of women on relief might have been totally forgotten.

The same circumstances that facilitated the contributions of women in New Deal policy-making positions also worked to the benefit of a second tier of women in the New Deal bureaucracy, women just below the level of presidential appointments represented by the women in the network. This second level of women administrators was broader and more extensive than the approximately thirty women who made up the network. Although their salaries and prestige were not as high as those of the women in the network (and probably less than those of comparable male coworkers), the excitement of serving in the New Deal infected this middle level of women bureaucrats just as much as it did Molly Dewson and Frances Perkins.

Historians have noticed that women generally fare better in bureaucracies and organizations when such groups are fairly new because inhibitions about using female talent tend to be weaker. Conversely, when bureaucracies become more entrenched and established, barriers to women's contributions stiffen. In the early years of the New Deal, women at all levels of governmental service benefited from the expansion of government programs; later in the decade, progress slowed. Yet the overall growth was impressive. Women's Bureau studies show that women's percentage of government employees grew from 14.3 percent in 1929 to 18.8 percent in 1939. Furthermore, women's rate of federal employment increased twice as rapidly as men's in the 1930s. Women's jobs were more concentrated in the recently established agencies than in older departments such as War, Navy, Justice, or Commerce. According to Women's Bureau figures for 1939, women's representation in the executive departments was 15.2 percent. This contrasted to women's 34.2 percent share in independent establishments, and their 44.4 percent in the seven newest independent establishments (which included the WPA). Of course, this expansion for women in the federal service did not mean that 175,000 women now had top-level civil service jobs. Then, as now, most of the women working for the federal government were concentrated in the lower ranges of salary and responsibility, especially in the clerical field.

While Women's Bureau studies claimed notable progress for women at all levels of the government bureaucracy, one black mark was Section 213 of the National Economy Act of 1932. A reflection of the tendency to make married women workers into scapegoats for unemployment, Section 213 prohibited both husband and wife from working for the federal government. While sex-neuter in its wording, the law's impact fell far more heavily on women than men, because wives' salaries were invariably less than those of their husbands. In all, some 1,600 married female government employees were forced to resign before the law was rescinded in 1937.

Nevertheless, while popular images portrayed eager young men flocking to staff the New Deal agencies, eager young women flocked to Washington as well. The collective story of this midlevel range of women who served in the New Deal awaits its historian, but several examples suggest the scope of increased opportunities for women in government service. For instance, women found many roles in the arts projects of the WPA known collectively as Federal One. The Federal Writers' Project had fourteen female state directors when it began, and the Federal Art Project provided an especially supportive climate for women artists and art administrators alike. A total of 8,000 women found employment on Federal One before its premature demise in the early 1940s.

Individual women, many at the beginnings of long careers in public life and government service, also found challenging opportunities. Caroline Ware joined the New Deal in 1933–34 as a special assistant to the Consumers' Advisory Board of the NRA, the beginning of her lifelong service to the consumer cause. Elinore Herrick rose to prominence in the National Labor Relations Board as a regional director, a position labor negotiator Anna Rosenberg (who was with the Social Security Board in the 1930s) would later hold. The Social Security Administration employed Maurine Hulliner as technical advisor to the Social Security Board and Lavinia Engle, a top Maryland Democrat, as educational representative. Marion Harron served on the Board of Tax Appeals, and Florence Kerr was a regional supervisor for the WPA before taking over Woodward's job in 1938. Lorena Hickok, one of the many newspaperwomen who flocked to Washington in the 1930s to cover Eleanor Roosevelt and other New Deal activities, signed on as a roving reporter for FERA administrator Harry Hopkins. Eleanor Roosevelt made sure that Lorena Hickok's graphic reports on relief conditions ended up on FDR's bedside table for his nighttime perusal. Dorothea Lange, working for the Farm Security Administration, matched Hickok's words with photographs vividly portraying the human impact of the Depression. This list, while by no means exhaustive, illustrates the important roles played by women throughout the New Deal bureaucracy, both in Washington and out in the field. Recognition of their contribution is long overdue.

THE NEW DEAL'S IMPACT ON WOMEN

In providing opportunities for women at senior and midlevel positions, the New Deal rates a very positive assessment. The New Deal's record on helping ordinary women, however, is more checkered. Both as workers and as members of families disrupted by the Depression, these women were in desperate straits. Since such women often lacked the opportunity to demand fairer treatment from New Deal agencies, their needs were often overlooked or slighted. And yet, the situation of many women was so desperate that any help, no matter how limited, was appreciated. This understanding is central to an evaluation of New Deal relief policies toward women.

The 1933 National Industrial Recovery Act, an attempt at industrial self-regulation through codes of production, was the keystone of the early New Deal recovery program. NRA codes affected more than 4 million women workers. The NRA codes had such a positive effect on women workers that the Women's Bureau concluded that enormous advances had occurred even in the relatively brief span of the law's enforcement. The Women's Bureau specifically cited the stabilization of deteriorating work conditions, which had characterized the early Depression, and the improvement of women's employment through wage and hours provisions mandated by each code. Women's wages were more affected by these minimum provisions than men's; since women earned the lowest wages, they had more to gain, even when the minimum wage was set at 25 cents an hour. Other aspects of the NRA drew vehement protest, especially the provisions in some one-quarter of the codes that mandated a lower minimum wage for women than men in the same jobs. Despite repeated protests from all the major women's organizations, these discriminatory features stood. The other major drawback to the NRA, in fact to all the New Deal welfare legislation, was that many women workers were left outside code protection. Domestic servants were an obvious (and numerous) example.

The Fair Labor Standards Act (FLSA) of 1938 made permanent many of the provisions of the temporary NRA, which had been ruled unconstitutional in 1935. The FLSA followed the precedent of the NRA and set wage and hours standards for both sexes, an important break from the older pattern of providing protection for women workers alone because of their presumed physical inferiority. FLSA wage and hours provisions proved especially beneficial to women workers in the textile and shoe industries, which came under the purview of the law. They offered little, however, to the majority of women workers who did not work in interstate commerce. Major areas of women's employment that were left outside the scope of the law were cannery workers, retail clerks, and domestic servants.

Another law, which made permanent the gains begun under the NRA, was the 1935 National Labor Relations Act, which extended federal support for unions begun under Section 7 (a) of the NRA. This governmental blessing of workers' right to organize encouraged the growth of the labor movement as a major force in American political and economic life, one of the New Deal's most far-reaching changes. Women shared in this progress: by the end of the decade, some 800,000 women belonged to unions, a threefold increase over 1929. Yet this record must be balanced against the large majority of women workers who still remained outside unions. Moreover, women were not exactly welcomed into the labor unions. Few leadership positions were open to them, and unions often collaborated with management in negotiating contracts with unequal pay and work provisions.

The story of women on relief is one of gradual improvement after a very dismal start. When people thought about unemployment, they invariably formed mental images of unemployed male workers -- few recognized that more than 2 million women were out of work as well. Only after Eleanor Roosevelt hosted a White House Conference on the Emergency Needs of Women in late November, 1933, did federal relief agencies seriously begin to take the needs of women into account. Still progress was slow. The Civilian Works Administration, designed to get the country through the winter of 1933–1934, gave women only 7 percent of its jobs; the Federal Emergency Relief Administration did little better. A further slap was that the pay on projects where women were concentrated averaged only 30-to-40 cents an hour, while the construction projects in which male workers predominated were guaranteed an hourly wage of $1.

The status of women on relief improved dramatically in 1935 with the establishment of the Works Progress (later, Projects) Administration. Women's percentage of WPA jobs ranged from 12 percent to a high of 19 percent, not too far from women's 24 percent representation in the general work force. On the Federal Art Project, some 41 percent of artists on relief were women. At its peak, 405,000 women were on the WPA, the responsibility of Ellen Woodward and her mainly female staff at the Women's and Professional Projects division. Yet the WPA had its drawbacks for women. Women found it harder to qualify than men, since only one member of a family was eligible. The WPA automatically assumed the man was the primary breadwinner: if a woman had a husband who was able but unwilling to work, the WPA still considered him the head of the household, making her ineligible for work relief. The WPA also continued the pattern of lower pay scales for women, and placed the vast majority of women in sewing rooms and canning projects. This stereotyped women's work demanded few skills and offered no training for more challenging (and remunerative) work when the Depression ended. Finally, the 300,000 to 400,000 women who benefited from WPA employment must be balanced against the several million women who still could not not find work.

Women in government and public life worked hard to increase recognition of ordinary women's needs on relief, but there were limits to what a small group of New Deal administrators and women's organizations could accomplish. The case of camps for unemployed women showed this dramatically. The Civilian Conservation Corps (CCC), one of the New Deal's most popular programs, sent 2.5 million young men off to the woods to live in camps and do reforestation work. The CCC was the only New Deal program limited by statute to men, which led critics to ask, where was the "she-she-she"? It was only due to the efforts of the WPA administrator, Hilda Worthington Smith, and Eleanor Roosevelt's timely offer to host yet another White House conference that a similar program for women won any support. It was a pathetically meager program compared to the men's: only 45 camps for 8,500 women were set up throughout the country. The program was abruptly terminated in 1937. It is hard to disagree with Hilda Worthington Smith's plaintive assessment: "As so often the case, the boys get the breaks, the girls are neglected."

The Social Security Act of 1935 did not so much neglect women as penalize them. In the general excitement over the passage of Social Security, several discriminatory features were written into the law. While the Act provided maternal and pediatric programs and aid to mothers with dependent children, it slighted women who did not work for pay outside the home, the great majority of American women. Until the 1939 revisions, which shifted the emphasis from the individual worker to the worker's family, a wife was not even entitled to widow's benefits if her husband died. After 1939, the widow received only half her husband's benefits. Moreover, there were no widower's benefits if the wife died, even if she had been contributing Social Security taxes at the same rate as a working man. The operative assumption for Social Security was that men were the primary breadwinners and heads of household; women were secondary earners, who were less entitled to protection. In addition to those discriminatory aspects, many groups of women, such as agricultural workers and domestic servants, were excluded from coverage entirely.

Few would have argued against the enactment of Social Security because of these discriminatory features: as with the relief policies, the overwhelming need for immediate federal action outweighed the limitations of specific laws. Historian Lois Scharf captured this response well: "Women protected by a discriminatory wage standard, who had never had a floor under their wages before, cared little for the sexist implications. For desperate women on relief, the sewing room represented survival rather than a sex-segregated handout." The same held true for Social Security.

When coming to a general assessment of New Deal relief policies as they affected women, one cannot escape the fact that many women (and men) were left outside New Deal protection. Nothing can change the discriminatory and indeed sexist assumptions behind many relief and recovery programs. Yet benefits and limitations must be weighed: is it more important that one-quarter of the

NRA codes discriminated against women or that three-quarters did not? Do we applaud the threefold increase in women in labor unions or bemoan the fact that so many women were still outside union protection? Whether one cheers the advances or harps on the drawbacks in large part comes down to an individual's ideological stance toward the New Deal itself. This in turn raises the perennial question of whether the New Deal could have made more sweeping reforms than it did, or whether it pragmatically accomplished all that it could within the context of America in the 1930s. For many historians, the New Deal provides more to praise than to condemn, and that judgment applies to women's treatment in the New Deal as well.

AN ASSESSMENT

The year 1936 marked the peak of women's participation in the New Deal. In the second term, progress was stalemated. The social and welfare programs, in which women administrators were concentrated, and which benefited ordinary women on relief, were cut back by an increasingly conservative Congress. Once women lined up in the Democratic camp in the 1936 election, they found themselves taken more for granted politically. Eleanor Roosevelt shifted her attention away from women's issues in the second term, and the network leadership was weakened by the retirement of Molly Dewson. Finally, as the political dialogue shifted from Depression to war in the late 1930s, women's contributions were in less demand. The unique congruence of factors that had set up progress for women in the early New Deal was already on the wane.

While some of the progress for women in the New Deal was temporary, women's collective stories still have much to add to historians' understanding of the New Deal, as well as to the contours of twentieth-century political history and women's history. The New Deal is perhaps the most studied period in American political history, and yet until recently women's roles in the period received hardly any notice at all. That an actively functioning network of women could have escaped the attention of historians who had scrutinized practically every nook and cranny of the New Deal suggests that women may have been a more active force in political life

than previously suspected. If women played such large roles in government and politics as far back as the 1930s, then perhaps women
have made contributions to public life in other periods as well. And,
since politics has traditionally been one of the areas least hospitable
to women's talents, this progress is even more remarkable.

The story of women in the 1930s also adds to our understanding
of New Deal historiography. One clear area of overlap is chronology.
Many New Deal monographs start with the excitement of the first
100 days, move into the administrative accomplishments of the first
term, and then describe stalemate, retrenchment, and decline after
1937. This pattern was perhaps best analyzed in James Patterson's
influential study of congressional conservatism in the New Deal.
The experiences of women follow a nearly parallel trail. The first
term was a period of exciting new innovations for women in government and politics—they shared in the experimental climate of the
early New Deal. Women's participation peaked in 1936 when the
network was at its height and women played large roles in the successful election campaign. After 1936, women's progress stalled, in
part because of attrition in the network but mainly because the New
Deal was stalemated. Since women were concentrated in the very
social welfare areas of the New Deal under the most severe attack,
they were especially hard hit by the changing New Deal.

The story of women in the New Deal parallels broader New Deal
historiography in other ways. Many historians have interpreted the
New Deal as the epitome of the liberal broker state, a stark contrast
to the single-interest, business-dominated government of the 1920s.
One of the New Deal's most lasting contributions was to open up
the political process to previously excluded groups of interests or
voters. As such, historians often speak of a New Deal for blacks, or
labor, or various ethnic groups. Equally, there was a New Deal for
women. This is not just because a group of high-powered women
took jobs in the Roosevelt Administration. These women advocated
and represented the interests of women in a direct and self-con-
scious manner. Molly Dewson's efforts in politics, for example,
strongly fostered such an awareness. The 1930s emerges as one of
the few times to date when women have been seen as a specific
group whose needs must be addressed in order to win their support.

There are especially strong parallels between the experiences of
women and of blacks in the New Deal. Both groups experienced
raised expectations and increased recognition during the decade.

Both groups found it necessary and efficient to develop informal networks in Washington to keep in touch with each other, and to advance the needs of sex or race at every possible opportunity. Actually, the Black Cabinet and the women's network shared more than just tactics: both were dependent on the support and help of Eleanor Roosevelt, without whom either group would have made far less remarkable progress. Both groups received somewhat more grudging support from Franklin Roosevelt, who responded to their requests in proportion to their increasing roles in the Democratic party and the New Deal coalition. Yet Franklin Roosevelt never gave either women or blacks anywhere near what they were asking for, or what, in fairness, they deserved. Both groups suffered from societal hostility toward their goals that contrasted sharply with the more supportive atmosphere they found in the New Deal. One final parallel might be that the activities of blacks and women in the 1930s were part of an historical process that culminated in the struggles of the civil rights and women's movements of the 1960s and 1970s.

There might be some who would say that the New Deal for women, either on the level of the network or the treatment of ordinary women by relief agencies, has very little to do with American feminism. The lack of a broad-based women's movement in the 1930s meant few voices were raised in protest against the unequal treatment of women in New Deal programs or in American society as a whole. The gains of elite women in the New Deal bureaucracy were the product of a propitious historical moment rather than the long-term development of feminism in the United States. Partial proof lies in the network's failure to institutionalize its gains. Another indication is the network's reluctance to address the contradiction between its belief in a democratic system based on merit and the obvious limits placed on women's advancement in American society. These women erroneously believed that if they did their jobs well, future barriers for women would tumble — a naive faith that offered little challenge to fundamental patterns of discrimination in American life. In this view, the story of women in the New Deal was one of a missed feminist opportunity.

While there is much to support such a negative interpretation of women's experiences in the New Deal, it remains unsatisfying. Women New Dealers were admittedly ambivalent about the priorities they assigned to issues specifically affecting women and those pertaining to broader social reform. For many women in public life in the 1930s, general reform concerns won out. Women's issues were squarely on their agenda, however, and they were willing to back up their convictions with action. Journalist Ruby Black captured this well when she said of Eleanor Roosevelt, "She talks like a social worker and acts like a Feminist." Women in the New Deal worked to promote more opportunities for women in public life and looked out for the interests of ordinary women hard hit by the Depression. This consciousness of women's interests shows one direction that feminism took in the postsuffrage years and places activities in the New Deal within a broader historical continuum that stretches from the suffrage movement to the revival of feminism in the 1960s. Feminism did not die after 1920. One of the areas in which it took root, however tentatively, was in the politics and government of the New Deal.

The impact of the New Deal on women in general, beyond those exceptional women who served in the New Deal administration, remains mixed. The treatment of women by relief agencies and New Deal policies parallels a pattern applicable to most aspects of the New Deal: those whom it helped never forgot the aid they received from the federal government, but many received little or nothing at all. This applied to both men and women, but women had to struggle even harder to get their due.

Yet women as a group did benefit from the policies of the New Deal: from Social Security, the NRA codes, the Fair Labor Standards Act, Aid to Dependent Children, and the WPA relief projects. For the most part, however, this progress for women came about not because of specific attempts to single out women for treatment, but as part of a broader effort to improve the conditions and economic security of all Americans. In the current metaphor, a rising tide lifts all ships equally. Women benefited not so much because they were women but because the federal government guaranteed the basic social security of all American citizens in response to the economic crisis of the Depression. While discriminatory features occasionally penalized women's interests, for the most part women shared in the salutory effect of this new legislation.

In the end, any evaluation of women and the New Deal must grapple with the irony that the New Deal's social welfare programs became institutionalized as the modern welfare state, while the positive gains for women were not. The federal government now has a controlling role in planning and managing the economy; it now guarantees, at least in theory, the basic economic and social security of all Americans from birth to death. The political process permanently includes such interest groups as labor, blacks, and minorities. Progress for women has proven more illusory. Unlike the popular support for the New Deal, there was no widespread interest in changing women's roles in the 1930s. Lacking a popular base to force recognition of women's concerns, women largely remained dependent on whatever benefits might trickle their way. For all the activities of the network on behalf of women and reform, the most long-lasting legacy of the New Deal for women may be the founding of the modern welfare state, which has improved women's lives along with men's.

The message that the New Deal experience offers to women is a contradictory one: organize as women in order to make your special needs known, but also work for broad-based reforms that will help all citizens. Eleanor Roosevelt addressed the same paradox in an April 1940 article on women in politics commissioned by *Good Housekeeping*: "Women must become more conscious of themselves as women and of their ability to function as a group. At the same time they must try to wipe from men's consciousness the need to consider them as a group or as women in their everyday activities, especially as workers in industry or the professions." Eleanor Roosevelt realized that it was not enough to let general social progress sweep women along with the tide: women must unite on issues of fundamental concern to them as women although women's interests were increasingly difficult to separate from men's. Whether women should organize independently from men to advance their cause or stress the similarities between the two sexes has been the crucial question of feminism in the postsuffrage age. The contradictions of women's experiences in the New Deal show how hard a question this is to resolve.

It is wrong to end on such an ambiguous note. Even if women in the New Deal did not solve all the problems of access to politics and government, even if New Deal programs sometimes slighted the needs of women, the 1930s still remains a period of important breakthroughs for women. The New Deal's experimental climate, which opened up opportunities for other previously excluded groups, did the same for women. Into the void stepped a group of women who showed conclusively and with great style how much women had to offer to public life. The social programs of the New Deal might not have have succeeded to the extent they did without the contributions of this spirited and well-trained corps of women. The New Deal certainly would have been a far less humane undertaking without their collective presence. Historians of the New Deal have much to learn from the experiences of American women in the of the 1930s.

SUGGESTED READINGS

Most of the material in this essay is drawn from Susan Ware, *Beyond Suffrage: Women in the New Deal* (Cambridge, Mass., 1981) and Ware, *Holding Their Own: American Women in the 1930s* (Boston, 1982). Other major sources on women in the 1930s include Alice Kessler-Harris, *Out to Work: A History of Wage-Earning Women in the United States* (New York, 1982); Lois Scharf, *To Work and to Wed: Female Employment, Feminism and the Great Depression* (Westport, Conn., 1980); Winifred Wandersee, *Women's Work and Family Values, 1920–1940* (Cambridge, Mass., 1981); and Susan D. Becker, *The Origins of the Equal Rights Amendment: American Feminism Between the Wars* (Westport, Conn., 1981). Useful introductions to women's history in twentieth-century America include William H. Chafe, *The American Woman, 1920–1970* (New York, 1972), and Lois W. Banner, *Women in Modern America: A Brief History* (New York, 1974). Lorena Hickok and Eleanor Roosevelt, *Ladies of Courage* (New York, 1954) provides a good overview of women's political roles in the New Deal and biographical vignettes of many of the prominent women New Dealers.

For specific women in the New Deal, the biographies collected in *Notable American Women* (Cambridge, Mass., 1971) and *Notable American Women: The Modern Period* (Cambridge, Mass., 1980) provide an excellent starting point. Eleanor Roosevelt has received the most biographical treatment: see Tamara Hareven, *Eleanor Roosevelt: An American Conscience* (New York, 1968); Joseph P. Lash, *Eleanor and Franklin* (New York, 1971) and *Eleanor: The Years Alone* (New York, 1972). Lash's books contain a wealth of information about the broad spectrum of women's activities in the New Deal as they coalesced around Eleanor Roosevelt. For Frances Perkins, see George Martin, *Madame Secretary* (Boston, 1976). Susan Ware is currently writing a biography of Molly Dewson. Eleanor Roosevelt, Frances Perkins, Mary Anderson, Rose Schneiderman, Hallie

Flanagan, and Florence Jaffray Harriman are among the New Deal women who published autobiographies describing their years in Washington. For Hickok's unsurpassed reportage on the impact of the Depression on ordinary Americans, see *One Third of a Nation: Lorena Hickok Reports on the Great Depression* (Urbana, Ill., 1981), edited by Richard Lowitt and Marine Beasley.